Fireworks

AIMER BOYZ

ISBN: 978-1-4834-1369-3 (sc)
ISBN: 978-1-4834-1368-6 (e)

Library of Congress Control Number: 2014910768

Lulu Publishing Services rev. date: 07/22/2014

Contents

Acknowledgments

Thank you to my husband for thinking I could write, to Terry and Gill for holding my hand throughout this daunting journey, to Lauri for putting her life on hold while she worked magic with my abysmal punctuation, to my family for not laughing at me, and to Chris Colfer for the inspiration that he is.

CHAPTER 1

Hello, I Want You

Steven stood entranced, head back, eyes on the exploding lights in the night sky. He watched the fireworks; Daniel watched him. They stood amid a crowd of friends and strangers, neighbours and family, all witnessing the pyrotechnic end of Canada Day.

They had met that afternoon at the backyard BBQ Daniel's sister threw every year. He hadn't wanted to go. He wasn't up to dealing with unwelcome advice and intrusive questions. *"Met anyone interesting? You've got to get out there again, Daniel. You're not going to meet anyone sitting at home!"* But, if he hadn't gone, his mother would have called and tried to pretend that she wasn't worried about him. So he had abandoned his plans for vegging on the couch with the air conditioning on full blast and a beer in his hand. Thank you, God! It scared him to think of how easily he could have missed meeting Steven.

❖ ❖ ❖

"What? No, you're coming." No way was Daniel skipping out on this BBQ. Sandy had plans and her brother was not going to screw them up. At thirty-six, four years older than Daniel, Sandy was the first-born and it showed. She always knew exactly what she wanted. She was persistent, and wielded the force of a Mac truck.

"I'm working on a deadline." Daniel tried to sound stressed but his sister wasn't buying it.

"Bullshit! It's July 1st, Canada Day, you've heard of it, right?" Sandy's question was rhetorical, not that she gave her brother time to answer it anyway. "No one in the whole freaking country is working. One o'clock, bring watermelon." She didn't bother saying goodbye.

Daniel heard the dial tone, and slapped his portable phone back into its base. Well, crap! It sucked being the youngest. Thirty-two years old, and his sisters were still telling him what to do. His family only believed in one thing: family. They weren't big on formal, polite facades. They all felt perfectly comfortable giving their opinions on each other's lives. There was only one rule: show up!

Post-shower, he stared at himself in the mirror over the sink and tried to do something with his hair. He was totally useless with hair products. After ten minutes of fussing, gelling, and tweaking, he looked like a static electricity experiment gone awry. *Fuck! They should take my gay card away*! He rinsed everything out, and finger combed the wet, wavy mess. *Good enough! It's only family anyway.*

He pulled on a T-shirt and cargo shorts, slipped his feet into Sperry Dock Siders, and started the perpetual hunt for his keys. *Shit! Where did I put them?* He could hear Karen's voice in his head. *Jesus, Daniel, it's not rocket science. Just put them in the same place every time. How hard is that?* At thirty-four, two years younger than Sandy and two years older than Daniel, his sister, Karen, was the middle child. She was intuitive and independent, and had never met an object that she couldn't organize, label, or sort the hell out of; OCD anyone?

Ah Ha! He grabbed his keys from the top of the microwave. Opening the front door, he caught sight of himself in the hall mirror. *Not good!* Faded T-shirt from some concert, cargo shorts so old they were missing buttons on half the pockets, and leather boat shoes that had never seen shoe polish. He shrugged and stepped out into the hallway, locking the door behind him. How good did he have to look to sit in his sister's backyard and let his nephew drop mustard all over him? He pressed the down arrow to summon the elevator and forgot about it.

Sandy's driveway was full, and finding a parking place on the street wasn't easy. Obviously, she wasn't the only one hosting a Canada Day BBQ. Parking six houses down, he climbed out of his car. *Way too freaking hot!* He slid his Ray-Bans over his eyes, grabbed the watermelon from the back seat, and pressed the lock icon on his key.

Halfway up the driveway, a dog started barking, and two kids came barreling out of the back yard.

"Danny!" His niece Lauren, who at five could easily outrun her three-year-old cousin, Rhys, reached him first.

Putting the watermelon down, he swung the little girl in a large circle, her hair sailing out behind her.

"Me too! Me too!" Rhys held his arms up. "Airplane!"

Daniel set his niece on her feet. "Lauren, baby, be a doll and make sure the watermelon doesn't roll out on to the street, while I give Rhys a turn." As he picked Rhys up, he couldn't help smiling at Lauren. She sat beside the watermelon with her arms wrapped around it. It wasn't going anywhere. He held his nephew at shoulder height, horizontal to the ground and twirled him around, making airplane noises; or rather, what Rhys thought were airplane noises. The kid didn't know yet that real airplanes didn't sound like sick lawnmowers coughing.

"Okay, Rhys. The airplane's tired." Daniel put his nephew down and picked up the watermelon. Rhys jumped up and down and tried to climb his leg, so he balanced the watermelon in his left arm, and held the three-year-old on his right hip. He made a big show of staggering under the combined weight of boy and watermelon, an act that earned him major laughs from the pre-school crowd.

"Honey, can you get the gate for me?"

Lauren ran ahead, giggling. "I'm Lauren, Uncle Daniel, not honey."

"Honey's your middle name." Daniel smiled a thank you to his niece as she held the gate open for him. "Didn't your mother tell you?"

"No, it's not!" Lauren knew her uncle pretty well; she didn't fall for his stories any more. "You're lying again." She let the gate slam shut behind her and ran full tilt across the back yard to the patio door. "Mom! Dad! Danny's here!"

A man in his mid-sixties with a receding hairline and Daniel's hazel eyes got up from his chair by the pool and crossed the lawn towards them, smiling at the circus act of watermelon and boy.

"Hey, Dad." Daniel shifted his nephew on his hip and smiled at his father.

"Let me help you with that." Brian peeled Rhys off of his son and sent him sailing through the air.

Nephew-free, Daniel scanned the backyard. His sister lived in what the real estate people liked to call an "established" neighbourhood, which really just meant old. The upside to a small, fifty-year-old house that needed a lot of work was a massive backyard with mature trees, a stone-paved patio where the BBQ and Picnic table lived, and a swimming pool, with enough lawn left over for the kids and dog to run around.

"Hi, Mom." He waved at his mother, sitting by pool, obviously on life-guard duty. His niece, having delivered the Daniel report, scampered back to the pool. "Bubby, you want to see? I can do the back float."

Turning his grandson upside down, Rhys shrieking with laughter, Brian carried the boy over to the pool. Karen's husband, Doug, grinned at Daniel as he fired up the BBQ. "Hey, man, I see you decided to come."

Daniel snorted. "Yeah, right! Like I had a choice."

Understanding completely, Doug nodded as he scrapped at the grill with a metal brush. "Glen was under orders to drag your ass over here if you didn't show."

Daniel rolled his eyes. Yeah, Sandy would have sent her husband to 'help' him get ready for the BBQ! Walking backwards on his way to the patio door, Daniel grinned at Doug. "Want to trade families?"

Doug laughed. "You've met my family, right?"

Daniel took the fifth on that one. He had met Doug's family and, yes, he didn't have pain-in-the-ass sisters, but his mother could teach sour to a lemon. He had never seen the woman smile, not even at her son's wedding. Karen had taken a black marker and drawn a happy face over her mother-in-law's grim visage in the family wedding photo; problem solved.

Crossing the patio, he tried to slide the screen door open with an arm full of watermelon, while his sister's mountain of a dog, Brady, jumped at the door from the other side. "Hey, Brady, sit boy."

"Brady, move!" Karen, a five-foot-two-inch ball of suppressed energy with Daniel's blond hair, shoved the excited mass of fur out of the way and grinned at her brother as she slid the door open. "Daniel! Such a surprise!"

"Yeah, you're shocked." Stepping into the kitchen, he looked around for an empty surface. "Where do you want this?"

Karen grabbed a salad bowl off the counter and plunked it on the table, clearing a space. "Here."

No, she wasn't shocked that Daniel had shown up. Sandy and an Act of God were pretty much synonymous. Plus, attending family functions was mandatory. Concessions were made for illness, in which case, of course, the family came to you. There was no escape, not for any of them, and her brother knew that.

Daniel dumped the watermelon on the counter and hooked his sunglasses into the collar of his T-shirt. Karen handed him a large, serious-looking knife. "Make yourself useful." While Daniel hacked into the melon, she started opening the cupboards over the sink. "I'm not sure where she keeps the platters."

"Cupboard on top of the fridge." Sandy, the *tall* sister at all of five feet three and half inches, with her mother's red hair, entered the kitchen carrying a case of soft drinks and glanced at the knife in her brother's hands. "Don't cut anything you may need."

Daniel raised the knife and advanced on his sister. "Well, I don't really need *two* sisters."

Sandy ducked and swatted at him. "Get off me, you moron!"

Glen, Sandy's husband, stood behind his wife, a cooler hoisted on one shoulder. "I know just how you feel, man, but Lauren still needs a mother."

"Nice!" Sandy, her green eyes laughing, glared at her husband. "A little more appreciation, please, unless you want to cuddle up tonight with your right hand."

Glen dropped the cooler to the floor and grabbed his wife. "I meant, 'Daniel back away from this angel!'" He nuzzled into Sandy's neck, blowing loud raspberries against her skin.

Karen laughed as Sandy struggled to escape her husband's teasing hands. "Glen, can you get a platter down for the watermelon? I can't reach them."

At just over six feet, Glen was the Jolly Brown Giant of the family; brown hair, brown eyes, with the patience and humour to handle the steamroller that was his wife. He popped the cupboard open and handed Karen a platter.

Daniel shook his head as he pushed the knife through the watermelon rind. "You are so whipped, man."

Glen shrugged as he flipped the cooler open. "What can I say?" He reached into the fridge and started to transfer cold drinks to the empty cooler, while Sandy moved more Coke into the spaces he emptied. They worked as a team, effortlessly in sync.

Karen piled the sliced watermelon onto the platter. "You want this outside?"

"Perfect, thanks!" Sandy grabbed a few bottles of water, closed the fridge, and followed her husband and sister through the patio door to the backyard.

The doorbell rang as Daniel rinsed the knife. "I'll get it." Wiping his hands on a dishtowel, he tossed it over his shoulder. His directionally challenged cousin, Allan, was always the last one to arrive. He had never yet made it to Sandy's house without getting lost. Daniel pulled the door open, words already tumbling from his mouth. "Allan, just get a freaking GPS already!"

The man standing on the door step was not Allan - so not Allan! He was pretty and perfect, which was not the same as pretty perfect, although he was that as well.

The man had chocolate eyes, framed by thick lashes Daniel's sisters would kill for, dark, wavy hair brushed back from a high forehead, and cheekbones sharp enough to be registered as weapons. He was beautiful. Not feminine, not with that jaw line and those shoulders, but beautiful all the same.

His red and white striped shirt, collar open at the neck, cuffs rolled with military precision, was teamed with light-washed blue denim shorts distressed by design, and preppy loafers buffed to a high gloss. He was a walking, breathing ad for Tommy Hilfiger. How the hell that shirt was crisp in this heat was a complete mystery to Daniel.

The small imperfections that proved him human; a slightly off-centre smile and an almost imperceptible bump on the bridge of his nose, only added to the overall impression of Oh! My! God!

Close your mouth idiot! You're doing a good imitation of a blow fish. "You're not Allan."

"No, sorry." Mr. Perfect smiled as he offered his hand. "Steven Monaco." He nodded to a house across the street. "New neighbour."

Daniel shook the proffered hand automatically, his attention snagged by lips that tilted in a microscopically crooked smile.

Steven withdrew his hand. "You're not Glen."

Daniel heard the unasked question and laughed, waving Steven into the house. "No, I'm Daniel Fine, Sandy's brother. Come on in." He closed the front door and led Steven through the kitchen. "Everyone's out back."

Daniel didn't have to say anything. His dropped jaw, and the quick but thorough visual strip-search he had given Steven at the front door, were tantamount to wearing a rainbow sticker plastered to his forehead. It was flattering but Steven wasn't particularly interested. The guy seemed nice enough, but he was a little old for the scruffy look and Steven had a fetish for neat. Trailing Sandy's brother through the kitchen, he eyed the baggy, bedraggled shorts the other man wore and felt it safe to assume that neat wasn't a high priority in Daniel's life.

Sliding the patio door open, Daniel called out to his sister. "San! Steven's here."

Playing tag with the kids and the dog, Sandy laughed as she spun Rhys over her head. "I win!" Turning at the sound of her name, she set her nephew back on his feet, and waved at Steven. "Gotta go, guys. Brady's it."

Crossing the lawn to the patio, she smiled at the two men waiting for her. Steven stood beside Daniel, hopefully a prophecy of things to come. Sandy had only talked to her new neighbour a handful of times since he moved in two weeks ago, but she already liked him better than her brother's not-so-lamented ex.

Daniel was not a man who was open to suggestion, certainly not about his personal life, and definitely not from his sisters. Stubborn to mule standards, he would be back in his car and gone if he thought she had engineered this meeting with Steven. To make sure he didn't get even a whiff of a set-up, Sandy casually separated the two men as quickly as she could.

"Steven, glad you could come." Sandy nodded at her brother. "You've met Daniel, I see. He's younger, but I'm better looking." She hip-checked Daniel; shoving him back a step, and took his place beside Steven. "This whole gang is just assorted family members. You know Glen and Lauren already. Come on, I'll introduce you to the rest."

Daniel watched his sister walk away with her new neighbour in tow, his eyes following the other man. Steven didn't have to say anything. His response to Daniel's eye grope had settled the gay/ straight question. That tilted smile, the hint of a challenge in his eyes, the look had said, "You like what you see?" The answer, of course, was Fuck YES!

Steven's inspection of Daniel had been subtle and swift, his eyes noting the mangled pockets of the ancient cargo shorts before returning to Daniel's face; no dropped jaw. Very aware that the bag-man-look had not won him major points with Mr. Perfect, Daniel grinned to himself. He was more than willing to take the offending clothes off, for Steven.

The man looked just as good from the back as he did from the front. Those shorts grazed an ass that Daniel wanted to become intimately acquainted with. Watching that ass, his mind removed the denim shorts, and his fingers curled at his side. He could almost feel the…

"You the short order cook, now?" Beer in one hand, BBQ duty delegated to Glen, Doug spoke at Daniel's shoulder.

Daniel startled in surprise; he had not heard Doug's approach. Retrieving his mind from Steven's ass, he turned puzzled eyes to his brother-in-law. "What?" Doug nodded at the dishtowel still on Daniel's shoulder. "Shit!" Daniel pulled the towel off his shoulder, twisting it in his hands, his eyes once again locked on Steven. *Nice first impression, Fine. Bad enough you're dressed like a refugee from Goodwill, but the rag on your shoulder, just fucking perfect!*

The two men were of a similar height, both hovering a few inches under six feet, with Doug carrying an extra thirty pounds on Daniel. Apart, each of them had woefully unkempt but unremarkable hair. Standing together, as they were, Doug's mass of unruly brunette curls next to Daniel's shaggy, blond waves, they looked like extras from the rock musical "Hair".

Doug watched Daniel track Steven across the lawn and raised his can of beer to his mouth, hiding his grin. *Oh, this is going to be good! That look alone is worth at least a couple of weeks of teasing.* "Didn't know prissy and uptight was your type, man."

"He's not prissy!" Daniel snapped at Doug but he never took his eyes off Steven.

Doug nodded. "Okay, I'll give you that but he's got anal retentive written all over him." He raised his eyebrows at Daniel. "And not your kind of anal retentive."

"Shut up!" Daniel hissed the words.

Doug laughed at him, and turned to watch the man Sandy was introducing to her parents. "I'll bet he colour-codes the towels in his linen closet."

"You can tell all that just by looking, can you?"

Doug took a sip of beer. "Yep, I'm married to the queen of OCD, remember?"

Daniel rolled his eyes. "She gave me this little plaque thing that I'm supposed to put on the wall by the front door." Daniel sounded exasperated and vaguely insulted. "Right!"

Doug scanned the backyard, making sure Rhys was still with his grandfather. His son had a habit of disappearing. Doug had lost him in the aisles of grocery stores more than once, not that his wife knew that. "Yeah, we've got one of those."

"And you use it?" Daniel didn't believe that for a second.

"Who? me? No. My keys go where they've always gone, on the night table with my wallet." Doug shrugged. "But it makes her happy, so…"

"Uh-huh." Daniel watched Steven's progress through the relatives.

Doug bumped his shoulder into Daniel's. "So, I guess you're going to be here a lot, huh?" Daniel turned; the question "why" in his eyes. "He lives across the street, right?" Doug grinned at his brother-in-law.

"Shouldn't you be making sure your son doesn't fall into the pool?" Daniel walked away, ignoring the laughter behind him.

Sandy lead Steven over to a group of people by the pool. An older couple in lawn chairs and a woman sitting on the pool steps laughed and talked together as they watched two kids in the water. "Mom, Dad, this is Steven. He just moved into the house across the street." Three sets of eyes turned to Steven, curious and friendly. "Steven, this is my mother, Julia, my father, Brian, and my sister, Karen." She pointed at the two kids in the pool. "You know Lauren, and that's Karen's son, Rhys."

"Pleased to meet you." Steven shook hands with Sandy's parents and smiled at Karen. "Sandy and Glen have been helping me learn my way around."

"Well, they've been here for almost six years; they should know where everything is by now." Julia looked at the young man her daughter had invited. *Are you the one? Can you make my Daniel happy?* Wrinkles creased around Julia's blue eyes as she smiled at Steven. Her red hair was threaded with grey, but the resemblance to Sandy was still strong. "How's the unpacking going?"

"It took a few days, but I finally got rid of all the boxes. I couldn't stand looking at them lined up against the wall." Steven moved his hands as he talked, eyes filled with the excitement of the first time home buyer. "This place is a lot bigger than my old apartment though, so it still looks kind of sad."

"If you need any help with bookshelves or towel racks or anything, give me a call." What remained of Brian's hair was grey, but his eyes were the same golden hazel as his son's. Stretching his legs out in front of him, he raised his arms out to either side, the very physical manifestation of relaxation. "I'm retired. I've got nothing but time."

"Are you serious? That would be great! I suck at handy man stuff. I tried to hang a shelf once, total disaster! Everything kept sliding off it!"

Brian laughed. "Got your phone?

Steven, apparently, had no problem admitting he didn't know everything and he could laugh at himself. Brian caught his wife's eye, and she smiled. That's all it took, a look, and Brian knew Julia was thinking the same thing he was. *This guy is nothing like Aidan.*

Steven pulled his Blackberry out of his pocket and typed in the numbers that Brian rattled off. "Thank you. I really didn't want to sign up for a Do-It-Yourself class at Home Depot." He slipped his phone away. "How should I pay you, by the hour?"

Julia laughed and pushed at her husband's arm. "Oh, honey, don't worry about it. I'd pay you for getting him out of the house."

"Thirty-nine years of marriage and absolutely no respect!" Brian shook his head at his wife, but the affection in his eyes was clear.

"Yeah, you're just miserable!" Sandy grinned at her father.

Karen looked up at Steven, her hand raised to shield her eyes from the sun. *Oh, Sandy was good!* She had to hand it to her sister. This guy was gorgeous. Of course, her opinion wasn't the one that mattered. "We went to one of the open houses before your house sold. Nice place."

"You didn't put in a bid?" Steven smiled at this pint-sized version of Daniel.

"No, it only has two bedrooms and we're planning on a brother or sister for Rhys." Karen shrugged. "We loved that it was across the street from Sandy, but it was just a little too small for us."

Steven nodded. "Yeah, my agent said that's why it was on the market for so long. There's just me, so two bedrooms are more than enough."

"The lot's a good size. You can always extend the house if you need too."

Steven laughed. "I can't even think about that right now."

"Mummy! Watch!" Lauren waded backwards, tugging her cousin with her. "Look, Rhys is swimming!"

"Way to go, Rhys!" "Good job, Lauren!" Both grandparents applauded, and Karen whistled. "Nice!"

Waiting until Sandy and Steven had walked away, Julia leaned closer to her husband and daughter, keeping her voice low. "What do you think?"

"What's he do, again?" Brian watched Steven as Sandy lead him across the lawn to meet Doug.

Karen kept an eye on the kids in the pool, as she answered her father. "He's a pharmacist, just moved here from Waterloo, originally from some place out west, I think."

"He seems nice." Julia watched Steven as he stood talking to her son-in-law.

Brian rubbed his hand over his chin. "He's nothing like Aidan, though." A major plus in Brian's opinion but, unfortunately, it wasn't up to him.

Julia nodded to herself, a satisfied expression on her face. "Exactly!"

When his fingertips wrinkled and his lips started to turn blue, Karen made Rhys get out of the water. She rubbed a towel over him and dropped a T-shirt over his head. He tried, and failed, to wriggle free as she slathered sunblock on his arms and legs. Finally managing to escape his mother, he chased Brady across the lawn, a pair of sunglasses in his hands and a determined look on his face. Brady, on four legs, easily outran the not quite coordinated three-year-old.

"Daddy! Brady won't listen to me." Rhys stuck his lower lip out and put his hands on his hips, a gesture he had seen his mother use more than once.

"What do you want him to do, buddy?"

"He has to wear his sunglasses."

Doug bit his lip to keep from laughing. Rhys wouldn't think it was funny, but oh God, he had to remember to tell Karen about this later. "I don't think dogs wear sunglasses, Rhys." Doug looked around for the dog. "Brady!" A hundred and ten pounds of long legs and black fur came barreling at him. "Sit!"

Hunkering down beside the dog, he held his hand out to his son. Rhys gave him the sunglasses, and Doug tried to put the glasses on Brady. "See, Rhys, his ears aren't the same as ours. The glasses don't fit around them. They won't stay on." Proving his point, Brady shook his head; drool and glasses went flying. Doug wiped his hand on his shirt as he stood up. "Yuck!"

Rhys wasn't convinced. "But Mummy's head hurts if she doesn't wear her sunglasses in the car."

Doug looked down at his son. "That's okay Rhys, Brady doesn't drive."

Rhys sighed with relief. "Okay." He turned and chased after the dog, sunglasses no longer an issue.

Flipping burgers on the grill, Glen eavesdropped shamelessly on his brother-in-law and nephew. As Rhys took off after Brady, Glen finally let himself laugh.

Doug turned at the sound and grimaced as he walked over to his brother-in-law. "Yeah, funny. I can fix everything now, but what am I going to do when he's ten or fifteen and he has real problems?" Doug leaned against the brick wall beside the BBQ, love and pride in every word he spoke about his son. "He thinks like a bloody lawyer!"

"Don't worry about it. He won't be talking to you when he's ten." Glen poked one of the burgers, testing the colour. "He'll have his head buried in Wii or Xbox or whatever the new thing is seven years from now. Then he'll be texting, then dating, then away at university."

"He's only three!" Doug had trouble dealing with the fact that his son was old enough for nursery school. He so did not want to think of him going off to university!

"Yeah, so enjoy it." Glen added some hot dogs to the grill, and nodded to his right. "What do you think?"

Doug followed Glen's line of sight to where Steven stood talking to Sandy. "Daniel took one look at the guy and practically hyperventilated."

"Really?" Glen looked over at Daniel, eyes thoughtful. "I'm surprised. I didn't think he'd go for him. He doesn't look anything like Aidan."

Doug shrugged. "Maybe Daniel doesn't have a type."

Glen moved his tongs over the grill, turning the wieners carefully. "Do we even know that this guy's gay?"

"You've met him, right?" Doug stared at his brother-in-law, constantly surprised at how clueless the big guy could be.

Glen looked over at Steven again. "It's not like it's written on his forehead. He could be metrosexual, or something. I don't know. My gaydar isn't great!"

Doug grinned as he watched Daniel trying to pretend that he wasn't watching Steven. "Well, Daniel must have gotten some kind of vibe because he's practically drooling."

Glen turned to look at Daniel, standing beside the picnic table, picking at a piece of watermelon, and pretending not to watch the new neighbour. He grinned at Doug and raised his hand in a high five.

Doug laughed as he slapped his palm against Glen's. "Family 1: Daniel 0."

CHAPTER 2

Fireworks

When the burgers were just the right amount of pink and the hot dogs crispy perfect, Glen waved his BBQ tongs. "Sandy! Food's done."

Tossing his empty Coke can in one of the blue bins by the backyard gate, Steven stopped by the BBQ, watching as Glen piled wieners and burgers on a platter. "Can I help?"

"Thanks." Glen held the platter out to Steven. "You want to put this on the kitchen table?"

"Sure." Crossing the patio, Steven jostled the platter to one arm so he'd have a free hand to slide the patio door open.

Daniel was in something of a quandary. He wasn't shy, and it wasn't that he had never picked up a guy before. Since his break-up, he had become a bit of an expert at talking guys into his bed. The problem was he'd never tried to cruise a guy in his sister's backyard before, right smack dab in family central. He couldn't just walk up to Steven and whisper something X-rated in his ear while he groped his ass. Well, he could, of course, but he had the feeling Steven would be pissed and he knew his mother would be appalled that her son could be so rude to a guest, not to mention the fact that if Steven told him to fuck off, his brothers-in-law would tease him about it 'til the end of time.

Plus, Steven was not exactly flashing the green-for-go signal at him. The man hadn't said a word to him since Sandy dragged him off to introduce him to the whole freaking clan. Daniel was damned if he was going to follow the other man around like a lost puppy. So, he sat at the picnic table, talked to his sisters, ate more watermelon than he wanted to, and watched and waited…

Seeing Steven crossing the patio, BBQ platter in hand, Daniel leapt to his feet, and beat the other man to the patio door. "Here, let me get that." Daniel grabbed the door handle and slid the door open for Steven.

"Thanks." Steven stepped into the kitchen and glanced at the table. "Does it matter where I put this?"

"Nah, wherever there's an empty space is fine. Sandy's not that picky." Steven put the platter down and Daniel tossed a bag of hot dog buns at him, motioning to a basket at the end of the table. As Steven tore the bag open and emptied the buns into the basket, Daniel did the same with the hamburger buns at his end of the table. "Now, if this was Karen's place," Daniel rolled his eyes, "whole other story! Karen plans her table settings as carefully as any military coup, and if you screw it up, there will be war."

Steven laughed. "I just met Karen by the pool. She seemed nice."

"Oh, she is." Daniel opened the fridge and tossed first ketchup, and then mustard, at Steven. "She's really nice. Do anything for you. She just thinks that everything belongs in its place. All the time! Everything!"

Steven placed the condiments in the centre of the table, *exactly* in the centre. "I'm a little like that myself. Sorry." He held his hands up in a 'don't shoot me' gesture. "Guilty."

Daniel nodded. "Yeah, Doug took one look at you and said you probably colour-coded your linen."

Steven looked down at his shirt. "Too much starch?"

Daniel smiled at the man he'd already filed under Mr. Perfect in his internal contact list. "Could be worse, at least you don't have a crease ironed into your shorts."

Steven twitched one of the napkins into an exact alignment with the cutlery, and looked over at the blond across the table. "So, I'm not a total head case?"

Daniel nodded. "Little bit, yeah." He looked directly at Steven. "Just enough to be interesting." And Daniel was interested, very interested.

Yeah, Steven got that, thanks. It was always an ego-stroke when someone found you attractive or, you know, wanted to get into your pants, whatever, but this guy looked like a work-in-progress and the only fixer-upper he had time for right now was the house across the street that he and the bank owned.

A small twitch of his lips, the merest beginning of a smile was all the reaction that Daniel got. "You guys just met me. For all you know I could have candy wrappers littering the floor of my car and empty beer cans scattered around the living room."

"Do you?"

Steven shuddered. "God, no!"

Daniel laughed, full out laughed. He threw his head back, and loosed a deep, rich roar that made Steven laugh with him. Laughter lit gold sparks in his hazel eyes and suddenly Steven didn't care that there were three buttons missing on the pockets of Daniel's cargo shorts.

On the other side of the glass patio door, in the backyard, Brady barked and rushed the gate to the driveway. "Brady, you fool. Sit!" Despite Brady's interference, Allan managed to unlatch the gate and push it open. "Hey, Brady. Sit down, crazy!"

Doug heard the commotion at the gate and turned to find his wife's cousin trying to shove Brady away. "Allan!" Doug shouted and heads turned.

Sandy grinned and pointed to the empty lawn chair beside her. "Only an hour and ten minutes late, you're getting better."

Brady jumping at his side, Allan walked over to the chair and collapsed into it. "I'm here!"

Glen closed the lid on the BBQ, reached into the cooler and handed Allan a beer. "What did you do this time?"

Allan twisted the top off, and took a swallow. "It's not my fault you live out in the middle of nowhere."

Doug laughed, and Glen shook his head. "We live fifteen minutes out of the downtown core, accessible from every major highway in the city. How the hell do you keep getting lost?"

Allan shrugged. "Well, I was at Cynthia's place last night. I've never come here from there before."

Glen groaned. "Unbelievable!"

Julia put her arm around her nephew. "Allan has more important things on his mind."

Doug smirked. "Yeah, like getting laid last night."

"Which one's Cynthia?" Brian scrolled through mental images of Allan's girlfriends. "I get them all mixed up."

"The tall blond with the ponytail, Dad." Sandy grinned at her cousin. "I thought you were seeing Jessica?"

"Well, yeah, but not just Jessica." Allan winked.

Doug stared at his wife's cousin. "I don't get it. You're not that good looking."

Allan looked wounded. "Yes, I am."

Shouts of laughter and jeers met this statement. Sandy stood and pulled her cousin out of his chair. "Come on, Casanova. Lunch is ready."

Lunch was a relaxed casual affair, everyone talking over everyone else. As the only one in the room not connected by blood or marriage, Steven didn't say much. His head constantly turned from one person to the next, as he tried to follow the multiple conversations, all of which were delivered with machine gun rapidity interspersed with laughter.

"So what happened this time? Miss your exit?" It was impressive actually, how many different ways Allan could screw up, and it was Daniel's pleasure to remind his cousin of every single time.

Allan started to answer but Glen beat him to it. "He only knows how to get here from his place, but he was coming from Cynthia's ..." Glen shrugged.

"Who says he knows how to get here from his place?" Doug jumped aboard the Allan-baiting train.

"Hey!" Allan's protest was pure form; he actually thrived on the attention.

"He only took one wrong turn when he came for Mother's day." Karen wasn't actually being supportive. She was simply supplying more ammunition.

Groans and smirks erupted around the table. Daniel turned to Steven, explaining what everyone else already knew. "He got lost coming from my mother's house, with my mother in the car, giving him directions!"

Steven looked at Allan. He shrugged, not at all upset by the routine ribbing. "Hey, it happens."

Brian squirted mustard onto a burger, and looked around the table, raising his eyebrows and drawing out his words sardonically. "All...the...time."

"What I don't understand is how you get to your girlfriends' places without getting lost." Doug frowned at Allan, clearly baffled by what he saw as an insurmountable problem. "Explain that."

"Well, most of the time, they pick me up." Allan smiled gently at Doug, obviously pitying someone who didn't understand how the world worked.

Steven looked from Doug to Allan to Daniel. "They?"

Daniel grinned. "Allan's a bit of a player."

Karen wiped ketchup off her son's fingers. "Yeah, a bit!"

Julia defended her favourite nephew. "Sometimes it takes a lot of looking to find the right one!"

"I just don't see the attraction. What am I missing?" Doug was an accountant. He liked definite answers, preferably in black and white. "Is it some kind of pheromone thing? Is he really that good looking?"

"Yes!" Sandy, Karen, and Julia answered as one, laughing.

Allan grinned at his cousins and aunt, pleased with their support. "Thank you, ladies."

"You're relatives, you don't count." Doug turned to Steven, directing his question to him. "What do you think?"

Steven gave Allan his full attention. He saw the blond hair that Daniel and Karen shared, but brighter, more gold than theirs, ocean blue eyes above the kind of smile you find in toothpaste ads, and a loose limbed tightly muscled body with narrow hips and broad shoulders. For a born and bred Canadian, Allan Fine certainly projected the perfect All-American image.

Allan smiled at Steven, a teasing glint in his eyes, and then his body language shifted subtly. He leaned into the table, focused on

Steven. Heated images of entwined limbs and twisted sheets played in his eyes as he invited the other man to make those images real. His eyes flicked down to Steven's mouth, as he allowed his own lips to open slightly. The whole table went silent and then Allan sat back. The spell broke, and he was once again the cousin they knew.

Steven blinked. He had never seen such an effective 'come hither' look delivered so effortlessly. "I think," He grinned at Steven, "that if you ever want to explore a different playing field, I'm across the street at number 8."

The table burst into catcalls and hoots. Everyone laughed; everyone but Daniel, who shot his cousin a narrow-eyed stare. Suddenly Allan wasn't that funny anymore. He hadn't physically fought with Allan since they were kids wrestling over the TV remote. Right now, he seriously wished he was nine years old again, so he could kick the chair out from under the lecherous lothario.

Ignoring the laughing adults, Lauren slid off her chair, and fed the rest of her hot dog to Brady. Eyes on his cousin, Rhys climbed out of his booster seat. He had appointed himself Lauren's shadow, where she went, he followed.

"Where are you going, guys?" Glen's voice stopped his daughter. Lauren turned, her hand behind her back, trying to pretend that she hadn't been on the point of sliding the back door open. "What's the rule?" Glen was proud of his daughter's independence, but no one was drowning on his watch.

"I can't go in the backyard without an adult when the pool is open." Lauren walked over to her father and leaned against his knee, eyes all pleading. "Come with us, Daddy."

Glen brushed Lauren's hair back. "Why don't you show Rhys your new iPad game while I help Mom clean up, and then we'll all go outside together?"

Steven found that he was a sucker for little kids with woebegone faces. "I can take the kids out, while you clean up." Steven smiled at Lauren. "We can keep an eye on Brady. Make sure he doesn't fall in the pool."

Imagining his hands around Allan's throat, Daniel wasn't paying any attention to Glen and Lauren's conversation, but Steven's offer snapped him into action. Grabbing Rhys, he swooped his nephew through the air, settled him on one hip, slid the back door open and smiled at Steven. "You and Lauren can keep an eye on Brady. I'll watch out for this one."

Brady and the two kids spilled into the backyard, trailed by Steven and Daniel. Her brother slid the patio door closed behind him and Karen raised her eyebrows, as she started to gather up the dirty dishes, her voice leaking sarcasm. "Well, he's just the perfect uncle today, isn't he?"

Sandy laughed as she loaded the dishwasher. "Obviously, he needed the right incentive."

Julia walked around the table and stood by the window, looking into the backyard, watching her son. She worried about Daniel. It had been almost a year since his breakup with Aidan and he still wasn't dating anyone. She didn't think he was even trying. He seemed to have given up on finding anyone to share his life with. Aidan had hurt him, she knew that, but she also knew her son. No matter what he said, Daniel wasn't happy. "Do you think he likes him?"

Glen laughed. "Oh, I think that's a pretty safe bet."

Brian moved to the window and wrapped an arm around his wife. "He's not in kindergarten anymore. You can't make play dates for him."

Doug stood at the patio door, watching the kids running around and the two men talking. "You can set up the play dates, but you can't make them play with each other." He grinned, and raised his eyebrows at his wife.

Karen groaned. "Yeah, we get it. So funny!"

Allan grabbed his beer off the table, trying to stay out of the way of the clean-up crew. "Wait. You guys set this up?"

"No." "Yes, totally!"

Sandy glared at her husband. "It is not a set up. Steven just moved in and he didn't have any plans for Canada Day so I invited him."

Glen snorted. "Right! Like you would have asked him if you thought he was straight!" Glen grinned at Allan. "Once she confirmed that he was single, she started plotting."

Karen packed the leftovers into the fridge. "Well, someone had to do something. It's not like Daniel is making any effort."

Allan took a swig of his beer. "Give the guy a break. Eight years! You don't get over something like that so fast."

Doug snorted. "Like you'd know?"

"Well, not personally, no." Allan loved that his perceived stud status made Doug crazy. There had actually been a female or two that had said no, but he didn't feel any need to inform his cousin's husband of that. "But, I've seen a lot of chick flicks."

As his relatives debated whether or not he was ready to move on, Daniel stood in the sunshine, watching his niece and nephew draw designs on the patio stones, thinking about the man standing next to him. No matter how many versions of 'Why don't you give me a tour of your new house?' he rehearsed in his mind, they all sounded exactly like what they were; thinly veiled suggestions of 'let's get naked'.

"When can we go swimming?" Lauren looked up from the patio stones, a purple stick of sidewalk chalk in her hand.

Daniel checked his watch. "Fifteen minutes."

Lauren turned to her cousin and relayed the information, voice full of authority. "Fifteen minutes." She glanced at the chalk in Rhys's hand. "You're colouring the tree red?"

Daniel smiled at Steven, lowering his voice so the kids wouldn't hear him. "I know that whole don't swim right after you eat thing is an old wives' tale. I'm just buying myself some time until Sandy or Glen get out here. They can take the kids into the pool."

"You don't like swimming?"

"Water's too cold. I'm a hot tub kind of guy." Daniel snagged a lawn chair and angled it towards the sun. "That's one of the reasons why I chose the building I'm in; indoor pool, hot tub."

"Nice! You use it a lot?"

Daniel turned to face Steven, gold flecks jumping in his hazel eyes. Steven already knew that meant Daniel was laughing even when he wasn't. "No. Not even once!" The rumbling laugh exploded, a sound that for some reason seemed to warm Steven from the inside out. "The building has a small gym too." Daniel sank into the chair. "Or so I've heard." He stretched an arm out and tugged a second lawn chair over for Steven. "Do you work out?"

Steven sat beside Daniel and tipped his head back to feel the sun on his face. "Does sitting on the couch eating Ben & Jerry's, and watching Bowflex infomercials count?"

"Which flavour?"

"Chocolate Fudge Brownie."

Daniel nodded. "Yeah, anything chocolate counts."

Steven grinned. "Then yes, I work out."

Oh, shit! That tilted smile at full force was aimed right at Daniel and he wanted to lick it off Steven's face. Daniel stared at Steven's mouth wondering if those lips would still be at a slight angle when they were wrapped around his ... *Fuck!* He had to see this guy again, somewhere, anywhere that wasn't here, surrounded by his freaking family.

Steven watched, fascinated as Daniel's eyes changed colour, the hazel shifting to gold. The wild mass of messy blond hair framing golden eyes, the fixed stare, the sudden tension in Daniel's shoulders; it all said predator. Daniel was suddenly mirroring some great jungle cat and Steven went still as an unexpected flare of want blazed in his groin. Maybe unpolished boat shoes weren't such a crime.

Allan slid the patio door open, interrupting the heated eye-lock. "Guys! Want anything? Beer? Coke?" He shook a wrapped ice treat at them. "Cyclone?"

"No, thank you." Steven smiled and Daniel shook his head. Allan slid the door closed behind him and stopped to look at the chalk Picasso the kids were making. "No cat?"

"No." Lauren wrinkled her nose. "I don't like cats."

"Nice tree, Rhys! Red leaves for Canada Day, very patriotic." Allan complimented Rhys as he burst the wrapping on his Cyclone open.

Rhys had no idea what patriotic meant and he wasn't at all interested in finding out. He held a finger up for Allan to see. "I hurt my finger yesterday." Rhys poked at his Sesame Street Band-Aid, looked up at Allan, and announced with the absolute seriousness of a three-year-old. "It bleeded."

"That's why he's colouring everything red." Lauren chose a green piece of chalk. "He likes blood."

Allan nodded. "Got it." He examined the chalk art. "If you want, I can take a picture when you're finished. That way when the rain washes it away, you'll still have it."

Lauren sat back on her heels, hands covered in chalk. "Okay."

Allan took a bite of his Cyclone and smiled down at the miniature of his cousin. "Good, find me when it's done." He walked around the patio picture, careful not to step on any chalk lines, and parked himself on the seat of the picnic table next to the lawn chairs Daniel and Steven were using. "I figure it's 50/50. Rhys is either going to be a doctor or a vampire when he grows up."

Steven looked over at the kids and smiled. Daniel took in the multi-coloured ice thing Allan was eating and laughed at his cousin. "How old are you?"

Allan took the treat out of his mouth. "Younger than you, dude!"

And he was, the little shit. Allan was two years younger than Daniel, and taller, and better looking. Sitting sideways on the picnic bench, Allan's knee was only inches away from Steven's, and that made Daniel twitchy with discomfort. "Here, take my chair."

Allan licked around the rapidly melting Cyclone. "Nah, this is fine."

Daniel stood. "No, really." He practically pushed his cousin off the bench and took his place.

With a shrug and a 'you're such a freak' look, Allan sank into the lawn chair. Steven wondered about the musical chairs act, but he didn't say anything. Pretending not to see the quizzical look, Daniel leaned back against the edge of the picnic table, angling his body so that his knee was almost touching Steven's. *Better, much better!*

Allan watched the possessive bit of body language and comprehension flashed across his face. He smirked at his cousin, and Daniel glared back. "So, Steven, what do you do?"

"I'm a pharmacist."

"Really?" Allan leaned forward in his chair, eyes betraying an oddly excessive interest.

"No." Steven shook his head. "Whatever you're thinking I can get for you. I can't."

"Stickler for the rules, eh?"

Steven nodded. "Yes, sorry, strictly by the book."

Allan glanced at his cousin. "Strict." He repeated the word, his voice dripping with innuendo. "Ow!" He glared at Daniel as he rubbed his abused shin.

"Oh, sorry, man." Daniel wasn't sorry. "Didn't see your leg there." He turned to Steven. "Hospital or drug store?"

"Drug store, you know that small independent pharmacy over on Cloverleaf? Less shampoo, more drugs. What about you guys?"

Allan laughed. "He's an unemployed, undiscovered author. I'm a photographer."

Daniel ignored his cousin. "I write for a few local magazines, mostly freelance stuff." He waved a hand, indicating Allan. "He chases women, and takes a few pictures."

"I do not chase women." Allan got up to toss his empty Cyclone stick in the garbage. "They chase me!" Pulling his phone out of his back pocket, he walked over to the kids. "You guys ready for that picture?"

Daniel moved back to the lawn chair Allan had vacated. "And they do too." He nodded at Allan. "I've seen it. All he has to do is smile and they're all over him. Fucker!" Daniel turned to Steven. "Not just the women either."

Steven's eyes went wide with surprise. "He plays for both teams?"

Daniel shook his head. "Not that I know of, why, you interested?" Teasing Steven, he asked the question lightly, but his heart beat like a caged thing, while he held his breath, waiting for Steven's answer. *Say no! Say no! Please, say no!*

Steven laughed. "Nah, I couldn't keep up with him." He shrugged. "I'm boring. I like the comfort of routine, a few friends, a shared meal, the same face over the breakfast table." He glanced over at Allan and turned, smiling at Daniel. "I think he likes the game. I don't."

I can do that. I can be that face over the breakfast table. Daniel squelched the insane image. *What the fuck?* "He does. He has the attention span of a four-year-old with ADD. He's always looking for the new, next, best thing." Daniel watched as Allan took pictures of the chalk drawing, laughing with the kids. "But he's not an asshole about it. He's honest. He's the first person I'd go to if I needed anything. He'll help, no questions asked. Even better, he won't tell you how to run your life which, in this family, is a freaking miracle!"

Steven laughed. "Pretty free with the advice around here, are they?"

Daniel grinned. "Hang around long enough, and you'll see for yourself."

And Steven did just that, he hung around. He stayed way past lunch and into the afternoon because he wanted to get to know his neighbours. Right! It had nothing to do with a shaggy blond in crumpled cargo shorts, absolutely nothing.

An intergenerational game of Frisbee with Daniel, Rhys and Steven on one team and Glen, Doug and Lauren on the other, ended in a draw because Brady took off with the plastic disc. Laughing, as Glen tried to pry the Frisbee from the dog's jaws, Steven glanced at his watch and did a double-take; 4:57 pm!

He hadn't really wanted to come. Spending the day with a bunch of strangers wasn't his idea of a good time. But, he didn't want to start off on the wrong foot with his neighbours, so he told himself to go make nice. He figured an hour and a half, two hours tops, and then he could go home and strip the disgusting wallpaper in his *en suite*. But the afternoon had passed in a blur of friendly teasing and family jokes. He felt surprisingly comfortable here, as if he had known these people forever. And, of course, there was Daniel.

Steven's eyes tracked the man, as he leaned over his mother's chair, making her laugh at something Steven couldn't hear. Beat-up boat shoes, cargo shorts that should have been relegated to the waste bin years ago, and a faded T-shirt; this was not a look that screamed 'responsible, got-my-shit-together adult'. It was a look that Steven felt could only be excused on a university campus. Not a look he found attractive in any way.

So, why was he watching the man? Why did he smile every time Daniel loosed that deep roar of a laugh? Why did he keep flashing on that look in Daniel's eyes earlier? Just thinking about the predatory lust in that focused stare had Steven's pulse jumping. Looking at Daniel now, he didn't see the ramshackle clothing and the messy blond hair. No, he saw the toned body under the Value Village clothes, the muscular legs above the dusty boat shoes, the wide hazel eyes set above a full lower lip that Steven wanted to sink his teeth into. Yes, in different clothes Daniel Fine could command some serious attention, or even better, no clothes at all. *Okay, time to go!*

Steven looked around for his hostess and found her sitting at the picnic table with her sister. "Sandy, thanks for today. I had a great time." Smiling at both women, Steven nodded at the diminutive blond sitting opposite Sandy. "Nice to meet you, Karen."

"Nice to meet you." Karen smiled at the man she was hoping would make Daniel forget Aidan had ever existed. "Enjoy your new place."

Sandy pushed Brady off her feet, and stood up. "I'm so glad you could come." She walked with Steven to the patio door. "I'm surprised you lasted this long. I know meeting so many new people all at once can be a pain." She slid the door open and Steven followed her into the house.

"You're family made it easy."

Sandy smiled as they walked through the kitchen. "They have their good points. They're a little opinionated, and they're not big on privacy, but they care." Crossing the foyer, she opened the front door. "Drop by anytime. My father wasn't kidding, you know. He's always happy to have a reason to get out his toolbox." Steven stepped outside and Sandy followed him on to the front steps. "He gets a little bored, now that he's retired."

Steven touched the pocket that held his phone. "I've got his number. I'll definitely call. Thanks again." Smiling, he started down the walkway.

Oh, no you don't. You're not getting away that easily! "Steven!" He turned at Sandy's call. "We're walking down to watch fireworks at ten. It's at the park at the end of the street. You want to join us?"

"Okay, sure." Steven waived and crossed the street. He liked fireworks. Hazel eyes, blond hair, a deep, rumbling laugh, and really nicely muscled calves had nothing to do with it. *Yeah, right!*

Sandy closed the door behind Steven and leaned back against it, triumphant. *You so owe me, Daniel Fine!*

The docked iPod in his bedroom blasted Steven's favourite playlist, as he danced around his small *en suite* methodically stripping wallpaper so bright it made him wince. He pulled the last offending piece off the wall, and stood back, smiling in satisfaction. Tomorrow, he'd clean the walls and splash on some paint. It shouldn't take too long. Thinking of time, he glanced at his wrist, which didn't help because he had taken his watch off before he started to fight with the wallpaper. Stepping into the doorway of the *en suite*, he checked the digital on his bedside table, 9:34. Damn! Stripping his grungy work clothes off, he beat his own record for fastest shower ever.

Unlike Daniel, Steven had no trouble finding his keys. Entering the park three blocks south, at the end of the crescent, Steven looked for Sandy and Glen. Okay, he was really looking for Daniel, but he wasn't admitting that, not even to himself. In the dark, it was hard to recognize anyone until you were almost on top of them. People were spread out, standing amid trees, sitting in lawn chairs, even lying on blankets looking up at the sky. A few stragglers, like Steven, were wandering in the dark looking for friends and family.

"Steven!! Over here!" Karen waved her phone, the screen glowing bright against the night.

Steven turned towards the yell and tracked the waving blue light. As he got closer, he could see Doug and Karen, Sandy and Glen and, yes, Daniel. "I didn't think I'd find you."

Sandy moved to stand in front of her husband, leaving a space for Steven beside her brother. "You're just in time. They've already fired the test shots. It won't be long now." Sandy was practically bouncing in place, excitement bubbling through her voice. "Fireworks are the best part of Canada Day!"

The music cut out. Anticipation spread on the air, as everyone looked up. When the first volley of noise and colour melted out of the sky, Steven looked at the blond beside him and found Daniel enjoying the spectacle as much as he was. Grinning at each other, they turned as one, looking up as the next rocket whistled into the air.

The first half of the show ended with an appreciative round of applause from the crowd. Waiting for the second stage of sound and fury, Steven noticed that Daniel had moved closer, now standing behind instead of beside him. *That doesn't mean anything. He's probably not even aware of it. He's watching the fireworks. It doesn't mean anything.* Eyes on the sky, Steven stepped back, stumbling in to the man standing behind him.

Daniel steadied Steven, one arm sliding across Steven's back, his hand resting on Steven's hip. "You, okay?" Daniel whispered the question against Steven's ear.

"Yeah, sorry." Steven tried to read Daniel's expression but it was too dark.

Daniel didn't move away. He kept his hand lightly curved over Steven's hip, his eyes on the fireworks blasting above them. If Steven wasn't interested, all he had to do was step away. But Daniel was betting that Steven was going to stay right where he was. He knew what that look meant, the one they had shared just before Allan interrupted them. He knew that for the rest of the afternoon, every time he looked around he found Steven watching him. Daniel had no idea why Mr. Perfect had suddenly gone from friendly to interested and he didn't give a shit. The man was right here, under his hand and Daniel wasn't going to mess that up with too many questions.

Steven stood still, under the hand that felt like a brand on his hip, arguing with himself. *What are you doing? You barely know this guy. Are you kidding me? Since when has that mattered? This is Sandy's brother. So, the fuck what? She's my neighbour, this could get awkward. Right! Tell me you don't like the feel of his hand on you. Tell me you don't want to feel more of…* Steven very subtly leaned back.

Daniel felt Steven press into him and his body didn't stop to consult his brain. Slipping his arm around Steven's waist, he pulled the other man flush against him, Steven's back pressed to his chest, Steven's ass tucked against his groin. He held his breath, waiting, hoping. Steven turned, smiled that slightly off-centre smile, and Daniel started to breathe again. *Yes! Oh, yes! We are so doing this!*

Steven stood entranced, head back, eyes on the exploding lights in the night sky. He watched the fireworks; Daniel watched him.

CHAPTER 3

Enquiring Minds Want to Know

The first day back after a long weekend was always a shit-storm of emails, phone calls, and employees who had trouble getting their heads back in the game. And, of course, the ever amusing switch-hitting necessary in the summer, as one staff member after the other took vacation time, just added to the mix of crazy. The day had been one long exercise in time management, and Karen was glad to see the end of it. Working through lunch, with a sandwich in front of her laptop, had not been the highlight of her career. Driving home from the office Tuesday evening, she took the first opportunity she'd had all day to call her sister.

Hitting the voice icon on her steering wheel, Karen spoke to her car. "Phonebook."

The dashboard screen switched to a display of her contacts, and her car spoke to her. "Please say a name."

"Sandy."

Her car got conversational. "Did you say, Sandy?"

Karen nodded, which was ridiculous because the car couldn't see her. "Yes." Sitting through a red light, she tapped her fingers against the steering wheel, listening to the phone ring.

"Hello?"

"So? Have you heard anything?" Karen didn't have to be any more specific than that, Sandy knew what she was talking about.

"No, and I can't call Daniel. I don't want him to figure out that Steven's being here wasn't exactly a coincidence." Sandy was dying to find out if her 'not a set up' had worked.

Karen flicked her right turn signal and switched lanes. "What about Mom? She calls him all the time. He won't suspect anything."

At the other end of the Bluetooth connection, Sandy started preparations for dinner. Opening the fridge, she pulled out a package of chicken. "She already tried. She called and rambled on about the BBQ, and Allan's craziness, and mentioned that Dad was really looking forward to helping out at Steven's place, and didn't he seem like a nice guy? Nothing. He said, 'yeah, he seemed nice' and changed the subject." She plugged the grill in and sprayed it with PAM. "Maybe we were wrong, maybe they didn't click."

Karen snorted as she passed a lumbering mini-van. "Right! When was the last time he volunteered to watch Rhys and Lauren? And did you see how close they were standing at the fireworks?"

Needing two hands to tear open the wrapping on the chicken, Sandy put the phone down and hit speaker. "Yes! They certainly looked comfortable!" She settled the chicken breasts on the grill and rubbed seasoning over them. "I know Aidan hurt him, but it's time. It's more than time!"

"Never liked him; pretentious asshole!" Karen pulled into her driveway. "I'm home. The guys are all playing soccer tomorrow night. I'm going to sic Doug on him."

"Good, that's good. Let me know if you find out anything. I really don't want to have to get up early and pretend to jog just as Steven's leaving for work!"

Karen laughed. "Nice! Bye."

❖   ❖   ❖

Wednesday afternoon rapidly turned into evening as Daniel stared at his blank computer screen. The words weren't coming. He couldn't concentrate. His eyes flicked to the date in the bottom right corner of the screen and he winced. He took pride in the fact that he had never missed a deadline in his life, but today, he just couldn't focus. His mind kept going back to that damn BBQ, those chocolate eyes, and how perfect Steven had felt pressed against him in the dark. *Fuck!* Giving up on his, as yet, non-existent article, he pushed away from the table, and took to pacing the living-room floor instead. *What the hell was I thinking? I can't do this. I'm not ready for this! Really? Not ready? You were plenty ready at the fireworks on Monday night. Shut the fuck up!*

Contrary to what his family believed, Daniel did not spend every night sitting at home missing his ex. After the break-up, he had done what every other self-respecting guy did when he got dumped. He hit the bars, credit card in hand, and got plastered. He hooked up with anything that moved because he could, because he wanted to obliterate the memory of Aidan, because he needed to prove to himself that there was nothing wrong with him.

The bodies of strangers helped him repair the ego that Aidan had decimated. Now, almost a year later, his self-concept and pride restored, Daniel no longer hit the clubs and bars with the same desperation. When he felt like it, when his own hand wasn't enough, he prowled Church Street. He was in control. He was safe on his island of one. He didn't need anything more.

Hook-ups he could do, one night stands that left with the sun, no problem. But he couldn't do this. He couldn't start something that could actually be something. *A movie? Dinner? Christ! A fucking date! What the fuck was I thinking? You were thinking that you wanted to…Fuck!* He ran his hand over the back of his neck. He was thirty-two years old, and in gay years that was ancient. Did they even call it dating anymore? Daniel paced into the kitchen and grabbed a Coke out of the fridge. He'd never really dated. In his undergrad years he'd just gone out with friends and dragged a guy back to his dorm whenever he could. Nothing was complicated, nothing was serious, it was all just fun.

Aidan had been serious, though. Daniel had been in the last year of his Master's program, and Aidan had needed a tutor for an English Lit course. Daniel had taken one look at Aidan and stopped looking at anyone else. Two weeks later, Aidan had moved out of the undergrad dorms and into Daniel's basement apartment off campus.

Crushing the empty can, he tossed it into the blue recycling bin. He understood the concept of dating, of course. He'd certainly seen most of his friends do it. He'd just never done it himself. How did anyone do that, sit at a restaurant table and eat and ask a lot of polite questions, when all they really wanted to do was get naked? At least, that's what he wanted to do. He wasn't so sure about Steven.

Thinking about Mr. Perfect, Daniel shut his computer down, and changed into his soccer uniform. He didn't know Steven very well, but he knew enough to know that the guy wanted more than bodies in motion. Sitting in Sandy's backyard, Steven had been pretty clear. He wanted the 'same face over the breakfast table', and Daniel wanted him. So, yeah, he was doing this.

Lacing up his soccer shoes, he grabbed his phone off the night table and started the ritual hunt for his keys. He checked the kitchen counters, the top of the microwave, and finally found them on the shelf under the flat screen in the living room. Locking the door, he couldn't help smiling as he thought of Steven, wondering if he had one of those key racks that Karen loved so much.

❖ ❖ ❖

Their soccer games were fairly competitive considering that more than half the team would never see thirty again. Limping off the field after the game, tired and dirty, Daniel promised himself, yet again, that he would start doing stretches before he played; next week, definitely.

"Danny!" Doug jogged passed him, grinning as he tossed the soccer ball from hand to hand. "You're supposed to kick the ball, man, not the ground."

Daniel shrugged. "Yeah, here's the thing. The damn ball keeps moving!"

Glen honked the horn of his SUV, and lowered the driver's side window. "Guys, let's go. If I'm not home by midnight, Sandy gets pissed."

Doug took shot gun, and tossed the ball into the back seat, very precisely aimed at Daniel's head. "What happens, Glen? Do you turn into a pumpkin?

Glen just grinned as he backed out of his parking space. "I like to find my wife waiting in our bed when I get home."

Doug shared a glance with Daniel in the back seat. Daniel asked the question for both of them. "Wouldn't she be in bed no matter what time you got home?"

"Right!" Glen snorted, as he turned out of the parking lot. "When we were first married, I came home late every time I hung out with the guys; two, sometimes three, in the morning." He stopped at a red light, and looked at Doug beside him and Daniel in the rear view mirror. "Sandy wasn't happy about it, but I was young and dumb, and I thought just 'cause we were married didn't mean I couldn't have a good time with my friends." Hitting his turn signal, he took a right at the lights. "Sandy started going out with her friends, her single friends. She came home at two in the morning, with phone numbers on cocktail napkins."

Doug's mouth dropped open. "No shit!"

"Oh, yeah!" Glen looked over at Doug. "I did not like coming home to an empty house and an empty bed, because my wife was out having fun with the girls." Glen pulled into a parking space in front of King Henry's Arms and cut the ignition. Three doors slid open and snapped shut as the men climbed out of the car. "So now I'm home by midnight and so is she." Glen pulled the heavy oak door to the pub open. "Besides, on soccer nights Sandy overdoses on Matt Bomer in *White Collar*, so I'm pretty much guaranteed some action if I get home before she falls asleep."

Doug went to the bar, while Glen and Daniel snagged a table near the large flat screen. They weren't going to watch anything, but the flickering screen acted like a homing beacon, drawing them in. Doug joined them carrying three bottles of Molson Canadian. Sliding one each in front of both Daniel and Glen, he sank into his chair cradling his own bottle. "So, Matt Bomer, eh? Sandy likes young, pretty gay boys?"

Daniel laughed as he reached for his beer. "Doesn't everyone?"

Laughing with him, both his brothers-in-law shook their heads in denial. Doug took a chug from his bottle and sighed with satisfaction. Catching Glen's eye, Doug signaled the start of 'operation yenta', and turned to Daniel. "You're the expert. I say Glen's new neighbour is gay, Glen says he could be metrosexual." Doug pointed his bottle at Glen. "His gaydar sucks!"

"Like yours is so great! You base everything on social stereotypes. It's not that simple, is it?" Glen turned to Daniel for support.

"Not always, no."

"But in this case, I'm right. The anal retentive across the street is gay, right?" Doug waited impatiently for Daniel's answer.

Daniel nodded. "Yes."

"Knew it!" Doug flashed Glen a triumphant grin. "Should have put money on it."

"You sure?" The whole conversation was bogus, of course. This was just Doug's lame ass attempt to find out if Daniel was going to see Steven again.

Hiding his smile behind his bottle of Molson, Daniel flashed on the way Steven had felt, pressed against him in the dark, lights exploding above them. "Pretty sure, yeah."

"You guys looked…" Doug raised an eyebrow and stressed his next word significantly, "*friendly* at the fireworks."

Thinking that Doug must have read his mind, Daniel shrugged. "It was dark. Steven tripped."

"Uh-huh." Doug wasn't buying it. "That's what you guys are calling it now, tripping? Isn't that what they used to say in the seventies, you know, flower-power, sit-ins, tripping on acid?" Doug tried, and failed, to make his next question appear casual. "You going to see him again?"

Daniel's eyes narrowed in suspicion. Since when did Doug play stand-in for Cupid? Never, that's when! This was Karen. The words were coming out of Doug's mouth, but the question was all Karen. "Fucking traitors!" Daniel slammed his bottle down on the table top. "What happened to the Bro Code?"

Glen pointed his raised bottle at Doug. "Told you he would catch on."

"I'm not an idiot! You guys never ask me about my relationships." Daniel traced quotation marks in the air, as he spat the last word out. "Something I've always really appreciated, by the way." He shook his head at them. "And now, you've gone over to the dark side."

Glen had the decency to look embarrassed but Doug just shrugged. "I like you Danny, but when I get home tonight Karen's going to be all over me about this Steven thing. And, no offense, but I'd rather have her all over me about me, you know? So, sorry about the Bro Code but..."

"I get it. Your wife's got you by the balls. I totally understand." Daniel's smile oozed sympathy as he commiserated with Doug.

Doug laughed as he raised his bottle, acknowledging Daniel's insult. "Not right at the moment, she doesn't, but I'm hoping later, yeah."

Daniel raised his right hand. "Stop! I don't want to know." Looking at both men, he leaned into the table. "Okay, you can go home and tell your wives that you tried. Tell them you asked and I said..." Daniel stared at his brothers-in-law, speaking to his absent sisters, "it's none of their fucking business!"

❊ ❊ ❊

Steven wasn't freaking out about his immanent date with Daniel. He wasn't thinking about Daniel at all, as he stood in his living room Thursday night, surrounded by the contents of several IKEA boxes. The various components seemed to be multiplying like tribbles as he stared at them in dismay. He picked up one of the white instruction sheets, and scanned it quickly. *I'm going to kill that kid. I'm going to drive back to IKEA, find that hormonal eighteen-year-old 'expert', and kick his ass! Easy! Easy for whom? NASA engineers?* There were twenty-one separate steps in the assembly directions, and that was for the small cabinet!

He sank onto the sofa, shoulders slumped, instruction sheet clutched in his hand. *What were you thinking? You can barely change a light bulb. Hanging a flat screen TV and three storage cabinets, no way!* He couldn't do it but, shifting on the couch he fished his phone out of his back pocket, he knew someone who could. Scrolling through his contacts, he found Brian Fine, and hit call.

"Hello?" Julia picked up the cordless phone on the kitchen counter.

"Hi, is this Julia?"

"Yes?" The voice sounded vaguely familiar, but Julia couldn't place it.

"Hi, this is Steven. I don't know if you remember me…"

"Steven! Of course, I remember you." *I remember you. You're going to be Daniel's Steven.* "What can I do for you, Steven?"

"Well, if Brian was serious, I could use a hand here." *And that's a fucking understatement!*

"He'll be thrilled. Hang on, I'll get him." Taking the phone with her, Julia practically sprinted into the living room, where Brian sat in his recliner watching animals eat each other on the Nature Channel. "It's Steven, for you." She handed her husband the phone and glued herself to his chair. She had no intention of missing a word.

Brian waved her back, but she shook her head, grinning at him. "Steven, how's it going?"

"Well, I'm standing in the middle of a bunch of shelves, and nuts, and bolts, and screws, and other things that I don't even know the name of." Steven groaned. "So, not good."

Brian laughed. "What are you trying to do?"

"I want to hang a flat screen TV, and three storage cabinets on the wall. The kid at IKEA said these things were easy to assemble. He lied."

"Well, if they told you it was hard, no one would buy them." Brian chuckled. "You want some help?"

"More than life itself!" Brian laughed again, a slightly different version of his son's laugh. Daniel's laugh was warm and deep, and it… *focus!*

"I've got a golf game tomorrow but I'm good Saturday. Does that work for you?" Brian glared at his wife, as she grabbed his wrist and leaned into the phone, so she could hear what Steven was saying.

"Please, whatever's good for you, you're doing me the favour!"

"Okay, nine Saturday morning. I'll bring some tools. Those little key things in the assembly package are a pain in the ass."

"Brian, thank you. Is there anything I can get for you, breakfast, lunch? What kind of coffee do you like?"

"Don't worry about the coffee. I can't tell one brand from the other. With any luck, we'll be finished by lunch. See you Saturday."

"Okay, Saturday. Thank you."

"Haven't done anything yet, kid."

"You didn't tell me to get lost, that's something."

"This is a two-dimensional favour, Steven. My wife wasn't kidding; she really is getting sick of me hanging around here. Bye." Brian handed the phone back to Julia. "You can go to Costco without me on Saturday."

"I can do a lot of things without you." Julia laughed and skipped away when Brian tried to grab her. Returning, she curled up on his lap in the recliner. "This is perfect! You can spend time with Steven, get to know him. Find out if he likes Daniel."

"I will not!"

"Brian Henry Fine! Do you want your son to die a lonely, bitter old man?"

"He's only thirty-two; he's got plenty of time. What do I look like some yenta from the old country?"

"You don't have to say anything. Just listen, and tell me if he mentions Daniel. Tell me exactly what he says." Brian started to unbutton his shirt. Julia stared at her husband, wondering if Alzheimer's was setting in. "What are you doing?"

Brian grinned at his bemused wife. "What, you're not going to make me wear a wire?"

❀   ❀   ❀

At his parents' house that Friday night, Daniel's sisters managed to drop Steven's name into the dinner conversation seven times. He knew that because he counted. Seated between his father and Glen, pretending to listen to their analysis of the latest PGA wunderkind, he heard that Steven ran three days a week, that he was planning on interlocking his walkway, and that he had replaced the cabinets in his kitchen.

"Sandy, I forgot to tell you." Julia placed a tray, loaded down with dessert plates and chocolate cake, on the dining room table. "That new neighbour of yours, Steven, called last night." She sliced pieces and popped them onto plates for Karen to hand out. "Your father's going over there tomorrow to help him hang something." Julia called across the table to her husband. "Brian, what are you helping Steven with tomorrow?"

Daniel paid careful attention to his slice of cake, cutting precision pieces in methodical rows, making sure to get exactly the same amount of icing on each forkful. He did not look up from his plate as Brian answered Julia. "Just a couple of wall-hanging cabinets and a flat screen TV; shouldn't be too much trouble."

Karen watched Daniel play with his cake. "You mean an entertainment centre?"

Brian shrugged. "I guess."

Sandy glanced at her brother, and raised her eyebrows at Karen. Karen nodded. *Yeah, got it.* There was no way a grown man needed to pay that much attention to keeping a few crumbs of cake on a fork.

Daniel could tell them. His father was going to be over at Steven's place tomorrow. He should say something. He could, he probably should, but he didn't.

He said nothing, because after thirty-two years in this family, he knew better. He so did not need his sisters weighing in on this, and his mother! God, no! They'd been, not so subtly, hinting for months now that he needed someone in his life. Telling them that he was seeing Steven tomorrow night would be like tossing a bleeding limb into a pool of sharks, a feeding frenzy! They would circle him, picking over his plans and suggesting better ones, totally high-jacking his date because intrusive wasn't even in their vocabulary.

It wasn't just about his nosy sisters, though. Pushing cake around on his plate, Daniel acknowledged the truth to himself. He didn't say anything about his date with Steven because the whole idea had him itching with nerves. Talking, not just the 'your place or mine' conversations he was used to, but actually talking, learning about each other; he didn't do this. Excess personal knowledge like birthdays, religious affiliations, or middle names weren't encouraged in the kind of hit-and-run relationships he indulged in. Half the time he didn't even bother to get a guy's last name. Yet, a few hours with Steven in his sister's backyard, a few minutes watching fireworks, and suddenly he was Freud. Stabbing his fork into the defenseless dessert on his plate, he visualized himself in horn-rimmed glasses, a beard and a German accent, Steven stretched out on a leather couch beside him. *"Tell me Mr. Monaco, tell me…"*

And fuck him, but he wanted to know. He wanted to know everything about Steven, from his first day in kindergarten to his first boyfriend. He wanted to know what music he liked, what movies he watched, what his favourite dessert was. He wanted to know what Mr. Perfect was like in bed, did he keep it all inside or did it all come tumbling out in gasps of profanity? Staring down at his plate, Daniel wondered how those chocolate eyes would look when Steven lost it, cum spurting over Daniel's hand.

Cock hardening inside his thankfully loose sweatpants, gut tense with a combination of nerves and anticipation, Daniel pushed his plate away. Tomorrow night loomed in his mind, a portal to various future possibilities, most of which scared the shit out of him.

❖ ❖ ❖

As it usually did, Saturday morning came way too freaking early for Daniel. He hated Saturday mornings. He hated them while he brushed his teeth. He hated them while he pulled on his work-out gear. He hated them while he clipped his bike to the rack on his car. He hated them while he dragged his bike off his car and waited for Allan to show up.

"Good morning! Great day, isn't it? Sun's perfect, sky's clear, these early mornings are awesome!" Knowing how much Daniel hated getting up early, Allan just had to rub it in. Ticking off Daniel was his default position and one of the major joys in life.

Daniel's sneer was nasty. "Who are you, the fucking weather man?" Glaring at his cousin, he locked his feet into the toe clips on his pedals and took off, Allan right behind him.

Fifteen minutes into their regular circuit, the path widened out and Allan brought his bike alongside his cousin's. "Is it safe to talk now?"

Daniel changed gears and grinned at his cousin. "If you can catch me!"

Three hours later, sweat drying on their bodies, and legs complaining of mistreatment, they fastened their bikes onto the roofs of their cars, and staked out a table at the park's café.

Daniel guzzled his iced coffee, and shook his head at Allan's whipped, candy coated confection. "You call that coffee?"

Allan licked a finger dripping with cream. "I call it nirvana!"

"You're such a girl!"

"Look who's talking!"

Daniel raised a lazy finger in a pointed salute, too tired to work up any real indignation. "Asshole!"

Allan stretched out in his chair, cradling his drink against his chest. "Finish the article?"

"Yeah, had to fight for this one though, absolutely nothing all week and then Thursday it just came together."

"Yep, inspiration's a bitch. Did you take a trip down to Church Street to celebrate?"

"Nah, I met Kevin for dinner."

"Kevin? Oh, right, the one with the hair. What colour is he now?"

Daniel grinned. "Well, he says now that he's Methuselah, which is Kevin speak for thirty, it's time to tone it down. He's gone back to his natural colour, although how he even remembered what it is, is beyond me. He kept the blue extensions though."

"He still with the same guy?"

"Didn't I tell you? He and Jonathan got married a few months back."

Allan shuddered. "Married! Why would he want to do that?"

Daniel shrugged. "He said they lived like they were married, they felt like they were married, so why not actually be married?" Daniel grinned at Allan. "Personally, I think he just wanted to register at Hudson's Bay."

Allan shook his head, smiling because, yeah, that sounded like Kevin. "Well, as long as he had a good reason."

Daniel stirred the ice cubes in the bottom of his glass. "Jonathan's in Vancouver on business, and Kevin's idea of cooking is peanut butter sandwiches, so we went for Indian." Daniel sucked on an ice cube. "What about you, boy wonder?"

Allan snorted. "I hit a wine bar with Caroline."

"Caroline? How do you keep their names straight?"

"I don't." Allan pulled out his Blackberry. "Thank God for smart phones. I keep their pictures in my contact list, so I can connect the name with the face." Allan laughed as he slipped his phone away. "I used to call them all 'honey' but that didn't work out so well!"

"They didn't appreciate the personal touch, huh?" Sarcasm thrummed through Daniel's voice as he laughed at his cousin.

Allan grinned. "I know! Some people are so sensitive." Squinting against the sun in his eyes, he angled his chair away from the glare, and looked across the table at Daniel. "You going to see that guy from Sandy's BBQ?"

"No comment."

Allan sat up in his chair, staring at his cousin, all avid interest. "Well, well. The dead walk again."

"Fuck off!"

❉ ❉ ❉

While Daniel and Allan had been chasing each other over the park's mountain bike trails, Brian had showed up at Steven's place as promised, tool box in hand. He started by running a stud finder over the living room wall. "Once we get the TV bracket installed, we can measure out how we want the wall cabinets spaced." He looked over his shoulder at Steven. "Then we get to the really fun stuff!"

Steven glanced over the IKEA collage decorating his carpet. "You really think we can get this done today?"

Brian fit a bit into his electric drill. "Piece of cake!"

Steven winced. "That's what the kid at IKEA said."

Brian knew what he was doing. By the time they stopped for lunch, the cabinets were assembled and on the wall, the flat-screen hanging between them. Steven closed the door on the delivery guy and dropped the pizza on the coffee table. "It looks great."

Hands on his hips, Brian stepped back, nodding in satisfaction, as he examined the wall. "Not bad."

"Not bad?!" Steven popped the box open and slid a slice onto a paper plate. "It's a work of art!"

Brian turned and took his plate from Steven. "After lunch, we can assemble the storage bench." He nodded to the pile of DVDs in the corner. "And you can get your collection stowed away."

Steven sat on the couch, his plate of pizza carefully balanced on his knees. "Good, the stack on the floor is making me nuts."

Brian scanned the titles as he sipped his beer. "Science fiction?"

"Yeah, I'm a real nerd." Steven shrugged his shoulders, his smile self-deprecating.

Brian came around the coffee table, popped the box open to take a second slice and sat beside Steven on the couch. "I've seen most of the Star Wars and Star Treks 'cause the kids were big fans. Still are."

"Yeah, I know. I'm seeing Star Trek: Into Darkness with Daniel tonight."

Brian nodded. "Yeah?" *Julia's going to flip out!* "I can handle the Star Treks but I drew the line at that Harry Potter stuff they wanted to drag me to."

❖　❖　❖

As lunch time came and went, Julia settled into the couch in the living room, magazine and teacup in hand. She flipped through pages, stared at pictures, and absorbed nothing because she was constantly glancing out the window watching for her husband's car. At the first rumble of the garage door opening, she was up and off the couch, on her way to the front door. Throwing it open, she stood in the doorway, waiting as he came up the walkway. "So, what did he say?"

Brian closed the door behind him. "He said 'Thank you for all your help.'"

Julia smacked her husband's arm. "What! Did! He! Say!"

Brian didn't often get to be the town crier. That honour usually went to his wife or daughters. Enjoying this novel experience, he took his time walking to his recliner, his wife nipping at his heels. "He likes science fiction."

Julia stood in front of Brian's chair, practically vibrating with impatience and curiosity. "So?"

"So he's seeing that new Star Trek movie with Daniel tonight." Brian grinned at the look on his wife's face.

"No!" Julia clasped her hands together, eyes shining with excitement.

Brian nodded, smiling at his wife's reaction. He hadn't seen that look since he gave her the diamond earrings on their 30th anniversary. He nodded. "Yes."

"Oh my God!" Julia turned and reached for the portable on the side table by the couch. "I've got to tell the girls!"

"Oh, no." Brian held his hand out for the phone. "Let me."

❈   ❈   ❈

After failing miserably to convince either Allan or himself that seeing Steven was no big deal, Daniel drove home, flopped onto his couch and pulled the tab on a Coke. Picking up the remote, he checked the time on the PVR, 3:30. He still had plenty of time to take a shower before he met Steven. The phone rang and he groaned as he leaned sideways to grab the portable off the end table. "Hello?"

"Good, you're home. Lauren needs a washroom, let me in."

"Hello to you to, Sandy." Daniel smiled as he hit six on the phone to unlock the condo entrance doors, always happy to see his niece. Powering up the Wii, he clicked over to the dance game Lauren liked. At the imperious knock on his door, he opened it, laughing as Lauren raced past him, down the hall to his washroom. "Wow! What did she drink?"

"Some sugary iced thing with raspberry that was taller than she is." Sandy tossed her bag on the floor and plopped down on the couch. She took in her brother's workout clothes and sweat-depressed hair. "Cycling with Allan?"

Daniel took the arm chair and put his feet up on the coffee table. "Yep. I hate getting up early on the weekend, but it's worth it to beat him every week."

"Of course, you're going to win! He can't take the lead; he'd never find his way out of the park."

"True." Daniel took a stab at being a host. "You want anything, coffee, some of mom's applesauce cake?"

"How come you have applesauce cake? I didn't get any."

"She likes me better?"

Sandy snorted, and smiled at her daughter as she walked into the living room. "You have time to say hello to your uncle now?"

"Hi, Uncle Danny." Lauren picked up the nearest Wii control. "Do you still have Rhythm Heaven?"

"Already loaded. Just hit play."

Sandy was more than happy to let Lauren and Daniel battle their way through the Wii games, while she checked Facebook and Tumblr on her phone.

"Yes!" Daniel scored a strike in Wii bowling, and punched the air in a victory dance.

"You're still losing." Lauren waited for her turn, control hot and ready in her hand.

"Maybe, but that was a strike. Eat my dust!"

Lauren ignored her uncle, totally focused on the game.

Daniel grabbed the phone on the first ring, eyes on the TV screen. "Hello?"

"Mom says you have applesauce cake?" Karen spoke into the metal grid in the lobby.

Daniel punched six, and dropped the portable back into its base, applauding as his niece did her own victory dance. "Way to go, Lauren!"

"Wrong number?" Sandy nodded towards the phone.

"No. Karen's on her way up." Daniel teased his niece as he stabbed at the control buttons. "You're going down, kid."

Sandy answered Karen's knock. "Hey, come on in. Lauren's kicking Daniel's ass at Wii bowling."

"He always had lousy aim." Karen hung her bag on the hall closet's door knob. "Hi, Lauren, how was art class?"

"I spilled paint on my cover-up." Lauren didn't take her eyes off the screen. "But mom says we have another one at home."

"Daniel, we're making coffee. You want some?" Sandy led Karen into the small kitchen.

"Yeah, black, two sugars." Daniel waved his control and grinned at his niece as pins fell all over the screen.

"Where's the cake?" Karen called from the kitchen.

"In the fridge."

Deciding that real cake beat digital bowling, Lauren clicked out of the game and grinned at her uncle. "Cake?"

Daniel took his coffee and leaned against the counter as Lauren filled them in on the trials and tribulations of day camp. Finishing her milk, she wiped her mouth with a napkin. "I'm going to play Rhythm Heaven."

Sandy put Lauren's empty plate and glass in the dishwasher. "Not too long, we've got to leave soon."

Reminded of the time, Daniel checked the green glowing numbers on the microwave, 5:15. *Crap! I've still got to shower and dress.*

Karen sipped her coffee. *Oh, this was going to be fun!* "Daniel, if you're not doing anything tonight, can you watch Rhys for a few hours? Doug has to suck up at some business dinner tonight, and he wants me to go with him."

Daniel was shaking his head before Karen even finished speaking. "No, sorry, can't."

"Two hours tops, I promise." Karen tried the puppy eyes that worked with her husband.

Daniel, however, was immune. "No can do, sorry."

Sandy popped the lid back over the remains of the cake, just managing to keep her laugh inside. "Why, what are you doing tonight?" She grinned at her brother.

"Yeah, Daniel." Karen was all wide-eyed innocence but a smile twitched at the corner of her mouth. "What are you doing tonight?"

Daniel looked from one knowing grin to the other. "Who told you? Allan? I'll kill him."

"Nope." Sandy laughed. "It wasn't Allan. I must say, Daniel, I'm hurt. That you would tell Allan before us, I'm crushed."

"Right!" Daniel snorted. "It couldn't have been anyone else. No one else knows."

"Uh-uh." Karen loved the confusion in Daniel's expression. "Dad knew."

Daniel's brow creased as he tried to work that out. "No, I didn't tell Dad."

"You didn't, but Steven did." Karen smiled, triumphant.

"Dad was over at Steven's this morning, remember, helping him put together his entertainment centre?" Sandy grinned. "Apparently, he didn't know it was supposed to be a deep dark secret."

Daniel sat back in his chair, dismay written across his face. "Mom knows?"

"Oh, yeah!" Sandy and Karen answered in unison, delighted at Daniel's expression of horror.

Karen put her coffee cup in the dishwasher, and smiled at her brother. "And she's thrilled." Leaning against the counter, she quoted their mother. "Steven's such a nice boy, with a good job. He'll be good for Daniel."

"Oh, God! Shoot me now." Daniel slumped in his chair, dropping his head into his hands.

"So, we thought you could use some help on this momentous occasion." Sandy tucked her chair under the table. "We can go through your closet, help you pick out a decent outfit."

"Yeah, Steven dresses well." Karen sniffed in disapproval. "You don't want to show up looking like a kid living on student loans, do you?"

Daniel glared at both of them. "Get out!"

Sandy laughed on her way out of the kitchen. "Lauren, time to go."

Lauren hit pause, and dropped her control. Joining her relatives in the foyer, she looked up at her uncle. "Can you get Harvest Moon for next time?"

"Lauren!" Sandy was not amused. "You do not ask people to buy you things."

Lauren looked at her mother, all wide, innocent eyes. "But Danny's not just people, mommy."

"That's right, mommy, I'm not just people." Daniel grinned at his sister, as he promised his niece. "Next time I pass a game store, how's that?"

Lauren nodded, happy. "It's good, you'll like it."

Daniel opened the front door and Lauren slipped out first. "Bye, Uncle Daniel." Lauren waved as she raced down the hall to the elevators.

"Lauren, don't get on without me." Sandy grinned at her brother and started down the hall after her daughter. "Have fun tonight!"

Karen turned in the doorway. "Sure you don't need any help getting dressed. I can choose a shirt…"

Daniel tried to close the door on her. "I don't think so."

"Daniel!" Karen bounced the door back with a nudge of her hip. "I like this guy. Be nice."

"Good bye, Karen." Daniel shut the door, and leaned against it, Karen's words echoing in the foyer. Yeah, he liked him too, that was the problem!

CHAPTER 4

Men in Black

Daniel would deny it to his last breath. Shackled to a wall, with a scary dude in a Freddy mask threatening to rip out his fingernails, he would deny it, but Karen was right. Increasingly frustrated, he flicked through the hangers in his closet. He pulled drawers open, and rifled through long forgotten birthday presents, but no luck. His whole wardrobe screamed starving student. How had he not noticed this before? Oh, right, because he worked at home and his computer didn't care what he wore.

Towel wrapped around his hips, hair still damp from his shower, Daniel stared into his mostly empty closet. He refused to meet Steven wearing the baggy sweat pants that were his daily uniform. He scanned the hangers: blue jeans, faded jeans, jeans that no longer fit, jeans that for some reason had shrunk to a really nerdy ankle length, one pair of grey dress pants that make him look like a Bar Mitzvah boy, and his interview suit. *Okay, jeans, that's better than sweatpants, right?*

He grabbed the newest pair, not that they were new, exactly. About three years ago, Aidan had flat out refused to go out in public with him unless he bought something that didn't look like he was going to the gym. Zipping up, he checked the mirror and exhaled in relief. They fit and the length was good. He turned and craned his neck to look over his shoulder. Not a bad ass for an old guy!

He ducked back into his closet, searching for shoes, not sneakers, shoes. Tossing decrepit runners and ratty sandals out of the way, he finally found a pair of real shoes. Bending over to grab the black lace-ups, he cursed as he heard the phone ring. He was tempted to ignore it, but what if it was Steven? What if he was cancelling?

"Hello?"

"Open up. It's me." The words were barely civil and the tone said 'now'!

Crap! Just what he fucking needed, sisters! He hit six, stomped to the front door, and shoved it open. Standing in the doorway, he waited for the elevators to spit his sister out. Karen had barely stepped foot in the hallway when Daniel started talking. Arms folded across his still naked chest, he glared at his sister. "Whatever it is that you think you have to say, don't."

"Yeah, yeah, got it." Karen ignored Daniel's glower as she walked down the hallway, stopped in front of him, and slapped a bag against his chest. "Black V-neck sweater, cashmere/linen blend, summer weight, goes with everything. And you won't look like a loser." She turned on her heel, marched back to the elevators, and pressed the down button. As the doors opened, she called down the hallway to Daniel. "You owe me a hundred and seventy-eight bucks."

❊   ❊   ❊

Humming the Star Trek theme, Steven stepped out of the shower and grabbed a towel. Rubbing a hand over his jaw, he decided to shave again. He wasn't thinking whisker burn and Daniel's pale skin; he was just fastidious about personal grooming, okay?

Padding over to his dresser, he opened the top drawer, and scanned the rows of neatly folded underwear. And yes, they were colour-coded, what did you think? He stepped into a pair of black Calvin Klein Bold: short, comfortably snug, and soft to the touch. He pulled on black socks and selected a pair of black jeans that were still draped in dry cleaning plastic. Ignoring all the preppy loafers, he opted instead for a pair of well-used black biker boots. His shirts, like everything else in his closet, were organized by colour. Sliding one of the black ones off its hanger, he shrugged into it.

Standing in front of the full length mirror on the back of the closet door, he rolled his cuffs three times, leaving his forearms bare. He snapped a black leather cuff around his right wrist, and nodded at his reflected image. A dark urban look, nothing like the preppy ensemble he had worn to the BBQ. He turned to leave the room and stopped...*Let's see what Daniel's made of.* Pulling a box off the top shelf in his closet, he sifted through it searching for...*Yes!* He had bought this online one night when he should have been sleeping, because really, who needed a complete set of Star Trek: TNG communicator pins? He chose two, fastened one to his shirt and pocketed the other. Grinning to himself, wondering what Daniel's reaction would be, he grabbed his wallet and phone.

Driving to the Cineplex, he wasn't particularly concerned about the evening. If there was no heat between Daniel and himself then, at least, he'd get to see the Star Trek sequel. If there was heat, well, then he wouldn't be going home as soon as the credits rolled. Turning left onto the Queensway, he found himself smiling. He had spent the last week imagining his hands caught in Daniel's messy blond hair, picturing his lips crawling up the back of those muscular legs, and wondering just what kind of ass Daniel had been hiding under that God awful pair of cargo shorts. He was betting on heat, because Daniel Fine had felt very, very good against his back in the dark last weekend. Steven was almost certain he would feel even better without his family standing right beside them!

❊   ❊   ❊

Daniel wanted to lean on his horn. A freaking giant of an SUV was blocking his lane in the parking lot. The moron driving it couldn't seem to back out of his parking space. He gritted his teeth as he envisioned ripping the man out of his behemoth and doing it for him. He didn't have time for this! He cursed under his breath and waited... and waited...and *fuck!* At this rate, he was going to miss the movie! Finally, thank you, movie theatre Gods! He zipped his car into the newly empty space, cut the engine, and bolted out of the driver's seat. Beeping the locks shut, he ran through the parking lot.

Slowing to a walk as he approached the circular cement steps in front of the multiplex, he scanned the few people waiting outside. He didn't see Steven. No one was wearing preppy loafers or starched cotton shirts. He started up the steps, thinking that Steven must be waiting inside.

"Daniel!"

The call came from behind him and Daniel turned to see a guy walking towards him, a fucking hot guy, with impossibly long legs encased in black denim, and black biker boots. He stopped in front of Daniel and held his hand out. "Daniel?" He smiled Steven's smile.

Daniel took Steven's hand and was pulled into a hug. He stepped back and grinned. "I didn't recognize you."

"Well, we're seeing *Into Darkness*, so voila!" Steven swept a hand down his torso, his lips quirking into his tilted smile.

Daniel's eyes followed Steven's hand, lingering over the firm chest, trim waist, tempting hips and…he jerked his eyes up to meet Steven's. "You look good."

Steven saw it; he couldn't miss it. It was there in Daniel's eyes: heat. *Oh, yes!* He also didn't miss the fact that Daniel had obviously made an effort tonight; the starving-student look was gone. The black sweater kissed Daniel's body, emphasizing his shoulders and skimming his abs. *Nice!* "So do you."

Daniel wasn't used to compliments. He actually blushed and Steven took pity on him. "I was here early, so I got the tickets." He started for the doors and Daniel fell into step beside him. "Oh, I almost forgot, here." Steven turned to face Daniel and pulled the communicator pin out of his pocket. "This is for you."

Daniel stared at the pin. He knew what it was, of course. He had just never seen one outside of a Sci-Fi convention. "You're kidding?"

Steven laughed as he pointed to the pin on his own chest. "Nope." He leaned into Daniel, pin in hand, challenge in his eyes. Daniel didn't back away. He allowed Steven to brand him with a geek pin and that said something about the man, something that Steven liked. It probably wasn't the most scientific of character tests but added to the hazel-gold eyes, melting laugh and really, really great legs, and yeah, Steven wanted to know this guy better, like, naked better.

Daniel went absolutely still as Steven's fingers shifted against his chest, pinning the communicator in place. He looked down at the dark head bent over the finicky task, and his hand went to Steven's hip naturally, as if it belonged there. Steven looked up, and Daniel saw it: heat. *Oh, yes!*

Steven lingered for a second, his eyes on Daniel's, his hand resting over Daniel's heart. With a smile and a quick pat to the pin, he pulled away. "Now, you're part of the Star Trek experience." He stepped back and they walked into the multiplex together.

The kid guarding the theatre doors checked their tickets and handed them 3D glasses. They found their reserved seats, just as the lights went down and the promos started. Staring at the screen, acutely aware of the man sitting beside him, Daniel found himself revising Steven's last comment under his breath. *"Now, you're part of the Steven experience!"*

※　※　※

Two and a half hours later, as the credits rolled and the lights came up, a smattering of applause from the die-hard Trekkers rang through the theatre. Steven turned to Daniel. "So?"

Daniel nodded. "Good."

They rose, threading their way between the rows of seats, Steven looking over his shoulder at Daniel walking behind him. "Not quite as good as the last one."

"Maybe, but the plot was a lot easier to follow." Daniel followed Steven down the theatre steps, his mind less on the movie and more on the man poured into the black denim in front of him. "I'm not so good with alternate time lines." They gave up on talking as they jostled their way through the exiting throng.

Once they joined the relatively free-flowing stream outside the theatre doors, Steven continued their interrupted conversation. "I had to see the last one twice. The side effects of time change always throw me."

"I'll probably see this one again. 3D really makes a difference. The space scenes were epic." Daniel stayed close to Steven, his arm hovering at Steven's back, so they wouldn't get separated in the crowd.

Steven nodded in agreement as they reached the glass doors to the multiplex. "It should definitely get a nomination for cinematography." He pushed a door open for Daniel.

Outside the theatre, they stopped on the top step and scanned the parking lot and the restaurants bordering it. Daniel turned to Steven. "Milestones, Baton Rouge, or the Dub Linn Gate Irish Pub?"

"Is it way too girly if I say I like the Bellini's at Milestones?" Steven didn't seem all that concerned about that possibility.

Daniel laughed. "Yes."

Steven grinned and fell into step at Daniel's side. They crossed the parking lot and entered the restaurant, still talking Trek. "Is it just me, or is Kirk getting shot down a lot more than he used to?"

"Yeah, this time around, Spock's got the girl."

"I like this new, improved Spock. He's a little more interesting; he doesn't always do what's expected."

Daniel pulled the door to Milestones open, pleased to find no one in line before them. "They've done a good job with the main characters. The connection between them is still there, just slightly tweaked."

"Table for two?" The hostess, with a headset imbedded in her hair, signaled a waiter.

"I'm Rafael. I'll be your server tonight." He guided them to a table and handed them each a menu. "Would you care for anything from the bar?"

Daniel flashed a grin at Steven. "Two Bellini's, please."

As Rafael left, Steven snorted. "Oh, right! Mr. Macho!"

"That's me." Daniel curled a bicep in jest, and Steven's eyes stroked the arm that his hand could not, at least, not yet.

Daniel snapped his menu closed. "I don't know why I even bother to look. I always order a hamburger."

Steven looked up from his own menu. "I know. I almost never try anything new. I hate being disappointed."

Daniel stared across the table at Steven. *"I almost never try anything new"*, *so not what I want to hear!* He really hoped the man was only talking about food.

Rafael returned with their drinks and placed one in front of each of them. "Do you need more time to decide or would you like to order now?"

Orders placed, Rafael and the menus gone, Daniel tasted his drink. "Not bad."

Steven grinned. "Sometimes the girls are right."

"Do not, under any circumstances, say that when my sisters are around!" Laughter threaded through Daniel's voice and his eyes sparked gold.

Steven smiled. "I'm an only child. I always wanted a brother."

"A brother sure, but sisters?" Daniel shook his head. "Believe me, you don't want sisters."

Steven couldn't agree; Daniel's sisters had been very nice to him. "Sandy's been very helpful since I moved in. She's even offered to wait for deliveries at my place if I'm at work."

Daniel's eyes widened with horror. "You wouldn't let her into your house when you're not there?"

Steven shrugged, that slightly crooked smile curving his lips. "Yeah, why not?"

"No, no, no!" Daniel leaned into the table, the teasing light in his eyes belying the seriousness of his expression. "You don't ever let Sandy, or, God forbid, Karen in your house unsupervised." He lowered his voice, and looked around the restaurant, as furtive as if he was about to reveal a national secret. "They will find out everything you didn't want them to know." He sat back and raised his arms in a gesture that denied any culpability. "I'm not saying how. And then, once they know your deepest, darkest secrets, and this is the worst part," Daniel leaned over the table again, locking eyes with Steven, "they will tell you how to run your life, every day, all day, forever!"

Steven laughed. "They're not that bad."

"Don't say I didn't warn you."

Rafael stopped beside their table, arms laden with platters. "Gentlemen, enjoy!"

"Thank you." Daniel nodded at the waiter and reached for the salt shaker. "What's your family like?"

Steven twirled his fork in his linguini. "How can I put this?" He smiled at Daniel. "My parents are whack jobs."

Daniel paused, his hamburger in mid-air, staring at Steven, the unasked question clear in his eyes.

Steven shrugged. "They're trying to make up for the fact that they were too young to get in on all the love-ins, sit-ins, and protest marches of the late 60s. Never mind the fact that all the really combustible ones happened in the States. We didn't have a war to protest."

"So they're like what, hippies?"

"More like wannabes. They say they're 'free spirits'". Daniel rolled his eyes. "They are so disappointed in me. They can't understand where they went wrong."

"Because you're gay?" It wouldn't be the first time that Daniel had heard of parents that weren't accepting, but it always pissed him off.

Steven laughed as he shook his head. "No, because I'm a pharmacist."

Okay, didn't see that coming. "They wanted you to be a doctor?" God knew that's what his parents wanted.

Steven snorted at how off-base Daniel's assumption was. "Doctor? Hell, no! They wanted me to be an artist, a musician, a freaking pottery maker, anything that doesn't say nine-to-five. I thought they were going to disown me when I applied to the Waterloo School of Pharmacy." Steven pointed his fork at Daniel. "They would just love you, though."

Daniel grimaced. "Right! A barely employed writer, who works out of his living room, and will probably never have enough money to put into an RRSP."

Steven laughed. "Yep. Creative, independent, not a 'capitalist, corporate drone'; they'd be all over you."

Daniel speared a French fry. "And my parents are just praying for me to get a steady job with health benefits." He smiled across the table into chocolate eyes. "The stork really screwed up!"

Surprise! Dating a la 'hetero' wasn't a complete waste of time. Contrary to Daniel's every expectation, he was actually enjoying himself. He was certain though, that what came naturally with Steven, would be tortuous with anyone else. They moved effortlessly in a continuous dance of words, from family to movies to music to their personal histories, as in schools, and jobs. Neither one of them wandered into the tricky area of past relationships. Daniel wanted to put that discussion off until just this side of never!

Steven was drunk on Daniel; what he said and how he said it, the way he moved his hands when he talked, the way his eyes shifted to gold when he got excited. The man across the table drew Steven in with every smile, and laugh, and touch. Daniel Fine was a 'toucher'. At least, he was with Steven. He constantly touched Steven as he talked, touched his fingers, his hand, his wrist. Once, he leaned across the table and grabbed Steven's arm. It didn't take long for Steven to realize that this wasn't a calculated routine, one that Daniel used with every guy. Daniel didn't seem to plan anything, not his life, not his career, not the words that popped out of his mouth. Steven wasn't even sure that Daniel was aware of how often he touched him. Daniel was impulsive, and smart, and funny, and Steven liked him, maybe even more than he wanted him.

"So, I hear my dad helped you put together an entertainment centre?"

"He's a miracle worker! No, really! He should have his own TV show."

"You told him we were seeing Star Trek tonight?" Daniel smiled, but Steven caught the definite scent of disapproval.

"Yessss. Why, shouldn't I have? Did you not want them to know you were seeing me?" Steven was suddenly stiff with hurt, his eyes going almost black with annoyance.

"No! God, no!" Daniel reached for Steven's hand. "It's not that!" Daniel played with Steven's fingers as he tried to explain. "It's just my family, you know. They can't mind their own business." Daniel looked across at Steven, into eyes that, he was relieved to see, weren't flashing dark fire anymore. "My dad told my sisters. They descended on me this afternoon, all excited, ready to dress me, like I was twelve years old or something." Daniel sounded aggrieved, and Steven had to laugh.

"Which one of them bought you the sweater?"

Daniel stoked his thumb over the back of Steven's wrist, gold jumping in his eyes as he grinned at Steven. "What makes you think this sweater is new?"

Steven turned his wrist out of Daniel's hold, and clasped his hand, entwining their fingers together. "Let's see, you already told me you work from home, you live in sweat pants, and I saw what you wore to your sister's last week. So, call it a hunch, but I think the sweater is new."

"Karen dropped it off just as I was getting dressed tonight." Daniel smiled, a slight hint of embarrassment lurking in his eyes. "Pathetic, I know, thirty-two years old, and my sisters still dress me."

"Gentlemen," Rafael materialized at their table, "please don't feel you have to rush, the restaurant stays open 'til one, but if you wouldn't mind paying now, I'd appreciate it. My shift ends at midnight."

Steven checked his watch. "Is that the time? I had no idea." He reached for his wallet, but Daniel shook his head as he handed his credit card to the waiter.

"I asked you, remember?"

Steven nodded as he slid his wallet back into his pocket. "Okay, I'll get it next time."

Daniel signed the receipt and locked eyes with Steven. "Next time."

Neither one of them noticed when Rafael left the table.

Walking back to their cars through the nearly deserted parking lot, their shoulders brushed with every step. They stopped next to Steven's car, standing just that touch too close. Steven's hand moved to Daniel's shoulder, as Daniel's hand moved to its already preferred spot on Steven's hip. They watched each other until it became clear that neither one of them was going to make the first move. Daniel stepped back, the words 'good night' almost on his lips, when Steven's hand clenched, fisting folds of Daniel's sweater. "I'll call you."

Daniel grinned. "Yeah."

Fastening his seat belt, Daniel took a left out of the parking lot, cursing himself the whole way home. *Fucking wuss! What the fuck is wrong with you?* He wanted Steven, he was almost certain Steven wanted him, so why was he driving home alone? For some reason all the glib lines he used with strangers just didn't feel right with Steven. Standing in the parking lot with Mr. Perfect, looking into those dark eyes, one well-used phrase after another running through his head, he had found himself mute. Steven wasn't some interchangeable trick and Daniel found that he couldn't say any of that crap, not to him. That realization had blindsided him, made his chest tight and his brain shut down. *Some fucking writer you are, dipshit! Couldn't string three words together? I want you. How hard is that?*

Steven headed home, driving by instinct, most of his attention on his own inner dialogue. *What the fuck is wrong with you? How could you just stand there? What are you, fourteen?* It had been awhile, what with the move and the new job, but he didn't think that he had forgotten how this worked. He ran his hand through his hair and stepped on the brake as the light turned red. He wanted Daniel, and it certainly seemed like Daniel wanted him. So, why was he driving home alone? *Why? No fucking reason, that's why!*

Checking the oncoming traffic, he pulled a U-turn in the middle of the street and headed back to the Queensway, and Daniel's apartment. He knew exactly where it was. Daniel had told him he lived in the new building with the Art Deco crown across from Bayview Village shopping centre. Driving on the quiet, after-midnight streets, Steven did not let himself think about Daniel's reaction. If he thought about that, he would chicken out, turn his car around and go home, home to an empty bed. Steven hit the gas. He was not going home!

❖   ❖   ❖

In his kitchen, Daniel leaned against the counter, eating Ben & Jerry's with a fork, directly out of the container. Ice cream was his comfort food and he needed a lot of comforting right now. He still couldn't believe that he had walked away from Steven. They could be in his bed right now, doing various unspeakable things to each other. *Fucking idiot! You did the right thing. Steven wants more than sex. He wants a relationship, something that has a longer expiration date than a liter of milk. You did the smart thing. You'll call him next week, and get together. Then you can get him out of his pants!* The ice cream was working, or maybe it was the image of Steven without his pants. Either way, Daniel started to feel better.

The phone rang, startling him into dropping his fork. Bending to pick it up, he glanced at the digital numbers glowing on the microwave, 01:08 a.m. *Allan! If you've lost your keys again!* "Hello?"

"Daniel?"

The voice was hushed, but he recognized it instantly. "Steven?"

"Yeah, it's me. Can I come up?"

"Of course." Daniel hit six and dropped the phone back in its base. He stared at the phone, trying to wrap his mind around the fact that Steven was here. *Here! Now!* He threw the ice cream container back in the freezer, the fork in the sink, and sprinted for the door, swinging it wide at the first quiet rap. "Hi."

Dark lashes hid the chocolate eyes, as Steven looked somewhere over Daniel's shoulder. "Hi."

"Is something wrong?" Concern leaked through Daniel's voice.

The lashes lifted, and Steven's mouth slipped into its crooked smile. "You forgot something."

"I did?" Daniel checked Steven's hands; they were empty. "What?"

Steven stepped across the threshold into Daniel's arms. "Me."

Daniel gathered Steven close, arms around his shoulders and lower back. Steven pushed his fingers through Daniel's hair and dragged his mouth into a kiss. Kiss is too tepid a word for an act that was all heat and need. They took turns, eating into each other's mouths, biting and sucking, inhaling each other. Past the scent and feel of Steven, over the roaring of arousal in his body, through the beat of blood at his groin, something knocked insistently at the outer reaches of Daniel's mind. *Door, door, door, the fucking door is still open!* Daniel swept one hand out and slammed the door shut.

Hearing the door slam behind him, Steven turned Daniel, backed him up against his own door, and shoved his sweater up. *Oh, yes! The clinging sweater hadn't lied.* Daniel's chest was edible, defined but not heavily muscled, a scattering of fine blond hair over his pectorals. Steven nuzzled into the warm skin, lips dragging up the centre line between Daniel's ribs before closing around one of the pale nipples.

Daniel's head fell back against the door as he arched into Steven, fingers grasping in the dark wavy hair.

Steven sucked and grazed his teeth over the taut nub, his fingers busy with the snap on Daniel's fly.

"Hey." Daniel closed his hand over Steven's. "I thought you wanted the same face over the breakfast table?" *Shut up! Shut up! Shut up! What are you trying to do, talk him out of this?*

Steven brushed Daniel's hand aside, sank to his knees, and pulled Daniel's zipper down. He looked up, directly into the hazel eyes above him. "I do want that. But until I find that," He curled his hand around Daniel's cotton covered cock, "I want this."

Daniel looked down at the solid certainty on Steven's face, the need in his eyes. *Oh, fuck, those eyes got even darker when ...* Steven squeezed and Daniel gasped, thrusting into Steven's hand. Steven freed Daniel's cock from its cotton bondage, as triumphant as if he'd won a prize. He licked the length and then swirled his tongue around the head. Daniel dropped one hand on Steven's shoulder, and curled the other around the back of his bowed head. There was something Daniel wanted to say, something... shit! He kept losing his train of thought. He finally managed to puff words out between breaths as Steven wrapped one hand around his shaft and slid his mouth down to meet his fingers. "I have...absolutely...no fucking problem with that!"

Lips and tongue sucked and lapped at Daniel's length, as Steven clenched his hands into Daniel's ass, finally feeling what he had been wondering about for the past week.

Daniel looked down at the dark head bent over him. *Oh, fuck, oh fuck!* Steven could do things with his tongue. *Oh, God!* Daniel could feel the rush starting to overwhelm him, and he didn't want that, not yet. "Steven, Steven, wait!" Steven looked up, letting Daniel's cock slip from between his lips. Daniel put his hands under Steven's arms and pulled him up. "I haven't seen you yet."

Smiling his off-kilter smile, Steven stepped back, hands pulling his shirt open, snaps popping one after the other down the centre of the black cotton. He balanced on one leg, then the other, tossing his boots. "So not a problem!" He unsnapped and unzipped, shoving his jeans down his legs. Kicking them off, he reached down to tug off his socks. Finally, he stood still under Daniel's stare, naked but for the black trunk shorts that hugged his body.

Perfect, the man was fucking perfect. Daniel didn't know what Steven's heritage was, but he was betting on somewhere warmer than Daniel's own mix of Russia and Ireland. Steven's skin tone probably looked sun-kissed even in the winter. Dark hair decorated his nipples and drizzled down to his waist band, nothing grizzly or fur-like, just enough to highlight his sleek runner's build. Daniel's hazel eyes shifted to gold, molten heat in his gaze as he stroked Steven's hip, his hand gliding on the soft black cotton. "I've never seen a real person who didn't look like a dork in underwear. But you," Daniel slid his hand off Steven's hip and grabbed a chunk of Mr. Perfect's ass, "you look fucking hot!"

Steven grinned, his tilted smile promising everything. "I look even better without them." Stepping back, hooking his thumbs in the waistband of his briefs, he slithered out of them. Hands on his hips, he smiled at the hunger in Daniel's look, and nodded towards his left. "Bedroom?"

"Huh?" Daniel reached out, one hand clenching into Steven's ass, the other stroking along the length of his cock, too busy playing to answer. "Beautiful!" Dragging his eyes off the rigid column of heated flesh in his hand, he looked into sultry midnight eyes. "Beautiful!"

Steven wound his arms around Daniel, and lost them both in a melding of mouths, and teeth, and tongues. Breaking the kiss, he tugged at Daniel's hand. "Where's your bedroom?"

Steven hit the bed first and shook his head as Daniel tried to follow him down onto the mattress. "Uh-uh!" Lying on his back, he crossed his arms behind his head, and grinned up at Daniel. "Clothes off!"

"What? Oh, right." Daniel pulled his sweater over his head and tossed it. Cursing, as he struggled to pull his shoes off without untying the laces, he lost his balance and fell onto the bed. "Shit!"

Steven laughed and Daniel growled at him. He finally kicked the shoes off, scrambled out of his jeans and underwear, and pounced. Straddling Steven, he locked their hands together, holding them above Steven's head, and bit across his chest. Steven arched into Daniel's lips, and hands, hissing out a breath as Daniel's teeth tugged at his nipples.

Daniel looked up to check Steven's response. "Sensitive?"

"Yes!" Steven moaned as his eyes slid shut. "Don't stop."

Curved over Steven, still holding his hands captive above his head, Daniel grazed his teeth over the taut peaks and nipped, gentle snaps of his teeth that made Steven writhe under him. Swirling his tongue through the hair delineating Steven's nipples, Daniel licked his way down Steven's body.

Steven opened his eyes, watching as Daniel rubbed his face through the thatch of hair at Steven's groin. *Oh, yes! So fucking hot!* Daniel's blond hair set against Steven's dark pubic growth was a surprisingly erotic image. Daniel's lips teased among Steven's curls, his mouth closing in on Steven's cock and Steven stopped caring about how it looked. *Oh, God! Yes!*

Releasing Steven's hands, Daniel settled himself between Steven's legs. Sliding his hands up thighs lightly covered with fine dark hair, he wrapped one hand around Steven's cock, pumping slowly. He cupped the other around Steven's sac, moving his balls gently, one against the other.

Raising his hips, pushing into Daniel's hands, Steven looked down at the naked blond kneeling between his thighs. Daniel had been lying when he said he didn't work out. He wasn't ridiculously ripped, but the man didn't spend all his time sitting at his computer; that much was obvious. He had a lean frame, the muscles in his shoulders and back rippling beguilingly as he bent over Steven, and his thighs…the man was like a well-kept secret, seriously hot under his appalling clothes. Stroking a hand through Daniel's hair, Steven decided that secrets were a good thing. As far as he was concerned, no one else ever had to know that Daniel Fine was stunning.

Steven felt good and tasted even better. His personal scent was intoxicating; Daniel could stay here nuzzling into the man for hours. His lips stretched around Steven's cock, Daniel looked up along Steven's body, to dark eyes staring back at him. Face flushed, hair falling over his forehead, Steven's eyes reflected Daniel's own need back at him. *So fucking perfect!* Abandoning Steven's balls, he traced two fingers over Steven's entrance, a caress and a question in the touch.

Steven bent his knees, drawing his legs back, opening himself for Daniel.

That was an invitation! Daniel thought he couldn't get any harder, but he was wrong. Fuck! "Yes?"

Steven tipped his hips pushing his opening against Daniel's fingers. "Yes."

Daniel read the desire and the trust in Steven's eyes, and suddenly it wasn't about him anymore. It was all about Steven, and giving him everything he wanted. Shifting to the side, he pulled his night table drawer open. Scrambling for lube and a condom, he tossed them on the bed. Eyes on Steven's, intent on his every reaction, Daniel covered him from shoulder to thigh. Staring down at Steven, he clasped their hands together, and pressed them into the mattress on either side of Steven's head. "Beautiful."

Colour tinted Steven's cheeks, as he tipped his head back, wanting Daniel's mouth. Steven set the pace, his hips pulsing up against Daniel, his cock brushing along Daniel's, his tongue sliding into Daniel's mouth. Twisting his hands out from under Daniel's, he pressed long strokes down Daniel's back.

Moans caught in the back of his throat, lips biting at Steven's, Daniel rolled, taking Steven with him, over him. He traced Steven's spine, and sank his hands into Steven's ass. He moved his thumbs down the crease, each pass deeper, separating Steven's ass cheeks, brushing over his entrance.

Steven tore his mouth away from Daniel's. "More, Daniel!" His eyes were dark fire, his breathing harsh as he pushed his ass against Daniel's hands. "More!"

Daniel watched Steven, drinking in his need, one hand scoring the sheets, searching blindly and finding. Snapping the lid on the lube open, he coated two fingers, circling around and over Steven's entrance, pressing, testing.

"Daniel!" *Oh, God, I need, I need, YES!*

Daniel plunged his fingers in, and Steven opened for him, thrusting back, grunting his approval. Rolling them again, he looked down into the dark eyes, his fingers finding and stroking over sensitive nerves. "Now, Steven?"

Steven's eyes slid shut as he grabbed his knees and pulled his legs back. That was all the answer Daniel needed. Not willing to leave Steven empty, Daniel grabbed a condom with one hand and tore it open with his teeth. He spat the wrapper away, and rolled the condom on one-handed, his other hand still busy, fingers stroking deep inside Steven. He slicked up, and drew his fingers out.

Steven whimpered once, feeling the aching emptiness, and then he was full again. Daniel thrust in slow, deep strokes, pulling back until the head of his cock stretched Steven wide, and then pushing back in. Slow, deep, steady; over and over until Steven wanted to scream with frustration. He arched his back, snapping his hips up, trying to force a faster pace. Daniel held his hips down, making him wait.

"Fucking move!" Steven's body was tense, arousal and annoyance blending in equal measure, as he glared up at Daniel.

Daniel gasped out a laugh, sweat breaking out along his spine, his breathing rough. "Not yet."

Steven didn't take orders, he didn't even like suggestions. He knew what he wanted. Narrowing his eyes, he clenched his ass. "Now!"

Daniel planted his hands on the mattress, on either side of Steven's shoulders, arms straight, holding his torso up. Staring into Steven's eyes, he snapped his hips, finally moving the way Steven needed him to; hard, fast, deep.

Steven cried out in relief; his eyes sliding shut. He clawed at Daniel's back, as Daniel's cock stroked exactly right, finding his prostate with every thrust. He arched his back, thrusting up, moving with Daniel.

Daniel's arms shook; his balls tight. Denying every screaming nerve ending in his body, he stopped thrusting.

Steven's eyes snapped open, his mind scrambling, trying to find the words to protest.

Supporting himself on one arm, Daniel pumped Steven's cock. His fingers a tight coil, sliding on pre-cum, he palmed the crown, rubbing the underside of the head with his thumb. He watched Steven, needing to see, to know...

Steven's mouth opened on a silent scream as he lost it, cum splashing over Daniel's hand.

Yes! Steven, as his climax smashed through him, was even more perfect! Dropping Steven's cock, Daniel grabbed the other man's hips, and pounded into him. Steven's ass pulsed around him, residual tremors rippling along Daniel's cock, pulling Daniel's orgasm out of him. "Steven! Fuck!"

Crawling back into bed, after tossing the condom, Daniel stretched out beside Steven and trailed a hand down his chest. "Okay?"

Steven grinned, his hand tracing Daniel's hip. "Well, it was only our first time. I'm sure we'll get better with practice."

Daniel laughed, the warm rumble seeping into Steven's skin. He flopped back on the bed, arms extended at his sides, hands open and loose. "Any better than that and I'll go into cardiac arrest!"

Steven smiled and curled his hand around Daniel's spent cock, his touch gentle. "It's late. I should..."

Daniel's arm snagged Steven, pulling him close. "No, you should stay." His fingers played in the soft waves of Steven's hair. "You have big plans for tomorrow?"

Steven tilted his head back on Daniel's chest, so he could see his face. "I was thinking of seeing Star Trek again?"

Daniel traced Steven's lips with a light finger. "Matinee?"

Steven nodded. "We can go back to my place after, if you want." He leaned up and whispered next to Daniel's ear. "There's a hot tub in the back yard."

Daniel grinned, golden sparks lighting his hazel eyes. "I'm really starting to like you."

CHAPTER 5

House Rules

Steven smiled to himself as he turned onto his side, careful not to dislodge the arm wrapped around him. Apparently, Daniel was always a 'toucher', even when he was asleep. He could get used to this!

More asleep than awake, Daniel tugged at the covers, and met resistance. He pulled harder, and heard a murmured complaint. His eyes snapped open. Lying beside him, hogging the blankets, head half buried under his pillow: Steven. Daniel smiled to himself and curled around the other man. He could get used to this!

Early morning light seeped through the spaces between the slats in the shutters covering the bedroom window. Steven raised himself onto one elbow to watch the sleeping man beside him. Daniel's blond hair was a disaster in the morning, and for some reason that made Steven smile. He traced a line across Daniel's chest and shifted closer, running his hand down, tracking the line of fine hair. His fingers teasing amid the fine blond curls at Daniel's groin, Steven was completely unsurprised when a rather significant part of Daniel woke up.

"Good morning." Daniel's raspy morning voice managed a whisper.

Steven looked up into sleepy eyes. "It's still early. You don't have to wake up yet."

Daniel looked down his body, to Steven's hand wrapped around his cock. "Apparently, I do."

Steven grinned. "Not all of you." He slid down the mattress and licked up the length of silken skin. With languid early morning strokes of lips and tongue, all warm wet friction, he slowly took Daniel in.

Daniel closed his eyes, and settled his hand on Steven's head. He stroked through the thick, wavy hair, and dropped his hand lower, loving the feel of Steven, the muscles in his back and shoulders, the warmth of his skin. Daniel's hips undulated against the mattress, pushing his cock up into the welcome of Steven's mouth. He could get used to this!

Steven bobbed his head, tongue swirling, mouth sucking, one hand wrapped around the base of Daniel's cock, the other stroking his own. Sunday morning in bed with Daniel, he could get used to this!

❊　❊　❊

At the sound of footsteps and clinking china, Steven stretched and pushed his arms back until he was leaning on both elbows. He watched as a naked Daniel got back into bed, carefully balancing a tray on his lap.

Daniel handed Steven one of the mugs. "Coffee?" Steven sat up against the pillow at his back and took the mug. "Is black okay? I can get milk if you want."

"No, I'm good." Steven examined the tray; two plates, two forks, two pieces of cake. "This is your idea of breakfast?"

Daniel shrugged. "It's my mom's applesauce cake." He looked at Steven, hazel eyes teasing. "For some reason, I'm in a really good mood this morning and toast just doesn't say happy the way cake does."

Messy bed hair falling into his eyes, white sheet skimming across his hips, Daniel Fine looked good, really fucking good! Steven now knew how that body felt; on him, in him, and he wanted more. Judging by the way Daniel had held him close even as he slept, had brought him breakfast in bed, and suggested they extend Saturday night into Sunday, Steven didn't think he was the only one who wanted more. His tilted smile grew into a grin as he looked over his coffee cup, at the man beside him. "Yeah, for some reason!"

Closing his eyes, Steven practically inhaled his coffee. The first cup in the morning was as close to a religious experience as he ever wanted to get. Caffeine need slated, he picked up his plate and took a bite of the cake. "It's good." He pointed his empty fork at Daniel. "You can't cook at all, can you?"

"Hey!" Daniel protested. "If someone else chops up the peppers and onions, I can make an omelet."

Steven snorted. "Oh, a real chef!"

Raising his hand in the air, laughter in his eyes, Daniel introduced himself. "Pampered Jewish Prince here."

Steven tapped his own chest. "Only son of crazy free spirits who didn't see the need for regular meal times."

Daniel shook his head as he forked a piece of cake. "Where do your parents live?"

"Now?" Steven opened his mouth around his next forkful of cake, and the memory of those lips closing around him was suddenly right there: vivid, tactile and so fucking real that for a heartbeat Daniel lost track of the conversation. "For the last five years or so, they've had a small farm outside of Kalona, BC. My father paints, my mother does pottery, and they grow medicinal marijuana."

Daniel's jaw dropped. "No way!"

"Yeah, they don't make any money at it. Health Canada only lets them grow enough for four clients." Steven shrugged. "It's like their personal charity."

Daniel finished his cake and put the empty plate back on the tray. "And my parents just write cheques to Sick Kids Hospital."

"That's good too." Steven slid his fork under the last piece of cake on his plate. "They're a little worried now though. The government is in the midst of changing the rules for growers. They'll have to apply to become licensed producers. It's going to mean a lot more paper work, inspections, regulations. They're not so good with rules." Steven put his plate back on the tray, and picked his mug up.

Daniel finished his coffee, put his mug on the tray, and leaning over the side of the bed, put the tray on the floor. "What will they do if this license thing doesn't work out?"

Steven finished the last of his coffee and held the empty mug out to Daniel. "Oh, they'll think of something. They always do."

Daniel put Steven's mug on the night table next to him and turned back to the man in his bed. He pushed the covers aside and slid down the mattress. Slipping an arm under one of Steven's legs, he laid his head on the other man's thigh and looked up into chocolate eyes. "You're one blow job ahead of me."

Steven's reached a hand down to sift through Daniel's hair. "I didn't know it was a competition."

Daniel turned his head and ran one finger along Steven's appreciative cock. "One I intend to win." His eyes on Steven's, he opened his lips and sucked Steven in.

A blow job was always good, it was pretty much the definition of the word, but that said, some were better than others. Daniel was better. Relaxing into the mattress, one hand stroking the nape of Daniel's neck, fingers pushing under the blond hair, Steven offered no direction. He didn't have to; Daniel seemed to be able to read his mind. Ratty clothes and scuffed boat shoes, Steven didn't care, Daniel could wear a fucking table cloth as long as he did this. *Oh, God!* Steven breathed out a low moan. *This!*

Steven was quiet, his body supple under Daniel's mouth, moving with him, small sighs and soft moans guiding Daniel. Remembering the angry glare and impatient demands from last night, Daniel smiled around the hard shaft in his mouth, tongue lapping just under the ridge, swirling and sucking. *Guess I'm doing something right!*

❖   ❖   ❖

Stepping out of the shower, Steven rubbed a towel over his hair and then wrapped it around his hips. The phone was ringing as he entered the bedroom, and since Daniel wasn't around, he answered it. "Hello?"

"Daniel, your father wants to know if the Star Trek movie was any good. His golf game got cancelled and he can't decide between that and Hangover III."

Steven swallowed, nerves tightening his throat muscles. "Oh, hi, Julia. Daniel's in the kitchen. I'll get him for you."

"Steven?"

"Yes." *Oh, shit! Daniel's going to be pissed.* Suddenly, he felt like a teenager caught out after curfew. He bit his lip to stop himself from babbling inanities. What was he going to say? I stopped by early on a Sunday morning to borrow a cup of sugar?

There was a long uncomfortable pause, as Julia digested what Steven answering the phone at Daniel's place at a little after ten on a Sunday morning meant. Her face split into a grin and she punched the phone in the air, as she danced a little jig on the kitchen tiles. "Oh, no need to trouble Daniel. What did you think of the movie?"

"It was good." Steven forced the words out, still uncomfortable. This was a new one for him; he'd never talked to a lover's mother while he stared at the sheets her son had fucked him on!

"So, it's worth seeing?" Julia wasn't uncomfortable at all. Steven answering Daniel's phone was Julia's definition of wish fulfillment, in technicolour!

"If Brian liked the first one, then he'll like this one." *One word after the other, it's called talking. Focus, the woman's going to think you're an idiot!* "The graphics are spectacular, 3D really makes a difference."

"Okay, thanks Steven. I'll tell him. Have a nice day, bye."

"Bye." But Steven was talking to air, Julia had already hung up.

Daniel walked into the bedroom, to find Steven standing by his bed, staring at the phone in his hand. "Automated sales call?"

"No." Steven shook his head, eyes apprehensive as he put the phone down and turned to Daniel. "It was your mother."

"Of course it was." Daniel rolled his eyes and wrapped his arms around the other man's waist, interlocking his fingers at the small of Steven's back. "Don't worry about it. It's not like we were ever going to be able to keep this a secret with you living across the street from Sandy."

"I'm so sorry. I'm just constitutionally incapable of letting a phone go unanswered."

Daniel leered at Steven's almost naked body. "Something I'm willing to overlook, considering your other sterling qualities."

Steven laughed as he tugged the towel off and tossed it on the floor. "Yeah?"

Daniel grabbed Steven's ass and pulled him in, pressing their bodies together. Leaning into Steven, he paused with his lips a breath away from that slightly tilted smile. "Yeah."

❊ ❊ ❊

Brian sat at the kitchen table, paper open in front of him, reading the movie reviews. He looked up, as Julia dropped the portable back in its base. "So, what did he say? Is it any good?"

Leaning against the kitchen counter, Julia raised her eyebrows at her husband. "Steven said it was very good."

"Steven? I thought you called Daniel?"

"I did call Daniel." Julia's grin beamed around the kitchen. "And Steven answered."

"Steven's at Daniel's place?"

Julia sank into the chair next to her husband's. "Steven answered the phone at Daniel's house at," She checked her watch, "ten past ten on a Sunday morning."

"So?" Brian had the feeling Julia was a step ahead of him somehow.

Julia shook her head, exasperated. How did he not get this? "What do you think? It's not like Daniel plays golf." As Brian continued to look blank, Julia threw her hands in the air. "Steven answered the phone at Daniel's house because he slept there last night." And just to make sure her husband got it, she added, "With Daniel."

"Oh." Understanding finally flashed across his face. "That's good, right?"

Julia smiled. "It's perfect!"

❊ ❊ ❊

They didn't make the 12:10 show. It was a near thing, but they managed to make it out of the condo in time for the 3:15 show. Apparently, putting clothes on could be just as erotic as taking them off, who knew? As the elevator doors swished shut, Daniel hit L for the lobby exit to Visitor Parking, and P for the underground Residents Parking.

"No sense taking two cars. Why don't we just take mine?" Steven wanted Daniel with him.

Daniel shook his head. "No. If we go in one car, you'll have to drive me home tonight."

"No problem. It's not that far."

"No, you've got to get up earlier than I do. I don't want you being sleep deprived because you had to drive me home."

Steven's smile tilted as his eyes laughed at Daniel. "Oh, but being sleep deprived because we're fucking is perfectly okay."

Daniel grinned. "Well, yeah."

After watching Spock and Kirk defend the world once again, Daniel followed Steven's car home, and pulled into the driveway behind him. Steven waited while Daniel locked his car and they walked to the front door together.

Daniel looked back at his car sitting in Steven's driveway, directly across from his sister's driveway. "Maybe I should put my car in your garage?"

"I think you're good. The neighbourhood's pretty safe. I leave mine out all the time."

"I'm not worried about the car. I'm worried about me." Daniel nodded at Sandy's house across the street and Steven laughed.

"Don't worry; I'll protect you from your sister."

Daniel got lost in the teasing light in Steven's dark eyes and the slightly off-centre smile that made him want to... He leaned in and kissed Steven's smile. "I like that."

"What?"

Daniel touched a finger to the corner of Steven's mouth. "The way your smile tilts, just here."

Steven laughed, as he fished his keys out of his pocket. "I hated it when I was a teenager. I spent hours in front of the mirror trying to force my lips into a normal, straight smile."

"Straight is highly over-rated."

Steven glanced over his shoulder and grinned at Daniel, as he unlocked the front door. "So true!" Pushing the door open, Steven stopped in the doorway, and turned to face Daniel. "Just so you know," He locked eyes with Daniel, "my house; I top."

Still standing on the threshold, Daniel blinked in confusion. "What?"

"When we're at my house, I top."

Steven stood, his body blocking the entrance and Daniel got the distinct impression that if he didn't agree, the door was going to slam shut in his face. "What is that, some kind of rule?"

Steven nodded, eyes determined. "Yes."

Okay, right there, major weird! Daniel had never heard anything so bizarre and he wondered what other dark surprises Steven hid behind his Mr. Perfect façade. "Okay, no problem. Now, let me in before Sandy sees me."

Steven closed and locked the front door as Daniel looked around the living room and whistled. "Wow! This is what you and my father put together?"

"Well, mostly your father. I just handed him stuff."

"Looks good." Daniel walked over to the entertainment centre, examining the hanging wall cabinets. Placing his hand on one, he turned to Steven. "Is this where you keep your porn?"

Steven affected a disdainful sniff. "I keep my porn where it belongs, on my laptop."

Daniel grinned, and stepped back to scan the titles of Steven's DVD collection. "All Sci-Fi, all the time?"

"Pretty much, yeah." Steven pushed the edge of one of the DVDs, aligning it exactly with its neighbours. "I didn't see any videos at your place?"

"No, I had a small collection, but I use the Movie Network and Netflix more, so I gave it away." And that was true to a point. What Daniel didn't say was that he gave the videos away because they hurt. Just looking at them, had caused Aidan flashbacks that made Daniel want to crawl under the covers and whimper like a child. No, he wasn't telling Steven that. "So where's this hot tub you promised me?"

"Let me get some towels." Steven headed for the stairs. "There are sodas and stuff in the fridge."

Daniel crossed the small hallway into the kitchen, opened the fridge, and called out to Steven. "You want anything specific?"

"Iced tea, please." While Steven plucked two beach towels off the bottom shelf in the linen closet, Daniel grabbed a bottle of iced tea and a can of Coke for himself. He pulled the tab on the Coke, and sucked up half of it while he stood at the patio doors looking out at the deck.

He was not freaking out. Okay, so last night had turned into today and, he glanced at the digital numbers on the stove, they were closing in on twenty-four hours together. Okay, he hadn't kicked Steven out last night, and Steven hadn't left this morning, it was no big deal. They weren't a couple, they weren't anything. They were just spending time together. He could do this.

Steven walked into the kitchen, arms full of fluffy towels. "You okay with the can, or do you want a glass?"

"Can's fine, thanks." Bracing the bottle of iced tea against his chest with the arm attached to the hand holding his can of Coke, Daniel slid the back door open with his free hand.

"Thanks." Steven walked onto the deck and dropped the towels on a lawn chair. He folded the cover over and shoved it off the hot tub, then hit the whirlpool button. "It's fairly private here, so you don't have to worry about a swimsuit." The words were casually innocent, but Steven was not. Holding Daniel's eyes, he pulled his shirt off, very slowly, playing peek-a-boo with the open sides of the shirt front. Now, you see skin, now, you don't.

Daniel put the drinks down, got comfortable in the nearest deck chair, and prepared to enjoy the show. Smiling in appreciation, he watched Steven's every move. "Too bad we don't have music."

Steven cocked one hip, did a slow obscene grind, and then pushed the other hip out, running his hand down his thigh. "I can improvise." He kicked the biker boots off, and slithered out of his jeans, pushing his socks off with the denim.

Daniel smiled at the sight of Steven in his underwear, yet again. "Deja vu."

"Not exactly." Steven turned his back to Daniel, speaking over his shoulder. "I was in a hurry last night."

He wasn't in a hurry now. Raising his arms above his head, he moved slowly, sensuously. Turning to face Daniel, he dragged his hands across his chest and down, hands ghosting over the waistband of his underwear. Eyes darkening as he watched Daniel watch him, Steven turned again and reaching back, glided his hands over his hips and down his thighs. He writhed sinuously, muscles in his shoulders and back shifting under his skin, hips undulating to a beat that only he heard.

Daniel's temperature rose just watching. His brain flashed pictures at him, memories from last night, plans for tonight. Focused on the barrage of mental images, he almost missed the end of Steven's act. Blinking the interior porn show down, he heard a splash and found his lover of just less than a day already in the hot tub.

Steven took his favourite corner seat, directly in front of the water jet that massaged his back. Spreading his arms out on either side, he rested them on the rim of the tub. "You're turn."

Daniel shook his head. "I don't think so!"

"You're not going to fall back on that old stereotype that Jews don't have any rhythm, are you?"

"It's not a stereotype if it's true." Daniel shook his head and flashed a smile at the man in the tub. "I can't dance, I'm not graceful, and I can't move my hips like you can."

"Not true. You moved your hips just fine last night."

Daniel actually blushed. "Shut up! That's different."

Something in Steven, something that he chose not to examine too closely, wanted to nudge Daniel outside his comfort zone. "Here's the deal. You at least try to strip, or I'm going to forget that I can."

"That's blackmail!"

Steven nodded, crooked smile morphing into a full out grin. "Yeah, it is. Is it working?"

Daniel considered never seeing Steven do that grind again and caved. Getting to his feet, he flashed Steven the middle finger salute.

Steven laughed. "Look, I'll help, okay? Just follow my directions. It's easy."

"For you! Not everyone grew up in an experimental bohemian family, you know."

"Oh, I think you have hidden potential, suburban boy."

And with Steven's eyes on him, Daniel thought that just maybe he did. "Okay, what do I do?"

"Turn around. Now, imagine a beat in your head. Move to that beat."

Daniel turned his back to Steven and grumbled loud enough to be heard over the bubbling water. "I told you I can't dance, right?"

"Stop thinking; just listen to the beat in your head and do what I tell you to do." Steven smiled as those last words echoed in his mind. They weren't premeditated, he hadn't planned on saying them but now that they were out there, he was surprised to find that he rather liked the idea of guiding Daniel.

Popping one shoulder, Daniel tilted his head first one way, then the other, his hands fidgeting at his side, obviously uncomfortable with the whole striptease thing, but going along with Steven anyway. Watching Daniel as he stood there, patiently waiting for instruction, Steven finally understood the attraction in Dom/Sub play. It wasn't about taking control, it was about giving it.

Daniel's decision to follow where Steven led spiked unexpected flares along Steven's spine. "Raise your arms. Cross them behind your head. Grab your T-shirt. Good. Now, using your fingers, pull the shirt up."

Feeling the T-shirt rising slowly, Daniel stopped when his hands were full of material and his back was bare.

"Okay, pull it over your head. Turn around. Drag your right hand down your chest." Steven licked his lips; Daniel moving at his whim felt like an illicit pleasure. He kept talking, the words binding Daniel to him, making Daniel his.

"I feel ridiculous." Daniel couldn't believe he was doing this. The tag line from an old anti-drug campaign ran through his mind, 'just say no!' He didn't want to say no, though, not to Steven.

"That's because you're still thinking. Close your eyes. Listen to the beat in your head. Undo your zipper, slowly. Fucking hot!"

Daniel heard the heat in Steven's voice and a smile crept across his face. He knew he looked like a fucking dork and he just didn't care. Steven's voice sounded like melted chocolate, dark and rich and heated from the inside out, because of him! From three meters away, without a hand on him, Daniel made Steven's breath hitch and he fucking loved that he could affect Mr. Perfect like that!

"Kick your shoes off. Spread your fly open." Daniel was a quick study, this time Steven didn't have to say slowly. "Think about fucking me."

Daniel's hips jerked, pelvis automatically thrusting. Eyes still closed, hands reaching out to grab phantom hips, he was in Steven.

"Oh, yeah!" Steven's voice rasped; need playing havoc with his vocal cords. "Hook your thumbs into the waist band of your underwear. Push them and your shorts down together."

One shove and Daniel felt the clothes slide down his legs, pooling at his ankles. He stepped out of them, fully erect, cock glistening with pre-cum.

"Open your eyes."

Daniel looked across the deck into dark eyes gone nearly black with want.

Steven intended to remember this forever; the light of the early evening sun on Daniel's body, the flush across his chest, his cock standing high and hard against the thatch of fine blond curls, and the arousal burning gold in his hazel eyes. "Beautiful! That was so fucking hot!"

Daniel snorted in disbelief, a blush running up his neck and sweeping across his face. "Shut up!" He stalked across the deck and climbed down into the tub. Sinking onto a seat across from Steven, he tipped his head back on the rim of the tub. Letting his arms float on the water, jets pulsing soothing streams around him, he closed his eyes and sighed in appreciation. "This is good."

Silently, Steven waded through the water, feet soundless on the floor of the tub. He straddled Daniel quickly, sliding onto his new lover's lap. "This is better!"

Daniel's eyes shot open, his head snapping up, as Steven sat across his thighs, their cocks sliding against each other in the water. He put one hand behind Steven's head and dragged their mouths together. "Yeah!"

❀　❀　❀

Dinner was Chinese take-out at Steven's kitchen table. Daniel's chopsticks hovered over the Szechuan shrimp on his plate, as he looked at the man across from him. "So what's with the house rules?"

Steven shrugged. "Just makes it easier, saves a lot of whining."

"Whining?"

Steven tipped his head to the side and changed his voice, obviously channeling someone else. "You topped last time. It's my turn." His voice dropped back to his normal register. "Or my all-time favourite," Cue the voice change, "but I always top."

Daniel laughed. "I take it you speak from personal experience."

Steven popped a shrimp in his mouth. "Oh, yeah." He grinned across the table at Daniel. "Those guys didn't last too long."

Daniel locked eyes with the man across the table. "I'm good with rules."

Across the street, Sandy peeked through the shutters on her living room window, portable phone at her ear. "His car's still there."

Rhys safely in bed, Karen was watching TV. "How long's he been there?"

"I don't know exactly. The car was there when I got back from a birthday party with Lauren. Mom's been calling me like every half hour for updates."

"I wish I could have seen her face when Steven answered the phone at Daniel's this morning."

"Yeah." Sandy laughed. "I can't believe she had to explain it to Dad."

"Dad! Please! If a golf club or a hammer isn't involved, he's oblivious."

Sandy grinned. "That came in pretty handy when we were teenagers."

"Remember that time when I was dating Carl? I came in at five in the morning and he believed me when I said that I was thinking about trying out for the track team, so I had to train before school."

"The make-up and high heels didn't give you away?"

"I don't think he even really looked at me. He just nodded and picked up the paper from the doorstep. God, I hope Rhys doesn't take after me!"

Sandy peeked through the shutters again. Daniel's car was still there. "Gotta go."

"Call me when he leaves."

"Yep."

Unaware of the amateur security detail observing the house from across the street, Daniel and Steven lay curled up together on Steven's couch, watching the credits role on Avatar. "I can't believe Sandy hasn't come over or called." Not that he wanted her there, God no! He just couldn't believe that she wasn't. "Maybe Glen has her tied to the bed."

Sitting between Daniel's legs, his back against Daniel's chest, Steven shifted, turning to see Daniel's face. "I think you're paranoid." He sat up, swinging his legs off the couch. "You want anything, coffee, beer?

Daniel shook his head. "No, thanks."

Steven's lips tilted into his crooked smile. "Ice cream?"

"What kind?" Daniel was picky about ice cream.

"What kind? You mean what flavour or what brand?"

"Both." Okay, he was a bit of a snob when it came to his favourite dessert. He wouldn't even bother with some generic convenience store crap.

"I've got Haagen-Dazs and Ben & Jerry's, maybe some Cold Stone Creamery. Almost everything has chocolate in it." Ice cream was a high priority in Steven's life too.

Daniel's eyes sparked gold. "Now, you're talking." He jumped up and pulled Steven to his feet, intoning in a robotic voice. "Take me to your freezer!"

They ate directly out of the containers, standing on either side of the kitchen counter. "Try this one." Steven held his spoon out for Daniel to taste. "It's Founder's Favorite."

Daniel's eyes slid shut as he savoured the ice cream. "Good, very good." He picked up one of the Ben & Jerry's containers. "This is my favourite though."

Steven nodded. "Yeah, it's hard to beat Chocolate Fudge Brownie." Turning his spoon over, he slid it out of his mouth upside down, licking the last drop of ice cream from the bowl of the spoon. "There's a great Gelato place around here. They do a perfect Peanut Butter and Chocolate, and their Cookies & Cream, unbelievable! Want to go?"

"Now?"

"Sure, they're open 'til eleven."

Daniel looked at the six containers on the counter and then across at Steven. "This isn't enough for you?"

Steven dug into a container of Gold Medal Ribbon. "No such thing!"

They didn't go out for Gelato, or down to Church Street for a drink, or over to the local pub to play pool. Daniel nixed every suggestion Steven made. Sitting on the kitchen counter, watching Daniel put the ice cream back in the freezer, Steven came up with another idea. "We could go dancing, lots of sweaty guys with their T-shirts tucked in their back pockets."

Daniel slid the freezer drawer shut. "And yet, somehow, that doesn't sound appealing." His voice dripped sarcasm. "Maybe it's me." Nudging Steven's legs apart, he stood between them, his hands on Steven's hips. "You know what I'd like to do?"

Steven put his hands on Daniel's shoulders and slid them up, curved around the sides of the other man's neck, thumbs brushing along his jaw. "What?"

Daniel traced Steven's smile with his finger. "I think it's time to test out those house rules of yours."

Steven slid off the counter into Daniel's arms, borrowing Daniel's words from the previous night. "I'm really starting to like you!"

❖   ❖   ❖

The Peeping Tom thrill had worn off quickly, and Sandy had retreated to her couch, her TV and her husband. Trying to watch *Breaking Bad*, she groaned when the phone rang, yet again. Pressing pause on the remote, Sandy read her mother's name on call display and picked up the phone. "Yes, his car is still there Mom."

"You'll call me when he leaves?"

"Mom, I'm not staying up all night stalking my brother."

"Sandy!" Julia was indignant. "We are not stalking your brother. We just care about him."

"Right! You care, I'm just nosy. I'll call you in the morning. Night, Mom." Clicking the portable back into its base, she curled up on the couch next to Glen. "I don't know which is worse; Mom worrying about Daniel because he's not dating or Mom worrying about Daniel because he is dating."

"Leave the guy alone. He's not a freaking soap opera." It was moments like this that made Glen realize how lucky he was to be an only child!

"I am leaving him alone. I haven't gone over there once have I?"

Glen looked appalled. "You wouldn't?"

"No, actually, I wouldn't." Sandy picked up the remote control and pressed play. "I wouldn't put it past my mother though."

❖   ❖   ❖

Even without the house rules, Daniel would know that Steven wanted to top tonight. He was different, a subtle difference, but it was there. He wasn't responding to Daniel so much as he was encouraging Daniel to respond to him. And Daniel was encouraged, he was encouraged a lot!

Naked, they stood wrapped around each other, Daniel's head tipped back so Steven could nip and lick at the base of his throat, his hands wandering over Steven's back and into his hair. Steven licked up, over throat and chin, taking Daniel's mouth. Catching Daniel's lower lip between his teeth, Steven pulled out of the kiss. Locking eyes with his lover, he lowered himself to his knees. Putting a hand on each of Daniel's hips, he urged Daniel to turn around.

Okay, not going with the tried and true here, then? Daniel turned easily because if Mr. Perfect wanted to play with his ass, he wasn't going to object.

Steven kissed the base of Daniel's spine and nipped the globes of his ass. He rubbed his face against the warm flesh, and moving his mouth to the top of Daniel's crease, licked a line straight down, between the cheeks. His thumbs spreading Daniel open, Steven's mouth followed the same path again, this time nuzzling in, lapping at hidden, secret skin.

Object? Who me? God no! Daniel moved his arms back, hands searching for Steven, needing to touch. Steven licked over his hole, and Daniel moaned, one hand locking onto Steven's shoulder.

Fuck! Steven could overdose on the way this man felt, on his scent, on the way he shivered into Steven's touch. He sucked at the tender opening, and blew on the heated skin. Daniel's head dropped down onto his chest, his eyes closing at the sensation, as Steven breached him with his tongue.

"Oh, Fuck!" Daniel's whispered words sent pulses of fire directly to Steven's groin. Sliding one hand around to the front of Daniel's body, he fisted the hard length, fingers gliding over silken skin. His tongue plunging into Daniel's ass and his hand pumping Daniel's cock, Steven drank in the sighs and moans that drifted on the silence in the room. *Yes, that's it baby. Quiver and moan and shake for me. Come for me.*

Daniel grabbed Steven's wrist, halting the hand pumping his cock. "Stop, I'm going to lose it."

Tugging on Daniel's hips, Steven turned Daniel around to face him. He looked up at Daniel and grinned. "Isn't that the point?"

Daniel never answered that question, because his mind disintegrated when Steven swallowed him down, taking him in to the back of his throat. The skilled tongue and perfect pressure had his balls curling up tight against his body in seconds. Daniel's hands clamped over Steven's shoulders. His breaths became harsh pants that talked to Steven.

Sliding a finger into his mouth, Steven rubbed it alongside Daniel's cock, coating it with saliva. Sucking hard on the tender crown, Steven thrust his wet finger into Daniel's ass.

Mouth falling open on a low moan, eyes clenched shut, hands pulling at Steven's hair, Daniel shot into Steven's mouth. *Good, oh God! So damn fucking good!*

Steven swallowed and swirled his tongue, gentle with Daniel's recovering cock. Letting Daniel's shaft slip from his lips, Steven nuzzled into Daniel's groin and pressed a kiss to his inner thigh.

Standing, he wrapped himself around Daniel and merged their mouths together. Drawing back, he smiled into eyes slowly returning to hazel as Daniel recovered. "Bed?"

"You couldn't have suggested that before you blew me?" Daniel grumbled as he collapsed onto the bed.

Steven straddled him, laughing. "Sorry, I'll remember next time."

Daniel reached a hand up to palm Steven's face, his thumb tracing the line of his jaw. "We're going to have a next time?" Part of him wanted Steven to say yes, but the part that was still broken from Aidan's defection was screaming in the back of his mind. *What the fuck are you doing? Haven't you learned anything?*

Steven turned his face into Daniel's hand and pressed a kiss into the palm. "Oh, I think so." The man liked ice cream, could debate the merits of *Star Trek Voyager* versus *Star Trek: Enterprise*, had a body made for Steven's mouth, and practically read his fucking mind in bed. Oh, yes, there was going to be a next time!

Daniel told the screamer in his mind to shut the fuck up! He wanted this man. Steven might be a major nerd and an OCD nutcase, but his brand of quirky made Daniel feel more alive than he had felt in years. From pinning him with a geeky communicator pin, to knocking on his door at one in the morning, to talking Daniel into doing a striptease, Steven was a shot of life that Daniel couldn't resist. Not to mention that the man was perfection done in shades of uptight and chocolate, with a body that Daniel wanted to live in. Yes, he wanted Steven so he shut the screamer down, shoved the fear and the past and Aidan into a metal chest locked under key and chain, and tossed it into the depths of his mind.

Steven leaned sideways, reaching over to his night table, slid a drawer open and grabbed a bottle of clear liquid. Smiling at Daniel, he flipped the top open and coated his hands. "I think you'll like this." Pressing his palms to Daniel's chest, he moved them over his ribs, leaving a trail of heat.

"Oh!" Daniel's eyes went wide. "What is…?"

"Warming lubricant." Steven spread the liquid over Daniel; across his chest, over his shoulders and arms. Daniel's skin heated under Steven's fingers and he sank into the mattress, boneless. Stretching

Daniel's arms out to the side, Steven slid his hands along their length. He rubbed the heat into Daniel's open palms, and laced their fingers together. Leaning over his lover, he dropped a kiss onto smiling lips. Retracing his path back across Daniel's arms, and down over his chest, he rubbed heat into his abdomen, just above his groin.

Daniel had long since melted into Steven's touch. His eyes closed as he drifted on the warmth Steven pushed into his skin. A sharp slap shocked him out of his torpid haze. "Hey!"

"Uh-uh, you're not falling asleep on me." Steven's eyes held a promise. "I'm not done with you yet." Throwing a leg over Daniel's body, he slid off the bed. Delving into the same drawer in his night stand, he took out a package of wet wipes and cleaned the warming lubricant off his hands. "It's perfectly safe to use internally, but I prefer creating my own heat."

Steven's words reminded Daniel of the night's agenda. He looked down in surprise when his cock twitched on his thigh, in total approval of that idea. Daniel, himself, was a little nervous. It had been a long time.

Steven climbed back onto the bed, bringing a condom and a tube of Astroglide gel with him. Dropping the lube beside them on the bed, he settled between Daniel's legs. He ran his hands up Daniel's inner thighs, framing his favourite play area. His fingers traced through the blond hair above Daniel's cock, while his thumbs rolled over his balls. Daniel's cock got very, very interested. *Okay, recovery time is officially over.*

Steven tugged on Daniel's hips, dragging Daniel's ass up onto his own thighs. He coated his fingers, and traced circles around Daniel's hole. "You've done this before, right?"

"Yeah."

Something in the way Daniel hesitated over that word brought Steven's head up. He looked into the hazel eyes and found the hint of nerves that Daniel was trying to hide. "How long has it been?"

Daniel looked away. He so did not want to talk about this. "Does it matter?"

Steven couldn't miss the wall that went up between them, even as Daniel's cock went down. *Okay, not going there!* "No."

Leaning down, he drew Daniel's hesitant cock into his mouth. He licked and sucked, until it reared back into happy and horny. He looked along Daniel's body, up into eyes gone golden with want, no wall in sight. Keeping his eyes on Daniel's face, monitoring his comfort level, Steven swirled his tongue over the head of his lover's cock while his finger pressed the rim of Daniel's entrance. He circled and rubbed the puckered skin, allowing only the tip of one finger to slip in.

Daniel cupped Steven's hip, stroking slowly. He hadn't done this in almost nine years, back before Aidan. His ex-partner had not been interested in topping. Daniel's forays into bottoming in his undergrad years had not been particularly enjoyable, so he hadn't tried to change Aidan's mind. He had no intention of telling Steven any of this. He wanted to pretend Aidan had never happened. He wanted to start over, to be born again. Looking into Steven's eyes, that's how he felt, brand new.

Steven drew off, and replaced his mouth with his hand. Stroking Daniel's length with one hand, he focused on preparing Daniel with the other. He pushed one finger in, and when Daniel showed no discomfort he added a second. He pushed both fingers into the man beneath him, reaching deeper, searching…

Daniel's body jerked. "Ah! Oh, fuck, I forgot…" Whatever else he had intended to say was lost as Steven pressed over his prostate again. He reached for Steven, his hips coming off the bed, nothing intelligible falling from his lips.

Steven scissored his fingers, stretching Daniel, and then added a third finger. He stroked the sensitive bundle of nerves until Daniel pushed back onto his fingers, wanting more.

Thank God! Steven couldn't remember the last time he had devoted so much time to prepping a lover. He didn't resent the effort, he wanted Daniel to enjoy this, but he was ready, so fucking ready! "Turn over." Steven reached for the condom packet.

Daniel rolled over and pushed up onto his knees. He heard the packet tear, and the rustle of sheets as Steven shifted on the bed, slicking himself.

Steven curved over Daniel's back, kissing across his shoulders, and nuzzling into his neck. Breathing in Daniel's skin, he felt the tension in Daniel's body and took a few seconds to centre himself, to step it down a notch and hang on to his control. Dragging his lips down Daniel's spine, he pulled back, and aligned himself, touching the head of his cock to Daniel's opening. His free hand gentled Daniel, stroking his side, cupping his hip. "Push back onto me. Take me in."

Steven's voice was force wrapped in velvet, thick with desire, and warm with concern. Daniel was certain he had never heard that exact combination before. Not with Aidan, not with anyone. Trusting that voice, trusting this man, Daniel moved.

Steven gasped as Daniel pushed back, his crown breaching the ring of muscle. "That's it, baby. Take me." He stroked Daniel's hips and thighs, soothing him. "Take me."

Daniel rocked back on his knees, pushing onto Steven's cock, taking him, taking all of him. Taking him and keeping him. Head dropping, eyes closed, he moaned. Steven was deep inside him, stretching him, filling him and Daniel felt whole somehow, as if he had found a missing part of himself. Fortunately, just as that thought slithered into his mind and before it had time to freak him the fuck out, Steven took his first careful thrust. The feel of all that hardness pushing against his inner walls and any thought he had ever had receded under a wave of *Yes! Oh, Fuck! Yes!*

"God, you feel good." Steven held Daniel's hips and thrust carefully. Daniel's walls fluttered around him, accepting, opening for him. Leaning over Daniel's back, he spoke close to his ear. "Now, Daniel, now we're going to fuck!"

With every thrust, Steven moved deeper. Long strokes, pulling back till the head of his cock stretched Daniel's hole, faster, harder. Moans and grunts filled the room. Sweat broke out along Steven's spine.

"God, so good! More! Harder! Please!" Words spilled out of Daniel, gasped out between his thrusts back onto Steven's cock. Steven slammed into Daniel, and Daniel slammed back. They moved together, no thought, no plan, just this, just feeling this!

Steven shifted to the side, sliding one arm under Daniel, wrapping his hand around Daniel's weeping cock. The slightly different angle, sent each thrust over Daniel's prostate. "Yes! God! More!" Daniel was still gasping out 'more', as he spilled over Steven's fingers. Steven fucked Daniel through the tremors of his orgasm, and then let himself fall into his own.

Daniel flopped onto his back as Steven disposed of the condom and came back from the washroom with a facecloth still warm from the hot water he had rinsed it in. Now he was the nervous one. Steven already knew that he wanted this to be more than a one-time thing. Daniel was impulsive and funny and easy to be with, not to mention intuitive and generous when the clothes came off. Steven liked the way Daniel reached out to touch him as they talked, he liked the way words and thoughts just seemed to erupt out of his brain without any kind of filter. He just plain liked the man. Daniel had felt good inside him last night, but Steven wasn't signing on to be an exclusive bottom, not for Daniel, not for anyone. *Please, God, let him be okay with switching!*

Sitting beside Daniel on the bed, he rubbed the cloth over Daniel's chest, and abdomen, and wiped between his legs. He didn't say anything, waiting for Daniel to speak first. Tossing the cloth into the laundry basket, he stretched out on his side next to the blond in his bed.

Daniel turned to look at him and Steven released a breath he hadn't been aware he was holding. There was no hiding the completely blown away expression in Daniel's eyes. "I didn't know..." His voice held wonder, surprise, pleasure. It was all there, written on his face. He didn't try to hide any of it from Steven. He was amazed, and overwhelmed, and grateful. Reaching over, he trailed one finger across Steven's tilted smile. "I'm a big fan of house rules!"

CHAPTER 6

Full Disclosure

Sidewalks burned through thin soles, asphalt stuck to the tires of parked cars, and across the GTA people locked themselves away in air conditioned comfort. It was the tail end of the summer, Labour Day weekend actually, and the city was melting.

Planting his hands on the edge of the hot tub, Daniel hoisted himself out of the water. Sitting on the deck, feet still submerged, he looked across the tub at Steven. "I need water, you want anything?"

"No." Steven held Daniel's eyes. "I've got everything I need."

They both knew Steven wasn't talking about dehydration. Daniel smiled, but he didn't reply. He couldn't. He swung his legs out of the tub, and stood. "Be right back."

It's not that he didn't like Steven. He did. It's not that he wasn't happy. He was! But he refused to look into the future. He couldn't start thinking that Steven was a permanent part of his life. Happily ever after didn't exist. That myth had exploded and died when Aidan had walked away from eight years as if they were nothing. Daniel would never be that trusting again.

Grabbing a plastic bottle out of the fridge, he twisted the cap off. Leaning against the sink, he drank his water and watched Steven through the kitchen window. Head tipped back, arms stretched out along the rim of the hot tub, eyes closed against the glare of the sun, Steven was a sight worth watching…and touching. In the quiet of the empty kitchen, alone with his thoughts, Daniel smiled. *Yeah, let's not forget touching!*

Steven's eyes were closed but he could almost feel Daniel watching him from the house. Shifting on the plastic bench, he moved so that the water jets blasted his lower back. He exhaled, one long breath, trying to distil the tension in his shoulders. Once again, Daniel had evaded his attempts to find out what the fuck they were to each other! Steven couldn't figure him out and it was starting to piss him off. He knew Daniel liked him; they'd spent every weekend together since Sandy's July 1st BBQ for fuck's sake. As far as he knew, Daniel wasn't seeing anyone else. But he could, they had not had any conversations about exclusivity. They had not had any conversations about anything of depth at all, ever. They went out or they stayed in, they caught movies at the Cineplex or watched TV, they laughed and they fucked and Steven was never one hundred percent certain that he was going to see Daniel the following weekend because Daniel never fucking said anything!

On the other side of the kitchen window, Daniel sipped his water and watched the man in the hot tub. Steven's skin had become darker over the summer even though he was almost religious about applying sunblock. He looked even more perfect than usual lounging against the froth and bubbles of the hot tub, the sun glinting off the water drops on his skin. Daniel glanced down his own body and grimaced, pale skin and sun, not a good combination!

Steven had been very subtle about it, but Daniel knew he wanted some kind of definition to their relationship. Daniel cringed even thinking the word relationship. He couldn't go there. He was happy here, like this, with Steven. No strings, no promises, no one gets hurt.

Daniel didn't hate Saturdays anymore. Oh, he still hated crawling out of bed early to go cycling with Allan, but he had extra incentive these days. The memory of Steven's lips on the muscles in his calves and thighs had Daniel throwing the covers back and climbing out of bed each Saturday, not exactly enthusiastic, but determined nonetheless. Saturday afternoons, were usually spent in Steven's hot tub, so yeah, he didn't hate Saturdays anymore. They spent Saturday nights together, at either his place or Steven's, which meant waking up together, which made Sundays pretty damn good too.

The doorbell rang as he tossed the empty water bottle in the recycling bin under the sink. Walking over to the kitchen table, he grabbed his shorts off one of the chairs, and stepped into them. The doorbell chimed again as he pulled his T-shirt over his head. *Give me a sec here!*

Expecting a duo of neatly dressed young men shilling for Jehovah's Witness, or an eight-year-old selling Girl Guide cookies, Daniel was surprised to find a woman on the doorstep. She had shoulder-length dark hair, brown eyes, a pretty smile, and a disconcerted look on her face when she saw Daniel. "Oh, hi, is Steven here?"

"Yeah, he's in the back. Come in." Smiling, he held the door open and stepped back, ushering the woman into Steven's small foyer. "I'll get him for you."

Retracing his steps down the hall and through the kitchen, he slid the patio door open. "Steven, someone's at the door for you."

Not expecting any visitors, Steven looked surprised as he climbed out of the hot tub and grabbed a towel, wrapping it around his waist as he crossed the deck. Sliding the patio door shut behind him, he looked at Daniel, eyebrows arched into question marks. "Who is it?"

Daniel shook his head. "No idea. She asked for you."

Steven shrugged, and started for the foyer. "They're always collecting for something around here, Teens against Drugs, Camp for Kids, last week it was...Stephanie!" Steven threw his arms around the woman and pulled her into a hug. "What are you doing here? Why didn't you tell me you were coming?" He released the woman, but kept her hands in his. "You're staying with me."

The last sentence, Daniel noticed, wasn't a question.

Stephanie laughed, a light bubbling sound that sparkled in the air and set Daniel's teeth on edge. "I'm interviewing for a new job. I didn't know 'til yesterday. Yes, I was hoping to but," She glanced over Steven's shoulder at Daniel, "I don't want to intrude."

"Oh!" Steven turned to Daniel, obviously having forgotten he was even there. "This is my friend, Daniel." Steven put an arm around Stephanie's shoulder. "Daniel, this is Stephanie."

Stephanie held out her hand to Daniel. "Steven's ex." They both laughed as Steven pulled her against his side.

Daniel shook hands, and smiled, and said all the right things. Steven dragged Stephanie over to the couch, sitting down beside her. Daniel took the arm chair, a smile on his face as their chatter rolled over him unheard. *Who the fuck was this woman who Steven felt comfortable hugging half naked? Ex? What the hell did that mean?* Daniel found that he was not happy, not happy at all, to be introduced as just a friend. *Whose fault is that asshole? It's not like you've exactly encouraged Steven to throw the word boyfriend around. What did you want him to say? This is Daniel, the guy I fuck but only on the weekends because he's too chickenshit to make it more than that.*

Watching the two of them, obviously close, jumping over each other's words, laughing, Daniel felt a grey cloud of cold, aching emptiness clench talons into his heart. "I should go." He stood up and forced a smile. "You have a lot of catching up to do."

"Oh, I'm sorry, we must be boring you." Stephanie smiled at Daniel. "It's just been a while, you know?"

No, he did not know! He knew nothing about this person and who she was to Steven, and that really pissed him off. "I can see that, no problem." He smiled at Stephanie and nodded at Steven. "I'll call you later."

Detouring into the kitchen to grab his shoes, he took the stairs to Steven's bedroom two at a time, snagged his wallet off the night table, and shoved it in his back pocket. He gathered his toiletries from the bathroom and tossed them into his overnight bag. Zipping the bag shut, he threw the strap over his shoulder, and strode from the room. Downstairs again, he ducked his head into the living room. "Nice meeting you Stephanie. Good luck with the interview." He nodded to Steven and practically bolted for the front door.

Steven watched Daniel's quick retreat and turned to Stephanie, "I'll be right back." He raced after Daniel, catching him as he was clicking into his seatbelt. Daniel lowered the window, and Steven leaned down to speak through the opening. "What are you doing?"

I'm getting the hell out of here before I say something incredibly stupid and you realize what an insecure nut job I really am! "Giving you time to catch up with your friend."

Steven stared, trying to read Daniel's face. "That's very considerate of you." He may as well have come right out and called Daniel a liar, because that's what the irony in his voice said. "We'll do that and then you can join us for dinner."

"No." Daniel shook his head. "You guys don't need me here. I'll call you tomorrow."

Laying his left arm along the length of the open window, Steven reached in and slipped a hand into Daniel's hair. Tilted smile very much in evidence, his fingers stroked the back of Daniel's neck. "Well, Stephanie may not need you here, but I do." He held Daniel's eyes with his own. "I want you here. I want you in my bed tonight."

Steven's voice lowered on the last words, and Daniel had to pull himself out of those dark eyes, and focus. *Right, Stephanie.* He shook his head again. "I don't think so, your friend just got here."

"So? I've got two bedrooms."

"You know I'm not exactly a morning person. There's no need to subject Stephanie to that." Daniel laughed, and started the engine. "I'll call you tomorrow."

Accepting defeat, Steven stepped back from the car. He watched as Daniel reversed out of the driveway, waved, and drove away. *Why don't I believe you, Daniel Fine?* Steven shook his head as he walked back into the house. It didn't matter, call or no call, he knew where Daniel lived!

Closing the front door behind him, Steven joined Stephanie in the living room. Curling one leg under him on the couch, he got comfortable. "Tell me about the interview."

"Oh, no," Stephanie shook her head, practically vibrating with curiosity, "you tell me about Daniel." This was the first she knew of a new man in Steven's life. He had not mentioned one word about Daniel in any of his emails.

Steven shrugged. "His sister's my neighbour. We've been seeing each other." His words said, 'no big deal', but he avoided Stephanie's eyes, his fingers plucking at the folds of the towel still wrapped around his waist.

Stephanie smacked his knee. "Uh-uh, try again."

Steven grinned; he had really missed this woman. No one knew him better. "This could take a while. You want something to eat, drink?"

"Ah, a drinking kind of story, my favourite kind."

"You still like Kahlua?"

An hour and two drinks later, Stephanie knew everything about Daniel that Steven knew, well, almost everything. "Maybe, he just wants to take things slow?"

"No." Steven shook his head. "Daniel wants to contain this, to keep a lid on it somehow, as if it's all going to explode in his face."

"And what do you want?" Stephanie already knew what Steven wanted, but she didn't know if he knew.

Steven looked at his best friend. "I want Daniel."

While Stephanie and Steven tried to solve the puzzle that was Daniel, the man in question was not dealing at all well with the sudden mystery that was Steven. Daniel drove aimlessly; brewing in a cocktail of pissed off, anxious and hurt, all topped off with a large dose of confused. Car stopped at a red light, he sat in the driver's seat oblivious, talking to himself. *Ex-what, ex-girlfriend, ex-lover? No fucking way could she be his ex-wife, Steven was only twenty-eight! People got married in grad school all the time.* The obscenely loud honk from the car behind him startled Daniel out of his head and back onto the traffic clogged city streets. Accelerating through the green light, he flashed on Steven's arm around Stephanie's waist. *Who the fuck was this woman?*

❖   ❖   ❖

Doug was doing father-son stuff with Rhys, which with a three-year old meant the PlayPlace at McDonald's and checking out the riding toys at Toys-R-Us, followed by ice cream. Karen was celebrating her ninety minute window of freedom in a bubble bath. A glass of chilled white wine sat happily beside Rhys' yellow plastic duckie. Eyes closed, she luxuriated in the heat of the water, the vanilla scent of the foaming bubbles, and the music from her latest iPod playlist.

Her cell phone rang and Karen groaned as she saw Sandy's picture on the screen. "I'm on alone-time, Sandy. Talk fast!"

"Daniel's car is gone." Sandy didn't have to say anything else. The whole family knew that Daniel spent Saturday afternoon in Steven's hot tub.

"Shit!" Karen pushed herself into a sitting position against the wall of the tub. "What happened?"

"I don't know!" Sandy paced her living room, staring out the window at Steven's driveway. "One minute his car was there, same as every other Saturday, and then it was gone." Sandy started to nibble at her nails, a nervous habit that she had never been able to break. "Steven's car is there and another one, one I don't recognize, but Daniel's car is gone."

"Did you call Daniel?"

"Yeah, that would go over well! Hey, Danny, why isn't your ass in Steven's hot tub?"

Karen laughed. "Yeah, maybe not." She stood up, water and bubbles dripping. "I'll see what I can find out." She hit end call and climbed out of the tub. Grumbling to herself, she dried off, and grabbed her robe. *You couldn't screw up your life any other time? You had to do it during alone-time?*

Dressed, waiting for the kettle to boil, Karen tried to think of a reason to call Daniel. He had been at the regulation Friday dinner at their parents' place the previous night, so she couldn't just call and say, "Hey, what's new?" She added a tea bag to her favourite mug. Maybe she could call to supposedly talk about their parents' approaching anniversary. Not an ideal excuse because she and Sandy made those kinds of decisions, but...the doorbell rang as she poured water over her tea bag. *Now what?*

Karen opened the door, shocked to find Daniel on the doorstep. *Wow! Think of the devil!* "Are you lost?"

"Funny!" Not that Daniel looked all that amused as he stepped past Karen, into the house.

Karen closed the door and followed her brother into the kitchen. "Well excuse me, but it's not like you're exactly a fixture around here. When was the last time you just dropped by? Try *never.*"

Daniel slid onto a stool and propped his elbows on the counter. "Okay, I get it. I'm a crap brother."

"I didn't say that." Karen opened the pantry to get a coffee disc. Daniel didn't drink tea. She tossed her tea bag, added milk and sugar to her mug, and waited for the Tassimo to spit out Daniel's latte while he sat lost in his own thoughts. He seemed surprised when Karen clicked his mug down on the counter in front of him. "Talk."

"It's no big deal." Except it was, of course, or he wouldn't be here.

Karen said nothing. She leaned against the counter, sipped her tea, and waited. Daniel was obviously here to talk; it was just going to take him awhile to figure that out. Her brother sat there twitching and avoiding her eyes. His lips separated but no sound emerged because he didn't know where to start or what to say. *Oh, yeah, no big deal!*

"A woman showed up at Steven's place today." Daniel caught Karen's eye and then looked down, muttering his next words into his mug. "He was really happy to see her."

"So?" Karen didn't see a problem here.

Daniel looked up, betrayal and hurt in his eyes. "She said she was his ex."

Karen sputtered tea down her shirt. "Steven was married?"

"I don't know." Daniel clenched his fingers around his mug. "He never said anything about this, this Stephanie."

Karen heard the accusation in Daniel's voice. *Oh, this is not good!* After Aidan, Daniel was firmly convinced that what you didn't know could and would hurt you. He would take this sudden emergence of a stranger and use it as proof that Steven couldn't be trusted. It was definitely time for some damage control.

"Oh, and you've told him about your ex?" She knew damn well he hadn't. Daniel got suddenly fascinated by the threads of colour running through the granite of Karen's counter top. Guilty as charged! "Let me guess. You haven't told Steven that you like him, you haven't talked about being exclusive, and you haven't told him anything about Aidan." Karen crossed her arms over her chest. "Why would he tell you fuck all about his own past when for all he knows, you think he's an alternative to masturbation!"

Daniel flinched. "He knows he means more to me than that!"

"Oh, he's psychic then?" Karen came around the counter and took the stool next to Daniel's. "What did you think, Daniel? Steven's what, twenty-five?"

"Twenty-eight." Daniel didn't see what Steven's age had to do with anything

"Okay, twenty-eight. You think you're the only person who took one look at him and thought, nice, I've got to get me some of that?" Daniel's lips twitched; it wasn't quite a smile but Karen counted it as a victory. She put her hand on his. "Of course, he's got a past. But that's all it is, a past."

"So you think I'm getting bent out of shape over nothing?" Daniel really needed a second opinion on this. He didn't want to be a paranoid prick but he had let a lot things slide with Aidan, assuming they meant nothing, and that hadn't worked out so well.

"Until, Steven tells you otherwise, yes." She slid off her stool and smacked a hand into Daniel's shoulder. "Of course, if you don't talk to him, then he can't tell you anything, can he?"

Twenty minutes later, Karen put Daniel's empty mug in the dishwasher and walked her brother to the front door. "Steven is not Aidan. You know that, right?"

Daniel slipped his sunglasses on and opened the door. "Yeah, yeah, I know."

Karen waved as her brother backed out of the driveway, closed the front door, and grabbed the nearest phone.

Sandy picked up on the first ring. "Hello?"

"He just left." Karen didn't have to say who.

"Nice. How did you get him to your place?"

"I didn't; he just showed up."

"That can't be good."

"Nope, he was losing it because some woman showed up at Steven's today saying she was his ex."

"No fucking way! How the hell does Steven have an ex-wife? He's just a baby!" To Sandy, anyone under thirty was a baby.

"He's twenty-eight, Sandy, not ten! She could have meant ex-girlfriend, not ex-wife. We don't know anything and neither does

Daniel." Karen paused, fingers playing with the Teno bracelet on her wrist. "Daniel's not good with not knowing."

"Yeah." Surprise was never a good thing, not for Daniel, not since that schmuck Aidan!

"I had to talk him down from the ledge. I told him that of course Steven had a past, that he had his own past he hadn't told Steven about, and that he should talk to Steven."

Sandy nodded, not that Karen could see her. "That's good."

"Yeah, no guarantee he's going to listen to me though. You know Daniel!"

They both fell silent, because yeah, their brother was a stubborn pain in the ass. "We need to know what Steven's thinking. If I'm doing some gardening in the front tomorrow, and Steven stops to say hi…"

Karen snorted. "You? You don't garden."

Sandy grinned, pleased with her own ingenuity. "Yeah, but Steven doesn't know that."

Steven knew that Stephanie liked Italian, so for dinner, they walked a few blocks over to a small family-owned restaurant aptly named "Mama Mia". After working their way through pasta, tiramisu, and an impressive sampling of the house wines, they linked arms and headed back to his place. Steven took comfort in the familiarity of the evening and the woman at his side. If you substitute pizza and beer for the pasta and wine, this dinner had been a replica of countless other nights from their college years: eating and drinking and talking about boys.

Unlocking the trunk of her rental car, Stephanie dragged her suitcase out and Steven set her up in the guest room. He brought her extra towels and left her to answer her emails and the increasingly frantic phone messages from her mother.

Stephanie grinned as she held out her cell. "Here, you can talk to mom."

"I don't think so!" Steven laughed as he backed out of the doorway.

"Coward!"

Walking into his own room, Steven checked the digital clock on his night stand, 11:42. He plucked the portable out of its base and scrolled through the missed calls, nothing. He checked his voicemail, nada. His cell had been ominously quiet all night. He wasn't surprised, disappointed yes, but not surprised. He knew Daniel wasn't going to call. Staring into the mirror as he brushed his teeth before bed, Steven grinned. "You're not getting rid of me that easily Daniel Fine!"

✻   ✻   ✻

Not so early on Sunday morning, Daniel stood in his kitchen, glowering at the empty shelf in his pantry where the cereal should be. *Okay, toast it is.* He considered making eggs to go with the toast, but that was way too much trouble. The phone rang as the Tassimo gurgled out his coffee. "Hello?"

"I have bagels." Steven rattled the bakery bag in his hand. "Bagel Haven."

Shit! Steven! He had meant to call Steven last night. On the drive home from Karen's he'd decided that his sister was right. Steven's past, Stephanie or not, was just that, past, and really none of his business. But every time he picked up the phone, he saw Stephanie in Steven's arms and he couldn't get past that image.

"Daniel?" Steven didn't know what Daniel's problem was, but he intended to find out.

"Yeah, sure, come up." He hit six and dropped the phone back into its base. Exchanging the ratty boxers he slept in for a pair of jeans and a T-shirt, Daniel opened the door at Steven's knock.

"I didn't wake you, did I?" Steven was a morning person, but he knew Daniel was not.

"No. Perfect timing, I was just thinking about breakfast."

Steven followed Daniel into the kitchen and put the bag of bagels on the counter. "They're still warm."

Daniel set two plates out and opened the fridge. "No cream cheese." He turned to Steven. "You want butter, jam?"

"Sure." Steven opened the bag and placed a bagel on each plate. "Bread knife?"

"What do I look like, Martha Stewart? Try a steak knife, first drawer."

Steven shook his head as he opened the drawer. "Barbarian!" He got out two butter knives and a steak knife. "Let me guess, no napkins?"

Daniel put butter and a jar of jam on the counter, and tore two strips off the roll of paper towels by the sink. "Sorry, you're going to have to rough it."

Steven folded the paper towels and tucked them under the rims of the plates. "You wouldn't have peanut butter would you?"

"Now *that* I have." Daniel opened the pantry and plopped a jar of Kraft peanut butter on the counter. "I hope you're okay with smooth. Lauren is in charge of the peanut butter and she doesn't like crunchy." Raising the pitch of his voice and pulling his features into a mask of disgust, he impersonated his niece. "Not the kind with pieces, Uncle Daniel. That's just nasty!" Steven laughed and Daniel reverted to his normal speaking voice. "Coffee?"

"Please." Steven cut both bagels, while Daniel popped another disc in the Tassimo. Daniel opted for jam, while Steven smeared his bagel with Lauren's peanut butter. He brought Steven his coffee and they pulled out the stools from under the counter and sat beside each other.

Steven didn't touch his bagel. He turned sideways on his stool and looked at Daniel. "I missed you last night."

Daniel swallowed too quickly and almost choked. He had not expected that! He had assumed that Steven would be pissed at him for not calling. He had been prepared for an argument. Suspecting sarcasm, he turned to read the other man's face. Steven smiled at him, eyes warm, completely sincere. For some reason, Steven's lack of accusation pulled the apology from Daniel that Aidan's hissy fits never had. "I didn't call. I'm sorry."

"Don't worry about it." Steven's lips tipped into his off-centre smile. "I knew you weren't going to call."

Daniel didn't like the sound of that. "You thought I was lying?"

"No." Steven shook his head. "I thought you were upset. You want to tell me why?"

Yeah Daniel, why? He sidestepped the question he didn't have an answer for and asked one of his own. "You and Stephanie seem close?"

So, Stephanie was the catalyst, but Steven already knew that. What he didn't know was why. "Oh, yeah, we go way back. My parents moved around a lot." Steven grimaced. "Lucky me, I got to spend my last two years of high school with a bunch of Neanderthals who drove flatbed trucks and thought a great Saturday night meant shooting at cans with their father's hunting rifles while they polished off cases of beer." Steven started on his bagel, licking at the peanut butter that oozed over the sides. "Stephanie saved my life." He grinned at Daniel. "Or, at least, my hair style, my clothes, and my dignity. If it wasn't for her, I would have spent most of every day with my head clogging the toilets in the boys' washroom."

"How did she get them to leave you alone?" Just a guess, but he didn't think that Stephanie had a black belt in Karate.

Steven shrugged. "She was my girlfriend. She forced the whole school to see intelligent and sensitive instead of gay. I owe her big time!"

Daniel wiped his hands on his paper towel and pushed his empty plate away. Holding his coffee cup, he swung sideways on his stool so that he was facing Steven. "So, when she said ex yesterday she meant...?"

"Ex-girlfriend? Yep."

"She knew you were gay?" Daniel didn't want to think that Steven had lied to Stephanie or to himself.

"Oh, yeah." Steven laughed. "She said the fact that I could look at the French teacher without drooling was a dead giveaway. Miss Gagnon was young, beautiful, and had all the right curves." Steven rolled his eyes. "She had those hormonal red necks tripping over their own feet, eyes glazed with teenage lust." He wiped crumbs off his fingers and leaned against the counter, facing Daniel. "We made a pact. I helped her with math and chemistry, and she helped me maintain the facade of a..." Steven sketched quotes in the air, "real man."

Standing, he tucked his stool under the counter and started to clear their dishes away, putting everything in the dishwasher. "If anyone wanted out of that place more than me, it was Stephanie! We bonded over our absolute disdain for everyone and everything in that town." He put the peanut butter back in the pantry and the jam in the fridge. "Of course, we looked like a couple; we were together all the time. We barely talked to anyone else." Following Daniel to the living room, he sank into the opposite side of the couch from him. "We went to UBC together. We don't see much of each other anymore, but we keep in touch." Steven smiled. "And that's Stephanie and me in a nutshell."

Don't ask. You don't need to know. It's got nothing to do with you. "So, you were just friends?"

Steven tipped his head to one side slightly. "You mean did we sleep together?" He smiled at some memory Daniel wasn't privy to. "We were young and curious, with no other outlet for our hormones than each other, so yes. We were lovers through senior year and part of our freshman year at University." Steven shrugged. "And then there were other options for both of us. I held her while she cried when her first boyfriend cheated on her. She took me out and got me smashed when I learned that hooking up meant the other guy disappeared as soon as he zipped up." Steven shook his head over his own naïveté. "Hard to believe that we were ever that young."

Daniel didn't smile. "You never said you were bi."

Steven heard the undercurrent of accusation in Daniel's tone. He saw the tension in his shoulders, the sudden distance in his eyes, and he didn't understand any of it. His story wasn't all that unusual, a lot of gay men had a woman or two in their past. "That's because I'm not. Why, would it matter if I were?"

Hell yes, it would matter! It was bad enough knowing that Steven was going to leave him for another man one day. He didn't need to worry about the women too! "No, of course not." Daniel dredged up a smile, but it sat awkwardly on his face, not nearly convincing enough. "It's not really my business anyway, is it?"

Steven averted his eyes, smiling softly as his fingers played with the material on the back of the couch. He looked back at Daniel. "I was hoping, after the time we've spent together, that you would think that what I do is your business."

Daniel heard what Steven was very carefully not saying. He even knew what Steven wanted him to say. He couldn't say it though, not now, maybe not ever. He couldn't say what Steven wanted to hear so he tried to deflect, to avoid the conversation all together. He was getting to be an expert at avoidance; he had been doing it for weeks. "I guess we don't know each other very well."

Steven waited, but Daniel didn't say anything else. He was sitting on the couch beside Steven, but he wasn't really with Steven, was he?

That's it? That's your response? We don't know each other very well? Maybe not, but Steven knew that Daniel wanted him. In the two months they had been doing whatever the hell they had been doing, that hadn't changed. What he didn't know was why Daniel drew a line in the sand that he couldn't step over. He didn't know why Daniel carried a huge sign that read, 'No Trespassers'.

He didn't know and he never would because Daniel didn't tell him fuck-all about anything that mattered. Steven stood and stared down into conflicted hazel eyes. "I would like to know you well." He reached down and put his hand under Daniel's chin, rubbing his thumb along the other man's jaw. "I would like to know you." He traced Daniel's lips with one finger and dropped his hand. Turning, he started for the front door.

He was already in the foyer before Daniel realized that Steven was not just leaving for the day, he was leaving forever. He raced after the other man, grabbing his shoulder and spinning him around. "Steven!"

Steven gave him a chance. He waited. He waited, and he watched as Daniel struggled to find words, fighting some inner battle that he couldn't tell Steven about. "You have to let me know you, Daniel. I don't think that's too much to ask." Steven turned and let himself out of the apartment, closing the door softly behind him.

CHAPTER 7

Issues

"Hi, Mommy!" Lauren waved as she rode her bicycle into the driveway. "Hi, Mommy!" Glen waved from his own much larger bike, as he followed his daughter to the open garage door. Brady trailed behind them, tongue hanging out of his mouth, drool dripping onto the interlocking bricks.

Kneeling on the grass in front of three very sad and tattered rose bushes, Sandy waved at her little traveling circus. "How was the park?"

"Cool! Brady found a dead bird!" Lauren kicked her bike stand into place. "Daddy took a picture with his phone. I'm going to tell Ashley." Lauren went running into the house and Glen walked over to his wife. Standing, and brushing at her knees, Sandy leaned into her husband.

"What are you doing?" In the six years they had lived in that house, Sandy had never once tried to garden.

Sandy motioned to the earth she had been digging at. "Duh!"

Doug looked at the freshly combed dirt, then around the front lawn, over their property, and their neighbour's, looking for clues to Sandy's sudden industriousness. Glancing across the street, at Steven's place, it finally clicked. "You're spying on Steven again!"

"I am not!" Sandy denied it vehemently, but her eyes laughed. "I just thought that if I was out here and Steven stopped to say hi..."

Glen wrapped his arms around his wife, pulling her back against his chest. "CSIS could learn a thing or two from you. Any particular reason you're haunting Steven today?"

"Daniel's car wasn't in Steven's driveway yesterday afternoon, or last night, or this morning." Sandy's tone made it clear that this was a disaster of epic proportions.

"He's probably working. You know how he gets before a deadline." Personally, Glen thought his wife was a little too involved in her brother's love life, but he knew better than to say so.

Sandy glanced over at Steven's place. She knew Daniel had freaked out yesterday over some woman from Steven's past, but she still hoped that Glen was right, and Daniel was just working. "Yeah, maybe."

Her gardening idea had been a complete bust. By the time she cleaned up from breakfast, found a gardening spade in the basement, and made it out to the front lawn, Steven's car was gone. Maybe he was at Daniel's? She really hoped he was at Daniel's!

Glen steered her toward the house. "It's almost time for lunch, and isn't Allan coming over to take a family photo this afternoon?"

"Right, I forgot about that." Sandy stopped on the first step and turned to look back at her husband. "How come you remembered?"

"Mind like a steel trap, babe." Glen opened the front door and stood aside for his wife to enter. "Also, Daniel made me put it in my phone last week after soccer. Allan told him that he wasn't lugging over all his equipment only to find no one home."

Sandy grinned. "Guess he hasn't forgotten the last time, huh?"

❉   ❉   ❉

Daniel stood in his foyer staring at his front door, the door Steven had just closed behind him. *Don't just stand there, asshole! Open the door. Catch him before he gets in the elevator. Stop him. Tell him...* He reached for the door knob and stopped. *Tell him what?* His shoulders slumped as he turned his back to the door, and leaned against it. It was better this way. God! He should never have started this. How had he thought he could do this? He couldn't be the man Steven wanted him to be.

Pushing off the door, he sat himself down at a dining room table littered with the detritus of his work: print-outs, files, assorted pens, highlighters, and computer paper. Opening his laptop, he clicked into his Word documents.

His article sat waiting for final editing, and waiting, and waiting. The words morphed into the slide show of Tumblr pictures that was his screen saver. The pictures melted on and off his screen unnoticed as Daniel focused inward. His past and his present flowed together, merging into a collage painted in hurtful hues. Aidan, the man he thought he knew, and Steven, the man he wanted to know. Both of them walking out and closing the door behind them, with Daniel left on the other side of that door wondering what he could say or do to bring them back.

❈   ❈   ❈

Lauren made the ideal subject for the camera. She smiled on cue, had no problem holding a pose, and for someone who hadn't started grade school yet, had a fairly good understanding of composition. Allan got a kick out of indulging her enthusiasm, taking shots with her favourite toys, encouraging her directorial debut. The family photo shoot turned into an homage to the five-year-old, but Sandy and Glen didn't seem to mind. Promising Sandy that he'd have the pictures ready within the week, Allan gathered his cameras and equipment and stuffed everything back into the trunk of his car. Walking around to the driver's side, he saw Steven coming out of his house, a woman at his side, a very nice looking woman. Since Allan considered beautiful women his *raison d'être*, he waved at Steven and crossed the street.

Walking up the driveway, he met Steven and Hello, Beautiful as they reached the bottom of the walkway. "Steven, hey." Allan grinned at Steven, and turned to soft hair, tempting lips and smiling eyes.

Steven rolled his eyes at the salivating puppy that was Allan. "Stephanie, meet Allan. Allan, this is my friend Stephanie."

Allan took Stephanie's hand in his, and conveniently forgot to let it go. "Here's one of the great things about Steven." He locked eyes with the woman before him, a smile tugging at his lips. "When he says friend in reference to a woman, you know it's not a euphemism."

Stephanie took her hand back, laughter dancing behind her smile. "We've already done the euphemism part."

Allan's eyes went wide and his gaze flicked over both of them. "What, just now?"

Stephanie laughed. "No, years ago, when we were kids."

"Really!" Allan stepped between Stephanie and Steven, and putting an arm around each of their shoulders, he urged them down the driveway. "Now, that's a story I want to hear." He stopped beside Steven's car. "Where are we going for dinner?"

Steven shook his head as he beeped the car open. You couldn't get mad at Allan; it would be like smacking a cuddly teddy bear that just wanted hugs. "We're going to that Irish place on the Danforth."

Allen's?" Allan opened the passenger door for Stephanie. "Great place, love it."

In the backseat, Allan leaned as far forward as he could, ignoring the bite of his seat belt. "So, you guys shared pails in the sandbox?"

"No, we don't go that far back." Stephanie turned and spoke to Allan through the space between the front seats. "Steven's family moved to our back of beyond hick town just as I was starting my junior year of high school. He saved me from terminal boredom."

"Nice!" Allan gave Steven's shoulder a congratulatory slap, not that Steven had anything to do with his parents' decision to move. "Teenagers: roiling hormones and curiosity!" Sighing dramatically, Allan turned to Stephanie, his blue eyes broadcasting a very flattering combination of appreciation and interest. "I take it this was your 'euphemism' stage?"

"Allan considers himself an expert on all things sexual." Steven spoke to Stephanie while he checked his mirrors before switching lanes. "Ignore his prurient curiosity."

"Really?" Stephanie sent Allan an assessing glance.

"I don't claim the title of expert." Allan tried for modesty. "I'd say I'm more of an enthusiastic student."

Stephanie grinned. "I'm a bit of an enthusiast myself."

Allan settled into the back seat, matching Stephanie's grin. "Yeah?"

Steven could practically hear the swords being drawn. "Great!" He muttered to no one who was paying any attention to him. "Just fucking fantastic!"

Steven held the door to the restaurant open and tugged Allan aside as Stephanie talked to the hostess. "She's my best friend."

Allan looked over at Stephanie. "I can see why. She's smart, funny, gorgeous, what's not to like?"

Steven hissed low enough that Stephanie wouldn't hear him. "That's not what I meant!"

Allan dragged his eyes off Stephanie and looked at Steven. "I know what you meant. I think she can take care of herself."

Steven glared at Allan. "Stephanie's honest, are you?"

Allan met Steven's eyes. "Yes." It was a promise, and Steven nodded, satisfied.

"Guys, they've got a table."

❖   ❖   ❖

Karen spent a good part of Sunday, when she wasn't chasing after her son or doing the housework she never got around to during the week, thinking about Daniel. She had tried his cell but it went straight to voice mail. He had been happier since Steven, happier than he had been in years. Not that he said word one about Steven. The only reason they knew anything at all was that Sandy lived across the street from the man Daniel would not admit to seeing. She didn't know why Daniel was trying to pretend that Steven wasn't important. Obviously the man meant something to him or Daniel wouldn't have shown up at her place yesterday looking so fucking lost. Why did she have this feeling that Daniel had not talked to Steven? Because she knew her brother, that's why. Throwing a Bounce sheet into the dryer, she set the timer, pushed start and walked into the kitchen, picking up the portable phone on the counter. "Did you talk to Steven?"

"No. The gardening ploy didn't work. His car was already gone by the time I got out there. I just saw him leave with Allan, and a woman I'm guessing is the one Daniel told you about." Sandy pulled lettuce, cucumbers, and tomatoes out of the fridge.

"Allan? Since when do Steven and Allan hang out?"

Sandy shrugged as she got a vegetable knife out of the drawer. "How the hell do I know? No one tells me anything. All I know is that Allan was here taking a family photo, and then he was getting in Steven's car." She started to chop up the cucumber. "Maybe Allan can find out what's going on."

Karen snorted. "Right, like Allan's going to notice anything that isn't attached to an XX chromosome!" She smiled as Doug walked into the kitchen, Rhys on his shoulders. "Gotta go. We're having dinner at Doug's parents' place."

"'Kay, bye."

❊   ❊   ❊

Allan wasn't quite as oblivious as his cousin thought. Okay, yes, he didn't devote a lot of his attention to Steven, but he was attuned to all things Stephanie. He noticed the concerned looks she sent Steven's way. She was subtle about it, just an occasional glance, as she and Steven regaled Allan with tales from their years at Red Neck High. He would have missed it entirely, if he hadn't been so focused on her.

"So, is this your first time in Toronto?"

"Yes." Stephanie tilted her head to the side, indicating Steven sitting beside her. "Steven played tour guide today. He whisked me through the highlights: the CN Tower, the Eaton Centre, Casa Loma. We walked the Beaches." Laughing, she slapped at Steven's arm lightly as she complained to Allan. "He told me about Bloor Street and Yorkville, but he wouldn't take me."

"Because I've seen you shop before." Steven grimaced. "No way am I spending two hours in Holt Renfrew looking at purses you can't afford anyway!"

"It makes no sense, I know." Stephanie laughed at herself. "I grew up in a small town that thought Reitman's was high fashion, so to actually be in the same room with designer bags that I've only seen in magazines, ecstasy! And don't even get me started on the shoes!"

"Sorry I'm not into designer drooling." Steven smiled at Stephanie's excitement. "But Toronto has more to offer than retail mania. There's a

dance club on Wellington that turns Monday nights into Saturdays."
He caught Steven's eye. "You know the C Lounge, right?"

Steven shook his head. "Heard of it, but I've never been."

"Dude, you've got to come." Allan smiled across the table at both
of them. "This place is great in the summer. They have a huge patio
with waterfalls, and fountains. The music is legendary." He looked at
Steven. "Call Daniel, we can all go together."

Steven's face totally shut down. Stephanie touched his arm, concern
in her eyes, and Steven twined his fingers with hers, constructing a
smile that looked plastic. "You go. Allan is a good tour guide." He
glanced over at Daniel's cousin, a more authentic smile tugging at his
lips as he teased Allan. "He spends more time in the clubs than he
does at home."

"Hey!" Allan looked at Stephanie and shrugged. "Why does he
make that sound like a bad thing?" They laughed and Allan steered the
conversation into a discussion of his favourite night spots. He didn't
mention Daniel's name again, and neither did Steven. Midway through
dinner, Allan's phoned vibrated with an incoming call. Caroline's
picture flashed on his view screen. He slipped the phone back into his
pocket, letting the call go to voice mail. As a matter of policy, Allan
always concentrated wholly on the woman he was with. To call or
text one woman while he was with another was not only rude, it was
counterproductive. A woman who felt neglected did not throw her
bedroom door open. Usually, Allan excused himself and answered
texts and calls from the safety of the men's washroom. Tonight, sitting
across the table from Stephanie's animated features, the thought never
even occurred to him.

❖　❖　❖

While Allan was offering to guide Stephanie through Toronto's night
life, Daniel was having dinner at Kevin and Jonathan's. He had
spent the afternoon peeling the label off a beer bottle, not watching
a Torchwood Marathon on the Sci-Fi network, and thinking about
Steven. He knew he was being a complete dick, Steven wasn't asking
for much. He just wanted to know how Daniel felt, and Daniel couldn't

tell him that because he was working very, very hard at not feeling anything. He wasn't going to set himself up for that kind of pain again. Kevin had called and Daniel had decided that he needed a break from hating himself.

"Vancouver's the ideal city. It's got everything: beaches and mountains. You can kayak, windsurf, bike, hike, ski." Jonathan passed the bruschetta to Daniel. "And it's queer-friendly. They even have Winter Pride, a ski week at Whistler."

Kevin wasn't impressed. "I don't ski."

Daniel laughed. Jonathan had been trying to get Kevin to think about moving to Vancouver ever since he got back from his last business trip. "No, but you drink and I hear that's what *après* ski is all about."

Jonathan twirled his linguini around his fork and glared at his husband. "You don't have to ski. I'm just saying you could."

Kevin mumbled around a mouthful of pasta. "I could ski here."

Jonathan snorted. "Right! 'Cause Toronto's known for its mountains."

Kevin put his fork down with enough force to clatter against the china. "I'm not moving to Vancouver. Now, stop boring Daniel."

Jonathan turned to Daniel. "Sorry, have I been ranting?"

"Oh, don't stop on my account. I love watching domestic bliss in action."

Kevin turned on his friend. "Just for that, you're helping me clean up after dinner."

Daniel shrugged. "I always help you clean up."

Kevin grinned. "Why do you think we keep asking you over?"

Two hours later, dishes done, kitchen clean and the better part of two bottles of wine polished off, Kevin and Jonathan walked Daniel to the front door. "Night sweetie, drive safe." Kevin kissed Daniel on the cheek and opened the door.

Daniel hugged Jonathan. "Don't stay up all night arguing about Vancouver."

Jonathan put one arm around Kevin's waist, and shoved Daniel out the door with the other. "We've got better things to do with our nights, dick head."

Daniel clicked into his seat belt and turned the ignition. Looking through the windshield, he waved at his friends. The two men stood framed in the open doorway, arms about each other's waists, Kevin's head on Jonathan's shoulder. They waved, and Daniel backed out of the driveway.

How do they do it? How any couple stayed together was a complete mystery to Daniel. Kevin and Jonathan, Sandy and Glen, Karen and Doug, even his own parents, thirty-nine years, how was that even possible? Every six weeks or so, Jonathan travelled on business, Vancouver, Calgary, Edmonton. Kevin didn't like it much, but he wasn't concerned. He didn't stay up nights worrying that Jonathan was going to come home from one of those trips and say, "By the way, I met someone. It's been fun, but it's over." How do you trust someone that much?

He had trusted Aidan. They had bought a small town house together when Aidan graduated from medical school. Their families had helped them move in. Daniel could still see them, Aidan and himself, that first night in their new home, talking late into the night, curled around each other in bed, making plans for a future that never came. The memory was still vivid, still painful, even now. Daniel blinked the memory back and gone.

Funny that, one minute he had a partner and a house, and the next he was alone in an empty condo. There had been signs which Daniel had totally misread. Aidan had been quieter than usual, a little withdrawn, certainly less interested in anything physical. Daniel had thought it was just the stress that came with being an intern, the long hours, the lack of sleep. He had tried to make it easier on Aidan, taking care of all the details of living, the laundry, the cooking, the bills. He did everything so that Aidan could work and sleep. It was only for a year, right? Daniel ground his teeth together. He still couldn't believe what an idiot he'd been. And that, ladies and gentlemen, is why he didn't believe in forever!

❄   ❄   ❄

Steven pulled into his driveway, and smirked at Stephanie as Allan scrambled out of the back seat fast enough to open her car door for her. Stephanie mouthed the words 'fuck off' at him before turning to smile at Allan, giving him her hand as she slipped out of the car. "Thank you."

"I'll pick you up tomorrow night, eight?"

"Sounds good." Stephanie waited as Stephen locked the car and walked around the hood to the passenger side, linking her arm through his. "You sure you don't want to come with us?"

Steven looked at Allan and patted Stephanie's hand in a theatrical version of avuncular. "No, no children, you go and have a good time. At my age, I can't go gallivanting around town on a week night."

Stephanie smacked his arm. "Shut up! You're only twenty-eight."

Steven started up the walkway, speaking over his shoulder. "Yeah, but that's much older in gay years."

"You better come with us then Steven, you've only got two years left to party." Allan laughed as Steven turned and flashed his middle finger.

Stephanie stepped closer to Allan, speaking low so Steven wouldn't hear her. "You don't mind if he comes, do you?"

Allan leered at her. "Not if you promise to grind up against me when the dance floor gets really crowded."

Stephanie laughed and followed Steven, walking backwards and calling out to Allan still standing in the driveway. "Or I could meet you in the men's room!"

Allan grinned and called up to Steven, already at the front door. "Steven, you have to come!"

Steven shook his head as he unlocked the door. "No, I don't!"

Stephanie waved at Allan and, still laughing, ducked into the house after Steven. Allan walked down the driveway, and crossed the street to his car. Fishing his car keys out, he glanced at Sandy's house, and let the keys drop back into his pocket. Skirting his car, he walked up the patterned concrete path to the front door and rang the bell.

"Allan?" Glen opened the door. "Don't tell me. We all have red eye and you have to shoot the whole thing over?"

"What? You don't want Vampire eyes? You should have said something." Allan stepped into the foyer. "Sandy around?"

"Yeah. We're just watching some stuff that's been piling up on the PVR. Come on in."

"Who was...?" Curled up on the couch, Sandy turned at the sound of footsteps on the hardwood floor. "Allan? You haven't got the pictures done this fast?"

"No." Allan walked around the couch and sat on the planked, wooden coffee table directly in front of Sandy. Glen sat beside Sandy on the couch and Allan addressed his question to both of them. "Have either of you talked to Daniel today?"

"No." Sandy shook her head. "We haven't seen him since Friday night at mom's place. Why?"

"I saw him yesterday, biking. He was going to Steven's after lunch, same as usual." Allan leaned forward, resting his arms on his thighs, his hands clasped between his legs, eyes moving from Sandy to Glen. "I just had dinner with Steven and a friend of his from high school, Stephanie. We were talking about going to C Lounge tomorrow night and I suggested that Steven call Daniel so we could all go together." Allan paused and Sandy knew she wasn't going to like whatever came next. "Steven pretended he hadn't heard me. His eyes went blank, and his face...something's wrong."

Sandy jumped up and started pacing. "I knew it." She waved an arm at her husband. "I'm going to kill him. He's finally happy again and he has to go and fuck it up!"

"Hey, how do you know it was his fault?" Glen liked Daniel, and relationships meant two people. "Maybe it was Steven. You don't know what happened."

"Right!" Sandy snorted, her opinion of that possibility very clear. "I know Daniel freaked out yesterday when this Stephanie person showed up at Steven's. Karen told him to calm down and talk to Steven." Sandy turned to Allan. "You were with them tonight. Is Stephanie someone Daniel has to worry about?"

"No." Allan was definite. He knew who Stephanie had been flirting with and it wasn't Steven. "They're close. They experimented when they were kids, but that's long over. They're friends. That's it."

Sandy nodded. "Okay, good. So what the hell happened?"

※　　※　　※

That's exactly what Steven had been asking himself all day, what the hell happened? After dinner with Stephanie and Allan, Steven walked into his room knowing before he even checked his voice mail that there would be no message from Daniel. If Daniel wanted to talk to him, he would have called his cell. He stripped off his clothes and tossed them in the hamper. Pulling on sleep shorts and an old T-shirt, he flopped down on his bed. Mashing a pillow up behind his head, he stared at the ceiling.

He'd known, he'd chosen to ignore it, but he'd known that Daniel needed to limit their involvement. It's not like there weren't enough signs. Daniel never called him during the week. They only ever got together on the weekend. They never made plans, because that would involve talking about the future, and Daniel never talked about the future. Not even anything as benign as, "The new Superman movie opens in two weeks, do you want to go?"

They were good together. They had fun together, whether they went out or stayed home. Even after all these weeks, the sex was still…Steven closed his eyes and groaned. The sex was still…better than anything Steven had ever known with anyone else. Daniel had found erogenous zones on Steven's body that Steven didn't even know he had. And yet, as good as the sex was, and it was sweat pooling, muscle trembling, scream inducing good, and as much as they were practically attached from Saturday afternoon to Sunday night, Daniel had never once suggested that they be exclusive. He had never asked Steven about his past relationships. He had never talked about his own relationships. And, most revealing of all, he had never said anything to encourage Steven to think that they were in any way a permanent thing.

So, yes, Steven knew that Daniel had issues, and he was okay with that. Everyone had baggage. He was more than willing to deal with a little drama and a past-not-perfect. Daniel was worth it. Steven was anal, no question. He was a classic, card-carrying nutcase. He liked lists and plans and little plastic organizers. He wasn't comfortable stepping back and letting life unfold in all its random glory. He would be more than happy to shake Daniel's life out, get rid of the garbage and organize it for him. But it was Daniel's call. He had to talk to Steven. He had to trust him. It really made the control freak inside Steven grind his teeth in frustration, but the next move had to be Daniel's.

He rolled off his bed, padded across the hall to the guest bedroom, and knocked on Stephanie's door. In response to the 'yes?' he heard through the door, he opened it and stuck his head in. "I'm thinking popcorn and a really ridiculous rom-com."

Stephanie closed her kindle and slid out of her sheets. "Crazy, Stupid, Love?"

Steven laughed. "You read my mind!"

❊   ❊   ❊

After Allan left, Sandy curled up beside Glen on the couch, but she just couldn't get comfortable. Glen hit pause and nudged his wife off the couch. "Go on, call Karen."

Sandy turned startled eyes to her husband. "What?"

"Right! Call your sister. Tell her all about the latest Daniel disaster. Work out some plan to fix your brother." Glen slipped his hand behind the back of his wife's head and pulled her into a kiss. "And then I want equal time."

Sandy grinned, and standing, snatched the portable phone off its base. She punched in numbers as she left the room. Glen shook his head and called after her. "Just for the record, I think you should stay out of it." He muttered to himself as he pressed play. "Not that anyone listens to me."

Karen watched the red digital numbers on the treadmill screen, stepping off when they finally flashed 20:00. She should do thirty minutes, but screw it, she was tired. Tomorrow, she promised herself as she climbed the stairs to the main floor. Yeah, right! In the kitchen, she opened the fridge and took out a bottle of water. She worked out at night after she got Rhys tucked into bed. Between work, Rhys, and trying to keep up with the housework, she needed the stress relief. Thank God Doug made dinner every night because she hated to cook. Swallowing half the bottle in one gulp, she walked into the family room.

"Hey, babe, call your sister." Doug turned from a rerun of The Big Bang Theory. "She called while you were on the treadmill."

"'Kay, thanks." Karen leaned over the couch and kissed the top of his head. Grabbing the portable, she walked into the living room, so her talking wouldn't disturb Doug. "Hey, Sandy, you called?"

"Have you heard from Daniel?"

"No, have you?"

"No. So you don't know if he talked to Steven?"

Karen shook her head, although Sandy couldn't see that. "I know he was going to talk to Steven when he left here. But I don't know if he actually did. You know Daniel, he's not so good with the whole talking thing."

Sandy sighed. "Well something happened. Allan was just here. He had dinner with Steven and that woman Daniel told you about. Her name is Stephanie, she's an old friend of Steven's from high school."

"Friend, or FRIEND?"

"According to Allan, they're just friends. Allan said he was talking about taking Stephanie to some dance club. He told Steven to call Daniel and they'd all go. He said Steven pretended he hadn't heard him. Allan thinks something happened."

"Shit! Why does he never listen to us? I'm going to kill him!"

Sandy laughed. "Yeah, that's what I said. Glen said maybe it's not Daniel's fault. Maybe it's Steven who screwed up."

"Oh, please! You don't think that for a minute."

"I know Daniel's scared shitless of being hurt again. We've got to fix this."

"How? We can't tell Steven what a prick Aidan was. Daniel would never forgive us."

"You're right, we can't tell Steven anything. We've got to talk to Daniel."

"I'll call him."

"Yeah, me too. Night."

* * *

Daniel didn't go home when he left Kevin and Jonathan's. He wasn't ready to face an empty apartment and a bed that still reminded him of Steven. He drove down Church Street and parked opposite a plethora of rainbow flags. Walking up the steps into the dark interior of a small night spot he had visited regularly pre-Steven, he crossed the room and straddled a stool at the bar. "Labatt Blue."

The guy behind the bar, wearing a tight white T-shirt and blue jeans, was vaguely familiar. He looked up from the drink he was pouring and nodded. He popped the cap on a beer and set it down in front of Daniel. "Been a while."

"Yeah, been busy." Daniel took a chug of his beer and turned on his stool to study the room. The bartender shrugged, and taking the hint, left Daniel alone. Daniel didn't want to talk to the bartender. He didn't want to talk to anyone. He didn't want to talk at all.

He watched two guys playing pool, and they watched him. He leaned back, elbows resting on the bar behind him, and raised one foot from the floor to the lower rung on the bar stool, a move that not coincidentally at all, tightened the denim along his thigh, and across his package. He sipped on his beer, and watched the two men at the table exchange looks. He didn't have a preference really. He would do either one of them, or both for that matter. He wanted up close and impersonal, and since he didn't know either one of them from Adam, they were perfect.

Daniel stood, set his beer down on the bar, and walked across to the pool table. The men leaned on their pool sticks, no longer playing, as they watched him approach. He stopped at the edge of the table and reached into his back pocket. Making eye contact with both of them, he laid two condoms on the wooden ledge bordering the green felt of the table. He turned and walked towards the washrooms tucked into a purposely dark corridor that ran the length of the bar.

Stopping near the end of the hallway, he leaned against the wall, and waited. He was vaguely interested to see which one of them would follow him. He wasn't twenty anymore, but his body was good. His blond hair, combined with the fact that he just didn't give a shit, pretty much guaranteed him some action. He tipped his head back against the wall, a cynical smile on his lips. If neither one of them joined him, well, there were a lot of bars and he was in no hurry. After all, there wasn't anyone waiting for him at home, now was there?

At the sound of footsteps, he pushed away from the wall and, turning, looked along the dark corridor to where light spilled from the bar area. Well, well, well, this was his lucky night, two for the price of one!

Hours later, the two men already a memory, Daniel staggered into the elevator in his building. It was after four in the morning and he was beat. The doors slid open and he lurched into the hallway. Staring at the key through blood shot eyes, he unlocked his front door. Closing the door behind him, he tossed his keys, not caring where they fell, and unbuttoned his shirt. He stripped as he walked to his bedroom, leaving the clothes littered behind him.

He brushed his teeth and drank water from the tap to swallow down two Tylenol. Turning the sheets down on his bed, he saw the red message light blinking on the phone on his nightstand, and he was suddenly wide awake, his heart jumping into his throat. That's all it took, just one tiny flashing light, and the person he had worked so hard to forget tonight, was front and centre again. *Steven!* He sank onto the bed, staring at the phone. *It's not Steven you asswipe! Steven won't call you ever again because you're a fucking moron.* He sat there staring at the phone, like a puppet with its strings cut, totally motionless, dead. He watched the numbers on his digital clock click over as minutes passed by unnoticed. He reached for the phone twice but snatched his hand back each time, leaving it untouched in its base. The message wasn't from Steven, he knew that, but if he didn't pick the phone up then he could continue to pretend that it was. And Daniel really needed to pretend. Sliding under the sheets, he turned his back to the phone, and closed his eyes.

CHAPTER 8

He Matters

Sandy set the temperature on the oven and pressed start. The phone rang as she opened the pantry door. "Hello?"

"Tomorrow's the big day. Is Lauren excited?" Julia stirred milk into her tea and got comfortable at her kitchen table.

"Are you kidding? She's had her backpack ready and waiting since last week. A new backpack too, because she couldn't possibly use the one she had last year in kindergarten!" Sandy's smile leached into her voice. She totally got how her daughter felt; she used to feel the same way every September. This year was especially exciting for Lauren. Grade 1 was a big deal when you were six. "She's worried that I'm going to sleep in tomorrow, so she made me set my phone alarm." Putting the phone down, Sandy hit speaker and continued the conversation as she grabbed flour and baking soda from the pantry. "When I drop her off at school tomorrow, I'll be lucky if she remembers to wave good-bye."

Julia laughed. "Is she wearing her new shoes?"

"New shoes, new clothes, new backpack." Sandy got out a mixing bowl and measuring cups. "She even asked me to do her hair in a French braid."

"No! You're going to take a picture, right?"

"I'll send it to your phone."

"Perfect! So, what are you up to today?"

"Making cupcakes. The PTA's organized a 'Welcome Back' bake sale at the school tomorrow."

"Need any help?"

"Nah, we've got enough volunteers, but drop by. We're setting up tables in the foyer at lunch time. Lauren can show you her new classroom."

"Same school as last year, right? Terry Fox?"

"Yeah. Come by about eleven-thirty."

"Perfect, that gives me time to not workout in the morning." Julia took a sip of her tea. "So, I take it Daniel's car was a fixture in Steven's driveway all weekend?"

Sandy winced at the happiness in her mother's voice. She had really been hoping Julia wouldn't ask about Daniel. "Not all weekend."

"They probably went to Daniel's place."

Sandy hesitated but she couldn't outright lie to her mother. "I don't think so, mom."

Julia's cup hit the table with a snap. "What happened?"

"I don't really know." Sandy leaned against the counter, phone in one hand, fingers of the other taping out her worry on the granite countertop. "Some old friend of Steven's showed up and Daniel blew it all out of proportion. You know how he gets, wondering what else he doesn't know about. He went to Karen's and she told him to talk to Steven. I don't know if he did, or what Steven said. All I know is that Steven, Allan, and this friend Stephanie went out for dinner last night and Allan says Steven got all weird when he suggested the four of them go to some club tonight."

"I'll get back to you." Julia hung up on Sandy and punched in Daniel's numbers.

❀   ❀   ❀

Daniel rolled over and blinked against the sun pouring in through the shutters he had neglected to close before crawling into bed. He groaned and pushed himself up against the headboard. Last night came back in more detail than he cared to remember: a pool table, two guys, a strange apartment, condoms. Okay, not his proudest moment but he hadn't done anything that would risk his health or anyone else's. Gold stars all around.

Stretching, he tossed the covers aside, swung his feet to the floor, and stopped. Everything stopped, except the perpetually blinking red light on his phone.

"You have seven unheard messages." The automated voice didn't know that Daniel's hands were sweating as he gripped the phone.

"Daniel, how did the talk with Steven go?"

"Hey baby brother, Steven's driveway looks naked. Where are you?"

"Did you talk to Steven yet? Call me."

"You have won a three day Caribbean cruise. Just call..."

"Daniel, why the hell aren't you answering your cell?"

"Dan, give me a call next week. I want to run some ideas by you for the next issue."

"Danny, Allan was over last night. Are you okay?"

The last question reverberated, bouncing back and forth like an old school Pac-Man, slamming into his brain as Daniel dropped the phone into its base. *Am I okay?* He pushed the thought away. *Nope, can't deal with this yet.* He needed a toothbrush, a shower, and coffee. He needed to not feel.

Wrapped in a robe, feet bare and hair a shambles after his shower, Daniel followed the trail of clothes dotting the path from his bedroom to his front door. Picking up his pants, he rummaged through the pockets, and pulled out his phone. Surprise, surprise! Missed calls from both his sisters. Why couldn't he be one of those lucky bastards whose family was so uncomfortable with homosexuality that they totally ignored the whole topic? Wouldn't that be nice!

Standing at the kitchen counter, he sorted through a pile of neglected mail as he drank his coffee. This morning avoidance was the name of the game, and he was winning until the phone rang flashing his mother's number across the screen. Generally, he didn't have a problem not answering the phone when he didn't feel like talking. But not answering the phone when his mother called? Daniel was pretty sure there was a rule about that carved into the stone tablets Moses dragged down the mountainside. Fucking call display! "Hello?"

"Daniel." Julia heard the sleepy still in her son's voice. "Don't tell me I woke you up. It's almost eleven."

"I had a late night."

"Working on a deadline?"

"No. I was out." Daniel knew he sounded like the fifteen-year-old he used to be but he did not want to talk about this. *Please, just let it go!*

Julia heard the 'I'm not telling you' in Daniel's voice and almost smiled. She knew that tone. Something was definitely wrong. "With Steven?" Of course, she knew he hadn't been with Steven, but she didn't want Daniel to know that.

"No. Played some pool, had a few drinks. No one you know."

"Oh, that's nice. It's good to get out with friends." Julia had no idea that 'had a few drinks' was Daniel code for screwed a stranger or two. Daniel tensed as his mother paused. His mother never called just to say hi. She wanted something, or she wanted him to do something, usually something he didn't want to do. "When are you going to ask Steven to Friday night dinner? He's going to think we don't like him."

Oh, fuck! I'm cancelling call display! "I'm not bringing him to Friday night dinner, Mom."

"Why not?" Julia smiled at the innocence she managed to inject into her voice. Really, acting wasn't that hard.

"Because he's not my boyfriend." *And I screwed up, did I mention that?*

"He's not your boyfriend? You've spent every weekend together for two months. What do you call that, Daniel Alexander Fine?"

Oh, shit! Not the middle name. Now, she's pissed. "We're just hanging out, Ma. He's a good guy. We're friends."

"Friends!" Julia snorted. "Yes, that's why when you're not sleeping at Steven's place, he's sleeping at yours. Right! And you guys get out your flashlights and read comic books in a tent in the backyard! You're not ten years old anymore, Daniel. Don't give me that crap. Friends! Bring him for dinner Friday." Julia hung up.

He really had to move! If he was in Vancouver or Halifax, he'd see his family twice a year and he wouldn't have to deal with any of this. Daniel tossed the phone on top of the mail, and thumped his coffee mug into the sink. *Yeah, 'cause it really sucks to have people in your life who care about you. Asshole!*

✿　✿　✿

Sandy was just slipping a tray of cupcakes into the oven when the phone rang. She set the timer and reached for the portable on the counter. "Hello?"

"If your brother calls to rant about what an interfering witch I am, don't be surprised."

Sandy laughed. "What did you do?"

"Me? Nothing!" Julia channeled William Shatner's less than subtle acting style. "I told him to bring Steven to dinner Friday night."

"Nice one, Mom!"

"Of course, he wasn't going to tell me that he'd done something stupid and Steven isn't talking to him. He tried to tell me that Steven wasn't his boyfriend! My God, the boy lives, breathes, and eats denial. What does he think? Steven's some kind of fuck buddy!"

"Mother!"

"Oh, please! I'm calling your sister. See you tomorrow, bye."

✿　✿　✿

Daniel spent the rest of the day hiding, from his mother, from his sisters, mostly from himself. If he wasn't such a screwed up mess, he could be spending Labour Day with Steven at the CNE, eating Beaver Tails, and funnel cakes, and watching the rides break down. Instead, he was here checking caller I.D., not returning his sisters' calls, and working on an article he was profoundly not interested in. It was a long day.

Late in the afternoon, he was rummaging around in the pantry looking for the new box of Tim Hortons Latte discs, when the phone rang yet again. He checked the screen before he judged it safe to pick it up. "Hey, Kevin, what's up?"

"Jonathan's making manicotti tonight. You coming over?"

"Sure, what can I bring?"

"Steven."

"Jesus Christ! Not you too!"

Two beats of silence preceded Kevin's drawled response. "Remind me why I'm your friend again." The words were spoken with Kevin's characteristic snippy sarcasm.

"Sorry, sorry. It's just my mother called this morning and asked me to bring Steven to Friday night dinner."

"So, what's the problem?"

"Uh, Steven's not exactly talking to me at the moment." Daniel was pretty sure he heard a quickly smothered gasp.

"Eight, bring wine and every single detail." Kevin wasn't extending an invitation; he was issuing an order.

"Kevin, I don't…" But Daniel was talking to dead air.

※　　※　　※

That evening while Daniel trolled the aisles at the LCBO looking for a bottle of wine to bring to Kevin and Jonathan's, Julia stood over the stove muttering to herself. "He's just a friend, Ma. Right! What does he think, that I was born yesterday?" Slashing her knife into the cutting board with more violence than any vegetable deserved, she turned as her husband wandered into the room. "Your son's a moron!"

Brian laughed as he walked into the kitchen and lifted the lid off a pot simmering on the stove. "What's for dinner?"

"Beef stew, and leave it alone, it's not ready yet." Abandoning the poor defenceless vegetables, Julia fished some cutlery out of a drawer and crossed over to the table. "Did you hear what I said?"

"How come he's my son when he's a moron?"

"Because I don't want to think that he got any of that from my side of the family."

"Right!" Brian sat at the table and pulled his wife onto his lap. "What's he done now?"

"I don't know!" Julia gritted her teeth in frustration, her back military erect, too upset to curl into her husband the way she usually did.

Brian stared at his wife. "You want to run that by me again?"

"I don't know what he said or what he did but Steven's not happy, so Daniel did something."

"You talked to Steven?"

"No."

"Then how do you know he's mad at Daniel?"

Julia bounced off Brian's lap and started pacing. "Because Allan had dinner with him and a friend of his and there's definitely something wrong between Steven and Daniel."

"Allan and Steven are friends now?"

"I don't know." Julia waved her hand dismissively. "It doesn't matter. Brian, focus! We're talking about Daniel here."

"Okay, Allan says there's a problem. Don't you think you should know what the problem is before you go blaming Daniel?"

Julia stopped pacing to glare at her husband. "Well, of course, it's…" An idea derailed her sentence. "Daniel won't tell me anything, but Steven might talk to you." She stepped in front of Brian's chair. "Does Steven golf?"

"No." Shaking his head in refusal and raising his hands as if to ward off his wife, Brian started backing out of the kitchen. "No way, Julia." He was so not being recruited into his wife's secret service! "Call me when dinner's ready."

❖   ❖   ❖

Stephanie spent Labour Day Monday preparing for labour, get it? She cracked herself up. She researched the company she was interviewing with, and its management. Thanks to social media, she now knew that the guy interviewing her tomorrow had two kids and climbed the CN Tower for charity every year. She tweaked her resume and then decided to take a break. Snapping her laptop shut, she went looking for Steven. She found him at the stove, throwing mushrooms into an omelet. "You sure you don't want to join us?"

Steven turned, laughter in his voice. "Yeah, I can just imagine how much Allan wants me there."

"He can deal." Stephanie shrugged. "Or, I can cancel and we can eat ice cream and watch a Star Wars marathon."

"Steph, I'm not suicidal. You don't have to babysit me."

Stephanie leaned against the counter and watched as Steven slid his omelet out of the pan and onto a plate. "How do you do that? I can never get it out in one piece. Mine always end up scrambled."

Steven winked at Stephanie as he ran water over the pan in the sink. "Like so many other things, it's all in the lubrication."

Stephanie laughed. "Well, you would know." Smiling, she took a seat at the table.

"Right!" Snorting out a laugh, Steven plunked his plate down on the table and took a seat opposite his friend. "Says the woman who carries lube in her purse!"

Stephanie shrugged. "My first boyfriend was gay. I learned a lot from him." She returned Steven's grin as they high fived each other across the table. Settling back into her seat, she studied the man across the table. "Do you think he's going to call?"

"It could go either way, I guess. It's like he's put up a perimeter fence. You can only get so close." Steven forked a section of omelet, as he considered the Daniel question. "I'm hoping that I mean enough to him that he'll consider lowering the gate." He transferred the egg to his mouth and swallowed. "I'm not expecting a call anytime soon, though."

"You're not going to try and convince him?"

"No." Steve shook his head. "He has to want this, us, me. If he doesn't, then I'll find someone who does."

"You okay with that?"

"I tried turning myself inside out for someone once, remember? It doesn't work. I like Daniel. I want Daniel, but he has to want me too. I can't make that decision for him."

"Still, for a control freak like you, it can't be easy waiting."

Steven's lips slipped into his tilted smile. "Oh, yeah, it sucks big time!" He glanced at the digital readout on the microwave. "Shouldn't you be getting ready?"

Stephanie looked over her shoulder and read the green digits. "Shit!" She jumped out of her chair and hit the floor running. "Shit, shit, shit!"

❀ ❀ ❀

Jonathan's manicotti, as always, was excellent. He was talented, no question, but Daniel often wondered if his skill wasn't born of a desire to duck out of clean-up duty. After dinner, the three men cleared the table and then, as he always did, Kevin kicked Jonathan out of the kitchen. "No, you cooked. We'll take care of the mess."

Jonathan, Daniel noticed, didn't put up much of an argument. "You realize that when he says we, he means you, right?" He was already backing out of the kitchen as he spoke.

Kevin hit his husband with a dishtowel and Jonathan left, laughing.

Daniel prepared himself for a barrage of Steven questions but Kevin nattered on about work. He taught English, Grades 10 through 12, and he'd been at school all week preparing for tomorrow, the first day back. Or, in Kevin speak, Black Tuesday. "Ah, it's a sight to behold, Daniel, teenagers as far as the eye can see; green hair, and nose rings, blue hair and tattoos, each and every one of them just dying to get the hell out of there!"

Kevin's one culinary talent was coffee. Thanks to some ridiculously expensive Italian machine he could make an award worthy caffeine confection. Kitchen restored to order, they brought their drinks into the living room. Jonathan swiped the game on his iPad closed and joined his husband on the couch. He took the coffee Kevin held out to him. "Thanks, babe."

Daniel inhaled his coffee heaven and took his usual seat across from his friends.

"Start at the beginning." Kevin pointed his mug at Daniel. "We're going to need all the details to help you figure out what you did wrong."

"I didn't do anything wrong!" Daniel defended himself as Jonathan rebuked his husband. "Way to be supportive!"

Kevin ignored them both, waving an imperious hand at Daniel. "Talk."

Daniel started with Stephanie's arrival, his sister's advice, Steven's showing up for breakfast. He told them every detail he could remember, relating conversations pretty much verbatim. "Steven said,

'I had hoped you would think that what I do is your business,' and I said, 'I guess we don't know each other that well. Then Steve..."

"Stop!"

Daniel halted mid-word, surprised at the interruption.

"That's where you screwed up." Kevin gave Daniel the kind of look he usually reserved for his more obtuse students. "What the hell is wrong with you? You have a guy in your life for the first time since that bottomless pit of conceit left. A guy you like; and you tell him that he doesn't matter to you!"

"I didn't say that!" Daniel looked to Jonathan for help.

Jonathan shrugged. "Yeah, you kinda did."

Daniel looked from one to the other, reading their faces. They weren't kidding, and if they *both* thought he'd screwed up, then maybe... "I did?"

They nodded, and just to be clear Kevin added an, "Oh, yeah!"

"Well, fuck!" Daniel sagged in his seat, elbows on his knees, and dropped his head into his hands. He stared at the floor and then looked up at his friends. "He matters to me."

Jonathan gave him a sympathetic nod. Kevin suggested, "You might want to tell him that."

※   ※   ※

Just after eleven, Julia closed the cover on her Kindle and turned the lamp on her night table off. Curled around her husband's back, her head between his shoulder blades, her arm around his waist, she closed her eyes and did not sleep.

"Stop worrying about it." Brian grumbled over his shoulder.

"How did you know what I was thinking?"

Brian snorted. "Like I don't know you're worrying about Daniel. How long have we been married?"

"What if he doesn't bring Steven on Friday night?"

"Then we'll sit him down at the kitchen table, put bamboo shoots under his nails, and make him tell us what the problem is."

Julia grinned in the dark and pressed a kiss into Brian's back. "Yeah, that might work."

❈ ❈ ❈

Stephanie opened her eyes to a room that wasn't Steven's guest room and the rhythmic sound of breathing that wasn't hers. Turning her head, she found a mound of body under the covers next to her and a tousled mass of gold hair. Allan! His name unlocked the missing link: last night, people, lights, drinks, dancing, bodies, sex. *Ah crap!* She hated waking up in other people's beds. She hadn't meant to fall asleep at all, not here. Pushing up onto one elbow, she peered over Allan's shoulder at the digital clock on his side of the bed, 4:13. Sliding out of the bed, she gathered up her clothes, and snuck into his *en suite*. She splashed water on her face and brushed her teeth with her finger.

In stealth mode, carrying the strappy killer heels she had worn the night before, she crept back into the bedroom. She scanned the carpet, the lone dresser, the shelf under the small flat screen. She crept through the room, picking up Allan's discarded clothes, looking for her sequined clutch.

"You dropped it on the floor, by the front door." Allan's sleep voice growled from the heap of sheets.

Stephanie shrieked and dropped Allan's pants, her hand on her heart as she spun towards bed. They stared at each other, the awkwardness of strangers after sex, somewhat eclipsed by the awkwardness of being caught trying to leave without saying goodbye. "I didn't want to wake you."

"You didn't. My bladder did." Allan climbed out from under the duvet. "You leaving?"

"Yeah." Stephanie sat on the bed and put her shoes on, tying the straps around her ankles.

Allan watched, half asleep but distracted by long silky legs. Stephanie stood, walked over to him, put her hands on his shoulders and air-brushed a kiss to the side of his face. "It was fun." Opening the bedroom door, she flashed a smile and was gone.

Allan yawned his way to the bathroom and back to bed.

❈ ❈ ❈

Wednesday night, Daniel laced up his soccer shoes with unusual anticipation. Shoving guys out of the way as he fought for the ball seemed especially appealing tonight. He had a lot of tension that needed to be exorcised. He'd been metaphorically kicking himself for days now, which was not nearly as beneficial as it sounded. Admitting that Steven mattered, at Kevin and Jonathan's, had made it all so much worse. He didn't want Steven to matter. He didn't want anyone to matter, ever again.

He grabbed his gym bag and scanned the living room. *Where the hell did I put them?* He flashed on Steven standing in the doorway, laughing at him, offering to drive if Daniel couldn't find his keys, his lips tilted just the way…Daniel shut the memory down. Sifting through the small mountain of paper that had somehow accumulated beside his laptop, he cursed as he heard the grating sound of metal sliding on wood, and grabbed his keys. *God, my life is a fucking mess!*

After the game, comfortable in their usual pub, Doug cradled his beer and nodded across the table at Daniel. "You owe me big time, Danny boy."

"Really? Cause the way I see it, if I hadn't blocked that guy on your left, you never could have made that goal."

"Not the game, dipshit. I saved your ass last night."

Daniel grinned at his brother-in-law. "You weren't anywhere near my ass last night."

"Damn right I wasn't and thanks to me, neither was your sister."

Daniel groaned. "Don't tell me. I don't want to know."

"We can only keep them off your back for so long, dude." Glen signaled the waiter for another round. "Maybe you should try returning their calls."

"Karen was this close," Doug held his fingers an inch apart, "to coming over to your place last night. It wasn't easy talking her out of it."

Glen traded his empty bottle for the full one the waitress brought. "I'm surprised you managed it at all."

Daniel nodded, he knew his sister. "Yeah, Doug, what did you say?"

Doug sat back in his chair, a smug look on his face. "I said she'd be really mad at herself if she interrupted you and Steven trying to work things out."

"Nice!" Glen tapped his bottle to Doug's.

Doug attempted modesty and failed miserably. "Sheer genius, I know."

❊   ❊   ❊

Driving home, Daniel dialed into a rock station and cranked the volume to headache levels. He couldn't hear himself think and that was exactly what he wanted, not to think. Stepping out of the elevator, Daniel found his cousin sitting on the floor in the hallway, his back pressed against the wall beside Daniel's apartment door. "How did you get in here?"

Allan looked up at his cousin and shrugged. "I just pressed all the intercom buttons until someone let me in." Climbing to his feet, he brushed his pants down and waited for Daniel to unlock the door.

Daniel waved him in and closed the door behind him. "What are you doing here? Shouldn't you be out with Caroline or Jessica or whatever the name of the week is?"

"Yes, you're damn right, I should be." Allan glared at his cousin. "And, I'm not!" He started for the living room. "You have anything to drink around here?"

Okaaaay! "Yeah." He tossed his gym bag at the louvered door that hid the washer/dryer combo in the kitchen. Grabbing two glasses, he tossed in some ice, and opened a cupboard by the sink. "Tequila or Vodka?"

"Vodka." Pacing back into the kitchen, Allan tapped an agitated beat onto the counter top.

Daniel sloshed vodka into the glasses and handed one to his cousin. "What's going on?"

"I have no fucking idea." Allan took his drink, knocked half of it back, and stormed into the living room. "This has never happened before."

"What's never happened before?" Daniel sat on the couch and watched his cousin pace.

"She didn't call."

"Who didn't call? Jesus Christ, Allan! Sit the fuck down. I'm getting motion sickness just watching you."

"Stephanie, Steven's friend." Dropping into an arm chair, Allan ran his hand through his hair, clearly aggravated or he never would have messed with perfection. "We went out Monday night. She had fun. I had fun." He looked across the coffee table at Daniel, completely unhinged. "And then she never called."

"Look, I know you're like some mega stud, but are you seriously telling me that no woman has ever not called you after a date?"

"Yeah, yeah, it's happened a few times. Sometimes people just don't click, you know."

"So what's the big deal?"

Allan was up again, too agitated to sit still. "The big deal is I never gave a shit before!" It was a tossup as to which man was the more surprised by that fact, Allan or Daniel.

Judging by the way his cousin was freaking the hell out, Daniel was leaning toward Allan. "So call her."

"I did!" Allan threw his hands in the air and stopped in his tracks, frustration and confusion practically vibrating in the air around him.

Did I miss the memo that said straight guys could be drama queens? "And?"

"And she said she was sorry but she had plans with Steven." Allan started pacing again. "So, I said 'no problem, I'll join you.' It's not like they're into each other. But she said no, Steven needed to talk and he wouldn't if I was there. Also, she was taking him down to Church Street and she didn't want the guys there to think Steven was with me and not cruise him. So, I said fine, what about tomorrow?"

Allan's lips were still moving but Daniel wasn't listening anymore. Guys cruising Steven, Steven leaning against a bar, smiling that tilted smile at someone else, Steven skin to skin with someone who wasn't him. Daniel set his glass down with a snap. *No fucking way!*

"She's leaving Friday." Allan was still rambling and pacing. "If she doesn't get the job she's been here interviewing for, I'll never see her again."

Daniel forced his mind away from the thought of Steven with some random stranger and focused back in on Allan. "You know it's the 21st century, right? Ever heard of little things like Skype, and Video Chat, and airplanes?"

Allan glared at his cousin. "Why am I even talking to you?" He started for the front door. "Fuck off!"

Ah, shit! Daniel caught Allan's arm before he cleared the end of the carpet. "Sorry, my bad, sit." Allan relented enough to perch on the arm of the couch. Daniel sat sideways on the sofa, facing his cousin. "I get it. It's not the long distance thing that's freaking you out. You like her too much, and you're fucking terrified of what that means. You aren't ready for monogamy and marriage and a house in the suburbs."

Allan was nodding before Daniel even finished speaking. "Yeah, man, that's it. I like her, but I don't want any of that other stuff. What the hell am I going to do?"

Daniel thought about the woman he had met at Steven's; funny, bright, a lot out of the ordinary. "Does Stephanie strike you as a 'cookie cutter' woman?"

"What?" Allan stared at his cousin. "What the fuck does that even mean?"

"I mean, you're assuming you know what she wants based on what you think every other woman wants. But Stephanie's not every other woman."

"You've got that right." Allan stood up and paced in silence as he thought about that. "So, I should tell her I like her, and see what happens?"

"Yeah." It didn't escape Daniel's notice that he was giving Allan the same advice Karen had given him.

"Yeah." Allan nodded. "Maybe." They walked to the front door together. "Hey," his hand on the door knob, Allan turned to look at his cousin, "what's the deal with you and Steven? I mentioned your name and he looked kind of sick."

Daniel sighed. "He doesn't want to do casual anymore. He wants it to matter."

"Do you like him?"

"Yeah." Daniel averted his eyes as he thought about just how much he liked Steven.

Allan watched the unhappy that Daniel was trying to hide. Daniel wasn't like him. He wasn't a player. He had never looked at another guy once when he was with that schmuck. He was programmed to want someone in his life who mattered. He was just afraid to try again. "Aidan already took eight years, man. How much more of your life are you going to let him have?" Daniel looked at Allan, surprised by the question. "Think about it." Allan opened the door, and let himself out.

※   ※   ※

Thursdays, for some reason that Steven had never figured out, were always busy and today had not been the exception to the rule. One of the techs had called in sick, which meant he'd had to do a lot of stuff he generally didn't bother with. There had been a question of drug compatibility for one of his regular clients, necessitating a round of calls to her various doctors. And then a vegan had come in with a list of prescriptions wanting to make sure that they didn't contain anything he was philosophically opposed to. Driving home, Steven just wanted to sit in his back yard and watch the squirrels get ready for winter, maybe order in Chinese, or pizza, or anything else that didn't involve him doing a damn thing. He pulled into his driveway, beeped his car locked, and started up the walkway. Wondering if Stephanie was going to be around for dinner, he slid his phone out of his back pocket, looked up, and froze.

Daniel sat in the red Muskoka chair on his porch. He stood, and took the one step down to the walkway. "Hi."

Steven glanced at his driveway, yep, just his car. "Where's your car?"

Daniel's nod indicated his sister's place. "I parked across the street." Yes, okay, it was the action of a chicken-shit coward but Daniel would take any advantage he could get and he was hoping that the element of surprise would work in his favour.

Glancing across the street as he tucked his phone away, Steven saw Daniel's car dwarfed, almost hidden, by Sandy's mini-van. Yeah, no surprise he had missed it. "Sandy kick you out?"

A smile twitched across Daniel's lips. "No. I came to see you. Can we talk?"

Steven nodded. "Sure." He stepped up onto the porch and unlocked his front door. "Come in." He closed the door behind Daniel and turned to find the man looking lost and awkward in the middle of the foyer. "Can I get you something to drink?"

"No." Daniel shook his head. "Thanks."

Clearly, Daniel was nervous, and that fact made happy bubble up through Steven's chest. A man who didn't give a shit didn't get nervous! Steven sat on the couch and smiled the off-centre smile that he knew Daniel liked. "You wanted to talk?"

"Yeah." Daniel followed Steven into the living room, but he didn't sit. He stood in front of the flat screen and looked over at Steven. "Yeah." He couldn't seem to make eye contact, choosing instead to stare past Steven's shoulder. "I'm sorry." The words were low, almost mumbled. Steven didn't say anything because he wasn't sure that he had heard correctly. Daniel met Steven's eyes, and repeated himself. This time the words were clear. "I'm sorry."

"Okay." Steven needed more than that. "Sorry about what?"

Daniel shrugged. "Pretty much everything." He came around the coffee table and sat down next to Steven. "I'm sorry I was such a dick about Stephanie. I'm sorry if I made you think you didn't matter to me. But most of all, I'm sorry for being such a fucking coward." Daniel paused, searching Steven's eyes. "I was with someone for eight years. We bought a house together. I thought…" He shook his head, editing himself. "It didn't end well." Daniel reached for Steven's hand. "I swore I would never go through that again and then I opened the door at Sandy's and you were standing there." He stroked his thumb back and forth over Steven's hand. "I'm sorry."

CHAPTER 9

Boyfriend

Steven looked down at their hands, entwined together, Daniel's on top of his. Turning his hand inside Daniel's hold, he pressed their palms flat against each other. Sliding his fingers down Daniel's palm, he wrapped his hand around the other man's wrist. Tightening his grip, his fingers a warm shackle, he held Daniel, keeping him. Daniel stared down at his hand manacled in Steven's grasp. His lips parted in surprise and his eyes jumped to Steven's. Neither one of them missed the symbolism. The grip said 'mine', and Daniel smiled.

Steven leaned into Daniel, pushing him back against the couch. They moved together, in a dance choreographed by passion and trust. As Steven moved over him, Daniel leaned back, head tipped against the edge of the cushion, looking up at the dark eyes that had haunted him for the last five days.

Straddling the man beneath him, Steven pinned Daniel's wrist to the back of the couch. Daniel reached up with his free hand, ghosting his fingers over Steven's face. Steven turned into Daniel's hand, and pressed a kiss to his palm. "I was going to give you a week."

Daniel traced Steven's lips. "A week?" He heard the words but they didn't mean anything, and he couldn't bring himself to care about that. The only important thing here was Steven. That Steven was talking to him at all was more than enough for Daniel. "For what?"

"To realize how fucking lucky you are to have me in your life." Steven nipped the tip of the finger tracing his lips and laughed at

Daniel's surprised hiss. He kissed the small hurt and then sucked the offended finger into his mouth.

The sarcastic retort Daniel wanted to make dispersed into forgotten as Steven stared down at him, lips wrapped around Daniel's finger. The image of his finger in Steven's mouth called forth other, more intimate, pictures and Daniel's hips lifted off the couch. Steven licked circles around the fingertip in his mouth, playing to the scene in Daniel's mind. He slipped his lips down to the first knuckle and then pulled back, rasping his teeth gently over the tip, as he released the finger. Snagging Daniel's wrist, he pressed it back against the couch, mirroring its mate on the other side of Daniel's shoulders. Holding both captured hands against the couch on either side of Daniel's head, he leaned over the man trapped under him and grinned.

Daniel turned his head, looked from one shackled wrist to the other, and smiled up at Steven. "Your house."

"Yes, it is." Steven lowered his head, his mouth a breath above Daniel's.

"Good." Daniel's whisper melted against Steven's lips. He couldn't move the hands that were still pinned under Steven's, but he didn't need his hands to touch the man above him. He tilted his pelvis up, pressing his cock against Steven's. The layers of clothing between them lent a teasing quality to the slide of straining flesh, a taste and a promise.

Steven moaned his approval into Daniel's mouth. He hadn't been, at all, as confident as his teasing words to Daniel implied. He had hoped, but he hadn't been anywhere close to sure that Daniel could let Steven know him, that he even wanted to try. But Daniel was here, and he cared, and that's all that Steven really wanted; that and this! Thrusting his tongue deeper, he moved his hips in counterpoint to the man under him. Mouth locked to Daniel's, he slid his hands off the pinned wrists and flicked the buttons on Daniel's shirt open.

Freed to wander, Daniel's hands glided down Steven's sides, and grabbed the hips rocking above him. Grinding up against Steven, breathing in his tongue and taste, Daniel couldn't even remember why letting Steven get too close had seemed like a bad idea. *Oh, right, Aidan. Fuck Aidan!*

Tearing his mouth away, Steven dismounted, pushed Daniel's legs apart, and slid to his knees between them. Wrapping one arm around his lover's waist, he set out on a quest of warm skin and tight muscles, biting and licking across Daniel's abs. Pressing one hand over the impatient bulge in Daniel's shorts, Steven looked up, eyes teasing, smile tilting just that little bit off-centre. "I think," He stroked the hard ridge under Daniel's shorts, "you missed me."

"Maybe," Daniel returned Steven's smile, "just a little." He managed to match Steven's teasing tone, but he wasn't fooling either of them. His body gave him the lie direct: hips thrusting, cock seeking Steven's hand. *Fuck, yes, I missed you! I missed us. I missed this!*

"Really?" Steven pumped Daniel through his shorts. "Doesn't feel like 'a little'."

Daniel laughed and reaching down, he traced his fingers through Steven's hair and along his jaw. "Stroking my ego, Monaco?"

Steven grinned, cupping Daniel's length, rubbing through the heavy cotton. "Among other things."

Daniel had envisioned many different scenarios on his drive over, everything from Steven throwing his arms around him to Steven throwing him out on his ass. But he had not predicted this: laughing, laughing as if the last five days had never happened. This man really was perfect!

Steven bit into the skin just beside Daniel's navel. He set his teeth deep enough to leave a mark. He smiled, lips brushing against skin, when Daniel moaned above him. His hands locking on Steven's shoulders, Daniel arched his back, offering his skin to Steven's teeth, pushing his cock into the hand working it through frustrating layers of cloth. Steven laved the bite mark, and sank his teeth again.

Sitting back on his heels, he tugged Daniel's sandals off. He popped the button on Daniel's fly, and pulled the zipper down. Daniel lifted his hips, and Steven pulled shorts and underwear down and off. Tossing them, he settled back between Daniel's legs and looked up at the mostly naked man on his couch. Daniel still wore his shirt, now opened down the centre of his chest. The column of skin visible between the vertical borders of cotton guided the eye down, down to strong thighs dusted with blond hair, and a luscious, leaking cock.

Steven smiled to himself, his hands sliding up Daniel's legs, eyes lit with satisfaction, pleasure, anticipation. *Yes! No one felt like Daniel, tasted like Daniel. Mine!*

Daniel stared down at the man between his legs. From this angle, he couldn't see the decadent eyes, but the slightly imperfect perfect smile was very much in evidence. Daniel took in the dark tousled hair, the blue polo shirt covering too much skin, and realized that Steven was still dressed. Reaching down, he grabbed the sides of Steven's shirt and pulled up, dragging it out of the black pants. Steven raised his arms and let Daniel strip the shirt off over his head. He nuzzled into Daniel's crotch and Daniel folded over Steven, skimming his hands over Steven's back and molding his ass. He traced Steven's shoulders, pressed down the length of his spine, and tried to slip under Steven's waist band to reach skin. Dragging his mouth away from Daniel's balls, Steven grabbed Daniel's hips and jerked him forward, so that his ass rode the edge of the couch. The new position tipped Daniel backward, and he caught himself on his elbows. "Hey, what…?" Any thought of protest flickered and died as Steven leaned in, and sucked at Daniel's entrance. "Oh, shit!" Daniel drew his feet up off the floor, his hands holding his legs folded against himself, giving Steven better access. "Fuuuuck!" The word emerged from Daniel's lips, more moan than speech.

Steven lifted his head. "Soon." Dipping back down, he licked over the tender opening, and thrust his tongue in. He held Daniel's ass in his hands and ate at his hole. He pushed into Daniel until his tongue started to complain of fatigue and Daniel was moaning and shaking in his hands. Drawing away, nipping at Daniel's inner thigh, he stood up.

Daniel let his feet drop to the floor and looked up, eyes wild, chest heaving. "Bedroom?"

Tearing off the rest of his clothes, Steven shook his head. "Uh-uh." He opened an antique box on the coffee table and took out two small packets. Stepping to the end of the couch, facing Daniel, he tore open one packet. "A little help here." Daniel slid down the couch, kneeling on the inside of the low arm rest, and took the condom from Steven. He stroked the condom down over Steven's shaft, as Steven broke the blister pack of lube open. "Down."

Daniel shifted onto his back, throwing one leg up along the top of the couch, dangling the other over the side. Holding the blister pack between his teeth, Steven yanked Daniel towards him, his ass riding the edge of the leather arm rest.

He had chosen this couch because of the arm rests. Wide, flat, only three inches higher than the couch, their minimalist styling had appealed to him. Possible sexual positions had not been a factor in his decision. Looking at Daniel now, though, spread out along the black leather, the cushioned arm rest presenting his ass like some perfect offering to the Gods of Fuck Me Now, Steven thanked the impulse that made him purchase this exact model.

Dividing the lube between his cock and his fingers, he stroked into Daniel. Two fingers worked Daniel open, then three. Daniel closed his eyes, his hands clenching into the black leather couch. He moved with Steven's touch, taking his fingers, wanting more. Steven watched Daniel writhe on his fingers, listened to his moans, and waited. His cock was more than ready, already dripping, and watching Daniel was the hottest thing he'd seen ever, but still he waited.

Daniel's eyes snapped open, glaring up at his lover. "What the fuck are you waiting for, an engraved invitation?"

Steven held Daniel's hips, pinning him down. He pressed the head of his cock to Daniel's entrance, teasing over the opening. "I waited for you all week."

Shock flashed over Daniel's face. "Payback? This is payback? Now?"

One hand anchoring Daniel's hip, one dragging his cock over Daniel's hole, Steven smiled down into frustrated hazel eyes. "You could say that, or you could say that I," Steven breached the ring of muscle surrounding his lover's opening, "missed you." He pressed in an inch. "That I wondered if I'd ever see you again." He thrust in another inch. "That you look fucking hot like this!" He stared into Daniel's eyes. "That I never want this to end." Steven snapped his hips, driving all the way home.

Daniel's back arched and his eyes snapped shut. "Fuck! More, Steven! More!"

Steven gave him more. That's what Daniel wanted. That's what he wanted. That's what his cock wanted. Right now, all three of them were ecstatic! Words morphed into groans and grunts. Sweat trickled down spines and gathered under the hair at the back of their necks. Their skin flushed, their breaths became pants, and they were aware of none of it because they were locked in another dimension where the only reality was reaching that final internal explosion.

One hand riding Steven's hip, fingers digging into his lover's ass, Daniel stroked himself off with the other. His cock slid through his grip to the rhythm of Steven's thrusts. Getting close, Daniel looked up at Steven. Dark, wavy hair spilled over his forehead, flopping into eyes that were dark, almost black with want.

Steven hid nothing as he held Daniel's eyes. He wanted this, this body yes, but even more, he wanted this man. "Go, Daniel. I want to see you." Steven watched as Daniel's eyes shut, his orgasm ripping through him, spunk coating his fist and stomach. Steven fucked Daniel through the after tremors, came inside him, and collapsed on top of him, folding over the man and the couch.

When he could move, he levered himself off Daniel and removed the condom. He tied it off, dropped it, and looked down to find hazel eyes lit with gold, the grin on Daniel's face matching the laughter in his eyes. "Make-up sex! HOT!!"

Laughing, Steven reached down, and pulled Daniel up, into his arms. They held each other, Steven nuzzling into Daniel's neck. "Yeah, well, don't get used to it." He nipped at Daniel's ear lobe. "I don't plan on any more major disagreements."

Daniel pulled back to look into Steven's face. He wound his arms around Steven's waist and ran his hand up the other man's spine, petting him. "I'm sorry."

Steven leaned in for a quick kiss. "I know."

While Steven went upstairs to change out of his work clothes, Daniel tugged his clothes on and wandered into the backyard. He lifted the cover on the hot tub, running his fingers through the water, wondering if Steven was going to keep it heated during the winter.

Steven slid the patio door open. "What do you want to do about dinner? Go out? Order in?"

Daniel smiled and crossed the deck to join him inside. "Why don't I make something?"

"Right!" The man couldn't cook a Pop-Tart!

"If you chop the veggies, I can manage a stir-fry." Daniel bumped his hip into Steven's, his version of a wink.

"So, I do all the work, and you get to say you made dinner." Steven tugged Daniel close, hand curled into the other man's waistband, thumb stroking his stomach.

Gold sparks lit in Daniel's hazel eyes, laughter rippling through his voice. "I was hoping you wouldn't figure that part out."

"Uh-huh." Steven turned and opened the fridge, getting out peppers and onions. "Fine, but you're cleaning the wok."

"You actually have a wok?" Daniel wasn't surprised at all.

"Of course." Steven opened a corner cupboard, took the wok off a shelf, and put it on the stove. "Why? What do you use?"

Daniel opened the pantry door, looking for oil. "Whatever pan I have that's clean."

Steven shuddered. "At least you use a clean one."

Daniel threw a dishtowel at him.

After the dinner that Daniel may or may not have made, the two men decided to watch the sun set from the comfort of the hot tub. The days were still hot this early in September, but the evenings were getting cool. "You going to keep this heated all winter?"

Steven insinuated his foot between Daniel's knees, and slid it up the other man's thigh. "Why? You plan on still being here three months from now?"

"Nice!" Daniel grinned, acknowledging Steven's dig. He wrapped his hand around Mr. Perfect's ankle, sliding his fingers up Steven's calf. "Why wouldn't I be at my boyfriend's place?"

Steven went still in the water. His eyes sought Daniel's. "We're boyfriends now?"

Daniel nodded. "According to my mother we are."

"What?" Steven wasn't laughing. He didn't want to joke, not about this.

Daniel slid off his seat and sloshed through the water to Steven's side of the tub. He sat in Steven's lap, his palms on either side of Steven's face, looking directly into his eyes. "I'm serious. You, me, boyfriends, no one else; I want to do this, do you?"

"Yes." Steven leaned into Daniel, their kiss the seal on the contract between them. Daniel slid off Steven and sat beside him in the water. He held his arm out and Steven cuddled into his side, throwing one leg over Daniel's thighs. "I don't like bumping into things in the dark of some stranger's bedroom, as I try to sneak out without out waking the trick of the night because God forbid, I might actually have to talk to him!"

Daniel laughed. "Yeah, I'm not going to miss that at all." Under the hot water and the bubbles, Daniel ran his hands over Steven's ass. Just thinking the word 'boyfriend' made Daniel smile. "We should get tested and then we can ditch the condoms."

Steven lifted his head off Daniel's shoulder and moved back until he could see Daniel's face. It was full dark now, only the lights strung along the fence allowed Steven to read Daniel's expression. "You ready for that?"

Daniel played with the swirls of hair at the nape of Steven's neck. "That's what no one else means, right?"

"We can be together without being exclusive, you know."

"Yeah, we could." Daniel thought about that, how it would feel coming to Steven after being with someone else, or worse, Steven coming from some stranger's body to his. "Nope, don't want that." He pulled Steven onto his lap, rubbing his hands up and down his boyfriend's back as he talked. "I was single for almost a year before I met you. I've had my fill of anonymous sex and a cavalcade of beds."

Steven read the sincerity in Daniel's face. He nodded. "Okay, but if we're ever with anyone else…" Steven trailed off but his meaning was clear.

"We'll suit up; agreed." Daniel rested his forehead against Steven's. "But that's not going to happen." *It's not going to happen, and if it does, Steven will tell me and we'll work it out. Steven isn't Aidan, Steven isn't Aidan, Steven isn't…*

Steven's hands rested on Daniel's hips, soaking up the fact that Daniel was here, in his arms, in his life. He slid his hands up through the water, fingers gliding on supple skin. He brushed his thumbs over Daniel's nipples, a small smile growing ever larger as he looked into the hazel eyes. "It must be very late now."

Daniel laughed. "Yeah, it's probably all of eight-thirty."

Steven grinned. "Time for bed."

Daniel slid his hands down Steven's back, and slipped them under his ass. "I was just thinking the same thing."

It took them a while to get out of the hot tub. Kisses and whispers, light touches and soft moans, smiles and bites; yeah, it took them a while. Daniel spun Steven in the water, took a swat at the ass he could barely see in the dark, and practically shoved Steven out of the tub. Standing on the deck, still laughing, Steven held his hand down to help Daniel climb out.

Grabbing towels from the lawn chairs on the deck, they dried off. Bent over, mopping at his hair with one end of the beach sized towel wrapped around his waist, Daniel looked up at Steven. "My mother's invited you for dinner tomorrow night."

Steven tucked his towel and rolled it securely at his waist. "You don't want me to come?" Steven had not missed the aggrieved sound in Daniel's voice.

Finished with his hair, Daniel fell into step beside Steven as they walked towards the patio door. "Of course, I want you there. It just really pisses me off, you know." Daniel slid the door open for Steven and followed him inside.

Steven glanced at Daniel as he closed and locked the patio door. "What?"

"That my mother knew I had a boyfriend before I did! How fucking lame is that?" They walked upstairs to the bedroom, Steven laughing as Daniel whined about his family. "I wish I had a family like yours, way the hell on the other side of the country."

Steven pressed into Daniel and dropped a kiss on his mouth. "No, you don't."

Daniel traced the tilted smile that inspired dark of night thoughts. "No, I don't." He pulled Steven's towel off. In the ensuing tussle of bodies and sheets, in the slide of skin on skin, Daniel's family was forgotten.

The next morning, Steven woke before the alarm and reached over to switch it off before it could wake Daniel. Rolling onto his side, he smiled at what he could see of his boyfriend: blond hair peeking out from under the duvet, one long leg that had escaped the sheets, muscles in thigh and calf very much on display. The correct names of the muscles escaped Steven; it had been quite a while since Grade 10 Biology, but he wasn't interested in technically correct anatomical terms anyway. He was interested in how those muscles looked when they shifted under Daniel's skin, how they felt against his lips and tongue. Just the thought of all that strength, those legs wrapped around him…Steven could feel his cock waking up, and that was just from thinking about the parts he could see. If he let himself dwell on the parts that were still under the covers, he'd never get out of bed. Glancing at the clock, he groaned and tossed the covers aside. Standing, looking down at Daniel, he had to smile. No question, with Daniel in it, his bed took on a whole first-scene-of-a-porn vibe that it just didn't have on its own.

Thirty minutes later, showered, shaved and dressed, Steven leaned over the bed and nuzzled the side of Daniel's face.

Daniel didn't open his eyes as he snuggled deeper into his pillow. "You smell good."

Steven chuckled. "You don't."

Daniel rolled over. "Hey, be nice to the guy with bed-head."

Steven ruffled the blond waves. "It looks good on you."

Eyes still half-shut, Daniel looked up at Steven and held an arm out. "Come back to bed."

Steven stepped back, shaking his head. "Some of us have to work for a living."

"I work." Daniel dropped the arm Steven had eluded, and snuggled back into the duvet. "I just work from home."

"Yeah, from your home." Steven pulled the pillow out from under his boyfriend's head, and smiled at the resulting barrage of swear words. He called over his shoulder as he left the bedroom. "Text me your parents' address."

With a groan, Daniel huddled back under the duvet. Right, Friday night dinner, with sisters who were going to be pissed that he hadn't called them back! Fun!

He was sitting at the kitchen table, eating breakfast and reading the news on Steven's iPad, when Stephanie rolled her suitcase into the hallway. She smirked at Daniel as she poured herself some coffee. "So, I see someone finally got his head out of his ass."

"Uh-uh, first rule in the Best Friend Handbook: You have to be nice to the boyfriend."

"Oh, so you're official now?"

"Yep." Daniel took a spoonful of cereal and grinned at Steven's ex. "Daniel and Steven sitting in a tree, K.I.S.S.I.N.G." Ridiculous happiness, apparently, made him turn into a four-year-old.

Stephanie joined Daniel, cradling the hot mug in her hands. Face serious and voice a little pained, she nodded at the blond across the table. "Yeah, I heard."

Daniel flushed. "Shut up. You did not!"

Stephanie laughed. "Nah, my room's across the hall, I didn't hear a thing."

"You were out with Allan last night?"

"Yep."

Stephanie didn't add anything to that single word, so Daniel changed the topic. "How did your interviews go?"

"Still too early to tell, but I've seen several layers of management, so I'm hoping. The company looks good, and the position involves a lot of travel, I like the sound of that." She sipped at her drink. "I'm keeping my fingers crossed." She nodded at the robe Daniel was wearing, Steven's robe. "You living here now?"

"No." Daniel shook his head. "I'm just not a morning person."

Stephanie glanced at the numbers on the microwave, 11:15, and laughed. "I guess not."

"What time's your flight?"

"1:40." She finished her coffee, and put the mug in the dishwasher. Daniel stood and walked with her to the front door. He nodded at her luggage. "You need any help with this?"

"No, I'm good." She smiled at Daniel as she leaned in to hug him. "Don't fuck up." She pulled the handle of her suitcase, and it followed her obediently. "You, I'm not worried about so much, but Steven's important to me."

Daniel laughed as he opened the door for her. "Yeah, I got that." As she passed him in the doorway, he touched her arm. "He's important to me too."

Stephanie searched his eyes, and nodded, satisfied with what she saw there. She stepped out onto the porch and started down the walkway to her car. "Tell Steven thanks. I'll text him when I get home."

Late in the afternoon, as Steven was helping a customer with questions she had about her rheumatism medication, his phone vibrated.

From Daniel: No point in taking two cars. Come to my place after work. I'll drive.

From Steven: K

He wasn't all that worried about dinner at Daniel's parents, he'd already met the whole family. He knew Sandy and Glen pretty well by now. Brian had really helped him out with the shelving system, and Julia hadn't sounded shocked when he'd answered the phone at Daniel's place back when they first got together. Steven didn't think it was going to be too awkward showing up as Daniel's boyfriend. He smiled remembering Daniel's exasperation. Apparently, Julia was all over that idea anyway.

Daniel was plenty worried about dinner at his parents. Not that they wouldn't like Steven, they already did. No, he was worried about his sisters. He couldn't care less about the load of crap he was under for not answering their calls. He was more than a little concerned, however, about what they would feel free to tell Steven, now that they were officially boyfriends. He knew his sisters and discretion was not in their vocabulary. They wouldn't just tell Steven stuff about him either, that was embarrassing, but to be expected. No, it was what they were going to tell Steven about Aidan, or about him when he was with Aidan. Yeah, that had him twitching a bit.

Leaning against his car, Daniel played a game on his phone, while he waited for Steven in Visitor Parking. At the hiss of tires on pavement he looked up to see Steven's car pulling into the space beside his. He exited the game, shoved the phone into his pocket, and laughed out loud when Steven reached into the back seat of his car and came out with flowers and wine. "Wow! Sucking up big time, Monaco!"

"I am not sucking up." Steven carried his loot around to the passenger side of Daniel's car and placed everything carefully in the back seat. "I am being a considerate guest." Steven buckled into his seat belt, ignoring the crack of laughter from the man in the driver's seat. "I was going to get chocolates too, but I thought that might be a bit much."

Daniel glanced at Steven, laughter lighting his hazel eyes. "Ya think?"

❖ ❖ ❖

At her grandparents' house, Lauren sat on the floor with Rhys, the Candy Land board game spread out between them. "If you get a double card, you get to move twice. Right, Zaida?" Both kids looked at their grandfather for confirmation.

Brian stared at the game, trying to remember, but it had been too long since he'd played this with his own kids. "Not sure about that. It doesn't matter much what the rules are exactly, as long as you both play by the same ones. That's what makes the game fair."

Lauren picked a card from the deck to find a picture of two purple squares. "See, I get two turns."

Rhys nodded, willing to accept whatever his older cousin said. Brian turned the TV off and sat on the floor with the kids. "Can three play this game?"

In the dining room, Sandy set the dishes out on the table, Karen following in her wake, laying out the cutlery. "I'm going to kill him. He shows up at my door, all pathetic and upset. I listen and try to help, and does he even have the decency to return my calls? Ingrate!" The cutlery snapped onto the table, small gun shots that replicated the heat in Karen's voice.

"You're just pissed because you don't know what happened." Sandy opened a drawer in the china cabinet and took out the linen napkins.

"And you're not?" Karen pushed the drawer shut, and opened the cabinet doors above it. They moved around the table and each other in a synchronized dance, the habit of years of Friday night dinners fully ingrained.

Karen placed the drinking glasses on her side of the table with exact precision. Sandy plopped hers down haphazardly, close enough to the plates. Karen walked down Sandy's side of the table and repositioned every glass. Knowing her sister's predilection for neat, Sandy could have been more careful with her glass placement. Likewise, knowing that her sister didn't believe in sweating the small stuff, Karen could have left the glasses where they were. But they were both just stubborn enough to insist on not changing one iota for the other. This little slight-of-hand had been going on for so long that neither sister even noticed it anymore.

Sandy put a salt shaker at either end of the table, and leaned closer to her sister. Checking the open archway into the dining room, making sure they were alone, she lowered her voice. "Daniel's car was parked in our driveway last night."

"What?" Karen looked up, the napkin she was folding forgotten in her hands. "Daniel's *car* was in your driveway but..." Karen's eyes went wide and Sandy grinned. "He was at Steven's!! Why didn't you tell me?"

"You were at work. I know you have those management meetings every Friday morning."

Karen didn't buy that. "Texting, you've heard of texting right?"

"I didn't want to say anything, okay? We don't know if this means anything. His car was there when I drove Lauren to school this morning. By the time I got back from running errands, it was gone."

The girls fell silent as Julia entered the dining room, carrying a pitcher of ice water. "I haven't heard anything from Daniel. The least he could have done is let me know if we're going to be one more for dinner." She set the water down at the head of the table. "I don't understand your brother. Where was he raised, in a barn? What if I don't have enough food?"

Sandy laughed. "Yeah, like that's even a remote possibility."

Daniel unlocked the door to his parents' house and led Steven into the foyer. He barely had time to close the door behind them before he was attacked by a little boy bomb. "Danny!" Now that Rhys was in Junior Kindergarten, the airplane game had been replaced by piggy-back.

Lauren, with all the dignity of a young lady in Grade 1, did not leave the game to go flying across the foyer. She granted Daniel a regal nod. "Hey, Uncle Daniel. Hi, Steven."

By the time Brian had levered himself off the floor, Daniel had swung Rhys up onto his shoulders. "Hold on, kid." Daniel went charging down the hallway, Rhys arms wrapped around his head, laughing and screaming. "Faster!"

"Steven." Brian held his hand out to the young man his son had abandoned in the foyer. "How's the entertainment centre? Shelves still on the wall?"

Steven shifted the wine to the crook of his left arm, balancing wine and flowers carefully, and shook hands with Daniel's father. "Still perfect. You did a great job." He passed the wine to Brian. "I hope red is okay, I didn't know what you were serving."

Brian didn't know much about wine, he was more of a beer drinker himself, but he took the bottle with a smile. "Thank you."

They both turned to watch Daniel run back down the hallway towards them, Rhys clinging onto his hair.

"Zaida, it's your turn." Lauren held the deck of coloured cards out to her grandfather.

Steven's attention was on the blond running towards him, his nephew held securely on his shoulders, his deep roar of a laugh melding with Rhys' high, gurgling tones. Brian watched Steven watch his son, and decided that neither man would miss him if he went back to the Candy Land game with his granddaughter. Placing the wine on the coffee table, he took his seat on the living room carpet, while Daniel swung Rhys down off his shoulders in the foyer. "Rhys, say hi to Steven."

Rhys put his hand out, the way the teachers at his Montessori school had taught him to. "Hello."

Steven shook hands, smiling at Rhys because how do you not smile at an almost four-year-old offering to shake hands? "Hello, Rhys."

"Well, look who's here." Karen and Sandy had seen Daniel go charging down the hallway, Rhys on his shoulders. Karen stalked up to her brother and stopped directly in front of him. "Rhys, go tell Daddy and Uncle Glen that dinner's ready." Rhys went tearing down the hallway to the basement door. Karen looked her brother up and down, and Daniel knew what the guys in a police lineup must feel like. "I used to have a brother; he looked a lot like you." Before Daniel could even think of a response to that, Karen turned her back on him. "Steven, nice to see you again. How's your place coming along?"

"Not quite there yet, but it's..." Steven paused, totally forgetting what he was about to say, as he watched Sandy pace a circle around her brother, slapping at his pockets.

Daniel tried to ward his sister off. "Stop that, what are you doing?"

Sandy reached into his back pocket and emerged triumphant with his phone. "So you do have a cell phone." Sandy smirked at her brother. "I was positive that you did." She ran her finger over the screen and it lit up. "And look, it works." She hit contacts, scrolling through the 'S' names. "And here's my number."

Daniel tried to take his phone back. "Okay, okay, I get it."

Sandy held the phone above her head and sent her brother a fake sympathetic glance. "Oh, I'm so sorry, was your phone stolen? Or maybe your battery died?" She smacked the phone into Daniel's hand. "Because you better have a damn good reason for not returning my calls."

Julia came out of the kitchen, oven mitts on her hands, and saw them all standing in the foyer. "Oh, good, everyone's here." She walked towards them, pulling the oven mitts off, beaming at Steven. "Steven, so nice to see you again."

Steven stepped forward, holding the flowers out to Daniel's mother. "Thank you for inviting me."

Julia pulled back a corner of the wrapping paper. "Steven, they're lovely. So thoughtful, thank you." Cradling the flowers in her arms, Julia turned and started for the kitchen. "Please, everyone, sit. Dinner's ready."

Behind her mother's back, Sandy smacked the back of her brother's head.

"Hey!" Glaring at his sister, Daniel rubbed his head.

"Mommy, what did Uncle Daniel do?"

Sandy took her daughter's hand and followed her mother. "It's not what he did, honey, it's what he didn't do."

Karen looked at her brother, her voice carrying all the warmth of a February morning. "That guy that you look like, the one who used to be my brother, tell him that he owes me an apology." She turned on her heel and trailed after her sister.

"Godiva chocolates?" Daniel called after her.

Karen turned and sent him an almost smile. "It's a start."

Turning to Steven, Daniel executed a half bow, one hand sweeping out in front of him. "Welcome to my world!" Keeping his voice low, he leaned into Steven as they walked towards the dining room. "It's not so bad once you realize that they're all about two meds short of an institution."

CHAPTER 10

Becoming Us

Daniel watched the road, but the traffic at this time of night was sparse, so he was free to devote most of his attention to the man sitting silent in the passenger seat. Steven hadn't said anything since they'd left Daniel's parents' house. The longer he remained silent, the more Daniel's mind conjured up ghosts of arguments past. Friday night dinners had been an ongoing issue with Aidan. Their 'discussions' on the subject were still clear in his memory. He so didn't want to go there again.

Steven didn't have a lot of experience with being 'the boyfriend' at a family dinner; his previous relationships hadn't panned out that way. Dinner tonight had been a replay of Sandy's lunch last Canada Day; the same verbal free-for-all, the same teasing closeness. Except tonight, Daniel's family had very casually enclosed Steven in their world. Living forty-four hundred kilometers away from the only family he had, Steven appreciated the warmth of the Fine clan. "Do you all get together every Friday night?"

Daniel glanced over at Steven. He couldn't tell if the innocuous question was a prelude to an argument or not. "Yeah, it's pretty much a command performance. There is a get out of jail free card, for cases of extreme emergency, like work commitments or conflicting social obligations."

Steven laughed. "You're lucky. Your family's great, warm, open."

"If you mean nosy, interfering, opinionated, and crazy, yeah, that's them."

"They're honest. You don't have to wonder what they're really thinking."

Daniel snorted. "No, you don't have to wonder about that. They're more than happy to tell you!"

Steven grinned. "Yeah, I noticed that. Why didn't you call your sisters back?"

"Because I'm not an idiot." Daniel negotiated a left hand turn into his apartment complex, just making the yellow light. "I was a mess after you left my place last Sunday. They would have tried to help."

"And that's a bad thing?"

Daniel hit the garage door opener on his visor. Waiting for the door to drag itself open, he looked at the man beside him. "Ever notice that when you've screwed up, the last thing you want to hear is that you've screwed up?"

Steven reached out and took Daniel's hand in his. "Yeah."

Driving into the underground Residents Parking, Daniel kept Steven's hand in his. He steered into his parking space one handed, and cut the engine. In the sudden silence of the car, he contemplated the man in the passenger seat. "I screwed up."

Steven's tilted smile slanted across his face. "And you won't be the only one. Just give me time."

Daniel grinned. "You mean you're not perfect?"

"Not even close." Steven unlatched his seat belt. "Promise." He flashed a smile at Daniel and opened the car door.

Walking to the elevators, Steven hooked a finger into a belt loop on the back of Daniel's jeans. "Do you think your family would mind if I come with you some Fridays?"

"Mind?" Daniel snorted as he punched the up arrow on the wall panel. "Yeah, I don't think that's going to be a problem!" The doors slid open and they stepped into the elevator. Daniel hit five, and turned to face his boyfriend, his back to the doors hissing shut behind him. He tugged Steven closer, arms loose around the other man's waist, hands clasped at the small of his back. "You realize that if you show up too often, they're going to expect you to propose."

❊   ❊   ❊

Singing a Pop 40 song that she didn't know all the words to, as she unpacked the dishwasher, Julia wasn't thinking proposals. She was thinking that Daniel finally looked happy again. Carrying a chair from the dining room back into the kitchen, Brian smiled at the woman mangling the lyrics to Katy Perry's *Last Friday Night*. "Happy?"

Julia dealt cutlery into their assorted slots and turned to face her husband. "Did you see them? I don't remember the last time Daniel looked like that."

"It's been awhile." Brian sat at the kitchen table, concern etching lines into his forehead. "Julia, don't get too attached to this idea of Daniel and Steven. It's only one Friday night dinner, and Daniel didn't invite Steven, you did. Don't read too much into this."

Julia grimaced as she put the last of the plates back in the cupboard. "I know. I'm not calling the caterers just yet." She joined her husband at the table. "Daniel's happy now, and that's all I care about."

❊   ❊   ❊

All Daniel cared about, right now, was the man walking at his side. They didn't touch, didn't speak, there was no obvious link between them as they covered the distance from the elevator to Daniel's condo door. It was there, though, there in the subtle frisson of anticipation that jumped from one to the other, there in eyes that touched, and held, there in instinctively matched strides. Unbidden, their pace increased with every step.

Steven crossed the threshold first, Daniel right behind him. He slammed the door shut, threw the lock, and grabbed Steven, turning him, and pushing him up against the door. Steven let his body flow into whatever position Daniel needed. He tipped his head back, his lips parted: an offering. Daniel took, tongue searching out every texture in his lover's mouth. Steven sucked on Daniel's tongue and they both moaned. Daniel's hands clenched on Steven's ass, pulling his boyfriend close, pressing into him, cocks mashing against each other through too many layers of cloth. Steven's hands played in Daniel's hair, migrated down his back, and slipped under the waistband of his jeans. Daniel dragged his mouth off Steven's. "My house."

Steven spread his legs wider, cradling Daniel between them. "Oh, I know." He clenched his fingers on Daniel's ass. "Fuck me."

❖   ❖   ❖

On the other side of the city limits, in suburbia, Doug carried a sleeping Rhys to his room and tucked him into bed. Leaving the night light on, and the door partly opened, he crossed the landing to the master bedroom. Karen rinsed her mouth and put her toothbrush in its cup. "Rhys okay?"

Doug pulled his shirt off and tossed it at the hamper. "Out like a light."

Karen leaned against the sink and watched her husband undress. "Did you see them tonight? Remember when we looked at each other like that?"

Smiling, Doug stepped close, running one hand under Karen's short sleep shirt. "I think I have a vague recollection."

❖   ❖   ❖

Daniel didn't remember his bedroom being so fucking far from the front door. Finally naked, clothes strewn over the carpet, he reached for the drawer in his night table. Grabbing a condom, he swiped the lube from its place beside the digital clock, turned to Steven and stopped, stopped moving, stopped thinking, stopped fucking breathing.

Steven was bent over the side of the bed, legs spread, ass raised, tanned skin appearing even darker against the white sheets. He looked over his shoulder at Daniel, eyes tempting, smile taunting, and swayed his hips slightly. "Want some?"

The inflaming words were the key, and like a clock-work toy that had been rewound, Daniel could move again. Tossing the lube and condom on the bed beside Steven, he sank to his knees behind his boyfriend. "Some?" Tracing Steven's hips reverently, Daniel lowered his head and bit into that perfect ass. Intending to leave a mark that would last for days, he sucked on the flesh caught between his teeth. Steven moaned, pushing back into Daniel's mouth and Daniel raised his head. "Some? Fuck no! I want it all."

✳ ✳ ✳

Across the street from Steven's empty house, Sandy brushed her teeth, pulled on an old T-shirt of Glen's, and padded into her daughter's room. Lauren looked like the angel she definitely wasn't, curled into her pillow, Elmo tucked under the covers with her. Leaving her daughter's door ajar, Sandy crossed the hall into her own room. She flicked the light switch off, and climbed into bed, nestling into Glen's side, under the arm he automatically held up so that she could do so. "Did you see them tonight? Did we ever look at each other like that?"

Glen's attention was on the golf channel, as someone recapped a particularly clever shot of Tiger Woods', but he heard enough to know that he should agree. "Probably."

Sandy stared at the flat screen, but she didn't see it. She saw, instead, the way her brother had watched Steven as he spoke, the way Steven had followed every move Daniel made. Smiling to herself, she sent her memory into the past, to when she and Glen were Daniel and Steven.

Something was off, wrong. It was too quiet. Sandy wasn't talking, and if nine years of marriage had taught Glen anything, it was that a silent Sandy was never a good thing. No longer paying any attention to the sports announcer, Glen tried to figure out what the problem was. He went over the evening, and drew a blank. She had been happy at dinner, not even really pissed at Daniel for not calling her back. She had been really happy to see Steven, to see Daniel and Steven together. *Did we ever look at each other like that?*

Doug pressed power and tossed the remote onto the bedside table. He rolled Sandy under him and looked down into surprised eyes. "We still do."

"What?" Sandy had no idea what he was talking about.

"Yes, we looked at each other like that." Glen smiled down at his wife. "And we still do."

Sandy smiled at the man she couldn't remember not loving. "Liar."

❖   ❖   ❖

No lie, Steven was the fucking hottest thing he'd seen, ever. Bent over his bed, eyes a dark demand, crooked smile inciting Daniel, inviting him to fuck the ass he'd been obsessed with since he'd first seen it walking away from him at Sandy's BBQ. Daniel could never decide which he liked more, fucking Steven or Steven fucking him. Fortunately, he didn't have to choose.

Standing behind his lover, Daniel plucked the condom off the bed and rolled it on. He ran his hands up the back of Steven's legs, and over the enticing ass. He drew his thumbs down the crease, rubbing over the beckoning entrance. Folding over Steven, he dropped kisses and bites along his shoulders, down his back. "Fuck, you look hot!"

Steven writhed on the bed, pushing his ass into Daniel's hands, wanting. Grabbing the lube, he pumped some into his hand, and reaching back, slicked Daniel's cock. One hand wrapped around the base of his lover's shaft, Steven guided Daniel to his entrance.

"You're not ready." One hand on Steven's hip, Daniel held himself away.

"Don't worry." Steven looked back at Daniel. "Let me try something."

It took a little adjusting to get the angle right. This time when Steven guided him in, Daniel moved with him. His hand still wrapped around Daniel's cock, Steven controlled the ride. He kept the strokes shallow until his body was ready to welcome the invasion. Releasing Daniel's cock, Steven stretched out on the bed, his arms above his head, his body Daniel's now.

Daniel was lost in Steven, lost in the way he felt, the way he sounded, the way he moved under him, for him. "Fuck, oh, fuck, you feel good."

"Yes." Rigid cock pressed into the mattress, tension rising up through his body, Daniel hard, so hard inside him. Yes, it felt good, bone-melting, breath stealing, world disappearing until there was nothing but the thrust of Daniel's body into his, major fucking good! "More!"

Daniel pried Steven off the mattress, one arm around his lover, holding him up, the other pumping his cock. He bit the curve between neck and shoulder, licked and bit again, and Steven exploded over his fist.

Dropping Steven back onto the bed, Daniel grabbed his boyfriend's hips, and pounded into him. He fucked Steven with deep, savage thrusts that would have sent him sliding across the mattress if Daniel hadn't been holding his hips in a death grip.

Steven chased the final tremors of orgasm, and turned his head to look back at Daniel. "Don't stop, God, don't stop."

So, of course, Daniel lost it. He collapsed over Steven, pressing his face into the dip between Steven's shoulder blades. As soon as he could get his legs to work, he got rid of the condom and crawled back into bed. One arm thrown over Steven's hips, he curled around his boyfriend. The word 'boyfriend' still made Daniel smile because he never thought he'd have this again, never wanted to have this again, until Steven. He trailed fingers down Steven's spine, and ghosted kisses across his shoulders. "You know, I don't think you understand the concept of bottom."

Steven laughed and turned his head to look over his shoulder at the man behind him. "You had a better idea?"

"No. That was pretty damn good!"

"Then shut up." Steven tucked himself back against Daniel, pulling his lover's arm across his chest, and closing his eyes. "Good night."

Daniel pulled the covers over them, hit the light switch on the wall next to him, and curled himself around Steven, smiling to himself in the darkness. "Night."

❈   ❈   ❈

The next morning being Saturday, Karen and Sandy decided to take advantage of the free babysitting at IKEA. They signed Rhys and Lauren into the playroom, watching as the kids dived into the pool of multi-coloured plastic balls. Karen linked her arm through her sister's. "Ice cream's on me."

Upstairs, in what IKEA called their bistro, but was really just a cafeteria, the sisters got themselves coffee, opted for Danish instead of ice cream, and settled down to an hour of adult only chat time.

"Mom's a genius." Karen blew on her coffee; she didn't want to pollute it with milk.

"I know. That worked out really well, didn't it?" Sandy swirled a finger through the icing on her cinnamon bun. "Happy all around: Daniel, Steven, Mom."

Karen sipped at her coffee. "I guess we'll never know what the problem was."

"Well, it's not like Daniel's going to volunteer that information, is he?" Sandy sat back in her seat, thinking. "But, you know, the next time Steven comes for dinner..."

❄ ❄ ❄

As his sisters plotted to interrogate his boyfriend, Daniel sat rubbing the shoulder he had pulverized during his weekly biking marathon with Allan.

Allan sucked the whipped cream off his hot chocolate and looked over at his cousin. "You want to go rock climbing?"

"No fucking way!" Daniel gaped at his cousin in disbelief. "I'm getting in my car and then in Steven's hot tub. My shoulder's killing me."

"Told you not to take that hill so fast, man." Allan expressed not one iota of sympathy as Daniel gingerly moved his shoulder in circles. "I don't mean right now. I was thinking in the winter, when the trails are too icy to ride, we can go rock climbing instead."

Daniel stared at his cousin. "What do you have, a death wish? I'm not climbing ice and rock in the dead of winter!

"Not outside, dipshit. Indoors, you know, climbing a wall, with central heating."

Daniel gave up on his shoulder and reached for his coffee. "Yeah, okay, sounds better than a stationary bike in a gym."

"I don't know." Allan pretended to consider the matter, before flashing a grin at his cousin. "Depends on the view at your gym."

"What are you, twelve? Is the next ass the only thing you think about?"

Allan snorted. "Like you don't?"

Daniel averted his eyes, staring down into his drink, but the words were clear. "Not the *next* ass, no."

"Steven's hot tub, huh?"

Daniel looked up. "Yeah."

"Steven's ass?"

Daniel couldn't have stopped the smile that blared across his face, not that he tried. "Yep."

Allan was happy for his cousin, but saying so was out of the question, way too estrogen heavy for him. "Nice ass?"

Daniel laughed. "World class!"

Allan grinned. Swirling his spoon through his drink to distribute the remaining whip cream evenly, he found himself doing the unprecedented, actually thinking about relationships. "So, one person…how does that work, exactly?"

Expecting more teasing, Daniel was surprised at Allan's question. The clever retort stuttered on his tongue and died unsaid, because it was obvious that Allan was serious. "I think that depends on the people involved."

Allan was not happy with that answer. "Duh!"

"No, really, there's the 'forsake all others', picket fence, 'joined at the hip' definition of couple and for some people that's the deal, that's what they want. But, that's not what it's about for everyone. I wrote an article a few years ago about successful long term relationships. I interviewed couples and asked them why they thought their relationships had lasted. I got so many different answers - anything from 'he never forgets to walk the dog' to 'she doesn't judge me'." Daniel shrugged. "There isn't just one way. This is about Stephanie, right?"

"Yeah." Allan didn't look too happy about admitting that.

"You saw her again."

"Yeah, I listened to my *older* cousin." Allan put rather more emphasis than Daniel thought was necessary on the world 'older'. "I saw her Thursday night, we talked. She told you?"

"I saw her at Steven's yesterday before she left for the airport. She didn't say anything, just that she'd seen you."

Allan nodded. "We had fun. She said she'd call the next time she's in Toronto." Allan plunked his empty mug down on the table.

"And?"

"What and? That's it." Daniel stared at his cousin, not saying anything, until Allan met his eyes, his own defensive. "What?"

Daniel snorted. "You're a photographer, you travel all the time. If you want to see her, see her."

Allan shook his head. "I can't do that."

"Why? Because she'll think you care?" God knew, Daniel wasn't an expert at relationships, but next to Allan he was a fucking guru!

Allan was pissed. "Look, I'm not an asshole, all right. I don't want her to expect…" Steven waved a hand at his cousin. "I don't want what you and Steven have."

"I thought you said you talked to her?"

"Yeah, yeah, I did. She's busy, new job, travelling. She's not looking for serious. It's all good." Allan shrugged. "I can't just go dropping in on her in Vancouver; that would be like, sending the wrong message. Not kosher, dude."

Daniel rolled his eyes. "Only you, Allan, could make liking someone seem like an immoral decision!" Standing up, Daniel pulled out his wallet; it was his turn to pay. "Now, excuse me, but Dear Abby has to go home to his boyfriend."

❖   ❖   ❖

Now that Daniel had stopped trying to keep Steven at a safe distance, their weekend-only thing had become a see-you-after-work thing. As the leaves changed colour in the cooling days of September, they got in the habit of spending most nights together, either at Daniel's apartment or Steven's house. As a couple, they embarked on a learning curve littered with surprises.

Taking a break one afternoon from the article he was working on, a nauseating bit of fluff about destination weddings, but hey, it paid the bills, Daniel texted Steven.

From Daniel: my place 2nite? Chinese?

From Steven: can't 2nite ttyl

Daniel stared at his screen. *What do you mean, you can't tonight?* Three words in a text and Daniel was in free-fall, imagining all the things Steven could be doing, all the things Aidan had done. Swiping out of his text screen, he checked the time on the home screen, 12:48. Steven, OCD case that he was, took his lunch at 1 p.m., every day, precisely. Twelve minutes and then he'd call; he needed to hear Steven's voice. It was much too easy to lie in a text. Not that he thought Steven would lie…*Steven isn't Aidan. Steven isn't Aidan. Steven isn't Aidan!*

Killing time, Daniel straightened the pile of papers littering his dining room table, tossed some junk mail in the waste bin in the kitchen, and made himself a cup of coffee. Walking back into the living room, blowing on the caffeine, he settled into a chair at the dining room table, and picked up his cell. 1:04, perfect. Daniel hit call.

Steven had just cleared the sliding glass doors of the pharmacy, on his way to lunch, when his pocket vibrated. Seeing Daniel's face pop up on his cell, Steven swiped his hand down the screen, his voice reflecting the smile on his face. "Hey, what's up?"

Daniel didn't even know how tense he had been until he heard Steven's voice and felt himself relaxing against the back of his chair. *See, nothing's wrong. You're such a fucking alarmist.* "What are you doing tonight, that's more important than doing me?"

Steven laughed. "Nothing, believe me."

Daniel believed him. He did, but, people lied, easily and well, and all the fucking time. Even people you knew well, especially people you knew well. "So?"

Steven sighed and stopped walking, tucking himself against a building out of the way of the sidewalk traffic. "I didn't want to tell you."

Daniel forced a teasing note into his voice, barely covering the panic snaking through his blood. "Let me guess, you're in therapy. I told you that sorting your underwear by colour is symptomatic."

Steven grinned at his phone, laughter in his voice. "No, I'm not in therapy, thank you very much!"

"You're not in some kind of religious cult, are you? Sneaking off to light candles and drink blood?"

"No, but you'd love me anyway wouldn't you?" Steven stared at his phone. *Oh, shit! What the fuck did I just say?*

Daniel laughed. "I don't know. I'm AB Negative, would that work?"

Oh, thank God, he thinks I'm joking. Daniel was just getting comfortable with the idea of 'boyfriend', the L word would scare the shit out of him. "What am I, some kind of vampire?" Squaring his shoulders, Steven took a deep breath and lowered his voice, embarrassment creeping into his tone. "Look, I take guitar lessons, okay?"

Daniel replayed that in his head, yeah, still sounded like guitar lessons. That couldn't be right. "Guitar lessons?"

"Yeah."

"You take guitar lessons?"

"Yes."

"I don't get it. What's the big deal? Why didn't you want to tell me?"

"I haven't told anyone, and I'm not going to. And neither are you. Not Sandy, not Karen, not anyone."

Steven was serious. Daniel had never heard that dark thread of steel in his boyfriend's voice before. He looked down at his lap, surprised to see his cock thickening along his thigh, very obvious under the thin fleece of his sweat pants. *Well, that's interesting.*

"Daniel?"

Steven's voice was still in that new authoritarian, demanding mode, and Daniel had to force his attention away from his inexplicably awakening cock, to focus on Steven's words. "I won't say anything." Daniel coughed, chasing the obedience out of his voice. "It's not like you're selling twelve-year-olds into a prostitution ring. What's with the cloak and dagger act?"

"Because the minute anyone finds out you're taking lessons, they want to hear you play. And I suck, big time. No one is going to hear me, ever."

Daniel laughed. "If you're really that bad, maybe guitar's not for you. Try something else."

"I am that bad, and I can't quit."

"Why not? Did they suck you into one of those, 'you save 30% if you sign up for two years' kind of deals?"

"No." Steven shook his head, not that Daniel could see him. It didn't make any sense, he knew that, but he just couldn't give up. "I don't quit things."

Silent, Daniel stared at the phone as he thought about that. He shouldn't be surprised. It fit right in with the persnickety housekeeping and the over-the-top neatness. "What about people?"

"Never."

Daniel liked the sound of that. Steven never quitting on him, sounded just about right. "Even if I sneak off to light candles and drink blood?"

Steven's voice was a warm, reassuring blanket around Daniel's insecurity. "Even then."

❖   ❖   ❖

Guitar lessons, and an as yet, unexplored interest in submission weren't the only surprises. It turned out that Steven and alcohol made an interesting mix.

Vegging in front of the TV one night, on his own because Steven was out with the pharmacy people celebrating someone's birthday, Daniel was surprised when his cell phone rang with Steven's face on the screen.

"Hey, having fun?"

"Yes. Everyone's here. We played a drinking game, lots of tiny, little glasses."

The drunk and happy in Steven's voice translated to fucking adorable! "Where are your colleagues?"

"At our table, taking bets on who I'm going to do." Steven turned on his bar stool very carefully, and waved at his co-workers. "They've heard rumours about back rooms in gay bars, and they want to know if they're true."

Daniel didn't miss the fact that his boyfriend was on the phone with him, and not in the back room with some faceless twink. "So, who are you taking into the back room?"

"You. I don't want to fuck anyone else. I want to fuck you."

Daniel laughed. "Well, I'm right here, babe."

"No, no, no. Come here. I want to do you here."

Alone in his apartment, Daniel smiled to himself. How cute was that? Steven was sitting in a bar, surrounded by new and different, and he wanted him. "Where are you?"

"In a bar on Church Street."

"Which one?"

"I don't remember. It has a rainbow flag outside."

"Steven, they all have rainbow flags outside. Ask the bartender."

"Oh, okay."

Daniel hit speaker on his phone and dropped it on his bed. He kicked his sleep pants off and shoved his legs into jeans. He could hear background noise, music, and a mumbled conversation. He stepped into his shoes, pushed his wallet into his back pocket, grabbed his phone, and started the hunt for his keys. "Steven?" He found the keys sitting beside the coffee maker and grabbed his leather jacket on the way out the front door. "Steven?"

"Dukes, he says we're in Dukes."

"I'm on my way. Don't fuck anyone till I get there."

"Why would I do that? I want you, Danny."

"Then stop drinking or you won't be able to get it up."

"It's already up." And Steven hit end call.

The grin was still on Daniel's face as he shoved the wooden door of Duke's open. Once his eyes adjusted to the darkened interior, he scanned the men at the bar, looking for dark wavy hair. He spotted Steven instantly, recognizing his boyfriend's posture on a subliminal level. He crossed the floor and slipped into the space between the bar stools next to Steven. "You called?"

"Danny!" Steven looked up at Daniel, his hair falling into his eyes, his face flushed with alcohol, and happy, and lust. "You're here!" Steven jumped up and on Daniel, the force of his embrace pushing Daniel backwards over the bar.

"Hey, watch the drinks. Take it somewhere else." The bartender snapped his towel at Steven's head to get his attention.

Steven backed off, grabbed the lapels of Daniel's jacket, and pulled him up, off the bar. Wrapping an arm around Daniel's shoulders, he dragged him towards the staircase at the end of the room. Not that Daniel needed to be dragged. There were only two things in the basement, the washrooms, and a storeroom with plenty of empty space for customers who wanted some privacy. Daniel was betting that Steven didn't need the washroom.

Two steps into the shadow-draped storage room, and Daniel was pushed face first against the nearest wall. Steven ignored the leather jacket, making no effort to remove either it or Daniel's T-shirt. His hands went right to Daniel's fly, unzipping and pushing the jeans down thighs that still made him drool. Daniel's jeans hit the floor, Steven's cock sliding between his ass cheeks seconds later. "Fuck!" Steven froze at Daniel's back. He dropped his forehead between Daniel's shoulder blades. "Jesus Fucking Christ!

Daniel turned his head, and looked over his shoulder. "What?"

"I don't have any lube!"

His wallet wasn't the only thing Daniel had remembered to bring. Pulling a blister pack out of his jacket pocket, he reached over his shoulder, and handed it back to his boyfriend. Steven snatched the packet and dragged Daniel's head back, smashing their mouths together. Grazing his teeth over Daniel's bottom lip, Steven pulled away and broke the packet open. Daniel rested his forehead against the wall, waiting as Steven slicked up.

"No." Daniel shook his head as Steven's fingers slid into him. "No, now, do it now." Daniel had been picturing this moment since Steven ended their call. He had thought of nothing else the whole drive down there. He had seen Steven sitting on the barstool waiting for him, and wanted him so badly he wouldn't have said no if Steven had wanted to take him on top of the fucking bar. And that image had Daniel's cock dripping. "God, Steven, now!"

Steven grabbed Daniel's hips, pulled his ass away from the wall, aligned himself, and drove into his boyfriend. Daniel gasped, and trapped a cry between clenched teeth. His fingers clawed at the cement bricks, as Steven thrust, hard and deep. *Oh, Fuck! This hurts. I can't...*

Steven wrapped his arm around Daniel's waist and pushed his right leg forward, shifting his weight, altering the angle of entry. Fireworks tore through Daniel. Pleasure blew the pain into nonexistence. "Fuck. Fuck. Fuck." Daniel grunted the words into the wall in front of him. He reached back with one hand, grabbing Steven's thigh. "Harder! More!"

Steven heard Daniel, but the words were far away, faint under the roar of his own need. "Mine. Mine, Daniel." He fisted Daniel, his hand slick on pre-cum and their combined heat. "Mine."

Daniel splattered over Steven's hand and the wall. He slumped into the brick, totally wrecked, absolutely destroyed, and insanely happy. "Yes, yours."

❊   ❊   ❊

Being a couple meant dealing with a few surprises about each other, yes, but it also meant change. And Daniel knew exactly what he wanted that first change to be.

Squeezing dinner in before a 7:10 movie one night, they decided on a burger place that was right next to the theatre. Daniel carried the tray with their burgers and drinks to the corner table Steven had staked out. He watched, with amusement and affection, as Steven unwrapped his turkey burger, a major production in origami. Folding the paper and running his hand over it, pressing it flat to the table, Steven looked up to find Daniel smiling at him. "What?"

Daniel shook his head. "Nothing." He took a bite out of his burger, still half submerged in paper. "My sister folds her paper out of the way like that."

Steven cocked his head to one side, eyebrows raised. "I'm going to pretend that you meant that as a compliment." He leaned into the table, his eyes broadcasting both promise and challenge. "If it was some kind of crack about my masculinity, then we're definitely going back to my house after the movie."

"About that," Daniel plucked an onion ring out of its carton, "I think we need to talk about your House Rules." He popped the onion into his mouth. "I get why you needed them before, but it's just us now." Daniel wiped his fingers on a napkin. "I'm impulsive, and your rules don't allow for spontaneity."

Steven put his burger down, eyes on Daniel's. "What do you want to do?"

Daniel reached across the table and clasped Steven's hand in his. "Can we just go with the flow, do what we feel in the moment, and not worry about whose place we're at?"

Steven's fingers clutched at Daniel's, and then he freed his hand to worry wrinkles into his paper napkin. Go with the flow, just the idea made him uncomfortable. Steven didn't 'flow', he made lists and organized things and planned. He couldn't do spontaneous, but Daniel could and Steven valued that ability too much to want to inhibit it in any way. Still, working without the parameter of rules made him nervous. "What if we both want the same thing?"

"I don't know. We can flip a coin or something." Daniel laid his hand over Steven's, stilling the nervous destruction of his napkin. "I know you like things structured, but I'd like our sex life to be more fluid. I don't want it to get boring."

Steven glared at Daniel. "I. Am. Not. Boring. In. Bed."

And that was the total truth. As regimented as Steven was in every other aspect of his life, in bed he was enticingly creative. And, not just in bed either. Daniel wasn't going to forget that drunk and happy booty call any time soon. He looked into his boyfriend's eyes, letting the heat show in his own. "No. I'll give you that. You're not boring in bed."

After dinner, in the dark of the movie theatre, Daniel glanced over at his boyfriend. Steven turned, and Daniel reached for his lover's hand, keeping it clasped in his own. *Mine! All mine, Steven Monaco. Every strand of wavy hair, every tilted smile, every secret guitar playing finger, every perfect inch of your body, mine!*

❉　❉　❉

In October, a little over a month into his new role as boyfriend, Steven faced his first relationship crisis. Walking through a mall on his lunch hour, getting more frustrated and anxious with every store he walked into and out of empty handed, Steven scowled at the date on his wrist watch. He had to find something today, preferably in the next forty-five minutes, because tomorrow was Daniel's birthday!

Shopping wasn't usually an issue for Steven; he had no problem buying what he liked. But this was different, this was for Daniel. If it was just a question of buying something that he would like for Daniel, he'd be done already. The stainless steel and black rubber Teno cuff, or the red Calvin Klein body thong, would both look fantastic on Daniel. They were things that he would appreciate, but Daniel, not so much. He needed to find something that Daniel would like!

Passing a Sony store, a memory clicked in; Daniel saying something about his laptop being too slow, or not having enough memory, something like that. Steven didn't remember exactly what the complaint was because he hadn't really been paying attention; computers didn't hold a whole lot of fascination for him. Daniel did like computers, though, and that's all that mattered. Steven walked into the store, and walked out twenty minutes later with the newest, sleekest, fastest laptop Sony made. Mission accomplished.

The next morning, found the birthday boy twitching in his sleep. Behind his closed eyes, inside his comatose mind, he was running. Bells rained down on him: large bells, small bells, brass bells and gold bells, all dropping down around him, crushing people and cars. Daniel ran. Looking behind him, he ran, frantic he ran, and still the bells smashed down around him, ringing...

His own murmuring woke him up, to the sound of the portable ringing in its base on the night table. "Hello?"

"Happy Birthday!"

Daniel pushed himself up on his elbows. "Thanks, mom."

"Thirty-three Daniel, I can't believe it!"

"You and me both, and don't remind me."

"Thirty-three is not old, and you don't look your age anyway."

"I hope not, I don't want anyone thinking I'm Steven's father."

"Well, aren't you a joy this morning? What kind of birthday cake do you want?"

Daniel scrubbed a hand over his face, finally starting to wake up. "Can you get that cheesecake with the brownies on top of it?"

"Yep, no problem. See you tonight, and get out of bed, it's your birthday!" Julia hung up.

Daniel stretched, climbed out of bed, and stumbled into the washroom. He stared at the mirror as he brushed his teeth, looking for the first grey hair. "Thirty-three sucks!" Shrugging into his robe, he groaned as the phone rang again. Grabbing it off its base, he flopped backwards onto his bed. "Hello?"

"Happy Birthday, Daniel. Did I wake you?" Just Steven's voice made Daniel feel better.

"No, my mother already did that."

Steven laughed. "You still in bed?"

"Why? You coming over?" Daniel rolled onto his side, smiling at a man who wasn't there.

"Yeah!" Steven snorted. "That would go over well around here. No, I'm not coming over."

"But it's my birthday; you have to be nice to me." Daniel wasn't above taking advantage of a calendar day.

"I will be very nice to you, tonight." Steven's voice went all dark on the last word, and Daniel smiled at the phone. "I put your present on the dining room table when I left this morning." Smiling, Steven hung up.

Grin plastered across his face, Daniel strode out of his bedroom, suddenly not minding being thirty-three at all. He didn't see it at first. Looking for a gift bag, or a wrapped box, he didn't see anything, just the usual accumulated work related mess cluttering up the dining room table. Scanning the table as he got closer, he noticed a birthday card sitting atop his computer. He picked the card up, smiling at Steven's scrawled birthday wishes and....*Holy shit! This isn't my computer. This is a brand new, silver, sleek beauty of a laptop!* Flipping the cover up, he saw the protective film still on the screen, and a quick start instruction manual. Glancing over the features and specifications he saw everything he ever thought he wanted. *This is fucking perfect, Steven must have....Steven! Where the hell is my cell?* He pawed through the mess and checked the coffee table and shelves in the living room before finally giving up and grabbing the portable by the couch.

Steven answered on the first ring. "Found it?"

"Steven! I love it! It's perfect but it's too expensive. You didn't have to do anything like this!"

Steven smiled at the happy in Daniel's voice. "Well, I did see a really hot red body thong by Calvin Klein, but I thought you'd like this better."

"Good call, since I have no fucking idea what a body thong is and I'm pretty sure I don't want to know."

"Maybe next year." Steven chuckled, possibly even happier than Daniel was. "I'll call you when I'm leaving. You want to meet at your parents' place, or should I pick you up?"

"Come get me." Daniel lowered his voice to make the double entendre clear.

Steven lowered his own voice. "Always." The word was a promise.

CHAPTER 11

Music Man

"I'd like to do Thanksgiving dinner here and invite your family. What do you think?" Steven speared a forkful of salmon as he looked across the dinner table at his boyfriend.

Granted, Daniel only had a vague idea of what was involved in preparing a Thanksgiving meal, but it was enough to convince him that no one in their right mind would want to do it. "Wouldn't it be easier to just go to my parents' place?"

"Easier maybe, but I want to do this. I'm at your parents' house every Friday. I'm starting to feel like a freeloader."

"You know they love it when you show up Fridays." Daniel didn't like where this was going.

"I know, and I appreciate that, so I'd like to return their hospitality." Steven aimed his crooked smile at his boyfriend. "You can help me cook. It will be fun."

"No, it won't." It was going to be a lot of work and Daniel didn't want any part of it.

Steven pushed his chair back, walked around the table, and slung a leg over Daniel's thighs, settling onto his lap. "I can make it fun."

Daniel's cock was saying, "Hell, Yes!" but his brain knew better. "Even you can't make cooking a meal for, what?" He added it up in his head. "Ten people, fun." His hands settled on Steven's hips. "Look, if you feel you owe my parents a meal, no problem, but the whole family? You don't have to do that."

"No, I don't have to." Steven flicked the buttons on Daniel's shirt open as he talked, slowly, one after the other. "I want to. Thanksgiving is a family holiday."

Daniel was getting desperate. "What about your family? Don't they expect you home for Thanksgiving?"

Steven laughed as he pushed Daniel's shirt off his shoulders. "Right! Like my family would do anything so mainstream. My father can rant for hours about a legislated holiday whose sole purpose is to thank a mass illusion." Steven ran his hands down Daniel's chest. "He takes his atheism very seriously."

Steven was joking, but for the first time it occurred to Daniel that perhaps growing up with such vehemently anti-establishment parents wasn't the nirvana he had assumed it was. He spread his hands out across Steven's back and pulled him closer. Nuzzling into Steven, he spoke low beside his ear, his hands clenching on his boyfriend's ass. "And just how were you intending to make cooking fun?"

Steven grinned and inched back on Daniel's lap. He slipped the button, and then unzipped his boyfriend's fly. "I don't know. We could cook naked?"

"Grills, and stoves, and sharp knives; I don't think so! I'm kind of partial to certain parts of my anatomy."

Steven petted Daniel's cock through his briefs. "Me too."

❊   ❊   ❊

The next Friday, at Daniel's parents' place, Steven invited everyone for Thanksgiving. "If that's okay with you, Julia?"

Daniel's mother smiled at her son's boyfriend. "Let's see: I don't have to do a thing. I can spend the day doing my nails and relaxing in the bath with a book, and after a day of doing nothing, I get to go to your house for a lovely meal that I didn't have to cook myself." She grinned at Steven. "Damn right, it's okay with me."

Standing, Julia picked up a platter to be refilled in the kitchen, and passing Daniel's chair, leaned down and stage whispered. "This one's a keeper!"

As Julia left the dining room, Steven sent a totally smug look his boyfriend's way.

"Better watch your back, Danny. Steven's going to replace you as Number One Son." Sandy laughed, teasing both her brother and his boyfriend. Steven, as Daniel's boyfriend and part of their Friday night circle, was no longer protected by guest status. Now, he was fair game.

"I know, right? He's making me look bad." Daniel sounded more proud than worried.

"Well, to be fair to Steven, making you look bad isn't hard to do." Karen grinned at her brother.

"Like you were going to volunteer to do Thanksgiving!" Daniel helped himself to another knish.

"Who me?" Karen shuddered. "No way."

"No, cooking isn't one of Karen's talents." Doug looked surprised at the death glare trained on him. "What?"

"And just what do you mean by that?" Karen wasn't amused.

"Steven honey, what can I bring?" Julia returned from the kitchen and set French beans in the centre of the table. "Fruit, dessert, salad? What would you like?"

The talk turned to Steven's Thanksgiving menu, and it was decided that the sisters would bring side dishes, and Julia would supply dessert. Glen offered to bring over some folding chairs and a card table to extend Steven's kitchen table. Doug said he had some wine hanging around, not to bother buying any.

Daniel sat back and watched his family become Steven's family. Watching his boyfriend interact with the Fine clan, Daniel clued into the fact that Steven wasn't just being polite. He wanted this; he wanted to be part of Daniel's family. Maybe Steven himself wasn't even aware of it, but Daniel would bet that there was a part of Steven that had always wanted this. Once again, Daniel found himself not envying Steven's childhood, not even a little.

Daniel wasn't the only one who picked up on the way that Steven was being assimilated into the family. Brian caught his son's eye, and nodded towards the group, more than pleased. Daniel knew what his father was thinking. Brian liked Steven, he was very pleased that Steven was making an effort to be part of the family, but his real priority was his wife. When Julia was happy, Brian was happy. Daniel understood that as he never had before. Completely in sync with his dad, Daniel nodded and returned to his Steven watching.

Through the end of dinner and over dessert, Daniel continued to watch what he could only describe as bonding. Steven fit in as seamlessly as if he had always been there, and Daniel couldn't help thinking that Aiden had not. In all the years they were together, his family had never really become Aidan's. Of course, Aidan had not been at all interested in becoming family, anyway. He had only ever come to dinner under protest, often late and always with some excuse to leave early.

Steven turned, still laughing at something Doug had said, looking for his boyfriend. Daniel got up and switched seats, taking the empty one next to Steven. He draped his arm over Steven's shoulders, and promptly forgot about his ex.

         ❊   ❊   ❊

"It won't be that bad." Steven took his watch off and set it on his night table. "All we have to do is babysit the turkey. How hard can that be?"

Daniel stood beside Steven's bed, kicked his shoes off and started on his pants. "Right! Stuffing, cranberry sauce?"

Steven tossed his shirt in the hamper and went into his *en suite* to brush his teeth. "No big deal."

Daniel folded his pants over the arm chair by the window, and stripped off everything else. He tucked his shoes under the chair and threw his underwear and socks in the hamper. Because it was Steven's house, Daniel made an effort to put everything where it was supposed to go. In a similar display of consideration, even though it made him absolutely insane, Steven did not tidy up at Daniel's place. Which explained why they spent a lot more time at Steven's place - well, that and the hot tub.

Steven walked out of the *en suite* as Daniel walked in, his hand brushing Daniel's ass as they passed. He hung his pants in the closet, stripped off his underwear and socks, and chucked them into the hamper. He hit the light switch on the wall, turned the lamp on the night table on, made sure the lube was within reach, and climbed into bed.

Daniel turned the *en suite* light off, and padded across the carpet. Steven watched him every step of the way, and because he did, Daniel's cock was at half-mast before he even got to the bed. Steven held the linens up, and Daniel slid in beside him.

Steven curled up, his head on Daniel's chest, his hand wrapped around his boyfriend's cock. Daniel stroked Steven's back, his hand eventually wandering down to the ass he loved. He clenched his fingers, squeezing, and Steven murmured in appreciation.

Slow languid caresses tonight, hands skimming over warm skin. Steven's fingers teased amid the thatch of hair at Daniel's groin, over his balls and along his cock, thumb gliding over the head. Daniel played with Steven's ass, fingers grazing lightly and clenching deep, as Steven nestled against him.

Daniel rolled on top of Steven, propped himself on his arms, and looked down into chocolate eyes. "My house?"

It wasn't his house, of course, and he didn't have to ask what Steven wanted; he knew his lover's body language by now. He used the words that had long since become part of their own private language, a shorthand, a code that expressed at once both who they had been and who they had become, together.

Hands grazing over Daniel's shoulders, Steven shifted on the sheets, sliding his cock along Daniel's. "Yes."

❖   ❖   ❖

Thanksgiving Monday, Steven got up early because, apparently, it took hours to cook a bird that big, who knew? By the time Daniel rolled out of bed, and wandered into the kitchen, the turkey was already seasoned and sitting in the largest roasting pan he'd ever seen. "Is that even going to fit in the oven?"

Steven looked up from the bowl in which he was mixing bread, chopped onions and spices, eyes widening in horror. "Shit! I didn't even think of that." He wiped his hands on a dishtowel and pulled the oven door open. Glancing from the roasting pan to the oven and back, he guesstimated the fit, removing one oven rack and shifting the remaining one to the lowest level. He hauled the turkey off the counter and laid it on the rack, sliding it in, and closing the door. "Just makes it!" Grinning in relief, he hauled the bird onto the counter again. "Remind me not to get a bigger one next year."

Daniel snuggled into Steven's back, his arms around his boyfriend's waist. "Let me get through this year first, then we'll see about next year."

Steven snorted. "You haven't done a damn thing yet; what are you complaining about?"

Daniel buried his head in Steven's neck, breathing in the scent of shampoo and Steven. "I got up, didn't I?"

Steven laughed. "A major effort, I know. You've got a choice; you can stuff this bird while I make cranberry sauce or you can knock the tables together and set up the folding chairs."

Daniel unwound himself from his boyfriend and leaned against the counter, studying the winged monstrosity in the roasting pan. "Stuff it? You mean put my hands inside that thing? Yeah, that's not going to happen!" He backed away from the bird. "I'll take care of the table."

Steven patted the bird, as Daniel escaped into the dining room. "Don't feel bad, he's a bit of a wuss."

Daniel stuck his head back into the kitchen. "I heard that."

※　　※　　※

Sandy popped over after lunch to drop off her side dish contribution, and to lend Steven a table cloth long enough to cover both tables. "Anything else you need? Wine glasses, drinking glasses, coffee mugs?"

"I think we're good, thanks." Steven snapped the table cloth open and Sandy helped spread it out.

"Where's Daniel?"

"He went back to his place to get his Wii and games for the kids."

Sandy nodded. "Smart, you can only expect them to sit at the table for so long." She took the stack of plates Steven had placed on the counter and walked around the table, setting them out. Steven balanced a tray of drinking glasses on one arm, as he walked counter clockwise to Sandy, placing one at each plate. "You've done this before?" Sandy nodded at the tray.

"Yeah, I was a waiter for four summers during undergrad." Steven opened a cupboard and Sandy watched as he transferred wine glasses to the tray.

"So, how did you talk Daniel into doing this?"

"What do you mean?" Steven retraced his loop around the table, this time with the wine glasses.

"There's no way this," Sandy gestured to the table and the turkey in the oven, "was my brother's idea."

"No. I said I wanted to repay your parents' hospitality, and Thanksgiving would be the perfect time to have everyone over."

"And he said, 'Oh yeah, great idea. I've always wanted to have ten people over for dinner'." Sandy's voice made it very clear how likely that was.

Steven's lips twitched. "Not exactly."

"Uh-huh, so my question remains, what did you say to convince him?"

Steven placed the last glass and set the empty tray on the counter. "Nothing." He caught Sandy's eye and grinned.

The grin told its own story but Sandy wanted detail. "But?"

"Well, I was sitting on his lap at the time." He raised his eyebrows.

Sandy nodded as a smile slid over her face. "Yeah, that would work." She started for the front door. "I'm going to try that the next time I want Glen to come to a Parent-Teacher meeting."

Steven opened the door for her. "You didn't hear that from me."

Sandy put her hand over her heart. "Nope."

❊   ❊   ❊

The cranberry sauce was a little watery, and one of the turkey wings was a bit too crispy, but no one really cared. Steven looked around the table; so many different emotions flowing one atop the other that he couldn't pin them all down. Happy, yes, but more; warm, comfortable, content? Yes, content. He had told Daniel that this was about thanking Julia and Brian, but now looking around the table, he knew there was more to it than that. Because his family didn't celebrate Thanksgiving, Steven's only experience of the holiday had been in high school, when Stephanie had invited him to her house. He hadn't specifically told Daniel why this dinner was so important to him, but he thought his boyfriend had figured it out anyway. This was his house, his boyfriend, his life, and bogus holiday or not, it felt ridiculously perfect!

Over coffee and dessert, as the kids played video games in the living room, the adults sat at the table trading horror stories of holidays gone terribly wrong. "Remember the time you forgot the turkey?"

Julia laughed at herself as she told Steven the story. "The kids were little, and I was doing it all myself. I prepared one dish after the other, and when they were all done I put the turkey in, but it was too late. It wasn't ready to eat until we were serving dessert."

"Didn't make a difference; she made so many other things that no one even noticed." Brian smiled at his wife.

"Hey, look what we found." Lauren and Rhys came around the corner from the hallway, carrying Steven's guitar between them.

Doug jumped up, and grabbed the guitar before the kids dropped it. "Here guys, let me help you with that."

"Is that yours?" "I didn't know you played." "Hey, play something for us." The comments tumbled over each other, everyone talking at once. The adults shifted their chairs around, turning towards Steven as Doug handed him the guitar.

Steven and Daniel stared at each other across the table. Steven's eyes were frantic with dread, his face the sick pallor that usually heralds a quick trip to the nearest porcelain bowl. Daniel rose from his chair; he didn't know what he was going to do, but he had to help Steven.

"Steven, play something?" Lauren plopped herself at Steven's feet, legs crossed as if she were sitting in front of a camp fire.

"Please!" Rhys leaned against Steven's leg, little fingers poking at the metal tuning keys.

Daniel sat back down, helpless, his eyes locked on Steven's. Trying to rip the guitar away from Steven and the kids would just make the whole thing worse.

"Do you know Itsy Bitsy Spider?" Lauren stared up at Steven, literally bouncing in place on the floor.

Sandy took in the frozen look on Steven's face, and reached over and touched her daughter's shoulder. "Lauren, Steven's tired. We can hear him play another time."

Steven blinked, and forced a smile for the two kids. "I'm just learning. I'm not very good yet. You sure you want me to play?"

Lauren clapped her hands and both kids yelled, "YES!"

Steven positioned the guitar, his hands finding their place on the strings. "I don't know Itsy Bitsy Spider. How about Twinkle, Twinkle Little Star?

"We know that one. That's good."

"Rhys, sit down. Steven can't play with you hanging on his leg like that." Doug tugged on the back of Rhys' shirt, and Rhys stretched out on the floor, on his stomach, the way he did when he watched TV. Steven looked across the table at Daniel. He shrugged and tried to smile, and started to play.

Daniel winced; his boyfriend had not been overstating the case. He was remarkably bad. The tune was barely recognizable but it was mercifully short.

Steven never looked up. He watched his fingering and winced every time he played the wrong note. Unfortunately, for Steven, his ear was actually fairly good, so he heard every wrong note loud and clear. His torture eventually ended, and his fingers stilled on the strings, his hands resting on the curved body of the guitar.

Lauren and Rhys clapped enthusiastically, which almost drowned out the silence of the adults. Lauren jumped up. "Can I do it? Show me."

"Lauren!" Sandy used her warning voice.

"Please, can you show me?" Lauren touched the strings tentatively. Rhys scrambled up off the floor. "Me too!

The petrified forest of figures around the table blinked back into life as Steven showed the kids how to position their fingers and strum the guitar strings. With the impromptu music lesson as background accompaniment, everyone pitched in to clear the table.

By the time the flush of embarrassment had faded, and Steven found the courage to look up from the safety of the kids and their questions, the borrowed card table and folding chairs were stacked against the wall ready for the return trip to Sandy and Glen's, and Julia was the only one at the table. "Where is everyone?"

"The golfers are glued to the flat screen; everyone else is in the kitchen."

"Do you think I'm old enough to take lessons?" Lauren looked up at Steven. "Do they make smaller guitars?"

"I don't know. I'll ask when I go for my next lesson, okay?"

Lauren nodded. "I'm almost six and four months." She walked backwards towards the kitchen, still talking. "Guitar's better than piano."

"Play Twinkle, Twinkle again, please." Rhys leaned against his grandmother's chair, and she scooped him up onto her lap.

"One more time, then I have to go help Daniel clean up." Steven smiled and started the song again.

Lauren had barely cleared the kitchen door before she was importuning her mother. "Can I take guitar lessons? Steven's going to ask his teacher if I'm old enough."

As Lauren and Sandy talked about lessons, Daniel stepped into the archway between kitchen and dining room, watching as Steven played for Rhys. It was sappy beyond anything he would ever admit to, but he couldn't make himself stop smiling at the Norman Rockwell picture; his mother with Rhys curled up in her lap, and Steven with his dark wavy head bent over the guitar. Turning back into the kitchen, he made sure to wipe the incriminating sentimental smile off his face before his sisters could tease him about it.

❖   ❖   ❖

"Thanks, Steven." "Night, guys." "See you Friday." "It was perfect, Steven, thank you."

Daniel closed the door behind his relatives, and Steven fell into him, burying his head in Daniel's neck. "Oh, my God, that was a total nightmare!"

"What are you talking about?" Daniel held Steven close, his hands making comforting circles on his boyfriend's back. "The turkey was great and your gravy didn't even have any lumps in it. Everyone had a good time."

"No, not that." Steven mumbled against Daniel's skin. "They heard me play." He pulled his head off Daniel's shoulder, his eyes burning with embarrassment and misery. "They heard me!"

Daniel threaded his fingers through Steven's hair and cupped the back of his neck. "I'm so proud of you."

"What?" Steven reared back, disbelief and outrage stamped across his face. "Then you're tone deaf and you need your hearing checked."

Daniel tightened his arms around Steven, holding him hostage while he explained. "I didn't say you played well, you know you didn't. I said I'm proud of you. You played because the kids asked you to. You could have made up some excuse, but you didn't. You did it for them, and you didn't have to. You sacrificed yourself to make Lauren and Rhys happy, and I've never loved you more."

Silence. Shock. They stared at each other, the words stenciled in block letters in the air between them. Daniel stepped back. "I didn't know I was going to say that." He looked Steven in the eye, his jaw firm as if he was meeting some challenge. "But I meant it. I love you."

Steven didn't respond. He searched the hazel eyes and found the truth staring back at him. The smile started inside somewhere, spread to his eyes, and filtered into the tilted slide of lips that etched itself onto his face. "If I had known that hearing me play would prompt you to say that, I'd have played for you weeks ago."

Daniel sagged with relief, releasing the breath he had not known he was holding. Steven leaned in and kissed him; slow, and warm. "I love you too."

They stood in the foyer, holding each other, trading soft kisses, tracing each other's faces and lips and hair. The musical chime of the dishwasher cycle ending thumped them back into the real world.

Steven turned the kitchen lights off, and arms around each other's waists, they took the stairs to Steven's bedroom together.

Naked, Daniel lay on his back on Steven's bed, his arms crossed behind his head, waiting for Steven to finish in the washroom. "You know, Steven, I think you have performance anxiety."

Steven poked his head out of the *en suite*, toothbrush in his hand. "What?"

"Performance anxiety, that's your problem."

"Hang on." Steven popped back into the *en suite* and came out, sans toothbrush. Just as naked as Daniel, he crossed the room and climbed onto the bed beside his boyfriend. "What the hell are you talking about?"

"You don't play badly at all." Daniel was proud of his own insightful perception.

"Please! I make the guitar sound like a cat caught on a roller coaster."

"No; not all the time, you don't. When you were teaching the kids, you didn't hit one wrong note."

"Big deal." Steven shrugged. "I just showed them a few chords, wasn't much I could get wrong."

"When you played Twinkle the second time around, you played just for Rhys, and you got every note right. You played it perfectly." Daniel waited as Steven replayed that last song in his memory. He smiled at the surprised look that crossed Steven's face. "See, I'm right."

"Maybe." Steven's smile morphed into a grin as he considered the possibility that he wasn't the world's worst guitar player. Still grinning, he straddled Daniel, pulling his arms out from under his head and pinning them to the mattress. "I prefer the term 'stage fright'." Lowering his head, he sucked at Daniel's lower lip. "Because," He nipped at Daniel's neck. "I don't have any," He pushed his leg between Daniel's, "performance anxiety."

Daniel wriggled the wrists caught in Steven's hands but he didn't try to break free. "Not that I've noticed, no."

Steven released Daniel's hands. "Leave them there."

Daniel had no problem with that. With Steven he'd discovered something about himself, something that had never come up with

Aidan. He found that he liked Steven in command mode. Not all the time, and not like the scary stuff in porn movies, but when Steven got bossy, Daniel got hot, end of story.

Steven scratched his teeth over a pale nipple, and raised his eyes to Daniel's. "My house."

❊   ❊   ❊

Thanksgiving over, the days got shorter and colder. November was grey in Toronto, not enough sun to make a difference, and no snow to brighten things up. It was full dark by the time Steven pulled into a parking space behind Daniel's condo. Striding through the foyer, he hit the up arrow on the elevator twice, as if that would make it arrive faster. He hated being late!

Using the key Daniel had given him, Steven unlocked the door to his boyfriend's apartment. "Daniel?"

"In here."

Steven followed Daniel's voice, stepping into the living room, as Daniel clicked out of his word document. "Sorry I'm late, I couldn't get away."

"Don't worry about it." They met in the middle of the room, Steven still wearing his coat. "It's not a big deal."

And therein lay one of the many differences between Daniel and himself. Daniel wasn't locked into schedules and clocks. This indifference to time was a quality that made him easy to be around and a major pain in the ass, both. To Daniel, five minutes late was on-time, to Steven it was five minutes LATE!

Reaching out, Daniel unbuttoned Steven's coat, and tossed it on the couch. "I called Kevin and said we'd be a little late." He twined himself around Steven, delving into the mouth that welcomed him automatically. Burrowing his fingers through Steven's hair, he tugged at the wavy strands and Steven moaned into his mouth.

Daniel smiled even as he dragged his tongue over Steven's teeth. It had taken him a while to figure it out, and it had been quite a surprise to Steven himself, but there seemed to be a direct connection between Steven's hair and his dick. A thought broke through the mist of sensual satisfaction, and Daniel wrenched his mouth off Steven's. "What if you go bald?"

Steven stared at him, eyes puzzled. "What?"

"What happens if you go bald? I won't be able to do this." Daniel tugged on Steven's hair.

Steven dropped his hands to Daniel's ass and squeezed. "Then you'll find something else." He sank onto the couch, dragging Daniel down on top of him.

Daniel grabbed Steven's shoulders, laughter lighting his hazel eyes as he grinned down at his boyfriend.

"What am I, some kind of Christopher Columbus, discovering new worlds for you?"

"Yes." Steven traced a finger over Daniel's cheek bone, his face suddenly serious. "You are my world."

They were very late for dinner.

❖   ❖   ❖

Janice Ranier, one of the pharmacy assistants at Cloverleaf, considered it part of her job to be perky and upbeat, even on the phone. She was a nurturer; friendly and helpful came naturally to her. Some clients, however, were more difficult than others.

"Good morning, Cloverleaf Pharmacy, Janice speaking." She recognized the voice immediately. It was pretty hard to miss that snotty, arrogant tone. "One moment, please." *Thank God he doesn't want to talk to me!* She hit hold and called to Steven working on the other side of the half wall that divided the dispensary from reception. "Steven, line one, it's your favourite doctor."

"Oh, be still my heart." Janice snickered as Steven stabbed at the lit button on his phone. "Aidan, what can I do for you?"

Steven purposely never used Aidan's title because he knew it annoyed the other man. "I'll have to look that up. How do you spell the name?"

Steven didn't have to look anything up, he knew exactly which client Dr. Aidan Blackthorn was calling about. He just liked messing with the arrogant jerk.

It was the pharmacy's policy to inform the prescribing doctor when they became aware that a client was taking conflicting medications. Clients quite often forgot to tell their doctors about all of the medications they were on. As a professional courtesy, they called the doctor involved and left the information with their support staff. Usually, within twenty-four hours a new prescription was called in. Occasionally, Steven got a call thanking him for the heads up. Out of all the doctors the pharmacy dealt with, Aidan Blackthorn was the only one who ever called looking to pass the blame. Steven had learned to keep a file, dates and signatures intact, on Blackthorn's patients.

"No problem, part of our service." Steven dropped the receiver back into its cradle. "You're welcome, asshole!"

The phone made a satisfying crunch as Aidan slammed the receiver down. God, he hated it when that prick was right! He scribbled a new prescription, and grabbed his coat off the rack in the corner. Stopping beside his receptionist's desk, he set the new prescription down beside her phone. "Salima, call this in, and then update the patient's file. I'm going out for lunch."

"Yes, doctor." Salima gave him a sweet smile, until the door closed behind him. Then she couldn't keep the snicker in any longer. God, she loved it when that pharmacist was right!

❖ ❖ ❖

Daniel tugged his coat collar closed around his throat, and ducked his head trying to avoid the worst of the biting wind. He probably should listen to Steven and get a scarf. In an effort to escape the weather, he pushed open the heavy glass door to Holt Renfrew, walked through the men's department, and took the escalator down to the underground stores and restaurants that would eventually take him to the subway.

A book title in a store window caught his eye, and he stopped to look at it.

"Daniel?"

Daniel turned slowly, hoping he was wrong, hoping…"Aidan."
Fuck! Five million people in this city, what were the chances?

Aidan hugged him, and Daniel was surprised by how much he remembered, and how much he had forgotten. Daniel's body recognized the feel of the other man, even his scent was the same. For a moment, the past rose up; its arms wrapped around Daniel. He returned the hug, and stepped back, surprised to find that he had to look up at Aidan. He was so used to Steven and he being almost the same height, he had forgotten how much taller Aidan was.

"It's been forever. You look great!" Aidan clapped Daniel's shoulder, grinning down at him. "I can't believe this! How are you?"

Apparently, Aidan had forgotten the last time they had seen each other. He didn't seem to remember slamming the door of their town house behind him, leaving a shattered Daniel, standing amid the ruins of their life. Daniel hadn't forgotten. He hadn't forgotten anything. "It's been awhile."

"Look, I was just going to get some lunch. Join me. We have to catch up."

Daniel looked at his ex, and thought, why the hell not? He had to admit he was curious. "Sure."

CHAPTER 12

Out of the Past

Aidan nodded at the Japanese restaurant next to the bookstore. "This okay for you?"

Daniel almost laughed out loud because some things never changed. "Get a bento box to go. I'll get something at the Chinese kiosk."

"Oh, right, I forgot you don't like sushi."

Daniel nodded. "Yeah." Aidan had never remembered. Steven never forgot.

They found an empty table near the edge of the food court. It felt surreal sitting here with his ex like this. He'd forgotten just how good-looking Aidan was. His memories had all focused on the lying, betraying, supercilious, schmuck part. The gorgeous part had somehow faded behind the catalogue of negatives that Aidan had become for him.

Glancing across the table at Daniel, Aidan opened his take-out lunch box. "So, how are you? How's the writing going?"

Daniel picked up his chopsticks. "Good. I've got a regular column now, and there are a few magazines that actually like my op-ed pieces." He took a bite of his Kung Pao Chicken. "How's your practice doing?"

"Good, really busy. Apparently, a lot of people are looking for a GP in this city. I may have to stop taking new patients for a while." Aidan shook his head as he caught a piece of runaway sushi. "I keep going through receptionists though. They don't stay very long."

Shocker, that! Daniel watched Aidan's hands as he maneuvered his chopsticks with a deft grace. So strange, he kept seeing those hands touching him, the image superimposed in a hazy mist over the hands carefully holding tiny bits of fish. Daniel blinked the ghost hands away. "How's married life?"

Aidan looked up, eyes not quite meeting Daniel's. "We never actually made it that far."

Daniel automatically checked Aidan's ring finger, yep, no ring. *How did I not notice that?* "What happened?"

Aidan dug back in to his lunch box. "Turns out Xavier had more of a social conscience than I was prepared to live with. He wanted to spend two years with Doctors without Borders. I didn't."

Daniel didn't know what to say to that. "I'm sorry."

Aidan nodded. "Yeah." He scanned the busy food court, and looked back at Daniel. "How's the family?"

They talked family and mutual friends, movies and vacation plans, and all the while Daniel's mind was carrying on its own separate conversation. *I don't fucking believe this! After years of ranting that marriage was for breeders, and gay men shouldn't force themselves into some hetero idea of love in a futile effort to appease the bigoted majority, Aidan had met someone, suddenly heard the charm of wedding bells, and left Daniel, for what? He had torn their lives apart for a man who wasn't even in his anymore.*

Leaving Aidan after lunch, with a totally insincere promise to keep in touch, Daniel walked through the underground PATH system to the subway. Staring unseeing at the ads along the top of the subway car, he thought about the irony that was life. A year ago, Aidan's leaving had totally gutted him. Now, he could kiss the man for walking out on him, best gift he'd ever given him!

As he walked across the parking lot from the subway station to his car, his cell phone set up a dance in his pocket. "Hey, pill pusher, what's up?"

Steven laughed. "You know pill pusher refers to doctors, not pharmacists, right?"

"Tablet tempter? Capsule coder?"

"And you call yourself a writer!"

"I do, and I am, byline and everything." Daniel pressed his key fob, and unlocked his car door.

"How did the meeting with your editor go?"

Daniel slid into the driver's seat and pulled the car door closed. "He has a hard-on for a new 'concept'. I'll do some research and see what happens."

"I just wanted to remind you, I won't be coming over tonight. I'm going out with the guitar people."

"You can drop by later."

"To watch you snore? I don't think so. You can survive without me for one night."

"Yeah, but can I survive without your cock?"

Steven laughed. "You've got a drawer full of toys, you'll manage."

Daniel lowered his voice, not that anyone could hear him in his car. "Call me when you get home and I'll tell you which ones I'm playing with."

Silence, as both of them did some visualization. Steven's voice snapped very decisively into Daniel's ear. "No. I'll call you when I get home, and I'll tell you which toys to use, and how to use them."

Daniel closed his eyes and sagged against the back of his car seat, his whole body responding to that voice, that picture in his mind. "Oh, yeah, that's better." He slipped one hand under his coat, reaching for... the siren scream of a fire engine hurtling past the parking lot, ripped Daniel out of his fantasy. "Jesus Christ, Steven, how the hell am I supposed to drive like this?"

"Carefully." Steven laughed and hung up.

Driving home, thinking of his boyfriend and their phone date, Aidan became the forgotten man.

※　※　※

After work, Steven fought city traffic to get downtown. Parking under Roy Thompson Hall, he crossed King Street and pulled the door to the Baton Rouge restaurant open, wincing at the cacophony inside. Too many people crammed into too small a space, the background music only added to the aural assault.

"Steven, over here." Annabelle Walker waved him over to a corner of the foyer well away from the blasts of cold that accompanied each person who stepped through the door.

Returning the wave, Steven weaved through the various customers cluttering up the foyer, waiting for friends or a table or both. Annabelle was a compact woman with a relaxed manner that invited you to join in the joke that was life. As the oldest of their small coterie of budding guitarists, she was their self-appointed leader. She stood flanked by Mario, a computer programmer who was taking lessons as part of a plan to serenade his girlfriend when he proposed to her, and Alton, the youngest of their group, who had talked the board of education into accepting the guitar lessons for course credit.

"I'm not late, am I?" Steven unbuttoned his coat as he reached his friends.

"No. Leslie's still looking for a parking space and our table's not ready yet." Annabelle shrugged. "We have a reservation, but apparently that doesn't mean too much around here."

"Dr. Blackthorn, table for two." The girl with the headset behind the hostess desk spoke into her microphone.

Steven rolled his eyes at his friends, all of them thinking the same thing. What kind of pretentious jerk gives his title to the hostess at a casual mid-range restaurant?

"Dr. Aidan Blackthorn." The hostess repeated her call.

"Of course!" Steven looked around, craning his neck as he tried to see around bodies and over people's shoulders. "I know this guy!"

"Dr. Blackthorn." A rather strident note of impatience had crept into the hostess's voice.

"I've never actually met him, but a few of his patients are clients at the pharmacy." Steven grimaced. "One call from him and I'm reaching for the Tylenol!"

By now, not just their group, but everyone crowded into the foyer, was looking around for the elusive Dr. Blackthorn.

"Wow!" Steven didn't have to ask Annabelle what she meant. The only reason he hadn't gasped out something similar was that he still hadn't managed to snap his jaw shut. The arrogant asshat from the phone calls was fucking gorgeous! Front cover of a magazine, I got all the lucky genes, gorgeous!

"I think I need to switch doctors!" Leslie unwound her scarf, as she reached their little group. She, like everyone else in the restaurant foyer, had seen who answered the hostess' call.

"He looks like an actor." Alton spoke with the kind of hushed awe you use when you unexpectedly sight a celebrity.

Aidan was tall, with dark hair, and a lean body that looked good even in a winter coat. Steven couldn't see the man's eyes, but judging by the Celtic colouring, he was betting on blue. He hated to admit it, but Dr. Aidan Blackthorn had a lot to be arrogant about.

"Walker, party of five."

❖　❖　❖

His stomach sent out a very insistent complaint, and Daniel checked the time on his laptop screen, 7:23. He hit save, clicked out of the various websites he had been scouring, and snapped his computer shut. Stretching, he walked to the kitchen and rolled his shoulder stiffness away as he opened the fridge, nothing. He spent most of his time at Steven's place with the result that all he had here was breakfast food, and he needed more than cereal. He picked up the portable and punched in Kevin's numbers. "Hey, you had dinner yet?"

"No. I had a late lunch with Jonathan before I dropped him off at the airport."

"Good. I'm starving. Meet me at the Shawarma place."

"I'm very comfortable on my couch, thanks. I've got a bag of nachos and *The Ultimate Fight Club*. I'm not going anywhere."

Daniel smiled to himself as he prepared to dangle the lure that would get Kevin off his couch and in his car in a heartbeat. "I had lunch with Aidan today."

Silence followed by a very emphatic, "Fuck you!"

Daniel laughed. "Eight o'clock." He hung up.

As Steven and his guitar class settled into their seats at Roy Thompson Hall, Kevin pulled off his gloves in Hannah's Shawarma. Scanning the tiny restaurant, he stalked over to Daniel's table and glared at his friend. "It's freezing out there." He complained as he unbuttoned his coat and threw it over the empty chair next to him. "You pried me off my warm, cozy couch." He sat across from Daniel. "This better be good."

"Oh, it's good." Daniel patted the menus on the table. "I already ordered for us."

Kevin dismissed that with an impatient wave of his hand. "Talk."

"Remember when Mr. Marriage is for Breeders left me to walk down the aisle with Mr. Right?"

"Yeah?" He remembered. He remembered what Daniel had been like back then, saying he was fine but shunning his friends, spending every night with strangers. Yeah, he remembered.

"Apparently, he wasn't so right after all. They broke up. Not only did they break up, they never got married in the first place." Daniel sat back in his chair, more than satisfied with the look on Kevin's face. "Xavier joined Doctors without Borders and left Aidan to go make the third world a better place."

Kevin shook his head, eyes wide. "I don't fucking believe it!"

Daniel leaned over the table and grinned at his friend. "That's not even the best part. Xavier actually thought that Aidan would go with him."

Kevin snorted. "Yeah, cause Aidan's just the kind of guy who likes to spend his time driving a jeep around in mud, and muck, in small villages in the middle of nowhere. The man couldn't make it through a day without Starbucks."

"He thought our town house in Mississauga was slumming." Daniel moved his Coke out of the way, so the waiter could put their plates down. "Thanks."

Kevin laughed as he salted his fries and passed the shaker to Daniel. "I love it!" He sent Daniel a pointed look. "Okay, this was almost worth freezing for. Did he look heartbroken and destroyed?"

"No, he looked pretty good, actually." Daniel took a bite out of his tinfoil wrapped pita. Kevin's eyes snapped to Daniel's face. *Please don't tell me you still have a thing for that jerkoff!* Daniel swiped his napkin across his lips and picked up a fry. "He didn't say how long ago they broke up. He's probably had time to recover."

"You're assuming he gave a shit in the first place." Kevin's voice was snide.

Daniel grinned. "No, don't try and be nice, tell me how you really feel!"

"He's a totally self-absorbed prima donna, a shallow shell of pretty covering slime."

Daniel laughed. "Nice! And so totally objective."

Kevin grinned. "Oh, and you're saying he's not an oblivious, navel-gazing, snot?"

"He had his good points." He did. He was a good diagnostician, he didn't pull wings off butterflies, or have lousy aim around the toilet, and he never forgot to pick up the dry-cleaning. Of course, most of it was his.

"Like what?" Kevin hated the way Aidan had demolished Daniel's self-confidence.

"He was easy on the eye, you have to admit that."

Kevin grunted. "Do not."

Daniel appreciated his friend's loyalty, but he couldn't help winding him up. "He was good in bed."

Kevin didn't want to hear that. "Miss him, do you?"

Daniel set his Coke down and picked up his sandwich, grinning across the table at Kevin. "Not even a little."

Later that night, Aidan no longer existed in Daniel's world, as he lay in bed, toys and lube spread out beside him, watching TV while he waited for Steven's call. At the first ring, he scrambled for the remote, clicking the TV off, and reaching for the portable on his night table. "Hey, how was the concert?"

"Incredible!" Steven kicked his shoes off and dropped onto his bed. "Amazing technique, he made the guitar weep."

"And that's a good thing?" Daniel smiled at the excitement in Steven's voice.

Steven pushed back against his pillows. "That's a good thing." He lowered his voice. "You know what else is good?"

Daniel had a few ideas of what would constitute good, but he was more interested in what Steven had in mind. "What?"

"When you do exactly what I tell you to do."

Daniel closed his eyes, as Steven's voice dark and low, raced along every nerve ending he had. His hand already skimming down his body, he breathed, "Yeah", into the phone.

* * *

A few days later, car keys in hand, Sandy was on her way out of the house, when the phone rang. Sighing, she juggled her purse, twisting it to get to the outside pocket where her cell lived. "Hello?"

"Hey, San, you know that pasta you brought to Mom's a few weeks ago, the one with the potatoes, and broccoli that Steven liked? Can you email me the recipe?"

Sandy laughed as she perched on the arm of the sofa. "Don't do it."

"What?"

"Don't poison your boyfriend."

Daniel brayed out a fake laugh. "Sooo funny! It's pasta, how hard can it be?"

"You're right. Even someone as kitchen challenged as you can handle it. I'll send it to you after I pick Lauren up from school. How did the meeting with your editor go?"

"How did you...oh, let me guess, you saw Steven."

"Did you know he lives across the street from me?" Sandy teased, laughter in her voice.

"He's thinking about moving."

"Shut up! He is not!" Sandy laughed. "So, editor?"

"Yeah, you know, same old. He didn't fire me." Daniel grinned as he remembered something more interesting than shop talk. "Oh, guess who I saw downtown?"

"Elvis?"

"Aidan."

It took a second for the name to sink in. "Aidan? Your Aidan?"

Daniel laughed, always happy to shock his older sister. "Well, he's not mine anymore."

Sandy glanced at her watch. "Shit! I've got to go. Give me two minutes, and I'll call you from the car. I want to hear everything." Shoving her cell into her coat pocket, she dashed out the front door.

Daniel poured himself a cup of coffee. He was still savouring the first sip when his phone rang.

"Where did you see him? Did you talk to him? How did he look? What did that bastard have to say for himself?"

He laughed, his sisters were a pain in the ass, but they were always on his side. "Where do you want me to start?"

"At the beginning, dipshit!"

❈ ❈ ❈

At his condo, that night, walking behind his boyfriend, his hands on Steven's shoulders, Daniel guided Steven into the dining room. "That's it, just a few more steps. Stop." Dropping his hands to rest on Steven's hips, he tucked his chin on his lover's shoulder. "Okay, open your eyes."

Steven's eyelids lifted on a decidedly different room. The ceiling pot lights had been dimmed and Daniel's laptop no longer lived at the dining room table. He had evicted it and set the table for two. Steven knew for a fact that Daniel did not own a tablecloth, much less matching napkins, and yet here they were, pristine white and obviously new.

Daniel stepped around Steven, slipped the plate off the top of the bowl in the centre of the table, and slid it underneath the bowl, revealing the pasta inside. He glanced at Steven as he poured the wine. "You can move you know."

Steven smiled and accepted the wine glass Daniel passed him. "Sorry, I thought I was in the wrong apartment for a minute there."

Daniel looked around the room, pleased with himself. "It looks good, doesn't it?" He walked around the table and pulled out his chair. "I'm pretty sure this will be the first time I've used the dining room table for, you know, actual dining." Sitting, he flicked his napkin open, and looked up at Steven still standing on the other side of the table. "You might want to eat before it gets cold."

Steven put his glass down on the table. "You cooked?"

Daniel nodded. "Yeah."

Steven talked as he circled the table. "You cooked? You didn't get Karen or Sandy or your mother to drop this off?"

Daniel laughed, because yeah, he could have done that. "No, I cooked."

Steven stood beside Daniel's chair and spread his hand indicating the room, the table, and the food. "You did all this yourself?"

The incredulity in Steven's voice was insulting. He was not completely incompetent, thank you very much. "You need proof? Here." He stuck his hand out, pointing to a cut on his index finger. "I got this chopping the broccoli."

Steven took Daniel's hand, touching the cut gently. "I believe you. I'm just surprised." He slid onto Daniel's lap. "It looks great." Steven brushed their lips together. "Thank you."

"It's noth…"

Steven kissed him again, insistent this time, molding Daniel's mouth to his own. Daniel's hands traced down Steven's back and up again, twisting into his hair. Steven moaned and pulled back. "Thank you."

"You're welcome."

Satisfied with that response, Steven smiled and dismounted. Walking back around the table, he took his seat across from Daniel. "I could get used to this."

"Don't." Daniel grinned as he picked up the bread knife. "It may never happen again."

Steven's mouth gaped open as he stared at the long, serrated knife in Daniel's hands. "I don't believe it! You bought a bread knife."

Flustered and a little embarrassed, Daniel cut into a crusty loaf of bread. "I couldn't sleep one night, and there was this infomercial on and…"

"And you remembered that I called you a barbarian because you didn't have a bread knife."

Daniel just shrugged and put two slices of bread on Steven's plate.

Steven spooned pasta onto both plates and caught Daniel's eye as he picked up his fork. "So, you think about me in the middle of the night, when you can't sleep?" He raised his eyebrows suggestively.

Daniel grinned. "Eat."

After dinner, they took their wine glasses into the living room, and settled into opposite ends of the couch, legs twined together. Steven looked at his wine glass and then across at Daniel. "Since when do you own wine glasses?"

Daniel grinned, raising his glass in the air. "Since about the time I own a tablecloth."

Steven raised his own glass in response, and then sipped at his wine slowly, his mind gnawing at a worry that had been plaguing him all afternoon. "My guitar teacher called today. He's planning a holiday concert, and he wants me to play. Well, he wants all of us to play."

"And?" Daniel asked, but he already knew the answer. Steven looked like he had been recruited for a session with budding psychologists and electrodes attached to sensitive areas.

Steven shot Daniel a glare that said, Duh! "I can't do it."

"Why not? I've heard you practicing, you're getting pretty good."

"You know my deal with stage fright, and this would be an actual stage. Not good."

"So, do your Jedi thing."

Steven laughed. "Jedi thing? You mean when I try to convince myself that I'm playing to Rhys?"

"It works, right?"

"It works in class, yeah, but at a real performance, in front of a real audience?" Steven shook his head. "I don't think so."

Daniel swirled the wine around in his glass, thinking. He looked across at Steven. "No problem. We'll put Rhys front row centre, and you'll play just for him. You'll do your Jedi thing, and you won't even see the rest of the audience."

Steven nodded slowly, considering. "That might work. Karen won't mind if you bring Rhys?"

Daniel snorted. "I'm not bringing Rhys. Karen and Doug can bring him. I'm bringing you."

"No, we can take him. Karen and Doug don't have to drive all the way down to the school."

Daniel shook his head. "Steven, we're talking about my family here. You know better than that."

"Oh, shit!" Steven was appalled. "They're all going to come, aren't they?"

Daniel grinned. "You're the one who wanted to come to Friday night dinner."

Lying in bed that night, Daniel could feel Steven still worrying. Rolling on top of his boyfriend, he worked his best Dracula impression. "Look into my eyes."

"That's so bad, where did you get that accent, Sesame Street?" Laughing, Steven shoved at Daniel's shoulder but he refused to move, starring down until with an exasperated huff, Steven capitulated and the dark eyes met his.

Still channeling the Count, Daniel intoned. "There is no concert. There is no audience." Daniel slipped his hand between their bodies and found Steven's cock. "There is no such thing as a guitar." Maintaining both eye contact and his accent, Daniel straddled Steven and fisted his lover's cock. "You will not worry about anything except fucking your boyfriend." He ran his thumb over the crown, catching a few drops of pre-cum, and trailed his bedewed thumb over Steven's bottom lip. "Say it."

Steven had already forgotten about the concert. He didn't even hear the hokey accent. All he saw was the heat in Daniel's eyes, and that's all he needed to see.

Reaching between Steven's legs, Daniel turned his hand, pressing the heel over Steven's balls, with his middle finger tracing over his lover's entrance. "Say it."

Steven pushed up into Daniel's hand. "I will not worry about anything except fucking my boyfriend."

"Damn right!" Daniel scooted back and knelt between Steven's legs. He leaned over his lover, taking him in, rubbing the head of Steven's cock along the roof of his mouth.

Steven looked down his body, watching. Daniel's lips wrapped around his cock; there was never going to be a time when Steven didn't want to watch that. He touched Daniel's face and Daniel looked up. Neither one of them looked away, until Daniel pulled off, and rolled onto his back pulling Steven with him.

Steven settled between Daniel's legs and worked his way down Daniel's chest, one lick, nip, and suck at a time. He nuzzled into the blond thatch of hair at Daniel's groin, nose, lips and tongue reveling in the feel and scent of this man, his man. Licking over the soft skin of Daniel's scrotum, he sucked the sac gently, feeling the balls shift against his tongue.

Daniel squirmed against the sheets, murmuring low sounds of encouragement, his fingers lost in Steven's hair. Steven licked up the underside of Daniel's cock, and sucked the crown into his mouth. Fist wrapped around Daniel's shaft, thumb tracing under the ridge, he sucked Daniel into the back of his throat.

"Steven!" Daniel shoved his hand under the pillow next to him and sent the lube sliding down the sheets to his lover.

Steven popped the lid open and Daniel brought his legs up, hooking his ankles over Steven's shoulders. Steven slicked his fingers and dropped the tube back on the bed. Kneeling between Daniel's thighs, he worked his lover open.

Grabbing the lube, Daniel slicked his hand, and reaching down between his thighs, wrapped his hand around Steven's cock. He stroked Steven while Steven's fingers pushed into him.

His hair falling into his eyes, Steven smiled at his boyfriend. "You keep doing that and I'm not going to make it inside."

"Yes, you will." Daniel grinned and tightened his fingers around the base of Steven's cock. Steven delivered a sharp smack to Daniel's thigh in retaliation. Daniel's surprised gasp turned into a laugh. "If you're trying to discourage me, you'll have to think of something else." But he moved his hands to the safer location of Steven's hips.

Watching Daniel's face, Steven curled his fingers and Daniel groaned, his eyes snapping shut.

"Look at me."

Daniel looked up into knowing eyes, eyes that knew him, eyes that he wanted to always know him. "I saw my ex yesterday."

Steven's fingers stilled inside Daniel, as his whole body froze. "The guy you lived with for eight years."

Daniel nodded. "Yeah." He tilted his pelvis up, pushing himself onto Steven's fingers. His eyes closed again, as he arched his back, fingers digging into Steven's hips. God! Steven felt so fucking good, in his life, in his bed, in him. Fuck! *Thank God, Aidan left me!* Holding onto Steven, needing him, Daniel didn't realize that he was pressing hard enough to leave finger-shaped marks on Steven's hips. "I'm so fucking glad he's my ex."

Steven felt the hands digging into his hips, felt the want in the hold, as if Daniel was trying to brand him. He stared down at the man beneath him, swallowing Daniel's words as if they were high octane oxygen. *Glad he's my ex, glad he's my ex, GLAD HE'S MY EX!* The words spiraled through him, detonating explosions of relief, elation, and triumph! Setting the head of his cock against Daniel's entrance, Steven slammed home, growling out their words. "My house."

Daniel caught the yell before it escaped and dragged Steven's head down as he raised his shoulders up. He gasped, "Yes", just before he sealed their mouths together.

The meaning encoded in those words, like their relationship, constantly evolved. Tonight they were a claim, and a vow.

❖   ❖   ❖

That Friday night at dinner, Steven mentioned the concert, intending to ask if he could take Rhys and Lauren to help with his stage fright. Before he had time to make that request though, the Fine clan went into action.

Lauren turned to her mother. "Can I wear my new dress, the one we bought for Hanukkah? Steven said it's a holiday concert."

Sandy smiled. "Sure."

"We're going to Steven's concert too, right?" Rhys tugged at Doug's hand, but Karen answered. "Of course, we're all going."

Daniel sent Steven a 'See, I told you' look, and Steven ignored him. "You don't all have to come. We can take the kids to the concert, and then out for ice cream or something, before we bring them home." He so did not need Daniel's whole family there. He wasn't sure that he wanted to be there himself!

Julia trained faintly puzzled eyes on her son's boyfriend. "Well, naturally, we'll all be there, Steven. We wouldn't miss it. Are your parents coming in from out west? Where did you say they live?"

Steven's eyes went wide and he just managed to turn his 'Fuck, No!' into a cough. "No, no I don't want them to fly all that way for a student concert. Really, it's just a bunch of students practicing. Most of us are only beginners. You don't need to subject yourselves to that."

"Oh, no, don't worry, Steven. We're coming to your concert. Can't have a holiday without a concert, right?" Steven's death glare was totally ineffective, bouncing harmlessly off Doug's grin. "I'll even record it for posterity."

Steven accidentally, on purpose, kicked Doug's shin as he crossed his leg. Doug just laughed. "What?"

"No, no, I'm on it." Glen grinned at Steven. "I bought this new video camera for the holidays. It's like tiny. I can try it out at your concert."

Steven glared at Glen, but before he could even think of a G-rated reply, Karen pulled out her phone and flicked through to her calendar. "What was that date again, Steven?" Steven watched in horror as everyone at the table did the same. He looked to Daniel for help, but his boyfriend just sat back in his chair and laughed at him.

"That's the Cosmo Music School, right, the one over on Dunlop?" Julia looked up from her phone.

Glen leaned over next to Steven's ear and whispered. "Give it up, bro. There's no way out of this."

Steven tried to smile at Daniel's mother, but he was sure it looked as artificial as it felt. "Yes. It's next Saturday afternoon, at three."

Julia frowned over her calendar. "I've got an appointment with my stylist, but this is more important. I'll reschedule."

"You don't have to do that Julia, really!" Steven looked at Daniel's father, but Brian just smiled in sympathy.

"Do you want me to bake anything for the concert? Should I call the school and see what they need?" Julia had already found the school's phone number in her browser.

Daniel finally decided to help his boyfriend out. "Don't worry about it, Mom. I don't think they want a bunch of people dropping food everywhere. If we need anything, we'll let you know next week." Putting an arm around Steven's shoulders, Daniel spoke low so only Steven would hear. "My mother's like a train, you can't stop her, all you can do is slow her down a little at a time. You'll get the hang of it."

Steven groaned and buried his head in Daniel's chest.

"Why is Steven crying?" Rhys was worried until Steven lifted his head and smiled at him.

"I'm not crying, Rhys. I'm just nervous about playing in front of so many people."

Rhys slid off his chair and walked over to where Steven was sitting. He leaned against Steven's leg and patted his hand. "Don't worry. It doesn't have to be perfect. Just do the best you can and we'll be proud of you." Rhys didn't understand why everyone laughed. "That's what Mummy always says."

After dinner, Sandy stood at the kitchen counter talking to Steven over her shoulder, as she stacked dessert plates on a tray. "Daniel was pretty surprised to see Aidan, huh?"

Steven pushed the fridge door closed with his shoulder, his hands full of cake. "Aidan?"

Sandy added napkins to the tray. "Aidan, Daniel's ex. He told you he saw him downtown last week, right?"

"Yeah, he told me." Smiling at the memory of what they had been doing when Daniel told him, Steven opened the fridge again. He took out the bowl of fruit that no one ever ate, but that Julia was convinced had to be served.

Sandy opened the cutlery drawer. "When he told me he had lunch with Aidan, I nearly dropped the phone. I don't think they've seen each other since they broke up." Sandy piled dessert forks onto the tray.

Steven uncovered the fruit bowl, tossing the plastic film into the trash. *Lunch? Daniel didn't say anything about lunch.*

Sandy picked up the tray and started out of the room, speaking over her shoulder to Steven. "Aidan Blackthorn! Thank God, we've seen the last of him."

Steven stood perfectly still, and watched as the fruit bowl fell out of his hands and exploded all over Julia's beautiful tile floor.

CHAPTER 13

Not Perfect

Driving home after dinner, Daniel was animated, laughing, one hand on the steering wheel, the other drawing punctuation marks in the air, as he told Steven about the emails he'd received in response to his last article. Beside him, in the passenger seat, Steven was quiet, smiling occasionally, mostly just looking through the car window, staring at the lights perforating the darkness of the city night.

"Hey, you okay?" Daniel reached for Steven's hand.

Steven turned from the window, and twined his fingers through his boyfriend's. "Yeah, just tired."

"Sure, you're not freaking out about the concert?" Daniel squeezed Steven's hand.

Steven grimaced. "Well, I wasn't." He smacked Daniel's hand away, laughing as he snarked at him. "Thank you very much for reminding me." Daniel grinned at him before turning to check his side view mirror and switch lanes. "Your family, they're like the Three Musketeers, aren't they?"

Daniel glanced at Steven as he negotiated the off ramp. "What do you mean?"

"You know, 'All for One, and One for All', the Musketeers' motto."

Daniel nodded. "Yeah, that's us, I guess." He flashed Steven a look, all raised eyebrows and teasing smile. "My sisters and I are the Three Musketeers, I take it. So, who does that make you, Leonardo DiCaprio?"

It took Steven a few seconds to make the connection between the Titanic star and the French king's Musketeers. *"Man in the Iron Mask?"* Steven shook his head. "Sorry, wrong colouring." He reached out and tugged at Daniel's hair. "Not like Goldilocks over here."

Daniel swatted his hand away. "Goldilocks!" He manufactured a very impressive scowl which might have been intimidating if the lights sparking gold in his eyes hadn't evolved into a rumbling laugh. "That would be California Blond to you."

"Right!" Steven's eyes lit with laughter as he teased the man behind the wheel. "Is that what it says on the bottle?"

Daniel tossed his head, shaking back the messy blond locks. "That's what it says in my DNA, dude!"

At Daniel's place, Steven hung his coat in the front hall closet and tried not to wince when Daniel walked into the living room and threw his own coat over the back of the couch. While his boyfriend dumped the contents of his pockets on the dining room table - cell phone, wallet, keys - Steven quickly grabbed Daniel's coat and folded it neatly, smoothing his hand over the material as he draped it over the couch again.

Daniel turned to find a precisely folded coat and a boyfriend looking a little guilty and a lot adorable. He looked pointedly at the coat, and then at Steven, eyes crinkling around a teasing smile. *You folded my coat.* His boyfriend shrugged. *Sorry, couldn't help it.*

"Coffee or ice cream?"

Steven tilted his head a little, considering. "Both? Have you got that espresso fudge chunk one?"

Daniel laughed. "I do."

Steven picked up the remote as Daniel walked into the kitchen. He settled into what had become his side of the couch, and flicked through the channels. Now that he was alone, he was free to torture himself. *Aidan fucking Blackthorn! Daniel's ex! What had Daniel seen in that arrogant asshole?* Steven dropped the remote on the couch and leaned over, elbows on his knees, hands raking through his hair. He flashed on the image of Dr. Aidan Blackthorn standing in the crowded restaurant foyer. *Fuck! Aidan Blackthorn was a walking wet dream. A blind man would know what Daniel saw in him!*

Generally, Steven was comfortable in his own skin. He liked himself, and that was enough most of the time, but not tonight. Tonight, insecurities he hadn't felt in years came slithering out of dark places in his mind and leeched into his soul. Succumbing to a surge of masochism, he compared himself to Aidan, giving the leeches even more ammunition. Aidan was taller and magazine perfect and a doctor, with the income and prestige that came with the title. *Fuck!* Steven's inner self folded his arms over his head and curled up into a ball, trying to protect himself from the battering of his own mind.

Enough! Get a grip. Aidan's gone, done, over. He was stupid enough to lose Daniel and now Daniel's in my life, in my bed. Steven focused on the memory of Daniel from a few nights back, eyes dark with arousal, skin flushed, breaths rasping as he writhed in his arms. He replayed the words Daniel had gasped out, as he arched into Steven's body. "I'm so fucking glad he's my ex!" That memory defeated the demons and sent them slinking back into the darkness.

Picking up the remote, he relaxed back into the cushions. He wanted Daniel and Daniel wanted him, and Dr. Aidan Blackthorn was nothing more than a shadow in Daniel's rear view mirror.

Daniel's phone emitted three high pitched chirps, skittered over the dining room table, and relapsed into silence as the freezer door closed and Daniel called out from the kitchen. "You want chocolate sauce?"

Steven turned and, raising his voice a little to carry into the kitchen, spoke over the back of the couch to Daniel. "No. I'll take my ice cream straight up, thanks."

Daniel's phone set up its little table dance again. "You want me to get that?"

"Sure." Daniel tossed the ice cream back into the freezer and grabbed spoons out of the drawer. Sticking one in each bowl, he carried their ice cream into the living room. "My editor really needs to get a life. Who sends texts this late on a Friday night?"

"It's not your editor." Steven stood by the dining table, staring at the text messages on Daniel's phone. He held the phone out to Daniel. "Something you want to tell me?"

His eyes puzzled, Daniel put the ice cream bowls down on the coffee table and reached for the phone. He read the texts and snorted. "Yeah, right!"

From Aidan Blackthorn: R U free tomorrow?

From Aidan Blackthorn: lunch at Harbourfront?

Tossing his phone down, he picked up his ice cream and settled into his corner of the couch. "Like that's going to happen!"

Steven stepped over Daniel's legs, *en route* to his side of the couch. As he bent to get his bowl, Daniel's phone chirped again. Steven grabbed the phone before Daniel could get to it and opened the text message.

From Aidan Blackthorn: Is Sunday better for you?

He passed the phone to his boyfriend. "He seems pretty insistent."

Daniel read the message and looked up at Steven. Holding his boyfriend's eyes, he very deliberately turned his phone off.

Steven watched as Daniel leaned over and put his phone on the coffee table. *He didn't answer him. Why didn't he answer him? Two letters, it would only take two letters, N and O. Why hadn't he said NO?* The demons were back in full force. Steven stood staring at the phone while insidious whispers tore him apart. *Why the sudden texts? Or were they sudden? Maybe this wasn't the first time. Daniel didn't tell me everything, did he? He certainly didn't tell me that he had lunch with Aidan. That, I would have remembered!*

"Steven?" Daniel looked up at his boyfriend still standing in front of the couch. "Did you change your mind? Decided to go for the chocolate sauce?"

Steven didn't give a flying fuck about chocolate sauce! "Why does Aidan think you're getting together this weekend?"

Daniel licked his spoon, completely oblivious to the fact that Steven was one thought away from a nuclear meltdown. "No fucking idea."

"You must have said something." Steven pointed at the phone. "He's texted three times in like five minutes."

Daniel shrugged, Aidan was an asshat, but fortunately, that wasn't his problem anymore. "He said 'we should keep in touch' and I said 'sure'. But that's just, you know, what people say. I didn't mean it."

Steven stared at the man on the couch. "And just when, exactly, do you mean what you say, Daniel?"

Daniel took in the frigid in boyfriend's voice, the hostility in his eyes, and finally clued into the fact that Steven was fucking furious. His spoon dropped into his empty bowl with a sharp clink. "What?" Steven was the locus in a storm of incensed, waves of pissed off shimmering around him. *What the fuck just happened?* Daniel surged to his feel, dumped his bowl on the coffee table and reached for his boyfriend. "Steven, what..."

Steven sidestepped Daniel's hands. "Why didn't you tell me you had lunch with Aidan?" Daniel paused, surprised at the question, he had told Steven, hadn't he? Trying to remember, he hesitated too long and Steven's demons erupted. "Do you need more time to think of something that sounds like you mean it?"

Steven turned and strode out of the room.

Not this time, no fucking way! Daniel hopped over the couch and beat his boyfriend to the front door. Arms crossed over his chest, he blocked Steven's exit.

"Move." Steven's tone was ice.

"No, not until you tell me why you're so fucking pissed."

Steven feinted right, and Daniel moved left, stalemate. Steven went left and Daniel moved to thwart him. "Get out of the way!"

Daniel didn't move. "Tell me what's wrong."

"What's wrong?" The ice cracked, releasing the cauldron of emotion that Steven had been suppressing since he dropped the fruit bowl all over Julia's kitchen floor. "What's wrong? Oh, absolutely nothing, except the fact that you had lunch with your ex, a man you shared your life with for eight years, and you never told me. You also forgot to mention that he's texting you. For all I know you've been seeing him for weeks." Steven was way past any rational thought processing, the words just erupting out of him. "And I wouldn't blame you because he's fucking gorgeous!"

The cascade of words abruptly cut off, as Steven's eyes went wide with shock, appalled at what had spewed out of his mouth. They stood staring at each other, the last sentence echoing in the sudden silence.

Daniel unfolded his arms and shrugged. "Well, yeah, but he's a bit of a dick."

It took a few seconds, but the import of those words finally sifted through the hurt and the anger. Steven choked out a laugh. "He is?"

Daniel grinned. "Oh, yeah." He took a step forward. "Is it safe to touch you now?"

Embarrassed at his uncharacteristic outburst, Steven avoided Daniel's eyes as he looked down, pushing his fingers through the hair at the back of his neck. "Yeah, sorry." Totally mortified, he finally forced himself to look at Daniel as he tried out a shaky smile. "God, I'm so sorry. I warned you that I wasn't perfect, remember? I told you that you wouldn't be the only one to screw up." Steven closed the space between them, lips curving into his patented tilted smile, heralding the teasing light in his eyes. "I admit I was just trying to make you feel better. I didn't actually think that I was going to screw up or become a fucking operatic ode to jealousy, but apparently, I have." Leaning into Daniel, he shook his head, dismayed at his own irrationality. "When Sandy said Aidan Blackthorn tonight, I just lost it."

Daniel slid his hand along Steven's back, soothing both of them. "You know him?"

"He's the doctor I told you about, the asshole who calls the pharmacy."

"Yeah, that sounds like Aidan."

"He's an arrogant shit." Steven pushed away from Daniel, his hands resting on Daniel's hips. "And you were with him for eight years?" Incredulity pulsed through every word.

Daniel winced. "Long story." He steered his boyfriend back into the living room. "This needs alcohol. What can I get you?"

"Beer."

"'Kay." Daniel pulled Steven into a kiss, molding his boyfriend's body to his. "Don't go anywhere." Pressing a palm to Steven's chest, he pushed lightly, watching as Steven fell backwards onto the couch.

Steven laughed as he fell. "Not going anywhere." Turning in his seat, he watched as Daniel loped into the kitchen. Steven wasn't good with rampant emotions; they weren't neat, they weren't tidy. Unless he was naked, and more often than not even then too, Steven liked to be in control. But, Daniel didn't seem fazed in the least. With a few words he had punched a hole through the miasma of hurt strangling Steven and now Steven was sitting here laughing. Yes, he definitely needed to keep this man around.

Returning with the beer, Daniel sat sideways on the couch facing Steven. Turning the bottle in his hands, staring at the label, he tried to decide where to start. "Aidan was my first boyfriend. Until you, he was my only boyfriend. Before him, and after him for that matter, there were just hook-ups and casual lovers. We met at school. I was a grad student tutoring for extra money, and he was an undergrad looking for a tutor." Daniel smiled, thinking of the young men they once were. "And that was it, he moved in with me two weeks later." He took a slug from his bottle. "It was good. For the first few years it was very good. Yeah, he was a little self-involved, and a bit oblivious to other people's feelings, but he was charming and funny, and always so contrite when you called him on his insensitivity. He was..."

Steven gestured with his beer bottle. "Fucking gorgeous."

Daniel nodded. "Yeah, fucking gorgeous."

"So what happened?" It was like picking at a scab, it hurt, but you couldn't resist the impulse. Steven didn't want to hear this, but he had to know.

Daniel shrugged. "I guess the same thing that happens to everybody: time, life. I was working at crap jobs, writing whenever I could, trying to get someone to publish my stuff. Aidan was in med school. We never saw each other. I was scared shitless, convinced that I would be busing tables for the rest of my life. Aidan was always studying. We were both tired and stressed, and it just seemed to fall apart. The longer Aidan was in med school, the more of a God complex he developed. By the time he graduated and started interning, he was pretty smug. He started making cracks about my 'career'."

Lost in the past, Daniel spun his beer bottle between his fingers, remembering hurtful comments and bitter arguments. "By then we had bought a town house together but there was very little laughter any more, and neither one of us was charming." Daniel grimaced. "At least, not to each other." Staring into his beer, he ran one finger around the lip of the bottle. "Magazines started to accept my pieces, and I quit the crap jobs to write full time. Aidan was always at the hospital, always on call." Daniel snorted. "Or, that's what I thought." Leaning to the side, he put his beer on the coffee table and pushed Steven's bowl of melting ice cream aside. "I came home from dinner at my parents' one Friday night, and Aidan was waiting for me, bags already packed. He had met someone else." Daniel shrugged. "That was the end."

Steven stretched an arm out and cupped the back of Daniel's head, pushing his fingers into the blond hair. "I'm sorry."

Putting an arm around Steven's waist, Daniel dragged Steven onto his lap. "I'm not."

Seeing the truth of those two words in Daniel's eyes, feeling it in the warmth of the hand on his lower back and in the possessive clasp of the other on his hip, Steven allowed himself to come home. He sealed his mouth to Daniel's, tongue searching, claiming, keeping.

Daniel slid his hands down Steven's back, curled them under his ass, and dragged his boyfriend closer.

Straddling Daniel, one leg bent at the knee, squashed between Daniel's thigh and the back of the couch, Steven anchored himself with the other leg, foot flat on the floor. He leaned into Daniel, eating at his mouth, pushing him backwards over the armrest. He broke the kiss by degrees, slowly, pulling away with a tug on Daniel's bottom lip. Scraping his teeth over Daniel's jaw, he took small bites down the side of his neck, and sucked his way back up, sinking his teeth into the adjacent earlobe.

"Ow!" Daniel jerked his head away and laughed up at his lover.

Steven smiled and leaned back, tracking his hands down Daniel's chest.

Laughter still lingering in his eyes and smile, Daniel snaked his fingers inside Steven's pants and tugged his shirt out. Turning his head, he offered up the other ear to his boyfriend's gentle torment.

Steven traced the outer shell, and blew lightly into the centre, before biting down on the lobe. Daniel shuddered beneath him. He sat back, pressing his ass down over Daniel's cock, his lips tilting into the smile that Daniel loved. He caught the hem of Daniel's sweater in his fingers. "Too many clothes, Daniel mine."

Daniel raised his arms over his head, and Steven pushed the sweater up and off. "I like that." Daniel reached up, unbuttoning Steven's shirt.

"What?" Steven traced Daniel's nipples with his thumbs.

"Daniel mine, I like it." Daniel pulled Steven's shirt open and pushed it off his shoulders. "It makes me feel like I belong to you."

Steven shrugged out of his shirt and tossed it on the floor. He tapped his finger over Daniel's heart. "Daniel Mine, it would make a great tattoo, right here."

Daniel shook his head, laughing up at Steven. "I don't think so."

Steven floated one finger down Daniel's arm, circled his wrist, tracing over the pulse point. "Or, you could put it here, on your inner wrist, subtle, discrete."

Daniel snorted. "Right! That's what I need, 'Daniel Mine' inked into my skin, like I'm some kind of Alzheimer's patient!"

Steven laughed, but a small part of him wasn't joking. He really wanted some kind of physical claim on Daniel, some mark or brand or … *Geez, insecure much?* "Okay, what about just 'mine'?"

Daniel reached up, cupped Steven's face, and looked directly into those dark eyes. "Steven, I'm not going to forget. I don't need a tattoo to remind me. It's already written on the inside."

Steven nodded, embarrassed at being caught feeling so needy. "Sorry." He ran a hand through his hair, trying to shove the inadequacy away. "Sorry, but fuck, Daniel, did it have to be Aidan Blackthorn? I couldn't stand the arrogant prick even before I knew he was your ex. And he's beautiful, and a doctor, and a lot taller than me. I'm borderline cute and only a pharmacist. Forgive me for feeling a little paranoid."

Daniel shot up, grabbing Steven's shoulders and pushing him down onto his back. Stretching out on top of Steven, he aligned their bodies exactly. "I don't want you any taller, we fit together perfectly." He snapped his hips, thrusting down, his cock pressing into Steven's. "See? Perfect!" He snapped his hips again and Steven moaned, arching into him. He ground their mouths together, owning Steven.

Breaking off, he stared into Steven's eyes. "Like I give a fuck what you do to earn a paycheck. You could sit home making that pottery your parents love so much and you'd still be the most important thing in my life. I know what you do for me." Leaning to one side, he grabbed Steven's hand and held it captive under his, pressed over denim and cock. "What you do to me."

The words kept coming as he spread Steven's legs, knelt between them, and worked Steven's belt open. "You never forget that I don't like sushi. You show up at my parents' place every week because you know it means a lot to me. You remember when I have meetings with my editor, and you actually give a shit about my writing." Daniel slid Steven's zipper down, slipped his hand under the black boxers, and wrapped his fingers around his lover's cock. "You are not," Daniel squeezed just that little bit too hard and Steven hissed, "borderline cute." He ran his thumb up Steven's length, and flicked it over the crown. "You have a smile that starts my heart. You have eyes that," His fingers stilled as he flipped through the Rolodex of words in his mind, "intoxicate and beguile me."

"Beguile, really?" Steven's smile tilted as he teased the blond kneeling between his legs. "Intoxicate, okay, but beguile? That's still a word, like, in this century?"

"Shut up," Gold flecks danced in Daniel's eyes as he grinned at his boyfriend, "the guy with the Master's Degree in English Lit, still talking here." Pleased that his totally dated, entirely romantic, word choice had provoked the laughter he had hoped to hear in Steven's voice, Daniel continued on his quest to remove every single Aidan related insecurity festering in his lover's mind. Tracing delicate circles around the head of Steven's cock, he locked eyes with his lover. "You have a body that...Fuck, Steven, I want you. I look at you and I want you. I think about you and I want you. I just fucking want you, all the time!" He leaned over Steven and licked at his lips. "You make my cock hard every single time you say my name." Daniel sat back on his heels, still stroking Seven's shaft. "You taught me how to like myself again." He leaned down and sucked Steven's crown into his mouth. He grazed his teeth over the head and licked a circle around it. Lifting off Steven, he smiled into the dark-as-night eyes beneath him. "You make me believe that I'm worth loving."

Steven brushed Daniel's hair back, ghosted his fingers over his lover's cheek. "Not fair. You're a writer. How can I compete with that?"

Daniel grinned. "Good, huh?"

Steven snorted. "Good? You just picked me up, dusted me off and made me new again, only better, with more glitter." Eyes teasing, he worked Daniel's belt and zipper open and set his cock free. He trailed a finger down the silken skin and cupped Daniel's balls. "You're not all talk." He fisted Daniel's cock. "Are you?"

Daniel's eyes went wide, his mouth dropped open in shock. "Fuck you!"

Steven was a Pandora's Box of surprises tonight. He was like an iceberg, all the really interesting parts hidden beneath the surface. Daniel loved that he got to see this Steven, and he wanted to see more. He definitely needed to keep this man around.

Steven smiled his lopsided smile and tugged gently on Daniel's scrotum. "Please!"

In Daniel's bedroom, on Daniel's bed, Steven pushed up onto his knees as Daniel snatched the lube off the night table. Crawling up the mattress, he grabbed onto the headboard and turned his head, looking back at Daniel, hair falling into his eyes, smile wicked. "I want to feel it."

Lube in hand, Daniel knelt behind Steven. "Is that a challenge?"

Turning to face the headboard, Steven swayed his ass, deliberately taunting the man kneeling behind him. "Let's see what you can do."

Grinning, Daniel delivered two sharp smacks, one atop the other. Steven jerked in surprise, knocking his head against the wood of the bed frame.

"That what you had in mind?" Daniel rubbed over the red splotch on Steven's ass.

Steven looked over his shoulder, trying to see his ass. "Not really. I was actually thinking of something a little more internal."

"Internal." Daniel slicked two fingers and pushed them into tight heat. "Like this?"

"Ahhh!" A shudder rolled down Steven's spine, and he dropped his head between his arms. Using the headboard for leverage, he pushed into it, and snapped his hips back, engulfing Daniel's fingers. "Yes. More!"

Daniel slid his fingers out, a slow dragging movement, and sent them back in just as slowly.

That's not what Steven wanted, he wanted hard, and fast, and now! Shifting impatiently, he repeated himself. "More, Daniel."

Daniel chose to tweak that authoritarian demand. He pumped his fingers into Steven, even more slowly and gently than before.

Steven growled. "Daniel! Fuck me. Now!"

Daniel snarked out a sarcastic, "Yes, Master." But he pulled his fingers out, slicked his cock, and digging his fingers into Steven's hips, thrust into his boyfriend.

"Fuck!" Steven yelled, his fingers clenching into the headboard. He bucked back, taking Daniel's cock, taking Daniel, needing Daniel. Pushing against the headboard, he slammed back, impaling himself on the hard cock pounding into him, skin slapping against skin. Steven fucked Daniel, as Daniel fucked him. "Yes, Daniel, yes! More!"

"Yeah!" Daniel bent over Steven's back, and bit into the skin just over his shoulder blade. He sucked at Steven's skin, pulling hard, marking him. Kneeling up again, he slipped an arm under Steven, wrapping a hand around his cock. "Fuck!" Daniel could feel the tension in his thighs, his sac tightening. He squeezed his eyes shut, blocking out the visual, trying to stave off the inevitable. He didn't want this to end, ever!

He tried. He tried to slow it down, to draw out the intensity but Steven reached back and grabbed his thigh. "Fucking move!" One hand still wrapped around the headboard, Steven rammed himself back onto Daniel's cock.

"Aaagh! Fuck!" With the hand not curled around Steven's cock, Daniel reached for the headboard, his hand landing centimeters from Steven's, and pounded into his lover.

"Daniel!" Steven slid his hand along the headboard until he could clasp Daniel's hand, twining their fingers together, two hands locked as one over the curved wood of the bed.

Daniel bent to Steven's neck, opened his mouth over skin damp with sweat and bit down. Steven cried out and shot over Daniel's fist and onto the sheets. Chest heaving and legs shaking, Daniel followed Steven over the edge.

Spent, sated and sleepy, Daniel lay on his back, his hand gliding lazily down Steven's spine. "Have you always been a bit of a dictator in bed?"

Steven lay curled into Daniel's side, head on Daniel's shoulder, one leg thrown across Daniel's thighs.

He nodded, his cheek sliding back and forth on Daniel's skin. "Yes and no. I guess I've always felt that way, but with you, I can say it out loud." Steven trailed his fingers across Daniel's chest, tracing gentle circles around his nipples. "The more you respond to it, the more I feel free to do it." He pulled his head back, to see Daniel's face. "It seems we've created a vicious circle. Does it bother you?"

"I like to do things my own way, I might be a smidgen on the stubborn side, and I hate people telling me what to do." Daniel palmed Steven's ass. "But when we're naked, or getting naked, or even thinking about getting naked, and you go all director on me, I get hot." Daniel squeezed a chunk of Steven's ass. "My cock goes into overdrive in, like, seconds. It freaked me out a little a first. But when it comes to sex, I'm a big believer in the maxim 'if it feels good, it is good'. Plus, it really dials back the stress factor, because I don't have to wonder what you want, or worry that I'm doing something you don't like. So, does it bother me? No." He trailed his fingers along Steven's crease. "And, of course, I don't have to listen to you."

Steven lifted off Daniel's chest, so he could see his boyfriend's face. "You don't?"

Daniel smiled at the teasing tone in Steven's voice, the laughter in his eyes. "No, I don't."

Steven curled back against Daniel's chest. "But it's better when you do."

Daniel nodded, dropping a kiss onto the dark waves of Steven's hair. "Sometimes, yeah."

Hands wandered idly, languid fingers stroking, as they held each other, wrapped in a cocoon of blankets and warmth. Daniel traced slow strokes through Steven's hair and down his back. "Let's just go where the need takes us. It's worked pretty well so far." Rolling over, he tucked Steven under him. "If it feels good…"

Steven pushed his hands into Daniel's hair, and dragged his head down. "It is good." He kissed the words against Daniel's lips, a smile lingering on his own even as he fell into sleep.

As usual, morning came bright and way too early for Daniel. "Come on, get up." Steven ripped the covers off the blond trying to hide under his pillow. "You're going to be late."

Daniel tried to grab the bedding back but Steven held it out of reach. He tried glaring at his boyfriend, but it was hard to get up a really good glare when he was still half asleep. "Go away." Daniel curled himself around his pillow, snuggling into it.

"You're going rock climbing, wall climbing, whatever it is with Allan, remember?" Steven stood beside the bed, wearing his winter running clothes: heavy sweats over a long sleeve thermal T-shirt.

Daniel opened one eye, and squinted at the digital clock. "It's still early. I hate you."

Steven sat on the bed and tickled his fingers across Daniel's ass. "Ah, but do you hate my waffles?" He lowered his voice, whispering seductive words like, "maple syrup, strawberries, and that mocha latte you like."

Daniel rolled over, blinking up at Steven, a smile spreading across his face. "You made waffles?"

Steven smiled at the sleepy mess of naked man. "Yeah, and they're getting cold, so snap it up."

By the time Daniel went to the washroom, shrugged into his robe, and stumbled out of his bedroom, Steven was ready to go. Jacket and hat already on, he clipped his iPod in place, and popped the ear buds in. "Meet you back at my place later." He tugged his gloves on. "I'm going to fire up the hot tub."

Yawning, Daniel walked with Steven to the front door. Crossing the threshold, Steven pulled Daniel into a quick kiss and grope. "Go climb something."

Leaning in the doorway, Daniel called down the hallway after Steven. "Can I climb you later?"

Steven turned and laughed as he walked backwards to the elevators. "Always."

Closing the door as Steven disappeared into the elevator, Daniel let the smell of coffee and waffles lure him into the kitchen. Steven's House & Home presentation pulled a smile onto his face. The man was a disgustingly chipper morning annoyance, but he made a mean breakfast! Before him, like a mirage in the desert, sat a placemat, napkin, coffee, orange juice, and waffles with the promised strawberries and syrup. Shaking his head in wonder, Daniel pulled his chair out from the table. Reaching for the cutlery, he found a note twisted around his knife and fork. It was just a torn piece of computer paper, blank except for a happy face drawn in the centre and a small heart in the bottom right hand corner, flanked by Steven's initials.

Goofy smile lingering, Daniel smoothed the paper out, laying it on the table beside his plate. As the waffles and syrup melted against his tongue, he 'read' his note. Breakfast done, dishes piled in the sink, the way he always left them when Steven wasn't around, he patted the note on his way out of the kitchen. Finishing his coffee as he dressed, he glanced at the digital clock on his night table. "Ah, shit!" Hurrying into the kitchen, he chucked his mug in the already full sink and started the annoying hunt for his keys. "Where the fuck did I put them?"

Shoving his hands into the pockets of his winter coat, he pulled out his gloves, and *thank you Master of the Universe*, his keys. Opening the door, he hesitated on the threshold. *Okay Fine, but you're never telling anyone you did this. You hear me, Fine?* Racing back into the kitchen, he grabbed the note, and ran back down the hall, folding the note and slipping it in to his wallet, as he went. Locking the door behind him, he shook his head at himself. *When did you turn into such a fucking girl!* Waiting for the elevator to come, he decided that it had happened the minute Steven shook his hand at his sister's BBQ, smiled that crooked smile and said, "You're not Glen."

※　※　※

Rock climbing wasn't as much fun as biking, at least, not for Daniel. Allan, on the other hand, loved it. You go up, you come down, even he couldn't get lost, plus, he got to make fun of his cousin. Daniel was hilariously awkward on the wall, moving from one hold to the next like a geriatric with arthritis. Oh, yeah, Allan loved rock climbing! Shaking his head, Allan watched Daniel examine the wall in front of him. "You're such a wuss. That eight-year-old is climbing faster than you."

Carefully sliding his foot over to the next hold, Daniel looked up at Allan. "I am not a wuss, I'm a klutz. There's a difference."

Holding his tether cord taut, Allan pushed off the rock wall. "Klutz, yeah, that's so much better. Get a move on."

"What's the rush?" Daniel methodically switched hands, and stretched his right arm up for the next hold. "Let me guess, there's a female involved."

"Yep." Allan grinned. "I'm picking Stephanie up at the airport in," He glanced at his watch, "two hours."

Taking a break, Daniel rested against the rock wall. "Really? Steven didn't tell me."

Allan suddenly got very interested in scanning the wall. "No?"

Daniel stared at his cousin, his nosy detector on high alert. Allan sounded way too innocent and Allan was never innocent. Tucking himself close to the wall, forgetting the possible fall to his death, Daniel let curiosity lure him up the next set of holds, until he was hanging next to his cousin. "Steven didn't tell me because he doesn't know, does he? Stephanie didn't call him because she isn't staying with him." Daniel pulled the next sentence out with all the drama of a magician flourishing a rabbit from a top hat. "She's staying with you!" Allan actually blushed, and Daniel crowed with laughter. "Fuck! It's finally happened. She's got you housebroken!"

Opting for a non-verbal response, Allan slapped a hand into Daniel's shoulder, shoving him off the wall.

Daniel swung in the air, holding onto his tether cord, laughing at his cousin. For once, he didn't even think about crashing to his death. "And here lies Allan Fine, buried under the size seven stilettos of Stephanie Baranski."

"Fuck off!" Allan pushed off the wall and lowered himself to the floor. Unhooking his harness, he handed it to a kid in jeans and a Wacky Walls T-shirt. He glared up at Daniel still hanging in midair. "And she wears size six and a half stilettos, asshole."

Daniel cracked up again, his shaking shoulders set his tether cord spinning, causing him to twirl in a slow circle. "You know what size shoes she wears! Man, you are so screwed!"

Allan glared up at his cousin, as a Wacky Walls employee towed Daniel to a stop. "Get your ass down here, or you're having lunch alone." Allan stalked off.

Daniel rolled his eyes at the Wacky Walls guy helping him out of his harness. "Drama queen!"

CHAPTER 14

No Regrets

Later that afternoon, hot tub set to stun, Steven stood in his kitchen staring at his boyfriend. Disbelief splashed across his face as Daniel pulled his winter coat on over his naked body. "What are you doing?"

Ignoring the zipper, Daniel held the coat closed by pulling the front edges together and crossing his arms over his chest. "Do I look like some kind of deranged survivalist? Bare skin and minus Celsius, I don't think so! Goose bumps are not a good look on me."

"It's a whole, what, three meters to the hot tub?" Steven shook his head. "If you leave your coat on the deck, it's going to be one large leather ice cube by the time you get out of the tub."

Daniel grinned. "Not if you bring it back into the house for me."

Steven laughed as he padded naked to the sliding door. "Let me guess, I'm supposed to freeze my ass off running into the house to get your coat for you?"

Daniel ran a hand down Steven's back and palmed his ass. "That's the plan."

Steven snorted as he pulled the patio door open. "God, you're such a wuss!"

Daniel huddled into his coat, wincing as the cold air hit him. "Winter sucks!" He sprinted across the deck, shrugging out of his coat as he reached the tub, and tossed it at his boyfriend.

The coat tumbled through the air and slid across the deck, almost making it to the patio door. Darting out, Steven picked it up, and dashed back into the house, dropping it onto the nearest kitchen chair. Sliding the door closed behind him, he ran across the deck and jumped into the steamy water. "Anything else I can do for you?" The polite words only highlighted the underlying tone of bitchy sarcasm.

"No, thank you." Daniel smiled appreciatively, because snarky sounded good on Steven. He closed his eyes and leaned his head back on the edge of the tub, relaxing into the warm welcome of the swirling water.

"Did you tackle Climbers Climax today?" Steven stretched a leg out and rubbed the side of his foot over Daniel's calf.

"Nope, not my fault though. Allan was in a hurry." Daniel opened his eyes and looked across the tub to where Steven lounged, submerged in liquid heat. "He had to pick Stephanie up at the airport."

"Taxi duty!" Steven laughed. "They must be getting serious."

"She's staying at his place." Daniel tossed the words out, already grinning, anticipating Steven's reaction.

"No way!" Steven gaped at Daniel. "We're talking about my Stephanie, right?"

Daniel grinned. "Not yours anymore, babe."

"She never, I mean never, stays with a guy. She says it gives them ideas."

Daniel nodded. "I know. We're talking Allan here, the original 'this is just for fun, don't bother learning my middle name' guy." Slinking down on the molded plastic bench, he slid his legs along Steven's, planting his feet on either side of his boyfriend's hips. "He's really got to work on his sense of humour." Daniel complained, his tone all injured innocence. "I could have killed myself today! He pushed me off the wall!"

Steven rolled his eyes as he stroked his hands along Daniel's calves. "Wearing a harness and hooked up to a tether cord? I don't think so. What did you say?"

"Nothing," Daniel smirked, "much. I just said that Stephanie had him housebroken."

Steven groaned. "And he didn't think that was funny? Quelle surprise!"

"He deserves a dig every now and then." Daniel didn't feel one shred of remorse. "Giving you bedroom eyes." He clamped his legs around Steven.

"What?" Allan was Daniel's cousin and Stephanie's sidekick, whenever she was in town. That's all he was, as far as Steven was concerned.

"You don't remember?" Daniel remembered it, clearly, and he couldn't believe that Steven didn't.

"No." Steven shook his head. "Allan's straight, like uber straight. He's not interested in me."

Daniel captured Steven's hands, twining their fingers together. "Then he shouldn't have given you his 'come fuck me' look."

Steven jerked his hands away, denial ready to leap from his lips, when his mouth twitched on the beginnings of a smile and false compassion spread across his face. "I knew it. It was only a matter of time. Working on your own, only a laptop for company. Delusional is an occupational hazard for writers, right? Don't worry, I know a great therapist."

"You don't want to go there, Monaco. I'm not the one who has anxiety attacks when a shirt is hung on a hanger backwards."

"I don't have anxiety..."

Daniel interrupted Steven's protest. "Not the point. At Sandy's BBQ, the day we met, Doug asked if you thought Allan was good looking and Allan gave you the look." Daniel didn't think about that look often, but when he did, it still pissed him off. Allan was not only family, he was one of his best friends. He knew the look didn't mean anything, but because of it he took extra pleasure in needling Allan whenever he could. Not that needling each other was anything new, they'd been goading each other since they could walk, but that look gave Daniel more incentive.

Steven did a mental backtrack; Sandy's house, Daniel, family, lunch... "Oh, my god! That was nothing. It was a joke." He slipped out of his molded plastic seat and waded across the tub to his boyfriend. "I had totally forgotten that." His tilted smile was very much in evidence as he straddled Daniel. Laughter sparked in his eyes, as he linked his hands around Daniel's neck, and dropped a kiss on his forehead. "But you remembered." Steven grinned. "Why is that, I wonder?"

Reading the knowing look on Steven's face, Daniel shrugged, trying to distance himself from any accusation of jealousy. "I've got a good memory."

"Uh-huh." Steven trailed his hands down Daniel's arms, and ran them up his chest. "Remind me, Daniel." Steven practically purred the words, just next to Daniel's ear, as he pressed his ass down in Daniel's lap. "That look, was it something like this?" Lifting Daniel's chin, looking directly into his eyes, Steven let Daniel see every thought, every intention, everything that he wanted to do to him, with him. He loosed the leash on his desire and watched as it poured out over *his* Daniel. He leaned into his lover, and licked at Daniel's lips. "Is this the look you mean?"

Daniel groaned and pulled Steven close, crushing their mouths together. He slid his hands down Steven's back, and molded his ass. He wanted everything this man could give him. He wanted everything Steven's eyes promised. They had to get out of this swirling wet, like now! Dragging Steven to the side of the tub, Daniel climbed out on to the deck...and immediately jumped back in. "Shit!" He glared at Steven. "It's fucking freezing out there."

Laughing at his boyfriend, Steven leaned back in the water and, kicking his legs out, let them drift on the bubbles. "Ah, poor baby, do you need your coat?"

Not surprisingly at all, yes, Daniel did need his coat. Complaining profusely about spoiled suburban princes who were total wusses, Steven climbed out of the hot tub and sprinted into the house. Quickly dragging a towel over himself, he returned to the hot tub, carrying Daniel's coat and another towel. "Dry off first, moron, or your coat is going to get soaked."

Daniel hoisted himself onto the deck and Steven tossed the towel around Daniel's shoulders, rubbing his back, chest and arms dry, while his boyfriend stood there shivering. Securing the towel around Daniel's waist, he handed Daniel his coat and laughed as the blond huddled into it. "You sure you grew up here?"

Daniel gave him a dirty look. "Yes, I grew up here, in a house with central heating." He swung an arm out indicating the backyard. "Not outside in the cold and snow!"

"It's not snowing." Steven smiled because apparently a disgruntled, shivering, blond wuss made him happy.

"How are you not cold?" Daniel pulled Steven against his chest and tried to make the coat close over both of them.

Steven wrapped his arms around Daniel, under the coat. "I am cold. I just don't care because I know what you're going to do to warm me up."

Daniel looked into eyes that held all the heat he needed. "Yeah?"

Steven wedged a hand between their bodies and closed it around Daniel's cock. "Yeah."

Daniel pushed into Steven's hand. "Tell me."

Steven spoke quietly, his voice raspy with arousal, his hand stroking Daniel's cock. Daniel went absolutely still, afraid to move. He didn't want to miss even one of the X-rated whispers that slithered down his spine and made him tight, and hard, and hot. God, so hot! He forgot he was outside. He forgot everything, everything but Steven's hand, Steven's voice, Steven's words. The words were lava flowing through him, searing him from the inside. The words made his cock throb. It wasn't just the sensual images that Steven burnt into his mind, it was the fact that Daniel knew they weren't just words. Steven could and would do everything he promised. "Stop!" Daniel jerked his head sideways, away from Steven's teasing lips. Panting, trying to slow himself down, he rested his forehead against his lover's. "Stop talking, please!"

Surprised and concerned, Steven moved back, so he could see Daniel's eyes. "You don't like it?"

"Like it?" Daniel managed a shaky laugh. "So not the problem. But I refuse to spurt all over the deck like some randy teenager, before I even touch you."

Relieved, Steven stepped back, out of Daniel's arms. He folded Daniel's coat around him, one hand holding it closed. "Then I think you should touch me." He sent Daniel an Allan-worthy 'come get me' smile, turned his back on his boyfriend, and started for the patio door.

Daniel watched his boyfriend walk away from him, because with clothes or without, Steven was worth watching. He feasted on the set of Steven's shoulders, the slide of his hips, the truly glorious ass that…the cold filtered through the lust, and Daniel charged after Mr. Perfect.

They never made it to the bedroom. Daniel couldn't wait that long. Sliding the patio door shut behind him, he tossed his coat onto the floor and grabbed Steven. His chest pressed against Steven's back, he slid his arms around his boyfriend. One hand traced a line between Steven's nipples, thumb smoothing over nubs still raised from the frigid air. The other glided south, the fingers stroking over his lover's abdomen and reaching into the thatch of dark hair. He nipped into the curve of Steven's neck and across his shoulders. "You taste good. You feel good."

Steven dropped his head onto Daniel's shoulder and moved his arms back, sliding his hands up and down Daniel's thighs. "I am good."

"And so modest." Daniel smiled, his lips whispering over winter-cooled skin. Turning Steven around, he knelt on his coat, and nuzzled into the dark curls at Steven's groin. Inhaling, he found Steven's scent almost completely obliterated by the medicinal smell of the hot tub chemicals. The eau-de-swimming pool wasn't anywhere near as entrancing as Steven's personal body aroma, but it did lend a holiday vibe to the sensory experience. One hand stroking up the back of his boyfriend's thigh, Daniel mouthed around and under Steven's cock, nuzzling into his balls. He pressed into the sac with his tongue, tracing one globe and then the other, sucking them gently into the warmth of his mouth. He danced his fingers over his lover's entrance and along his perineum, while his tongue and lips played with the delicate skin covering Steven's balls.

This never got any easier, and Steven suspected that it never would. He was always torn, caught between two versions of utopia. Daniel on his knees, blond head bent over Steven's groin; the image alone could yank cum right out of Steven's body! He needed to drink in that sight like he needed to breathe, but Daniel's mouth on him set off a domino effect; his spine liquefied, his head fell back, and his eyes slid shut. He could lose himself in the heat of Daniel's touch, or he could watch, but, apparently, he couldn't do both at the same time.

His hands on Daniel's shoulders, Steven fought to keep his eyes open. Daniel clenched his hands into Steven's ass, and licked a line up the underside of Steven's cock. He sucked the head into his mouth and slid his mouth down, down until his nose brushed the dark hair at Steven's groin, and Steven lost the fight. His eyes snapped shut, his hands fisted in the messy blond hair, and his head dropped back. "Fuuuuck!" Daniel smiled around Steven's cock. That word breathed out on a soft sigh wasn't a profanity. It was a futile attempt to express the sheer sensual sensation, the pure pleasure that Steven felt in Daniel's touch. Eyes closed, fingers sifting through Daniel's hair, Steven's sigh whispered on the air. "Daniel mine."

Daniel hummed his agreement along Steven's length, and Steven shuddered for him. Daniel moved both hands to Steven's ass, and holding his mouth still, urged Steven to fuck him. Dropping his hands back to Daniel's shoulders, Steven pumped into Daniel's mouth. He wasn't rough, and he didn't push for more than Daniel could comfortably give. He felt the head of his cock slide along the roof of Daniel's mouth and nudge into his throat. He pulled back, and pushed forward again, repeating the inner glide.

Looking up at Steven, Daniel could see that his lover was close. His eyes were shut tight, the thick lashes dark against his flushed skin; most telling of all, his mouth was a tight, thin line. As if Steven could feel Daniel's gaze, his lashes trembled, and fluttered open. Their eyes locked as Steven nudged into Daniel's throat. Lost in the dark chocolate of Steven's eyes, Daniel swallowed, and Steven poured into him. Daniel drank as Steven pulsed against his tongue. Crossing his arms low on Steven's back, he nuzzled into his lover, curling closer as Steven grew smaller within his mouth.

Steven stroked Daniel's shoulders, eventually sliding one hand into his hair and tugging gently. Daniel let Steven slip from his lips, and sat back on his heels, his cock hard and wanting. Steven leaned two fingers against Daniel's right shoulder. A slight push and Daniel was on his back, on top of the coat he had been kneeling on. Settling between Daniel's legs, Steven hooked his arms under Daniel's knees, and dragged Daniel's ass up off the floor and onto his lap.

They were similarly sized; Daniel's cock perhaps a fraction wider. His lighter skin tone gave his aroused cock a delicate flush; a marked difference from Steven's own darker hue. The deep pink shade, especially when it was dew kissed with drops of pre-cum, as it was now, made Steven lick his lips, every single time. He wrapped his hand around the base of Daniel's cock, and ran his thumb over the crown. "I love your cock, it's fucking edible."

Okay, not something you hear every day but Daniel was more than willing to take the compliment. Grinning at his lover, he snapped his hips, pushing his cock through Steven's hand. "Hungry?"

Steven tilted his head to one side, considering. "I could manage a, what does your mother call it, a nosh?"

Daniel groaned. "Jesus Christ, Steven, do not talk about my mother when we're fucking. I can't afford the therapy."

Steven laughed. "No problem." He leaned down and licked a line from base to tip, sucking the crown in, popping it in and out of his mouth, carefully gliding his teeth over it. Letting the head slide free, he licked circles around the shaft exactly as if Daniel were an ice cream cone.

Daniel was more than ready to cum and this playful licking was not going to get him there. "Steven?"

Steven stopped licking, smiling at the impatience in Daniel's tone. "You know I'm a slow eater."

Daniel raised a hand and smacked Steven's arm. "Don't play with your food. It's not polite."

"So I shouldn't do this?" Steven swallowed Daniel down in one long slide.

Daniel's back arched off the floor. "Oh, fuck!" He drifted down on to the coat again as Steven sucked, dragging his mouth up Daniel's shaft. "Yes, that!"

Steven sucked a finger into his mouth, rubbing it along Daniel's shaft, and Daniel moaned. Steven plunged the saliva coated digit into his lover. One deep thrust, and his hooked finger, more by luck than design, pressed against Daniel's prostate on the first try. The wet, hot, sliding friction of tongue and lips on his cock, combined with the internal glide over sensitive nerves, and Daniel didn't last long.

Cum splashed over Steven's tongue. He dialed back the intensity, sliding both finger and tongue in a gentle rhythm, soothing Daniel through the residual tremors. Daniel reached out, sent a hand up Steven's arm and into his hair. Steven pulled off and stretched out beside his boyfriend.

Into the almost silence of laboured breathing, Daniel's phone sang out; its tone muffled under layers of coat and bodies. Ignoring the unwelcome sound, Steven rolled onto his side and Daniel rolled to face him. Steven traced Daniel's lips with one finger and Daniel's hand followed the curve of Steven's hip. The phone rang out again and Daniel glanced down, to find his coat vibrating under his knee. Reaching down, he wrestled with his coat pocket and pulled his phone out. He stared at the screen for a second and then handed the phone to Steven. "You want to answer him?"

Puzzled, Steven took the phone, glanced at the text message, and sat up abruptly. He read the text again and looked over at Daniel. "You sure you want me to answer this?"

Daniel grinned, stretched out on his back, and linked his hands behind his head. Totally unconcerned, he looked like he was going to take a nap on the beach. "Yep."

Steven raised his eyebrows. "I can say anything I want?"

Daniel nodded. "Go for it."

Steven read the message again, face expressionless.

From Aidan Blackthorn: Tonight? Woody's? 9:30?

Daniel watched, amused, as Steven frowned at the screen, considering various possible replies. Decision made, he flashed a grin at his boyfriend and sent his fingers flying across the touch screen. Done, he turned the phone around so that Daniel could read his typed response.

From Daniel Fine: Steven here. Sorry, Daniel can't come out to play tonight, or any other night. He's grounded for the rest of his life, or until we get tired fucking each other, whichever comes first. Don't hold your breath.

Daniel laughed; a short bark of surprise. "Holy shit!"

"Too much?" Steven sounded concerned but his eyes were dancing.

"No, no. It's perfect." Daniel hit send, tossed the phone, and pushed Steven down on the floor, straddling him. "Succinct, precise, clear; pretty impressive for a pharmacist."

Steven slid his hands up Daniel's arms, stroking across his shoulders. "The subject matter inspired me."

Daniel stared into the chocolate eyes, wondering, reassessing his concept of who Steven was. "You're a possessive little shit, aren't you?"

"Yes, only child, remember? We don't like to share." He smoothed his hands down Daniel's back, and clenched them into his boyfriend's ass. "I'm not kidding when I call you, 'Daniel mine', you know."

Daniel nodded. "Yeah, I'm getting that loud and clear." He shifted until he was stretched out on top of his lover, his arms crossed over Steven's chest. "Lucky for you, I'm a needy, insecure asshole who gets off on that kind of thing."

Steven raised his head enough to brush his lips across Daniel's. "See, co-dependent neurotics. We're obviously made for each other."

Daniel laughed; a low, warm rumble that made his chest vibrate against Steven's. Lowering his head, closing in on his lover's lips, he was startled when his phone peeled for the third time. They both froze, staring at each other. Daniel shook his head. "Nah?"

Steven shrugged. "Maybe he can't take a hint."

Daniel rolled off Steven and grabbed his phone. "A hint, you call that text a hint?" Opening the new text, he smiled in relief. "It's Kevin. They're thinking Pegasus and then maybe Zipperz. Want to join them?"

"Zipperz?"

"Dance club."

Steven's smile tilted. "Where we can grind up against each other in public? Absolutely!"

Daniel shook his head, as he texted Kevin. "Possessive and kinky." He hit send, dropped the phone, and crawled back over his boyfriend. "Thank god I went to Sandy's BBQ!"

❖　❖　❖

At dinner that night, laughing and more than a little proud, Daniel told Kevin and Jonathan about the Aidan texts and Steven's in-your-face response. Jonathan just grinned, but Kevin almost choked on his drink. As Daniel pounded on his back, Kevin sputtered, his eyes on Steven. "You told Dr. Gorgeous to go fuck himself?"

Steven shook his head. "I didn't say that."

Kevin waved that inconsequential detail away. "You did." He held his hand out to Daniel.

"What?" Daniel slid his drink closer to Kevin. "You won't like it."

"Not the drink." Kevin repeated the 'give me' gesture. "Your phone."

Daniel pulled his phone out, glanced at Jonathan and Steven, and with a shrug handed it over.

Kevin flicked through screens until he found Aidan's texts. "Oh, this is too fucking good!" He passed the phone to his husband. "Can you imagine his face?"

Jonathan read the text and nodded to Steven as he handed the phone back to Daniel. "Nice!"

Kevin looked around the table as he raised his glass, "To the memory of Aidan Blackthorn, a man who never saw a mirror he didn't like."

Not unusual for a Saturday night, the club was packed, too many bodies, too close together, and much too hot. The air was thick with the collision of too many scents, too many sweating men. The music was so loud that Steven could feel it reverberating through him. None of that mattered. In fact, none of that existed because Daniel was pressed up against him. His lips marking Steven's neck, his hard cock pressed against Steven's. Daniel danced, sinuously weaving his body a breath away from Steven's.

Practically shouting to be heard over the music, Steven talked to the blond temptation in his arms. "I thought you said you couldn't dance."

Daniel shook his head, laughing. "I can't dance."

"What do you call this?"

Daniel tucked his head alongside Steven's, his lips at Steven's ear. "Foreplay."

Steven clenched his hands on Daniel's ass. "Oh, fuck!"

Daniel licked into Steven's ear. "Soon!"

Not soon enough! It took fucking forever to get home. Steven cursed every red light, ready to explode by the time he locked his front door behind them. He strode into his bedroom, ripping his clothes off and dropping them on the floor, before grabbing the lube off the night table. Turning, he found Daniel still almost fully dressed, folding his sweater neatly, and placing it carefully on a chair seat. "What the fuck are you doing?"

Daniel glanced at Steven, smiling as he slowly unbuttoned his shirt. "Getting undressed."

"In slow motion?" Two hours grinding against each other at Zipperz was more than enough foreplay for Steven.

Daniel shrugged out of his shirt, and proceeded to hang it carefully over the back of the chair. He glanced at Steven as he slipped off his shoes and placed them neatly under the chair. "I know how you like to keep things neat and tidy." He unzipped and slowly drew his pants down. "I know how important it is to you." He sent Steven a sly grin.

The grin was what did it, what finally broke through Steven's haze of lust. "You bastard!" Steven gaped at Daniel. "You're doing this on purpose."

Daniel smirked at Steven as he folded his pants and laid them on top of his sweater. "Ya think?"

Steven shook his head, laughter in his voice. "You're going to regret this, Daniel mine."

"Really?" Daniel didn't look worried as he slowly slid his underwear down his legs.

Steven nodded. "Really." He raised his eyes from Daniel's cock, and grinned at his boyfriend. "Hands on the seat, ass in the air." The words hit the air with military precision. Steven would have done a drill sergeant proud.

❖   ❖   ❖

Snuggling into his sheets Sunday morning, his eyes still closed, Daniel smiled remembering the previous night. Steven was wrong. Daniel didn't regret it. He didn't regret anything about last night. He didn't regret the grinding in the club, or the surreptitious stroking in the cab on the way back to Steven's. He especially didn't regret the slow reveal that had yanked Steven's chain so spectacularly.

Stretching against the sheets, Daniel grinned with satisfaction. If that's how Steven reacted to a little teasing, Daniel was going to have to do it more often. Steven had retaliated in kind, making Daniel wait forever to come. It had been so fucking hot, that Daniel didn't even cringe at the memory of himself babbling, pleading, begging Steven. No, he didn't regret anything.

Rolling over, he buried his face in his boyfriend's pillow, inhaling the scent that was Steven. He had every intention of slipping back into sleep, until he caught the aroma of coffee and what was that, biscuits? The thought of golden brown morsels of heaven dripping in butter dragged Daniel out of bed and into the washroom. After taking care of his bladder and his teeth, he stole Steven's robe off its hook behind the bathroom door and stumbled into the kitchen.

"It's alive!" Transferring a baking sheet from the oven to the counter, Steven smiled at his boyfriend. No one should look that cute still wearing bed hair.

Daniel snuggled into Steven. "You made biscuits."

"I did." Using a spatula, Steven worked the biscuits off the baking sheet and onto a plate. "And eggs, and bacon."

Glancing over at the table set for two, covered serving plates hiding the eggs and bacon, Daniel suddenly felt better about mornings. "Anything I can do?"

Steven nodded at the fridge as he carried the biscuits over to the table. "Orange juice."

Daniel filled their glasses, returned the container to the fridge, and took his seat across from Steven. Plucking a hot biscuit off the serving plate, he smiled at the cook. "You're spoiling me."

Steven grinned as he slid eggs and bacon onto Daniel's plate. "No, I'm not. You're doing the clean-up."

Daniel bit into a biscuit and closed his eyes, savouring the delicious. "No problem."

"What's your schedule like around the end of the month?" Steven poured himself some coffee, and held the carafe out to Daniel.

Daniel nodded. "Not too bad. Most of the stuff I'm working on isn't due till mid-January. Why?"

Steven filled Daniel's mug. "I've been thinking, Hanukkah is over and you don't do Christmas, so why don't we go away for the holidays?"

Daniel thought about that. "I don't do Christmas, but you do. Don't you want to spend Christmas with your family? I'll come with you." Daniel snapped off a piece of bacon. "I've never met your parents."

Steven grimaced. "Yeah, they're making noises about meeting you too." He smiled across the table at Daniel, his eyes teasing. "I'm going to put them off as long as possible. I don't want to take any chances."

"Chances?"

"Yeah, that you'll meet my parents and start to wonder if the crazy is contagious."

"They can't be that bad."

"No." Steven cut into his eggs. "They're good people. They're generous and they practically invented the term social conscience. They try to save everyone and everything; animals, people, the planet." Steven shrugged. "Of course, their methods are questionable, often illegal, but they mean well. They're just as outspoken as your family, but they have no concept of normal."

Daniel laughed. "You think my family is normal?"

Steven gave him a pointed look. "Do they grow marijuana?"

"Okay, I'll give you that one." Daniel popped a forkful of eggs into his mouth. "I have to meet them eventually, you know."

Steven nodded. "I know, but not this year." He grinned at Daniel. "They're spending Christmas zip-lining in South America, so sorry."

"Yeah, I can tell." Daniel stole a piece of bacon off Steven's plate. "Okay, Christmas, you, me, sunblock, and an island?"

Steven laughed. "You, me, a roaring fireplace, and lots of snow?"

Daniel recoiled. "Don't tell me you ski!"

Steven pointed his fork at his boyfriend. "Let me guess, you don't?"

Daniel broke open a warm biscuit. "It was decided after I ended up in the hospital three years in a row, that skiing is not something I should do."

Steven's eyes went wide. "You had skiing injuries three years in a row?"

Daniel shook his head, his eyes lit with laughter. "I don't think you can call them skiing injuries, not technically, since I never made it to the slopes."

Steven sat back in his chair, wiped his mouth with his napkin, and prepared to be entertained. "Oh, this should be good."

Daniel grinned. "The first year, I slipped on the ice getting out of the car and sprained my ankle. The second year, I tripped over Karen's ski boots and fell down the stairs." He pointed to a small white scar just under his hair line. "Eight stitches. The third year, I sat hanging in the air for an hour and a half, while they tried to get the ski lift working again."

Steven interrupted. "That didn't put you in the hospital."

"Well, no, not exactly. But by the time they finally got the lift to move again, my leg had fallen asleep and when I tried to get off the lift, I stumbled and lost my balance." Daniel shrugged looking slightly embarrassed. "I rolled down the hill, got tangled up in my skis, and bashed my head into a rock hidden under the snow." He smiled. "Concussion."

Steven stared at him. "Oh, my, God! Your poor mother!"

Daniel snorted. "Right! You'd think I'd get some sympathy, wouldn't you? No, they were all too busy being pissed at me for ruining their holiday. They called a family council and voted me out of any future ski vacations."

Steven broke his last piece of bacon in two and handed one half to the blond bottomless pit across the table. "Don't worry. I can take care of you."

Daniel grinned at Steven and popped the bacon into his mouth. "Yes, you can." He raised his eyebrows, sending Steven a suggestive leer. He wasn't talking about skiing.

Steven laughed as he got up and started to clear the table. His phone pealed out a series of beeps, and he grabbed it off the counter on his way to the sink. He read the text, and looked over at Daniel. "Steph. She wants us to have dinner with her and Allan tonight?"

"Sure." Daniel gathered up the dishes and glasses, and carried them over to the dishwasher, as Steven sent his response. He stacked the plates in their racks, put the glasses on their ledge, and snapped the door closed. Leaning against the counter, he pulled his boyfriend close, his hands linked behind Steven's back. "You know, you can take care of me on an island too."

Steven linked his arms around Daniel's neck. "I can take care of you anywhere." His lips tilted into the smile that Daniel loved, his voice a threat and a promise. Daniel moaned and licked into Steven's mouth. Steven wound his hands through Daniel's hair, as Daniel slid his palms down Steven's back. Steven broke the kiss, and backed out of Daniel's arms. He threw words over his shoulder, as he walked out of the kitchen. "I just want to see you on a dogsled."

Daniel blinked, his face a mask of 'please, god, he didn't really say that!' "What? Steven?...Steven?"

CHAPTER 15

Past Imperfect

Friday night dinners chez Fine were not quiet, orderly meals. Everyone talked at the same time. Three or four simultaneous conversations, all of them loud, were par for the course. To have even a hope of being heard, you had to be fast. You listened for the slightest hesitation between words and jumped in. It had taken Steven a few weeks to figure it out. It was a little like surfing; the ocean never got completely still, but you waited for your chance to slip your board in and coast on the waves. Like any other skill, it required practice. Steven had fallen off his board a time or two in the beginning, but he could surf with the best of them now.

"Uncle Daniel, we're going skating tomorrow. You want to come?" Rhys had an unfair advantage when it came to being heard, his voice was higher than anyone else's.

Daniel shook his head, as he smiled at his nephew. "Sorry Rhys, I can't. Steven and I are going away for a few days."

Yes, he was looking forward to it. Just the two of them away from everything and everyone, yes! But, dogsledding, really? What happened to sitting by a fire, drinking themselves silly, and crawling all over each other in bed? Isn't that what winter resorts were for? Dogs, sleds, and speed...crap! Who was Steven, some kind of gay Evel Knievel? Handing over control of life and limb to ten dogs tied to a sled, how was that a sane idea?

"Somewhere with Pina Coladas, I hope." Karen's idea of heaven was an island with babysitting.

Steven smiled across the table at Daniel's sister. "This place probably leans more towards Hot Buttered Rum and Apple Cider."

Karen's mental image went from palm trees to fir trees, and her nose wrinkled in distaste. "Why, where are you going?"

Daniel sat back in his chair, waiting for the fallout that he knew was inevitable. Unknowing innocent that he was, Steven blithely walked into the minefield. "Maple Hill."

."No way!" Karen's exclamation was loud enough to break through the other conversations. Everyone turned to see what the commotion was.

Sandy had heard Steven's answer, but she didn't believe it. Daniel didn't 'do' winter, certainly not winter outside. Her brother was like some great Grizzly bear, he hibernated during the icy months. Looking from Daniel to Steven, she drew what she thought was the only possible conclusion. "We're not paparazzi. You want to be alone, okay we get it. You don't have to lie about it."

Daniel rolled his eyes. "We're not lying. We're going to Maple Hill Resort. What's the big deal? People do it all the time."

"Other people, yes." Karen shook her head. "Not you."

Steven glanced around the table, at a sea of incredulous faces. "Daniel told me about the ski thing. Don't worry, we're not going skiing. We've booked for snowshoeing and dogsledding."

Groans and laughs, then everyone spoke at once. It was like standing under a waterfall, with a cascade of words instead of water.

"Dogsleds? Flying over the snow behind a pack of dogs, oh yeah, that's much better than skiing!" "Oh, I don't know, Steven. Do you really think that's a good idea?" "Maple Hill has a doctor on staff, right?" "He can do the snowshoes, maybe. He can walk, almost."

Daniel raised his middle finger at that last remark. With a quick jerk of her chin indicating the kids, Karen pushed his hand down.

"What's snowshoeing?" Rhys tugged on his mother's arm to get her attention.

While Karen explained what a snowshoe was, Daniel leaned over, his voice pitched for Steven's ear. "You okay?"

Steven kept his own voice low. "We don't have to do this. If this is freaking you out, we can find an island."

Daniel shook his head. "They're freaking out, I'm not." His voice was definite as he smiled into Steven's concerned eyes. "I'm going to be with you."

"Awesome!" Walking on top of the snow sounded like a great idea to Lauren. "Can we go to?"

"No." Glen used his 'don't even think about it' voice. "We're going skating, remember?"

Conversation veered into various plans to keep the kids from being bored during the holidays. Steven volunteered to bring his guitar over when Daniel and he got back from the resort. He had gotten into the habit of giving Lauren and Rhys little mini lessons. The kids liked it, and it helped with his stage fright.

"That would be great Steven." Karen nodded at the chocolate-eyed brunette sitting beside her brother. "But you'll probably be busy."

"No, I don't have to be back at work 'til after New Year's."

"Not work." Karen shook her head, a smirk twitching at the corner of her lips. "You're probably going to want to spend time with Daniel in the hospital."

"Karen!" Julia was not amused. "That's not funny! Maple Hill is a beautiful resort. Daniel and Steven are going to have a lovely time. I'm sure of it." She wasn't sure at all, that was obvious in the nervous look she shared with her husband.

"Yeah, I don't know, dude. Dogsleds at your age?" Three years Daniel's senior, Doug was just messing with his brother-in-law.

"Be careful on the blades, dude." Daniel stressed the 'dude', smiling at Karen's husband. "The ice is awful hard on old bones."

"Maybe we should get him kneepads, like the kids have." Glen believed in equal opportunity teasing. He didn't want anyone to feel left out.

"Kneepads!" Doug snorted. "I can skate circles around you, old man." Glenn had turned forty and Doug didn't let him forget it.

"I didn't know," Daniel's voice was suspiciously innocent, "that you were a figure skater."

Doug knew an insult when he heard one. He couldn't give Daniel the response he felt that remark deserved, not in front of his son and niece. Fully aware of the words Doug was holding back, Daniel grinned.

Doug nodded, ceding this one to Daniel. Locking eyes with his brother-in-law as he picked up his glass, he drawled, "I'm versatile."

Steven choked and Daniel laughed as he pounded on his boyfriend's back. He gave Doug a thumbs-up. "Nice!"

With the kids' bedtimes in mind, Karen and Sandy left early. Daniel and Steven were the last ones to leave. Brian had fallen asleep in his recliner and Julia walked them to the door. "Ma, don't worry." Daniel zipped up his coat and reached into his pockets for his gloves. "I won't even go near a ski lift!"

Julia nibbled on her lower lip, a nervous habit. She glanced between the two boys. Men, she corrected herself, they're men now, not boys. She shoved her hands into her pockets to keep from dragging Daniel away from the front door and locking him in his old room.

Steven shrugged into his coat and wrapped his scarf around his neck. "I'll keep an eye on him, Julia."

Julia nodded and tried to smile. "I know. I know you will, Steven. It's just..." Hands working on instinct, she reached up to button Steven's coat. "You have no idea how quickly he can get into trouble. One minute he's fine, and the next we're calling 911."

"Ma, I'm not nine years old anymore!" Daniel understood that his mother was worried but this was just embarrassing. He was a grown man and he didn't need his boyfriend to babysit him. Steven was four years younger than he was for fuck's sake!

Hands on her hips, Julia turned on her son. "Oh, and when you had to be carried off the soccer field two years ago, how old were you then?"

Daniel growled with exasperation. "That was an accident!"

"They're all accidents, Daniel. That's my point!"

Steven slipped his hand into Daniel's. "We'll call you as soon as we get back from Maple Hill. Will that help?"

Julia turned to the young man she already considered a son-in-law. "Yes. That would help a lot." She glared at her son, and touched Steven's shoulder in gratitude. "Thank you."

Daniel rolled his eyes, and opened the front door. Steven leaned down and kissed Julia goodbye. "See you next week. Don't worry."

"Oh, Steven, I almost forgot." Julia hugged Steven. "Happy Christmas!"

"Thank you. And we'll call, don't worry."

Striding down the walkway, Daniel started gripping as soon as the front door closed behind him. "Can you believe them? I'm an adult. I pay rent and taxes. I do my own laundry. I'm not that uncoordinated disaster of a kid anymore! I bike on dirt trails," Daniel vented as he popped the lock on the car door, "with hills and everything." He slid into the driver's seat and slammed his door closed. Snapping into his seat belt, he jabbed his key into the ignition. "I play soccer, and rock climb, well, wall climb and…"

Daniel's vent cut off mid-rant, as Steven leaned into him. Placing a hand along the side of Daniel's face, he angled Daniel's head to one side and kissed along his jaw. "And you don't end up in the hospital every time you move. I know." Steven smiled as he sucked his way down the side of Daniel's neck.

"I don't." Daniel grumbled even as his arms closed around Steven. He sank one hand into his boyfriend's hair, and trailed the other down his back, over the cashmere winter coat.

Steven dropped a quick kiss on Daniel's mouth and moved back into his own seat. "They're just worried about you." He clicked into his seat belt.

Daniel muttered as he turned the ignition key. "They should all mind their own business."

"Right!" Steven snorted. "'All for One, and One for All', remember? You are their business." Reaching over, he slid his hand up Daniel's thigh, successfully distracting his boyfriend. "I bet you can move all over me, and not fall out of bed once."

Daniel clasped his hand around Steven's, twining their fingers together. "Well, that depends." He grinned at his boyfriend as he backed out of his parents' drive way. "Are you going to lie perfectly still and let me fuck you?"

"Lie perfectly still?" Steven cocked his head, pretending to consider it. His lips tilted into that slightly off kilter slide. "Nope."

Daniel switched into the passing lane, and hit the gas. "Good answer!"

❊   ❊   ❊

The next morning, soft flakes coated the windshield as they drove into cottage country. Not enough to make driving hazardous, just enough to create the perfect holiday atmosphere. Daniel watched as they left civilization behind, small towns became occasional homes until finally they were driving through a vast empty, snow and trees as far as the eye could see. He turned to the man behind the wheel and smiled. "This is going to be great!"

"Holy shit!" Daniel dropped his bag and stared around their hotel suite; massive king size bed, cozy couch in front of a fire place and, tucked between two pillars, a hot tub with a view of snow-covered mountains. "How much is this costing you?"

"There was a discount for online bookings." Steven parked his bag on the bench at the end of the bed. He wasn't lying, exactly. The resort did offer an online discount, just not for this room.

On a small table beside the fireplace, Daniel found two champagne flutes, a corkscrew, and a bottle of bubbly. Brandishing the bottle, he grinned at Steven. "Wow! They think of everything."

Patrolling the room, Steven glanced into the *en suite*, to find a glassed in shower stall big enough to hold a party in, equipped with a rainfall shower head and a myriad of nozzles scattered along the walls. A selection of L'Occitane bath products lined up along the marble counter by the sink and a stack of white towels fluffy enough to dive into completed the look of luxury. "Yeah, they do." Smiling at the image of a naked, water-streaked blond pressed up against the shower tiles, Steven turned to find Daniel struggling with the cork on the champagne. "Need some help?"

The cork slid free and Daniel shot Steven a proud grin as he poured golden bubbles into the flutes. Handing one to Steven, Daniel took a tour of the room. Stopping beside the hot tub, he took in the winter wonderland scene on the other side of the window and turned to his boyfriend. "I feel like a Trophy Wife!"

Steven sipped his champagne and watched Daniel. "And that's a good thing?"

Daniel kicked off his boots and, being careful with the champagne, stretched out on the bed. He sipped from the crystal flute, glancing around the room and out over the mountains. "I could get used to it. Look at this place!"

Steven put his glass down on the night stand and sat on the bed to unlace his boots. Shucking them off, he crawled over to his boyfriend. "You know the thing about a Trophy Wife is," Steven took a sip from Daniel's glass, and placed it beside his own glass on the night stand, "she has to give it up to the guy who pays the bills."

Eyes lit with gold flecks of laughter, Daniel slid down the mound of pillows until he lay under Steven. "Yeah? Sign me up." Reaching out, he traced his hands through Steven's hair, grazed over his cheekbones and along his jaw. Staring at Steven's mouth, he ghosted a finger over the tilted smile. Steven kissed the finger at his lips, nibbling at the tip.

It was a little thing, nothing really in the grand scheme of all things sensual, just lips and teeth tugging on his finger. But looking into Steven's eyes, it felt like more, it felt like everything.

Steven watched the smile light in Daniel's eyes and spread across his face. It was a little thing, a smile, but this smile from this man, felt like home.

Sliding his finger free, Daniel wrapped his hand around the back of Steven's neck and pulled him into a kiss. As their mouths connected, their bodies slid along each other, legs and pelvises aligning, clicking into place like pieces of a puzzle. They fit.

Steven broke the kiss and rolled off Daniel and onto his back. Daniel moved automatically, tucking himself along Steven's side. "I'm thinking this place has possibilities." Steven's voice was low, his arm across Daniel's back. "You'd look really good pressed up against the marble in that shower stall."

Daniel tipped his head back to see Steven's face. "Yeah? You'd look good naked, stretched out on the carpet in front of the fireplace, the light from the fire flickering over your skin."

Steven's hand moved to Daniel's ass. "Mmmm."

Daniel settled back against Steven's shoulder and cupped Steven through his jeans. "I bet the view from the hot tub would be even better with me pounding into you as we watch the stars."

Steven groaned and squeezed Daniel's ass. "Fuck! You're good at this."

Feeling a little smug and a lot pleased, Daniel grinned at Steven. "Writer, remember?"

Steven pulled one of Daniel's legs across his own. "Excellent, excellent career choice."

Hands stroked idly, the silence comfortable between them. Staring at the ceiling, Steven thought of something else, an addition to the to-do list for their mini-vacation. "I want to hold hands on the rink tonight and kiss under the trees. I never got to do that in high school."

Daniel sat up quickly, staring down at Steven. "Skating? You want to go skating?"

"It's lame, I know but..." Steven averted his eyes, looking into the past. "You get older, and you move on." He turned back to Daniel, eyes dark, smile sad. "But you never really forget do you?" He twisted his fingers into a crease in Daniel's jeans. "I was fourteen, hanging around an outdoor rink with kids from my class, pretending to laugh when everyone else did. I didn't want to be in the snow on the outside of the boards, passing around a bottle that someone had stolen from their parents' liquor cabinet. I wanted to be on the ice, inside the boards, skating with Jimmy Muldoon. I wanted to hold his hand as we skated. I wanted him to smile at me," Steven laughed softly, laughing at the boy he had been, "the way he was smiling at Angela DiMarco."

Rolling onto his side, facing Daniel, he threaded his fingers through his boyfriend's. "So, yes, tonight I want to skate with you. I want you to hold my hand. I want you to kiss me under the trees as we walk back to our room." He looked at Daniel, eyes vulnerable, hesitant. "Okay?"

Daniel wanted to wrap Steven up, to protect him from every future hurt and every past memory. He felt honoured to be the person this man shared himself with. He tightened his fingers around Steven's, a silent acquiescence. "This Jimmy Muldoon, I'm better looking, right?"

❉ ❉ ❉

They spent the afternoon exploring the resort, beating each other in the Video Arcade and losing money in the casino. After dinner, they wandered down to the rink and took a stab at re-writing Steven's history. Neither one of them had been on skates in over ten years, so they weren't particularly graceful. Their laps around the ice engendered more laughter than romance, but, they did hold hands. Returning their rental skates, they walked through softly lit, snow-swept paths back to their room. Daniel tugged Steven off the path and into a cluster of trees, pressed him up against the trunk of a denuded maple, and gave Steven the kiss that Jimmy Muldoon hadn't.

Steven closed his eyes and moved into Daniel, at least as far as their puffy parkas would allow. He rested one hand on Daniel's shoulder, and curled the other into the heat of his neck. They kept the kiss slow and sweet, almost chaste, as if they were both fourteen again. They stood wrapped around each other in the winter night, under the trees and the stars.

Steven stepped back. "I'm fucking freezing!"

Back at their room, Steven stopped Daniel before he could close the door. "Wait." He took the Do Not Disturb sign off the door knob and switched it to the outside of the door. Daniel nodded, shut the door, and clicked the lock. Staring at each other, they unbundled themselves. Hats, and gloves, and parkas dropped onto the floor. Daniel kicked his boots off and bent to help Steven unlace his. The rest of their clothes went flying, a small snowstorm of extraneous material.

Daniel stroked his hands down Steven's sides, and palmed his ass. "Fireplace or hot tub?"

Steven trailed a hand over Daniel's chest, thumb playing over a stiffening nipple. "Fireplace." He watched as Daniel walked over to the fireplace and pulled the screen open. "You know what you're doing?"

Shaking his head, Daniel stepped back, motioning for Steven to take his place. "Opening the screen, that's all I've got." He watched as Steven jiggled with the logs, added tinder and struck a match. "Let me guess, Boy Scout?"

Sliding the screen shut, Steven laughed. "Nah, that's way too middle class for my folks. No, we did our own camping. They liked to sit around a fire at night and sing. My father played the guitar."

Daniel stepped behind Steven, pulled him close, and tucked his chin on Steven's shoulder. "Is that why you're learning to play?"

"Maybe." Steven's voice was soft as he stared into the flames. "Maybe." He turned in Daniel's arms and slid his hands down his boyfriend's back. Raising his eyebrows, he smiled suggestively. "You were saying something earlier, something about the firelight flickering over my skin?"

Watching Steven's face, Daniel stroked over his hip, across his thigh, and palmed his sac, rolling the glands gently. "I was?" He pumped one long slide down Steven's shaft and drew back with a smirk. "I think I said something about you lying naked on this carpet."

Steven lay down and stretched his arms above his head, settling into the carpet one muscle group at a time. Eyes half shut, smile molten, he looked up at Daniel and let his legs fall open.

Daniel looked down at Steven, at tousled curls, and heated eyes, at a body lit in light and shadow by the teasing touch of fire light. Beautiful, God, so fucking beautiful, and his! Steven writhed on the carpet, needing, and Daniel went up in flames. Sinking to his knees, he moved to cover Steven, and was stopped. Steven strong-armed him, his hand planted firmly in the middle of Daniel's chest. "Forget something?"

Daniel blinked, his mind a room full of static, his body screaming at him. "What?"

"In my bag." Steven nodded to the bench at the foot of the bed. "Lube."

It took a second for Steven's words to penetrate. "Fuck!" Daniel growled and dragged himself off his boyfriend. Leaping across the carpet, he pulled the zipper on Steven's bag with a violence it didn't deserve. Riffling through the clothes, he found Steven's leather shaving kit, and flipped it open. Grabbing the lube, he almost tripped over his own feet getting back to his lover.

Kneeling between Steven's thighs, he slicked his fingers. Steven propped himself up on his elbows, and planted his feet flat on the floor, knees bent. He lifted his lower body off the floor; legs spread, ass in the air.

One hand palming Steven's ass, Daniel pushed two fingers in, feeling Steven clench around him. Steven looked along his body, watching Daniel, feeling Daniel stretch him open.

Daniel lifted his eyes to Steven's, letting Steven see him, see into him. "You always feel so fucking good."

"Mmmm." Steven tipped his head back and pushed his ass down on Daniel's fingers. Eyes closed, he fucked himself on Daniel's fingers, and Daniel shuddered, watching, wanting. "More, Daniel mine. More." Steven's words came out on a sigh, barely heard over the hiss and crackle of the fireplace.

Daniel added a third finger, and Steven opened around him, for him. He watched Steven. Head back, eyes closed, firelight glowing on his chest, hips thrusting, fucking himself on Daniel's fingers, and his cock... Daniel licked his lips, and bent his head, curling over Steven, swallowing him down.

"Oh, fuck." Steven pushed at Daniel's shoulder, but Daniel didn't move. Any previous plan melted into oblivion. Now, he wanted this. He wanted Steven to come like this, on his fingers, in his mouth. He wanted Steven to lose it, for him. He slid one arm under his lover's back, helping Steven to hold himself high. He thrust his fingers in deep, hard, fast, fucking Steven, fingers gliding over his prostate, bringing him.

Acquiescing to Daniel's inclination, Steven spread his arms out, clenching his fingers into the carpet. Daniel's fingers worked Steven, lightning touches, and Steven went rigid. Sucking hard, fingers pumping, Daniel built the heat, and tension, and need. "Daaaaan," Steven snapped his hips, pumped into Daniel's throat, and lost it, "ielll!"

Daniel swallowed and licked gently, only reluctantly letting Steven slip from his lips. Flopping down beside his boyfriend and rolling onto his side, he watched as Steven came back to himself.

Steven turned his head, glared at Daniel, and whacked his arm. "You were supposed to fuck me."

"Ow!" Daniel grinned, rubbing at his arm. "Yeah, I know." He tried the look that had always won his teachers over, all smiling eyes and innocent charm. "Change of plan?" He curled his fingers into a fist, and rubbed it down Steven's side, digging into the dip above his hip. "I mean, wouldn't it get boring if I always did what you told me to?"

Surprise flashed across Steven's face as he thought about that. Rolling onto his side, he propped himself up on one elbow. "Okay, I'll give you that, but don't make a habit of it."

Feeling like he had managed to talk himself out of detention, Daniel nodded, a slow smile spreading across his face.

Steven fisted Daniel's cock. "Now, what are we going to do about this?"

Daniel flopped onto his back. "Anything you want."

Steven muttered to himself as he slid his hand along Daniel's shaft. "I should leave you to take care of this yourself!" As the words hit the air, and the image formed in his mind, Steven realized that was just what he wanted, to watch Daniel bring himself off. Giving Daniel's cock one last pat, Steven slid himself along Daniel's body, and spoke low against his ear. "Touch yourself." Daniel's eyes went wide with surprise. *Nope, did not see that coming!*

Steven chuckled at the lack of enthusiasm marching across Daniel's face. "I want to watch you. I want to see you let go. You're beautiful, you know, like that." Tugging Daniel up with him, Steven urged him onto the couch. Sitting with his back against the arm rest, his legs stretched out along the length of the couch, Steven settled Daniel between his legs. One arm held Daniel close, the other slid along Daniel's thigh. Daniel tucked his head back against Steven's shoulder, and stretched his legs out along Steven's.

Steven bent his head, speaking low next to Daniel's ear. "Show me." He traced over Daniel's hip, and thigh. "Show me, Daniel mine. I want to watch you." Steven's voice was hushed velvet, his lips brushing Daniel's ear, his breath heating the side of Daniel's face. He whispered words that went directly to Daniel's cock. He licked Daniel's neck, nipped at his ear lobe, and never stopped murmuring incendiary words into Daniel's ear. He built Daniel's desire the way he had built the fire. He set the tinder and lit the match. Daniel moaned as heat scorched through his balls and poured into his cock.

Daniel's hips jerked, and his hand was suddenly fisted around his shaft, pulling. "Steven?"

"I'm here, Daniel mine. I'll always be here." Steven cupped Daniel's sac, thumbing over his balls, and Daniel's eyes slammed shut, his lips opened on a gasp, and everything spilled out of him. Eyes still closed, he lost himself in the feeling, and found himself in Steven's words. "Beautiful, Daniel mine, so beautiful."

Melted into nothing, Daniel stretched and curled into Steven and the couch. "Uh-uh, get up, we can't fall asleep here. We're not pretzels." Grumbles and protesting groans were Steven's only answer. It took a few elbow pokes and a threat to tip Daniel onto the floor but eventually they were huddled together under the thick duvet, tucked against a mountain of pillows, watching as the fire died down.

"Anyone else I should know about besides Jimmy Muldoon?" Daniel was curious. Steven was turning twenty-nine in March; there had to have been someone.

"You want a blow-by-blow account, or rather a blowjob-by-blowjob account?" Steven's smile tilted and his eyes laughed. "It could take a while."

Daniel laughed. "I bet! No, just give me the highlights, the guys whose names you actually remember."

Steven huffed, a total pretense of mortally offended dignity. "I am not a slut, Mr. Fine!"

"No, you're the man who makes my dick hard."

Steven laughed, his eyes crinkling at the corners, his smile delighted. He shoved his shoulder into Daniel's, and Daniel shoved back. They rolled around the bed, wrestling with the sheets and each other, until Daniel pinned Steven's hands to the mattress. "Talk."

Steven laughed up at Daniel. "Okay, okay, get off me, Hulk Hogan!" Daniel let Steven go, and pulling the covers back around them, they settled against each other, linked at shoulder, hip and thigh. "Well, you know high school was a bust, boy-wise, I mean. Undergrad was a lot more fun; more boys, more sex, more boys." Steven shrugged. "You know how it goes. Grad school was starting all over again; new province, new school, new people."

Steven paused, his hand reaching for Daniel's, and Daniel knew this was it. This was the story he wanted and didn't want to hear. "My first co-op placement was at an independent pharmacy, a small chain of three stores. The owner was an established pharmacist, a graduate of the school. He was close to forty, I guess; smart, striking, hot. One smile from him and my life was perfect. If he complimented my work, I was in heaven." Steven shook his head, wincing at the thought of the boy he had still been back then. "When he asked me out to dinner, I thought I'd won the lottery." Steven went silent, starring down at the sheets, seeing nothing, remembering everything.

Daniel waited. He waited until Steven's stillness started to scare him. "Steven, it's okay, you don't have to…"

Steven jerked back into the present, his hand clamping around Daniel's. "To this day, I don't know if he was just messing with me, trying to break me or if he was trying to make me over, into a previous lover or his ideal partner." He shook his head. "I don't know and I never will." He turned his hand in Daniel's, twining their fingers together. "Over a period of two or three months, I went from thrilled to miserable. I couldn't do anything right; my hair, my clothes, the way I spoke, the things I said. I found myself constantly apologizing, and trying, trying to be better, to be what he wanted." Steven turned to Daniel, his face haunted. "He didn't hit me or rage at me, nothing like that. He was patient, almost gentle. He always looked so disappointed, though, and he would give this small sigh of defeat, as if my failures hurt him."

"Bastard!" Daniel didn't even know the man but he wanted to kill him.

Steven flashed Daniel a watery smile. "Yeah, it would have been better if he had just hit me. Then I would have left. I wouldn't have kept trying to be someone else for him." Cuddling into Daniel, Steven buried his head in Daniel's neck. "I'd like to tell you that I smartened up and dumped him, but that's not what happened. My placement ended, and I went back to school. I was such an idiot. It never occurred to me that we were over. When he didn't call me, I called him. I left messages at the stores, at his home, on his cell." Steven shook his head, his cheek rubbing against Daniel's skin. "I finally went to his house. He opened the door and he looked at me like he was trying to remember how he knew me. He said, 'Can I help you?' as if I were some door-to-door salesman." Steven went silent again, his fingers curling against Daniel's chest, his thumb stroking over a nipple.

"You're the pharmacist, tell me what I need, and I'll drive to Waterloo and slip it into his coffee." Daniel wasn't entirely sure that he was joking.

Steven smiled and tipped his head back to see Daniel's face. "You and Stephanie think alike." Steven pushed away from Daniel and sat facing him. "I went back to school and fell apart. If it wasn't for Steph, I would have flunked out. She flew out to Waterloo and stayed with me. She got me drunk and then got me to class. She told me he was a douchebag, and a controlling sadist. She got me the name of a therapist and made me go."

Steven looked at Daniel, a smile tilting his lips, laughter brightening his dark eyes. "The last week before she went back home, she staged a reign of terror. Every day when I came home from class, she would greet me with some horrible thing she had done to him." He laughed, and Daniel had never been so happy to hear anything in his life. "She slashed his tires and spray painted his front door. She had twenty pizzas delivered to his house at two in the morning. She snuck into one of the stores, posing as a cleaning lady, and broke into the files. She copied some Bell statements, and as the *pièce de résistance*, just before she flew back home, she had telephone service cancelled to all three locations." He grinned at Daniel. "I took her to the airport myself. I wanted to be sure she got on the plane. I was so worried she'd be arrested that I stopped feeling sorry for myself for a few hours."

Tucking one hand under Daniel's leg, Steven ran his fingers over the calf muscles he loved. "It was almost a year before I could be with anyone. When I finally got my head in a better place, there were a few friends with benefits, nice guys. We still keep in contact. Hookups when I needed the release." Steven shrugged. "I graduated, moved here, and met you." Looking at Daniel, his tilted smile stayed on his lips but his eyes got serious. "I don't change myself for anyone, not any more. I won't, not even for you. I can't."

Daniel's heart hurt, literally. Blood pulsed in his ears, tears stuck in his throat, and his chest was tight. He pushed away from the pillows, locking eyes with Steven. "You don't have to change for me." He reached for his boyfriend's shoulders, dragging him close, rolling over and tucking Steven under him. "You know what I thought the first time I saw you standing at Sandy's door? I thought you were perfect. I still call you that," Daniel tapped his temple, "in here, I call you Mr. Perfect."

Steven's smile turned into a full-out grin. "You do not!"

Daniel shrugged, but he held Steven's eyes, not taking anything back. "Yeah, I do. I'm not saying you are perfect, don't get all puffed up. I'm just saying I think you're perfect."

Steven laughed, and touched Daniel's face with tender fingers. "Even when I make you skate in the cold?"

Daniel nodded. "Yeah."

"Even when I'm a little dictatorial between the sheets?"

Daniel grinned. "Hell, yes!"

"Even when I redecorate your bedroom?"

"Nice try!" Daniel shook his head, laughter threading through his voice. "The only thing you're touching in my bedroom is me."

Steven stared up at Daniel; searching, looking for...He didn't know what he was looking for exactly. He had never told anyone about his experience with the pharmacist from hell, anyone but Stephanie. Not even his parents knew. Even now, after the therapy and the years, Steven still thought he should have been stronger, smarter. It had taken a long time to forgive himself, to put it behind him. He didn't want Daniel to see him as defective somehow, less. Searching Daniel's face, looking into his eyes, that's what he was looking for, disappointment, disapproval, disgust, but he didn't find it. Looking up at Daniel, he found a man who wanted him, him, not some hypothetical version of him, but him, just the way he was.

Propping himself up on one arm, Daniel pushed a hand through Steven's hair and tugged, smiling when Steven's hair thing kicked in, and the man hardened under him. *Yeah, Steven was fucking perfect just the way he was!* Snapping his hips, he ground against the man in his arms. *Perfect!*

Steven clenched his hands into Daniel's ass cheeks and pulled, spreading him open. Daniel tugged on Steven's hair again and Steven arched into him. They thrust against each other, cocks trapped between their bodies, sliding together, slick with pre-cum and body heat. Steven circled Daniel's hole, tapping, asking. Daniel bent his head and took Steven's mouth, eating at his lips, breathing 'yes' into his mouth. Steven pushed his finger in, and Daniel tightened his fist in Steven's hair, pulling hard.

They made a satisfying mess. Exhaustion, more from the emotional trip back in time than any physical exertion, crashed down on them. One minute they were stretching against each other, smiling and laughing, arguing about who was going to get up to get a warm facecloth. The next they were comatose, still locked in each other's arms.

CHAPTER 16

Snowshoes and Dogsleds

Steven, as usual, woke before Daniel. Leaving his boyfriend buried in a pile of blankets, he dragged the hotel robe on, and padded into the *en suite*. Brushing his teeth, he considered the decadent shower but elected to wait for Daniel. He'd feel lost in there by himself. Staring in the mirror, he stroked his jaw and decided that vacation meant he didn't have to shave.

He needed coffee, like now! Acting on the assumption that any resort thoughtful enough to provide champagne would be smart enough to know that caffeine addicts needed their morning fix, he checked the cabinet beside the flat screen and yes! Playing with filters and tearing open packets, he made two coffees. Adding sugar to Daniel's, he carried them both over to the night table on his side of the bed. Crossing the room, feet silent on the thick carpet, he pulled the curtains open, letting in snow, and trees, and sun. Smiling at the perfect winter scene, he piled his pillows against the headboard and crawled back into bed, tucking the duvet around him. Coffee in hand, Daniel at his side, nothing to do, and nowhere to go; life just didn't get any better than this!

"Ugh!" Eyes still closed, Daniel turned away from the window. "Who let the sun in?"

Steven picked up Daniel's mug and held it out towards his not-quite-awake boyfriend, letting the aroma of coffee speak for him.

Daniel's eyes blinked open, hand automatically reaching for the elixir of life. "Coffee?"

Steven pulled the mug out of reach. "Uh-uh, sit up first."

Stretching, moaning and shoving his hair out of his eyes, Daniel pushed himself back against the headboard and held out his hand. Smiling, because really only Daniel could take something as simple as waking up and turn it into a major production, Steven gave the man his coffee. Sitting back against his pillows, he sipped at his own brew and waited for Daniel to work his way to coherent.

"God, it's quiet." Daniel stared out the window at snow, and snow, and more snow. It felt like he and Steven were the only two people in the world.

"Mmmm." Steven finished his coffee, put his mug on the night table and slid down the bed. He wrapped himself around Daniel, pushing the duvet away and laying his head in Daniel's lap.

Daniel played with Steven's hair, as he sipped his coffee. "We should do this more often."

"Take vacations?"

"Well, that too, sure. But, I meant, this; lying in bed together, taking our time, not rushing about first thing in the morning."

Steven snorted. "This from the man who starts his day at ten!"

"Yeah, but you're not there." He slid his hand across Steven's shoulders and down his back. "This is better."

"Yeah, it is." Yes, it was, Steven thought, his arm wrapped around Daniel's thighs. This was better, this was everything.

Daniel drank his coffee, his free hand playing in Steven's hair and over his skin. Steven's fingers traced patterns on Daniel's thighs. They were quiet together, wrapped in warmth and each other. Eventually, Daniel sipped his way to some smattering of energy and put his empty mug down on the night table. "I need the washroom." He shifted out from under Steven's head and slipped out of bed. He didn't bother with the hotel robe and Steven appreciated that omission, really, really appreciated it, until the *en suite* door closed between them.

Wondering about the weather, Steven turned the bedside radio on and "Joy to the World" surged into the room. *Right! It's Christmas.* By the time Daniel came out of the washroom, Steven was singing along to "Grandma Got Run Over by a Reindeer".

"That is one serious shower." Daniel grabbed his bag off the floor and tossed it on the bed. "I hope it comes with an instruction booklet. Did you see all the nozzles on that wall?" Rummaging through his bag until his hand closed on a wrapped box, he looked across the bed at Steven. "Close your eyes."

Seeing that Daniel's hand was still inside his bag, obviously hiding something, Steven snapped his eyes shut, a smile spreading across his face. "What did you do?"

Tossing his bag back on the floor, Daniel sat on the bed beside Steven and put the present in his hands. "Happy Christmas!"

Steven blinked down at the red wrapping and green plaid ribbon. "Daniel, you didn't have to do this."

"Yeah, yeah." Daniel gave that remark all the attention it deserved. "Open it!"

Steven, being Steven, took his time un-wrapping his gift, folding the paper neatly. "We already exchanged gifts at Hanukkah." Not opening the box, he looked at Daniel. "I feel terrible. I don't have anything for you."

"Really?" Daniel leered at Steven. "I'm pretty sure you do."

"Asshole!" Still laughing, Steven opened the box and moved the tissue aside. "Oh!" He reached into the box and carefully lifted out an Inuit carving in soapstone, two huskies waiting beside a sled. "It's beautiful." Steven ran his fingers over the dark stone, cool to the touch, smooth.

"I didn't know what to get you. I saw this at a gallery downtown and I thought…"

"It's beautiful. It's us and this." Steven waved his hand indicating both the room and the whole vacation. "I can hold the memory in my hands." Steven leaned over the small sculpture and kissed Daniel. "Thank you."

Daniel stretched out on his side, his head resting in his hand, watching Steven pack the dogs carefully back into their box. "I thought it was a little more original than getting you a snowman."

Steven set his gift on the night stand and climbed on top of Daniel, smiling down at him. He was truly touched at the thought Daniel had put into this present because he knew that shopping was not Daniel's idea of a good time. "It's beautiful, and I love it, and you're still getting on the real thing tomorrow."

"Crap!"

*   *   *

Their morning was perfect, their afternoon, not so much.

"We're lost." Steven stopped trudging behind Daniel and scanned the snow draped forest around them, looking for something, anything that would tell him where the hell they were.

"No, we're not." Daniel turned, his snowshoes leaving web shapes in the snow.

"We're going in circles. I told you we should have taken a map."

"Like a map would help. Do you see any street signs?" Daniel didn't know exactly where they were, but he wasn't too worried about it. "We just have to follow the path markers."

"Well that's the problem isn't it?" Steven glared at his boyfriend. "We've run out of markers, and these fucking trees all look the same." *They were going to end up on the six o'clock news, 'Two men missing at Maple Hill.'* Daniel was not Steven's favourite person right now.

Daniel laughed. "If it all looks the same, what makes you think we're going in circles?"

"I don't know." Steven threw his hands out in frustration. "Because I'm getting dizzy!"

Daniel grinned. Apparently, Steven's need to keep everything in its place extended to himself. Daniel wasn't at all surprised to find that his boyfriend craved the comfort of a paper grid. He understood the unease behind Steven's snippy sarcasm. And, of course, a flustered Steven hiding his nervous behind a veneer of annoyance, his chocolate eyes spitting aggravation at Daniel, was just way too cute! "Hey, I'm the over-protected Jewish prince. You're the one with the outdoor creds."

Steven glared at Daniel. "We went camping in the summer! With maps!"

Padding back through the snow to stand beside Steven, taking care not to trip over their snowshoes, Daniel put his arm around his disgruntled boyfriend. "Don't worry, I won't let the bears get you."

Not amused, Steven stepped out from under Daniel's arm. "I will. I'll say, 'There he is. Chew on him. He's the one who said we didn't need a map.'"

Daniel laughed as Steven turned his back on him and stomped off through the snow. Following in the webbed tracks his boyfriend indented into the pristine white, Daniel inhaled the beauty around them. "This is amazing. It's like walking through one of those pictures in a tourism video, you know, The Great White North!"

Steven stopped walking and shoved his annoyance aside long enough for him to see what Daniel saw; snow-covered fir trees and stark-branched maples stretched unendingly before them, a world carpeted in white, the snow sparkling like diamonds where the winter sun caressed it. "You're right. It's incredible!" He turned and smiled at Daniel, eyes laughing. "And if we don't find a marker in the next ten minutes, I'm going to push you over a cliff and leave you there 'til spring!"

Eyes scanning every tree trunk, looking for the painted paw prints that were their markers, they walked in near silence. The only sound the rustle of their clothing and the 'shush' of the snowshoes.

"Daniel!" Steven's voice was a soft gasp, as his arm reached back for his boyfriend.

Daniel held Steven's arm as he froze beside him. "I see them." He spoke in a whisper.

They stood absolutely still, hardly daring to breathe. Directly ahead, not more than fifteen meters away, three deer stood atop a small ridge. Majestic, they surveyed their realm, and then at some unknown signal, they turned as one and loped off into the forest, fleet and graceful.

"Okay, that you don't see in the city." Daniel's voice was filled with awe.

"Totally worth being lost in the arctic." Steven grinned, suddenly ridiculously pleased with the universe, with his life, with the man standing in the snow beside him.

Returning Steven's grin, Daniel took the lead. "Arctic! We're like two hours north of the city." He turned to look at Steven. "And we're not lost."

Daniel was right. They weren't lost. Steven was both happy that they weren't going to lose any toes to frostbite and pissed that Daniel had been right. They found a plethora of path markers: blue, red, and yellow-painted paw prints. Following the red markers, they ended up back at the main building, starving, just as the setting sun was painting blue shadows on the snow. Stuffing gloves into their pockets and unzipping their coats, they waited for the hostess to find them a table. "This way, please, gentlemen."

Hanging his coat on the back of his chair, Steven checked his watch, as he took his seat. "It gets dark so quickly up here."

Daniel opened his menu. "No neon lights." Deciding on the gnocchi, he snapped his menu shut. "They should give you little badges, you know, 'I survived Maple Hill'."

"Please!" Steven rolled his eyes. "We went for a walk in the snow, on the grounds of the resort. We didn't trek the Himalayas."

"Big talk from the man who wanted to call out the RCMP." Teasing lights danced in Daniel's eyes.

"I wouldn't think of bothering the RCMP." Steven looked up from his menu, tilted smile lurking at the side of his mouth. "Isn't there an army base around here?"

"Why?" Daniel leaned across the table and took Steven's hand. "Looking for a guy in uniform?"

Steven stared at Daniel, his eyes flicking over his shoulders, and down his body, picturing all those luscious muscles covered by a dress uniform, the blond hair glinting under the peak of a military cap. "Not just any guy, no."

Smirking at the expression on Steven's face, Daniel patted his hand and sat back in his chair. "I am not enlisting for you, Monaco."

Steven didn't want to give up a perfectly good fantasy. "Halloween then? Air Force for you, I think, Navy for me?" He winked at Daniel.

"Or, I could wear a nurse's uniform? You know, like that 1945 Victory Kiss in Times Square, the sailor kissing the nurse? What do you think?"

Daniel stared at Steven, seeing himself in uniform bending Steven over his arm, Steven in nurse's whites. Heat ran up the back of his neck, and his cock twitched. Averting his eyes, he coughed, and his hands suddenly got very busy arranging his cutlery. *Yeah Daniel, what do you think?* "We'll see."

Hiding his smile, Steven signaled the waitress. Daniel was so damn cute when he was flustered.

Their dinner, like everything else at the resort, was excellent, not that Daniel noticed. He was too busy picking at his gnocchi, hoping for an avalanche or a blizzard, anything that would mean a cancellation of the tour Steven had booked for tomorrow. "So, what time is this dogsled thing tomorrow?"

"Try not to be so enthusiastic. I booked for the afternoon." He leered at Daniel. "I've got plans for the morning."

Daniel pretended to misunderstand. "Oh, you want to use the gym here?"

Steven pushed his knee into Daniel's under the table. "I have every intention of giving you a work out, yes."

Whatever response Daniel intended to make was interrupted by their waitress. "Would you like to see our dessert menu?" She smiled at both men as she refilled their coffee cups.

Glancing across the table at each other, they turned as one, and answered in unison. "Ice cream."

The waitress laughed. "All our iced desserts are made locally, exclusively for Maple Hill. This week's flavours are chocolate-cappuccino and caramel-peanut butter ice creams, raspberry and hazelnut gelati, and a green tea sorbet. They're all excellent. We've had guests buy coolers for their cars so they can bring their favourites home. Would you like to try something?"

Another shared glance, but this time Steven answered for both of them. "Chocolate-cappuccino."

From their table, they looked down on the fairytale-perfect skating rink, glowing against the dark of the winter night, ice gleaming under the lights, guests gliding gracefully or not so gracefully on flashing blades. A woman, dark hair escaping from under her hat, was trying to teach her boyfriend to skate. Daniel laughed with Steven. "We didn't look much better last night."

"No. Team Canada isn't going to be calling us anytime soon." Steven looked at Daniel. "We could give it another try?"

Daniel moved his leg under the table, brushing Steven's knee. "You want me to kiss you under the trees again?"

"Nope." Steven grinned and pressed his leg into Steven's. "I want to kiss you under the trees."

"Or, we could stay inside where it's warm, sit in front of that gigantic fireplace in the lounge, and you could buy me a drink?"

"Enjoy!" Their waitress placed an artfully designed plate of ice cream in front of each of them.

"Thanks." The waitress whisked herself away, as they picked up their spoons.

"Or," Steven dug into his dessert, "we can stay inside where it's warm, sit in front of that gigantic fireplace in the lounge, I can buy you a drink..." He licked his spoon suggestively and leered at Daniel. "And, I can feel you up under the table."

Grinning, Daniel pointed his spoon at Steven. "That's what I'm saying!"

Steven did not feel Daniel up under the table. Daniel did not take advantage of the intimate mood lighting in the lounge to fondle any part of Steven's anatomy. They sat in leather club chairs, drinks in hand, facing a small dais, and listened to the ubiquitous piano player.

The pianist talked between songs, an arsenal of jokes that he'd perfected over the years. He encouraged people to sing along with him, and a few voices emerged hesitantly from the audience. Most Canadians would rather enlist in the next tour of Afghanistan than sing in public, at least until a surfeit of liquor erased their inhibitions. Abandoning the rather lame sing-along, the pianist segued into a series of slow ballads. A couple, here and there, took a turn on the small dance floor.

The intro to an old Elvis song, one his father used to sing, had Steven looking from the dance floor to his boyfriend. Daniel read the question in Steven's glance, and held his hand out. What the hell? If anyone was offended, they could leave. As paying guests, Steven and he had just as much right to dance as anyone else.

Smiling, Steven rose from his chair, took Daniel's hand in his and led him to the dance floor. Swaying slowly together, Daniel thought that it was worth any fallout to see Steven this happy.

The pianist kept playing, and no one stalked out of the lounge in disgust. An older couple, probably in their late sixties joined them on the dance floor. Catching Daniel's eye, the woman smiled. "Aren't you guys a little young for Elvis?"

"My dad's a big fan." Steven smiled at the couple.

Her husband nodded. "This is old enough to be elevator music."

"Can't beat the classics." Daniel smiled at these people who didn't seem to care that two men were dancing together.

The woman laughed, and patted her husband's arm. "That's us, Michael, classics!" Her husband twirled her under his outstretched arm, and they moved away. The pianist crooned the chorus, and Daniel laid his head on Steven's shoulder.

Walking back to their room, Steven dragged Daniel off the path into a cluster of trees, Daniel muttering a litany of complaints. "There's something seriously wrong with you, you know that, right? It's freaking cold out here and we've got a..."

Steven pushed Daniel back against a tree trunk. "Shut up." He leaned in, and Daniel sighed into his mouth, tirade forgotten. They were both dressed for the cold, not a lot of skin was available, but Steven worked with what he had. He kissed along Daniel's jaw, and nibbled at the inch of neck that was exposed above his coat collar. Frustrated, he bit just behind Daniel's ear, and Daniel jerked in surprise, shaking the branches above him. A light powder of snow cascaded over them both.

Laughing, they pulled away from each other. Steven brushed snow off Daniel's shoulders. "Okay, maybe you were right."

"Maybe?" Daniel smirked at his boyfriend. "Maybe I was right?" Turning, they headed back onto the brick walkway that led to their room. "I'm always right. Who said we weren't lost this morning, huh?"

Steven shoved his shoulder into Daniel. "We were lost, you just got lucky."

"I knew exactly where we were."

"You did not!" Steven swiped his key card and opened the door to their room. "You had no freaking idea."

Daniel hung the Do Not Disturb sign, closed the door and pushed Steven back against it. "Maybe, just maybe," he unzipped Steven's parka, "we were a little bit lost." Dragging the coat off Steven's shoulders, he tossed it behind him. Pressing into his boyfriend, he bit at Steven's lower lip. He tapped Steven's thigh, and Steven spread his legs. "But it's exciting not knowing what's going to happen next, being just a little bit lost." Daniel ground into Steven; he wasn't talking about snowshoeing anymore.

Steven tipped his head back against the door and arched into his boyfriend. "Yesss."

Locking his eyes with Steven's, Daniel invoked their code. "My house."

Steven ran his hands down Daniel's back, and palmed his ass. "Your house."

Stepping back, Daniel grabbed the hem of Steven's sweater and pulled it up, over his head, and off. Head bent, fingers unfastening Steven's shirt buttons, he flashed Steven a dark look from under his eyelashes. "I'm going to make you scream."

Steven swallowed and his eyes went wide, almost black, with need. His hands clawed at Daniel's sweater. "Yes!"

Steven writhed, and moaned, and pleaded, and when Daniel finally slammed into him, he screamed.

❊　　❊　　❊

The next morning, Steven sat back against his mound of pillows watching as Daniel made their coffee, and brought both mugs over to Steven's side of the bed. "I feel like some medieval king, or Eastern prince."

Daniel snorted out a laugh. "What does that make me, you're harem boy?"

Steven smiled as he took the mug Daniel held out to him, letting his eyes wander his boyfriend's body. "Can't say I don't like that idea."

Daniel sipped his coffee. "Yeah?"

Steven grinned and leered at Daniel. "Yeah."

"Then shouldn't I be doing this?" Daniel put his mug down on the night table, and kneeling beside the bed, he bowed his head.

Oh, my God! Steven clutched his mug, suddenly feeling his pulse everywhere, blood pounding at his wrists and in his ears, and pouring into his cock.

Keeping his head lowered, Daniel flashed a look up, and laughed out loud at the mixture of lust and shock on Steven's face. Rising to his feet he took the mug out of Steven's hands and placed it beside his own. "You looked like you were going to drop it." Sitting cross legged on the bed, he smirked at Steven. "Should have known you'd have a dominance kink."

Steven shook his head, face flushed, eyes still wide. "I didn't know. I've never done any role play. I had no idea." He stared at his boyfriend. "You looked so fucking hot like that!"

Daniel crawled over Steven's legs, and lay down on his back beside him. "So, you want me to kneel for you, huh?"

Steven tried to read Daniel's eyes. "Not if you don't want to."

"Well, if you're going to keep looking at me like I'm sex on a plate." Daniel grinned and Steven sagged with relief. "You should see your face. Stop worrying so much. I'm a big boy; I can say no if I want to."

Steven slid down the mattress, tucking himself against Daniel, hiding his face in his boyfriend's neck. "You must think I'm such a perv."

Daniel threaded his fingers through Steven's hair, closed his fist, and tugged. Steven reacted the way he always did; his eyes closed and he melted into Daniel, thrusting his cock against Daniel's thigh. "I think you're my perv."

❖ ❖ ❖

The twenty minute minibus ride to Northern Experience, the dogsled tour company, was just enough time for Daniel to think himself into a what-the-fuck-am-I-doing frame of mind. Staring out the window, he concentrated on not imagining all the ways this could go so horribly wrong.

The bus turned into a gravel courtyard and they could hear the dogs barking. The side door on the minibus slid open and the canine noise became inescapable. Steven grinned at him, eyes dancing with excitement, and Daniel smiled in spite of himself.

"Mr. Fine, Mr. Monaco?" A man with a clipboard called names off a list. "Okay, we're all here. Welcome to Northern Experience. It's a beautiful day, the dogs are raring to go, and whether this is your first time or your twenty-first time, we're going to make sure you have fun. I'm Sam; I'm going to be your guide today. If you all just go on inside to take care of the paper work, and then come back out here, I'll set you up with your sleds."

Waiting behind a family with two teenagers, Daniel dug his wallet out of his parka and turned to Steven. "You realize if I end up in the hospital, you're the one who'll have to tell my family, right?"

Steven rolled his eyes. "Nothing's going to happen to you. We've got a guide, and the dogs probably know the route blindfolded." Steven pulled his own wallet out. "Let me get this, you paid for the snowshoes yesterday."

Daniel took his credit card out. "You paid for dinner last night, my turn."

Steven frowned. "But I asked you, I wanted to take you away for a few days."

"You did." Daniel handed his card to the woman behind the desk and grinned at Steven. "And I may never forgive you."

His gloved fingers tight around the handles of his sled, his boots planted firmly on the skids, Daniel waited in line with everyone else as the staff checked the dogs' harnesses. The instructions had been simple; it sounded easy enough. Daniel was just starting to think that maybe he could do this when Sam yelled "Mush", and one after another the dog teams took off, and the sleds went flying!

Steven screamed a high-pitched shriek of surprise as his sled jerked and careened down the slope of the courtyard, his dogs anxious to catch up with the others. Daniel's laugh cut off abruptly as his own sled jumped into the race. Holding on, his legs braced against the skids, his hands gripping the handles, snow flying under the dogs' paws and trees whipping by, Daniel felt like he was on an amusement park ride. Not good, rides and he, not a good mix! Fortunately for the contents of his stomach, once the initial burst of speed dissipated, the dogs settled into a more moderate running speed. Steven was right; the dogs knew where they were going. Daniel didn't have to worry about 'driving' them. He could concentrate on the thrill of the experience, the beauty of the landscape, and not falling off. Of the three, not falling off had top priority.

At the mid-way point, Sam called a halt. Staff waited for them, ready with steaming mugs of hot chocolate. Steven hopped off his sled and ran back to where Daniel's dogs were bringing his sled to a stop. "Isn't this great?"

Daniel stepped off his sled, legs a little stiff, balance a little off. "Yes. I have to admit, it's probably one of those things everyone should have on their bucket list."

"Yeah, like skydiving, and hang gliding, and swimming with dolphins."

Daniel stared at his boyfriend. "I'm not going skydiving, don't even think about it."

Steven just grinned. "Maybe one…"

Daniel shook his head. "No, no day, never."

"So, what do you think? You guys okay?" Sam handed each of them a hot chocolate.

"This is the best thing I've done on vacation, ever." Steven blew on his drink.

"Yeah, we hear that a lot, which is great because that's what we're trying to do, give you a unique experience."

"How long have you been doing this?" Daniel couldn't imagine how someone wandered into this kind of work.

"I've been with this company for three years. I came to dogsledding as a hobby about ten years ago. I bought a Huskie. They're smart, high energy dogs. A walk around the block after work isn't enough for them. My vet suggested getting into dogsledding and I never looked back."

"Sam?" One of the teenagers, a girl about fourteen, had questions about the dogs, and Sam excused himself.

"Okay, no skydiving. But we can come back here next year, right?" Steven smiled, lips tilting into kissable.

"If I can make it through the afternoon without falling off the sled, or mangling myself in the harnesses, then yes, you can drag me back here next year."

Daniel heard his own words with a shock of did-I-just-say-that? Eyes wide, he looked at Steven. *Did you hear that?* Steven smiled and tipped Daniel's mouth closed with one gloved finger. *Yes, I heard that.*

"Okay, people, the dogs are ready." Sam called out and everyone started back to their sleds.

Daniel and Steven handed their mugs to a young woman wearing a hat shaped like a maple leaf. Steven nudged Daniel as they walked to their sleds. "You okay?"

Daniel thought about it. His blood was zinging around a bit but it didn't feel like terror. It felt like anticipation. He had said the words 'next year' and he was still standing. Apparently, he had no problem planning a future with someone, as long as that someone was Steven.

"Yeah, I'm okay." He smiled at the man who had become his future. "I'm good."

"Excellent." Steven bumped his shoulder into Daniel's. "Then, this summer, we can go hang gliding."

Daniel swatted at Steven's ass, or where Steven's ass should be under the parka. "No, we can't."

Despite Daniel's every expectation, he got through the whole tour without getting tangled in the rigging that attached the dogs to the sled, or falling off the runners, and he had the pictures to prove it! They made it back to their room, a little cold, a lot tired, but all in one piece. Steven unlocked their door and Daniel headed straight for the hot tub. Three hours of hanging onto a dogsled, fearing for life and limb, had his leg and arm muscles twitching. He turned the hot tub taps on full blast and started to strip. Tossing his coat and boots, he pulled his sweater over his head and found Steven leaning against the locked door watching him. "Enjoying the view?"

"I am." Steven followed Daniel's hands as they played with the button over his fly.

Daniel popped the button, and deciding to play the tease, he let his fingers hover over the zipper. "Not exactly the one advertised on the Maple Hill brochures."

Steven shrugged away from the door and tossed his coat on the bench by the bed. "No, it's not." He crossed the room and, pushing Daniel's hand away, lowered the zipper himself. "Let's keep it that way." Steven curled his fingers into Daniel's waistband, grabbing both jeans and boxers. One quick tug and Daniel was in his hands. Steven watched Daniel slide through his fist, the head of his cock pink and perfect. Glancing up to meet Daniel's eyes, Steven teased. "Pretty in pink."

Daniel tried to look affronted, but it was hard to feel insulted when Steven was palming the head of his cock. "I am not wearing women's underwear for you."

Steven laughed and moved his free hand to cup Daniel's sac. "No, I wasn't thinking Victoria's Secret. *Pretty in Pink*, it's an old movie title." Steven used both hands, working his lover's shaft and balls. Daniel's eyes slid shut, and he widened his legs as far as the jeans still hugging his thighs would allow. "Although, now that you mention it, you would look…"

Daniel's eyes snapped open. "Finish that sentence and you're going into the hot tub, head first."

Laughing, Steven released Daniel with one soft pat to his balls. He sat on the bed to unlace his boots, tossed them aside, and stripped quickly. Daniel was so focused on watching his lover's body emerge from under all the winter layers that he forgot the water was still running.

"Shit!" He twisted the taps to off, and hit the button for the whirlpool. Leaving his clothes in a pile by the side of the tub, he stepped into the heated welcome of the water. Slipping onto the molded seat, pulsing jets of comfort massaging everywhere, he sighed in satisfaction. Head back, resting on the rim of the tub, eyes closed, he heard Steven's hum of pleasure as he too stepped into the tub.

Steven relaxed into the water. "Hmmm. Too bad we have to get out soon."

Daniel didn't bother opening his eyes. "Who says?"

"We're going to get hungry."

Daniel rolled his shoulders under the jets of water. "Room service."

"You can't eat dinner in a hot tub!" Steven sounded scandalized.

Daniel opened his eyes and smiled at the horror in Steven's voice. "We could eat in front of the fireplace, in our robes. That way we won't have to get dressed." He leered at Steven. "Saves time."

"Lech!"

"Perv!"

Steven laughed and sank deeper into the water. "That's me." He hadn't been lying this morning, that whole harem boy thing had taken him by surprise. He had never even thought of anything like that, and had no idea that he would find it so fucking hot! There was something he did know about himself though, something he had never thought he could share with anyone. But Daniel's easy acceptance this morning and, even more, his reaction yesterday to Steven's suggestion of wearing a nurse's uniform…maybe, he could share this with Daniel. Sinking lower into the steaming water, he stared at the blond across the tub. *Maybe, one day…*

CHAPTER 17

Making it Work

"Call your mother." Steven turned the radio down, and checked his side view mirror before switching lanes.

Daniel turned to look at the man behind the wheel. The man who had woken him up early, not that he was complaining. "I can call her when I get home." No, he so wasn't complaining about that!

"You could, but you won't. You'll forget."

Daniel pulled his phone out, because yeah, Steven was right. He probably would forget. He scrolled through his contact list and hit call. "Ma we're…"

"Daniel! We'll be right there. What hospital are you in?"

"Ma we're…"

"It's not serious, is it? You didn't break anything?"

"Ma! I'm fine. I'm not in a hospital. We're on the 400 heading home. I'm fine."

Julia was silent for a moment. "Really? Let me talk to Steven."

Daniel rolled his eyes and hit speaker, holding the phone out to Steven.

"Julia, he's fine. Nothing even scratched. We had a great time."

They could hear Julia's sigh of relief. "Oh, that's so good to hear. I've been worried about you two all weekend. Steven, thank you for calling."

"Hey, I was the one who called!" Daniel felt he deserved some credit.

"Right!" Julia knew damn well who was responsible for the call. "See you Friday. Bring pictures."

"Bye, Julia." "Bye, Ma."

Daniel slipped his phone back into his pocket. He sat silent for a while, the traffic flowing by unseen as he thought about the weekend. "Thank you." He turned to Steven. "This was a good idea, more interesting than sitting on a beach."

"We can do the island thing too." Steven leered at Daniel. "I'm not averse to ogling you in the sun, or rubbing lotion all over you."

Daniel laughed. "All over me?"

Steven grinned. "Nude beach." Taking the exit onto the 401, he glanced over at Daniel. "You want me to drop you off at your place?"

"Yeah, I'll check my calendar and emails, grab some clean clothes, and meet you back at your place for dinner."

"You know, all this packing overnight bags, juggling our cars, deciding whose place we're sleeping at… why don't we just move in together?"

The question wasn't quite as spontaneous as Steven wanted it to appear. He had actually been thinking about this a lot. Economically, it made a lot of sense. They spent most of their time together anyway, why pay for two places? Saving a few dollars on rent was not the motivating factor behind his suggestion though. There was only one reason, and that reason was sitting beside him in the passenger seat, all blond hair and hazel eyes. Steven wanted a life with Daniel, and that meant living together. He had wanted this for a while now, but he hadn't thought that Daniel was ready to hear it. He glanced over at his boyfriend. *Are you ready? Do you want this, want me?*

Daniel stared at Steven, too surprised to say anything.

Steven took in Daniel's shell-shocked expression and quickly focused on the cars around him. "Just a thought, it's not a deal breaker. If you don't like the idea, no problem." Steven sent his boyfriend another swift look. "Think about it."

Daniel thought about it. His stomach twisting into a twitching knot of nerves, his 'Aidan baggage' screaming in the back of his mind, he thought about it. He had sworn to himself that he'd never live with anyone ever again. But, this was Steven, and they were practically living together already. As much as it made his heart go into overdrive with terror to admit it, he loved Steven, and he wanted a future with him. With this man, he wanted everything. "So, what are you thinking? That I move into your place?"

Oh, thank God! Steven's hands unclamped from their death grip on the steering wheel. He tried to rein in the excitement sizzling just under his skin, Daniel hadn't said yes, yet. "That makes the most sense, I think. You're place is too small, and I've got that extra bedroom that you can use as an office."

Daniel snorted. "You mean I'd better keep all my writing mess in that room, so it doesn't explode all over your dining room table?"

Steven grinned. "It sounded better the way I said it, but yes."

"I don't know, Steven. I'm totally incapable of putting anything in its place. I don't even understand how things have a place. You know I can never find my keys. That's going to make you crazy."

"Yes, it will." Steven smiled across the seat at the man sitting beside him. "I'm pathologically neat. I organize and label and sort. That's going to drive you nuts."

"Yeah." Daniel nodded and smiled at the man he still thought of as Mr. Perfect. "We're going to fight a lot."

"Probably." Steven took one hand off the steering wheel, and reached out to Daniel. "Is that a yes?"

Daniel took Steven's hand, twining their fingers together. "Yes."

❀ ❀ ❀

Condo sales were slow so Daniel decided to rent his place. A posting on the in-house bulletin boards of the magazines he free-lanced with, a few emails to editors, and it was done. Writers were a peripatetic group; someone was always relocating somewhere. Within hours, inquiries lit up his inbox. He chose a woman from New Brunswick because she needed a place right away and she wanted it furnished, which saved Daniel a lot of aggravation. His furniture was a collection of cast-offs from his sisters, not anything he would even consider bringing into Steven's perfectly colour-coordinated haven. In a matter of hours, he had emailed pictures of his place along with a contract, and received a scanned signature along with the first month's rent via electronic deposit.

In the first week of January, before he had time to digest the reality of it, Daniel found himself packing up his old life and starting a new one. Dropping an empty cardboard box by his bed, he pulled his closet door open. Grabbing armloads of shirts and pants, he tossed them, hangers and all, into the empty box.

Steven gasped in horror and reached into the box, rescuing the topmost shirt, and cradling it to his chest as if it was some hurt child. "This is your idea of packing?"

"Yeah." Daniel grabbed another stack of hangers. "Why?" He looked from Steven to the packing box, and back. He didn't see the problem. His clothes had to go from point A to point B, no big deal.

"Oh, my God!" Steven took the shirt he was holding and the clothes in Daniel's hands and laid them out on the bed. Bending over the packing box, he pulled out the rest of the clothes Daniel had tossed in. Shaking them out, he placed them with their fellows on the bed. "You go box up the other rooms. I'll do this."

Daniel watched as Steven methodically emptied his closet, placing everything on the bed. "There was something wrong with the way I was doing it?"

Steven whirled to face Daniel, the "Well, duh?" ready to slide off his tongue, but one look at his boyfriend had him wrestling the words back into his mouth. *No way! We're not having an argument, not today, not when Daniel is freaking out over the move and could still back out of the whole idea.*

Daniel was both annoyed and absurdly hurt by Steven's criticism. Rationally, he knew this was just Steven's symptomatic neatness kicking in, but it felt like a personal attack. The words, 'It's none of your fucking business how I pack my own clothes, asshole', huddled just behind his lips.

They stared at each other over the empty packing box, and Steven seemed to pick the words right out of Daniel's brain. "You're right. They're your clothes, not my business." He walked around the box, leaving the room and its contents to Daniel. "I'll check through the kitchen and see if there's anything..."

Daniel grabbed him before he could leave the room, burrowing into him, burying his face in Steven's neck. "I'm sorry."

Steven smiled as he soothed a hand down Daniel's back. "What are you sorry for? I'm the one who was being an ass."

Daniel pulled his head back, so that he could see Steven's face. "No, I overreacted. I know it was the mess you didn't like, not…" Daniel didn't finish that thought, he couldn't. It scared the shit out of him.

Steven's eyes went wide as he connected the dots. "Not you?! How the fuck can you even think that?" He held Daniel's shoulders, meeting his eyes. "Daniel, just so you know. You can leave your towels on the washroom floor, you can miss the hamper when you aim your socks at it, you can never, ever remember to hang up your coat, and I'm still going to want you in my life."

Daniel read the sincerity in Steven's eyes, and a slow smirk teased at his lips. "I can?"

Steven grinned, and slid his hand down to palm Daniel's ass. "I don't know. Can I spank you whenever you forget to put something away?"

Daniel's mouth gaped open, as he stared at Steven in shock. Chuckling at his reaction, Steven placed one finger under his chin and tipped his mouth shut. "I'm kidding."

Daniel backed up, out of Steven's arms and motioned to the packing box and the clothes on the bed. "You deal with this and I'll pack up the rest of my stuff."

Steven turned to the closet as Daniel walked out of the bedroom. He picked up a pair of runners and Daniel's one pair of dress shoes and arranged them neatly in the bottom of the packing box.

"Steven?"

Steven looked up from the box to find Daniel standing in the doorway. "Yeah?"

"Just so you know, domestic discipline, not going to happen. But, if you're very, very nice to me," Daniel turned and tossed the next words over his shoulder as he left the room, "we can talk about the spanking thing."

Smiling to himself, Steven bent to gather the rest of the shoes in Daniel's closet. *Oh, yeah, Daniel moving in was a fan-fucking-tastic idea!*

In the dining room, Daniel assembled a box, folding the ends into each other and taping the bottom. Putting the box on the floor beside the dining room table, he swept his arm over the tabletop, and knocked everything into its waiting depths. Grinning to himself, he surveyed the resultant mess. *Steven would have a heart attack!* He shut his laptop down, unplugged it, wrapped the black cable around it, and placed it and his wireless mouse into the box. Walking into the adjourning living room, he looked around trying to decide what to take. He grabbed pictures of his niece and nephew off the shelf under the flat screen, the dozen or so DVDs that had escaped his post-Aidan purge, and tossed them into the packing box. Carrying the still half-empty box, he headed for the kitchen.

Four hours later, boxes shoved into the trunks and back seats of both of their cars, green garbage bags taken down to the dumpster in the utility room, Daniel and Steven walked through the eerily impersonal apartment.

"You okay?" Steven was concerned; Daniel was way too quiet.

"I'm thirty-three years old, and I can put my whole life in a few boxes?" Daniel turned to Steven. "Isn't that the definition of loser?"

"No. It means you know what's important." Steven slipped his hand inside Daniel's open coat, over his heart. "You matter. Everything else is just," Steven shrugged, "stuff."

Daniel blinked, forcing back the moisture building behind his eyes. Turning towards the front door, Steven walking beside him, Daniel shot Steven a teasing look. "You seem quite attached to your stuff?"

"Well, yeah." Steven flashed a smile. "But then, I'm a bit of a princess. I like my creature comforts. I'm not as evolved as you are."

Opening the front door, Daniel laughed. "Right, that's me, evolved!"

At Steven's place, which was now also his place, okay, that was going to take some getting used to...at their place, they unloaded their cars and dragged the boxes into the house. Daniel dumped the last box, the one with his laptop and work related paraphernalia, on the desk in Steven's guest room, now his office, and wandered into the master bedroom.

Steven looked up from the box of clothes he was unpacking and smiled at the blond standing in the doorway. He waved a hand at the two walls of closets, one on each side of him. "A handy design feature; His and Hers closets. Well, in our case, His and His." He took one of Daniel's shirts out of the box, slipped it on to a wooden hangar that matched the ones on his side of the closet, and hung it up on Daniel's side.

Noting the matching hangars, Daniel had to smile. "I'm assuming you don't want my help?"

"I'm almost done. Did you get your office sorted?" Steven looked at Daniel as he hung the last shirt.

Daniel shook his head. "I'll do it tomorrow. I've had enough of pawing through boxes for one day."

Steven upended his empty box, collapsing the sides. "Good, I can help you organize it."

Daniel laughed. "No, you won't." He picked up the collapsed boxes and followed Steven out of the room. "You're going to stay the hell out of my office."

Turning on the staircase, looking back at Daniel, Steven pouted, eyes laughing. "You're kicking me out of a room in my own house?"

"No, I'm kicking you out of a room in our house."

"Our house." Standing in the foyer, at the bottom of the staircase, Steven reached out and curved his hand around Daniel's hip. "That sounds good, Daniel mine."

Daniel leaned the collapsed boxes against the wall and pulled Steven close. "You finished unpacking?"

Steven bumped his pelvis against Daniel's. "Why? Something you want to do?"

Daniel slid his fingers into Steven's hair, and angled his head. Steven's lips parted, and Daniel covered his mouth, sliding into warmth, coming home.

Steven broke the kiss, his hands already undoing Daniel's pants. "Bedroom?"

"No, here." Daniel dragged Steven's sweater away from his neck, biting into the curve between shoulder and neck.

Steven looked into Daniel's eyes, his hand wrapped around his lover's cock. "Okay."

They didn't waste any time; they didn't even undress properly. Rolling over the floor and each other, they shoved at jeans and underwear, and took turns sucking each other off. Maybe it was some kind of Moving Day Madness, maybe it was an expression of 'Oh, my God! We're living together' anxiety; whatever the reason, they were frenzied and fast! Mere moments later, they lay gasping together on the hardwood floor.

Curled into Steven, his hand still wrapped around his lover's cock, his own cock tired and resting along his thigh, Daniel felt the difference. It didn't make any sense really, he had spent many a night sleeping over at Steven's, they'd certainly fucked each other in most of the rooms, but logical or not, this was different. He didn't have to get up and go home, not tonight, not tomorrow. He didn't have to go home because he was home, and that thought made him smile. Rising onto his knees, he straddled Steven and leered down at his Mr. Perfect.

Steven lifted lids that felt heavy, to find Daniel staring down at him, his fingers tapping the head of Steven's cock. "What, again?" Steven didn't sound all that upset about the idea.

When they finally pulled their clothes back together, Daniel convinced Steven that moving day meant pizza. It was a time-honoured tradition that Daniel felt it would be unlucky to mess with. After packing up Daniel's life, unpacking it again, and trying to find a place for it all in his house, Steven was more than willing to bow to tradition.

Sitting on the living room floor, on either side of the coffee table, they shared a pizza, pulling pieces directly out of the box. Shaking his head, Steven smiled at the blond on the other side of the Pizza Nova box. "I don't usually do this."

Daniel grinned. "Just think of it as camping."

Steven handed Daniel a napkin. "No, I mean, when I'm home I cook."

Daniel looked appalled. "Why?"

"Because it's healthier, and it tastes better."

Daniel bit into his slice. "I don't know. This tastes pretty good to me."

"That's because you're used to pre-packaged garbage from the freezer."

Rolling his eyes, Daniel swiped his napkin over his lips. "How come I didn't know you were a health nut?"

"Getting tired of take-out doesn't mean you're a health nut," Steven wiped greasy pizza residue off his fingers and raised his eyebrows at his boyfriend, "it means you have taste buds."

"Right! " Happily 'tasting' the extra cheese and spicy tomato sauce, Daniel ignored the implied insult. "And you're just mentioning this now, after what, almost six months?"

Steven shrugged. "We weren't living together before."

Daniel popped a piece of pepperoni into his mouth. "Any other surprises I should know about?"

Steven raised his eyebrows and leered at his lover. "Lots!"

❊   ❊   ❊

For the first few weeks, they tiptoed around each other, being extra polite, smothering any hints of annoyance. Neither one of them wanted to risk an argument. They were both terrified that the other would change his mind, and realize that this couldn't work. Of course, that kind of artificial perfection couldn't last for long.

Unlocking the front door, his arms full of groceries, Steven almost tripped over Daniel's boots. "Shit!" Kicking the boots onto the mat they were supposed to be on, and pushing his shoulder into the door to close it, he turned to see Daniel's coat thrown over the couch. Gritting his teeth, he carried the bags into the kitchen.

Upstairs, Daniel scratched some notes on a scrap of paper and snapped his phone down on the desk. Opening a file on his laptop, he quickly typed in the pertinent points from the notes he'd made. Scrunching up the now unnecessary scrap of paper, he tossed it at the waste basket, and missed. Leaning back in the ergonomic desk chair that Steven had insisted he buy, he thought about his latest round of interviews. There was something there, something...

Daniel opened the top desk drawer and routed through it. Slamming it shut, he started through the second drawer. Not finding the newspaper clipping he was looking for, he pushed out of his chair, and walked around to the other side of the desk. Moving piles of books, and papers, and magazines around, he muttered under his breath. "It's here, I know it's here." Leaning over the desk, frantically shoving things aside, he became aware of the faint scent of Orange Pledge. "Fuck!" Stomping out of the room, he took the stairs two at a time, and blazed into the kitchen. "What did I tell you about touching stuff on my desk?"

Steven turned from a sink full of Daniel's dishes, and snarled at his boyfriend. "What did I tell you about leaving dishes in the sink?"

Daniel ignored that as irrelevant. "I can't find a clipping I need for my article."

Steven leaned against the sink, arms crossed, eyes black, and lips in a tight line. "Maybe if you organized things a little better, you'd be able to find what you need."

The condescending, needling tone in Steven's voice made Daniel livid. He paced across the kitchen, his voice rising loud enough to carry into the backyard. "I could find things just fine, until I moved in here!"

"Really?" Steven shrugged away from the sink, his eyes smoldering and his voice pitched to just above a whisper, the tone freezing Daniel where he stood. "Because I remember you looking for your keys every fucking time you left your apartment."

Face flushed, and a pulse throbbing at the left side of his temple, Daniel opened his mouth and... nothing. *Fuck! Fuck! Fuck! Steven was right. Fuck!* Nonplussed, he stared at his boyfriend, the sudden silence vibrating between them.

Steven's eyes warmed back to chocolate, and his lips twitched, as he fought back a smile.

Daniel snapped his mouth closed, and sagged back against the counter opposite Steven. "Well, fuck, if you're going to be right all the time, how am I going to win any arguments?" He peaked at Steven from under his eyelashes, trying for school boy charm. Laughing, Steven moved into Daniel's arms and Daniel nestled their heads together, cheek to cheek. "You're scary when you're mad."

"Me?" Steven tipped his head back to look at Daniel. "I've never heard anyone yell so loud."

"No one yelled in your house?" Daniel looked surprised.

"No, not really, there were only the three of us, and my parents are pretty mellow."

"Mellow, hmmm?" Daniel sounded thoughtful but his eyes were laughing. "Guess they don't sell all the weed, huh?"

※　※　※

Several weeks into their new living arrangement, while he was downtown for an interview, Daniel arranged to meet Allan for dinner. Cutting into his steak, he watched people scurrying by on the sidewalk, huddled into their coats and scarves trying to escape the cold. "It's fucking freezing out there."

Allan plucked a curly fry off his plate. "You know it's February, right?"

"So, I hear you conned some gallery into showing your work?"

"How did you…?" Allan narrowed his eyes at his cousin. "Steven."

"Yep." Daniel grinned. "Your girlfriend has a big mouth."

"She's not my girlfriend."

Allan's denial was fast and habitual, and Daniel wasn't buying it for a second. "No, of course not, you just know her schedule better than she does and you talk to her, how many times a week?"

"She doesn't even live here, asshat, we're not dating."

"Right, she lives half way across the country and you still see each other every month, but you're not dating!" Daniel grinned at his cousin. He really got a kick out of ridding him about Stephanie.

"Fuck off, Mrs. Monaco."

Daniel laughed. "Don't take it out on me that your girlfriend lives in Vancouver and you crawl into an empty bed every night."

"Who says I crawl into an empty bed every night?"

"Right!"

Allan didn't want to talk about what he and Stephanie were or were not doing. If he talked about it, he'd have to think about and, nope, not going there. "So, what's it like, domestic bliss?"

"Good, good. Steven's great." The words were right, but Daniel didn't meet Allan's eyes.

Allan stretched out one foot and kicked Daniel's shin.

"Jesus! What the fuck?" Daniel rubbed his leg and glared at his cousin.

"Don't wimp out on me. Spit it out."

"Yeah, 'cause you're the expert!"

"Just pretend I'm that bartender, the one with the dreads who thinks she's a psychologist." Allan wasn't just trying to be nice; he really did want to know what living with someone meant. There was absolutely no reason for his sudden interest in domestic harmony, none at all. "Spill."

Daniel put his knife and fork down, and pushed his plate away. "I've been here before, you know. It didn't work out so well last time."

Allan considered that for a moment. He wasn't particularly surprised to hear that his cousin was still haunted by that schmuck. "Steven is not Aidan. He's not looking for a live-in cheerleader to stroke his ego. He's looking to build a life." He gave Daniel a moment to process that truth, and then he reverted to the kind of teasing they were both more comfortable with. "Don't tell me that the sex has gone stale all ready?"

Even during February, arguably the coldest month of the year, Steven still went running. He was stubborn that way, plus, he hated gyms. Working up a sweat on a treadmill, watching TV, or listening to his iPod was tame and boring. Feeling one with the city, dodging cars and bicycles, nodding hello to the other addicted runners, that's what made him get out there. He needed the sky above him, and life happening around him, even if it was fucking cold!

Rounding the corner onto his street, finishing his run, he slowed his pace. Gradually bringing himself to a walk, he noticed Sandy's car pulling into her driveway. She climbed out of the car, beeping it locked, and waved at him. "Hey!"

Steven crossed the street. "You're up early."

Sandy sighed, a frown crossing her face. "Lauren wants to dance in competition. I think she's too young, but I told her she could try it. So now she's at the studio an hour earlier." She shook her head, brushing the worry away, and smiled at Steven. "So, how's it going? Daniel making you crazy yet?"

"Good, good. Daniel's great." The words were right, but Steven looked down at his feet as he said them.

Sandy took in his posture and averted eyes. "You have time for coffee? My Tassimo makes a mean Caramel Macchiato."

Steven laughed. "Sure."

Walking to the front door, Sandy faked a shiver. "I don't know how you can run in this weather."

"It's all in the layering." Steven waited while she unlocked the front door.

In the foyer, they hung their coats or, in Steven's case, about three layers of thermal running gear. "Where's Glen?"

Sandy grinned. "Saturday's his sanctuary day. He sleeps in as long as he can." She opened the cupboard over the Tassimo and took out two discs. "You're going to Allan's exhibit, right?"

Steven grinned. "Like Daniel would miss it! He put the date in his phone and mine. He's very proud of Allan, not that he has any intention of telling him that."

Sandy nodded as she removed one cup and slipped in the next disc. "Yeah, God forbid they say anything nice to each other."

Steven smiled as Sandy placed his cup in front of him. "Seems to work for them. Stephanie's coming in for the opening."

Sandy took her cup and joined Steven at the counter, pulling up the stool beside his. "I never thought Allan would be in a relationship."

Steven rolled his eyes. "Stephanie either. They both vehemently deny that they're in one."

Sandy laughed. "I know. It's so cute!" She put her cup down and turned to face Steven. "Okay, what's the problem?"

"What makes you think there's a problem?" Steven played with his coffee cup, turning it in precise circles on the counter top. He couldn't look at Sandy; he wasn't a very good liar.

Sandy snorted. "Two people living together, of course there are problems."

Steven's head popped up. "Yeah?"

Sandy snorted. "Well, duh! What do you think? You're living in some Disney movie?"

Steven laughed and decided that Sandy was exactly the right person to talk to. "I've never done this before, lived with anyone. It's…"

"Claustrophobic? No alone time because he's always fucking there?"

"Oh, God! It's not just me then? Other people feel like this?"

"Almost everyone. I'm sure half the pleasure of golfing, for Glen, is that I'm not there." Sandy grinned. "I disappear into a bubble bath or a book." She looked out the kitchen window, gathering her thoughts. "It takes a while but eventually you figure out what you need to do to still be you." Turning back to Steven, she met his eyes. "Being a 'we' is one of the joys of life. But there still has to be a 'me', or else…shit! Sorry, I'm not saying this right. Look, Daniel loves you, so you need to stay you. It takes two people to make a couple. Am I making any sense, here?"

"Yeah, actually. I've been feeling so guilty. I always wanted someone to share my life with, and now that I have him, I want to be alone! How wacked is that?"

"I know! Crazy, right? It doesn't make any sense. Human nature sucks!" Sandy grinned across the table at him, and Steven grinned back.

Glen wandered into the kitchen, in his bathrobe, scratching at his stubble. "Hey Steven, what's up?"

Sandy looked a question at Steven and he shrugged. *Sure.* "Steven's missing his alone time."

Glen opened the fridge, and got out a carton of orange juice. "Ah, honeymoon's over, huh?"

"I guess."

Glen got a glass and joined them at the counter. "Yeah, at the beginning you do everything together. But eventually, you start hoping you'll get a cold so you have an excuse to sleep in the guest bedroom."

Steven's eyes got wide, but Sandy laughed and swatted at her husband. "Don't scare the boy. He's new to this."

Glen grinned and drank his juice down in one gulp. He caught Steven's eye. "When you come in the door at night, you still want him to be there?"

Steven nodded. "Yes, of course."

Glen put his empty glass down, walked around the counter, and punched Steven's shoulder. "Then you're good, man." Leaving the kitchen, he called over his shoulder. "Gonna take a shower."

Raising one hand, indicating both her retreating husband and his refreshingly simplistic take on a complicated issue, Sandy smiled at Steven. "And there you have it, love defined. He's a regular poet!"

❀   ❀   ❀

The living together thing took some time, and a lot of tweaking, but eventually they got there. Surprise, surprise, the neat/slob divide wasn't the only issue. It wasn't even the major issue. Their misaligned sleep patterns presented more of a problem then they had anticipated. Daniel was a night person, and Steven was not. They knew this, of course, but it hadn't really been a problem until they moved in together.

In some ways, it worked out really well. Steven was long up and gone by the time Daniel pried himself out of bed, so he had the house to himself. In that respect, his life hadn't changed too much. He just worked from an office with a real desk, instead of from his dining room table.

Steven's daytime routine hadn't changed too much either. Well, if you didn't count the early morning blow jobs, or the times he talked Daniel into shower sex and then let him crawl under the covers and go back to sleep, or the fact that Daniel liked Steven to slide into him when he was still half asleep. Okay, waking up with Daniel's head on the pillow beside him seven days a week was a lot different, but, once he got dressed, his day was pretty much the same as it had been before Daniel moved in.

The nights were more of a quandary. Daniel was never ready to go to sleep when Steven was. He was more than happy to go to bed when Steven wanted to, or the couch, or the floor, or the kitchen counter for that matter, but to actually sleep when Steven wanted to, no.

"Where are you going?" Steven's voice was groggy, his eyes closed.

Shit! "I thought you were asleep." Daniel smoothed the hair back at Steven's temple.

Steven snuggled into Daniel. "I felt you move."

Ah crap! Daniel put his arm around Steven and tucked his head back beside his lover's. "Shhh. Go back to sleep."

Steven rolled onto his back and stared up at Daniel. Not that he could see much, they kept the room borderline black. "You're going to sneak out on me again, aren't you?"

Daniel sighed, and rolled onto his side, facing his boyfriend. "Fuck, Steven, I'm just not tired."

"That's because you didn't get out of bed till ten."

"I know that!" Maybe it was juvenile, but Daniel didn't want his life to be programmed. He liked being awake when most people were asleep.

Steven heard the impatience in Daniel's voice. Maybe he was being unfair, Daniel shouldn't have to change for him but..."I like having you here beside me."

"I know." And he did, he felt the same way. Just not at, Daniel glanced at the digital on the night table, 11:42. "Hang on." Throwing the covers aside, he padded out of the bedroom. Steven propped himself up on his elbows, and looked at the greyish outline that marked their open bedroom door. He heard Daniel go down the stairs, and a minute later come rushing back up. Carrying his iPad, Daniel jumped back into bed. He settled himself, sitting with his back against the headboard. "Come here." He pulled Steven's pillow next to him and patted it, motioning for Steven to lie down. "Close enough?"

Steven curled into his pillow and tucked his head against Daniel's hip. He brushed his hand over Daniel's thigh and tucked it between his lover's legs, his knuckles grazing Daniel's cock.

"Hey!" Daniel swatted the top of Steven's head. "You're supposed to be sleeping." He swiped his iPad on and popped his ear buds in.

"What are you doing?"

"Watching Netflix." Daniel ran a hand through Steven's hair. "I'm a fucking genius. You don't have to sleep alone, and I get to watch TV. Win, win!"

Steven's hand curled around Daniel's cock, giving it slow, warm strokes.

The Game of Thrones flashed unnoticed on the small screen, as Daniel looked down at the hand on his cock. "Steven?"

Dark lashes lifted as Steven looked up at Daniel, his smile tilted ever so slightly, his eyes teasing. "I'm awake now."

Daniel pulled the buds out, and tossed the iPad. "Why the fuck didn't you say so?"

❅ ❅ ❅

Nutrition was another area of contention between them. Like their conflicting sleep patterns and their disparate conceptions of neat, nutrition demanded negotiation. Left to his own devices, Daniel ate like the college kid his wardrobe suggested he was. If it was frozen, disgustingly full of toxins, and had the sugar content of a whole bakery, then Daniel loved it.

"Put that back." Steven stared his boyfriend down. "You can't live on that stuff."

Daniel sent him a disbelieving look. "Who are you, my mother?"

Steven grabbed Daniel by his belt buckle and pulled him in. "I'm your partner and if you drop dead from a clogged artery in the middle of fucking me, I'm going to be pissed!"

Daniel grinned. "Okay, that's hot!" He took the offensive package with the bacon and cheese and enough cholesterol to destroy his heart valves and put it back in the freezer. "You know, you could have saved us both a lot of aggravation if you had said that in the first place."

"Uh-huh." Steven pushed the grocery cart and Daniel fell into step beside him. "So you're telling me to skip any appeals to your intellect and go straight to your libido?"

Totally incapable of resisting a setup line like that, Daniel flashed his boyfriend a sideways look from under his eyelashes. "Well, not straight no, I don't think that would work." Daniel cocked his hip, throwing Steven off balance. Steven laughed and shoved his shoulder into Daniel. Daniel danced away, and then bounced back. He glued himself to Steven's side, connecting their bodies from shoulder to hip as they walked through the store.

"What?" Steven glanced at the man practically stuck to him.

"Partner, huh?"

Steven stopped walking and stared at the blond beside him. *Are you fucking kidding me?* "What the fuck did you think we were?"

Daniel curled his hand into Steven's side, just above his belt. "No, I know we are. I just never heard you say it before."

Steven's lips tipped into the smile Daniel loved. "Moron!"

After a heated debate over which Mini-Wheats were better, brown or white frosting, they called it a draw, and added both boxes to their cart. Standing in line at the cash, Steven glanced at Daniel. Lowering his voice, he leaned closer. "I've never heard you say it, either."

"No?" Daniel started to unload their cart onto the conveyor belt.

"Hi, how are you?" The teenaged cashier had green hair and a silver stud in her tongue.

"Good, thanks." Daniel pushed their now empty cart ahead of them, and he and Steven watched as the cashier checked everything through the scanner.

"Sobeys points card?"

Daniel shook his head.

"Your total is $178.50. Credit or Debit?"

Daniel smiled at the girl and leaned into the counter. "My partner has the credit card."

The word blindsided Steven. His face flamed. He was so rattled it took him three tries to get his credit card into the reader.

Daniel leaned against the counter, grinning as Steven messed up his code and the cashier sent him an impatient look and started the transaction over. He smiled at the teenager behind the cash. "He's shy."

"Uh-huh." She didn't really care; she just wanted her shift to be over. Ripping off the receipt, she handed it to Steven. "Thank you for shopping at Sobeys."

Steven took the receipt, folded it precisely, and filed it with the other receipts in his wallet. He put one hand on the cart and grabbed the back of Daniel's neck with the other. Leaning into his partner, he growled into Daniel's ear. "Just wait 'til we get home."

Grinning, Daniel ducked out of Steven's hold. "Give me the car keys. I drive faster than you do."

❖   ❖   ❖

Amid the laughter and the yelling and the working things out, they discovered that not everything required compromise. More often than not, they were completely in sync.

Sitting in the hot tub one night after dinner, Steven looked across the swirling water at Daniel, trying to decide if 'maybe, someday' was today. He thought Daniel would be okay with it, he hoped Daniel would be okay with it. He had always kept this part of himself to himself. There had never been anyone he wanted to share this with, anyone he trusted enough. But, now there was Daniel and Steven wanted to explore this with him. Daniel wouldn't...

"Babe, I can hear the fuses blowing from here. Just tell me." Daniel laughed as surprise stamped itself onto his partner's face. "Steven, do you really think that after all this time, I can't tell when you're freaking out about something, that I don't know you by now?"

Steven grimaced. "Funny you should put it just that way." He looked at Daniel and tried for a smile. "The night you moved in, we were eating pizza and I said I didn't like to eat too much junk food. You asked if there were any other surprises you should know about and..."

"You said 'lots'. Yeah, I remember." Daniel stared at Steven, wondering where he was going with this. "So?"

"I was thinking." Steven waded across the tub, and slid onto the seat with Daniel. Turning sideways, he hooked one leg over Daniel's knee.

Daniel didn't like hearing the hesitancy in Steven's voice. "Whatever it is, I'm not going anywhere babe."

Steven took a deep breath and spat it all out at once. "I'd like to wear something, uh, you know, different." He fluttered his hands over his chest, and Daniel got the message; different meant feminine. "Just sometimes." He sent Daniel a nervous glance, hiding behind his lowered lashes. "If you don't think that's too weird?"

Holy shit! Daniel had never thought of cross-dressing, and drag acts had always seemed cheesy to him, but this was Steven, and images of what he was offering burnt across his mind. He ran with his imagination, picturing how Steven would look, what he would wear. Caught up in what could be, he forgot to answer his boyfriend.

As the painful seconds of silence ticked by, Steven began to wish that he had never said anything. He felt too vulnerable, and almost paralyzed with embarrassment. "Too weird, right?" Pretending a nonchalance he didn't feel, he moved to unwrap himself from Daniel.

"No!" Daniel grabbed Steven and pulled him onto his lap, holding his hips to keep him there. "I was just surprised. Give me a minute here."

Steven laid his hands on Daniel's chest, palms flat, feeling his heartbeat. "Bad surprised?"

"No, I just never thought about this." Daniel stoked his thumbs over Steven's hips, as he tried to read his boyfriend's face. "You've done this, umm, wearing different things before?"

"No." Steven shook his head and looked directly into Daniel's eyes. "I've always wanted to, but I never trusted anyone enough."

Daniel felt those words like a punch to the gut. He didn't believe in fate. There was no master plan. There was only luck, a haphazard convergence of possibilities. Looking into Steven's eyes, Daniel felt like a lottery winner. He was awed, and humbled, and grateful for the gift that was Steven. "Thank you."

Steven's smile tilted, as his arms slipped around Daniel's neck. "For what?"

"For letting me in." Daniel framed Steven's face with his hands. "You make my life."

Steven offered his mouth, and Daniel took it. They were gentle with each other, one warm sliding kiss melting into the next. Dragging his lips off Steven's, Daniel slid his hands down his lover's back, pressing him closer. "When?"

Steven tipped his head, eyes confused. "When what?"

"You know, when are you going to wear the, uh, different stuff?"

Even if Steven couldn't read the heat in Daniel's eyes, or hear it in his voice, he couldn't miss the hardness growing under him. "You want me to?" Steven's eyes danced as his smile teased, he already knew the answer.

"Yeah." Daniel nodded, as his fingers curled around Steven's hips. "We can go shopping tomorrow. Do you know what you want, where to buy it?" Mental pictures lit fires in Daniel's mind. He wanted to see Steven like that, like now!

Steven slid backwards on Daniel's thighs, so that he could wrap his hand around the shaft that was begging for attention. "I already have a few things. I bought them for me, because I like them. I've never worn them for anyone though."

His hands gripping under Steven's ass, Daniel started to rise, lifting Steven with him. "Here? You have them here?"

Steven laughed and smacked Daniel's shoulder. "Sit down, idiot! I'm not putting them on now."

"Oh!" Daniel sank back into his seat. "Why not?" Even to his ears, that had sounded like a whine.

Steven grinned at the disappointment on his boyfriend's face. "Because I'm a little freaked right now." Leaning in, he laid his head alongside Daniel's, his lips next to his lover's ear. "I could tell you about the pieces I have." He drawled the words out, dark and low. "I could describe them for you." Steven sucked down the side of Daniel's neck, as he pumped his cock. "If you want?"

Daniel groaned, his hips snapping up, pushing his cock through Steven's hand. "Yesssssss." The word emerged as a long, drawn-out sigh.

Steven moved his head back to see Daniel's face. "Or, maybe not. I don't want to ruin the surprise."

"You fucking tease!" The words lost a lot of their bite because Daniel couldn't stop rutting into Steven's hand.

Steven grinned. "Not nice, Daniel mine." Dropping Daniel's cock, he slid off his lap and stood in the swirling water. "Turn around. Kneel. Lean over the edge of the tub." His voice stern, Steven rattled off the orders, each word a gun shot. "Ass in the air."

Oh, fuck! How does he do that? Steven could change from one breath to the next, from cozy kitten to dark lord in a heartbeat. It was the biggest fucking turn-on ever! Steven was everything Daniel could ever want and more.

"Now!"

Daniel scrambled to obey, because Steven telling him what to do made his cock ache.

Coating two fingers with saliva, Steven leaned over his boyfriend. Wrapping one arm around Daniel's waist, he fisted his lover's cock, tugging almost painfully hard. He pushed his fingers inside Daniel, thrusting in and out, searching. Yes! Daniel gasped, jerking in Steven's hands. Rubbing over the sensitive nerve cluster, he nipped bites into Daniel's shoulder. Keeping his voice low, his words spoken next to Daniel's ear, he painted pictures in Daniel's mind. "I don't have panties, Daniel mine. I don't like them. I have corsets. They cinch my waist, and frame my ass." Daniel moaned beneath Steven, thrusting his ass back, pushing down on Steven's fingers. "I have a white one in satin. It's soft and sensuous. It clings to me. I look fucking amazing." Steven sank his teeth just behind Daniel's ear. "I have one in leather, Daniel mine, black leather."

"Oh, fuck!" Daniel shot his load over Steven's hand, and sagged against the tub. Smiling with pleasure at Daniel's reaction, his own cock insistent, Steven sank down beside his boyfriend. Breathing hard, eyes still blown with lust, Daniel turned around. "You weren't just saying that, were you? You actually own corsets?"

Grinning, Steven nodded. "Yes, I actually own corsets."

"Black leather?" Daniel really, really wanted that one to not be a figment of Steven's imagination.

"Yep." Steven could feast for days on the look in Daniel's eyes. "It has laces down the back that you can pull," Steven moved his hands, miming tying laces, "tight."

Daniel's lips parted, as that picture lodged in his brain. He slid off his seat and kneeling in the water, he pushed Steven's legs apart. Pressing his hands under his partner's thighs, Daniel lifted Steven, raising his cock above the water line. Steven reached back and hooked his arms over the edge of the tub, floating on the water so Daniel didn't have to hold him up. Daniel bent and sucked Steven in to his mouth. He swirled his tongue, and wrapped a hand around the base of Steven's shaft. Pulling off, he glanced up at Steven. "Tomorrow?"

In bed that night, Daniel pulled Steven close. Steven wrapped an arm and leg around Daniel, and Daniel rested his head against Steven's, one hand stroking Steven's back. He thought about Steven's earlier revelation, and the harem boy thing they discovered at Maple Hill. He thought back to the beginning of their relationship when he had first realized that Steven going all 'I'm in charge' on him was fucking hot. He smiled remembering when he figured out that tugging on Steven's hair turned the man liquid in his arms. He ran his fingers through Steven's hair and smiled when Steven murmured in appreciation. "You think twenty or thirty years from now we'll still be surprising each other?"

Steven tipped his head back to look at Daniel, not that he could see much in the dark. "I think we'll be surprising each other in the nursing home."

Daniel laughed. "We should buy stock in Pfizer. They make Viagra, right?"

They learned to compromise, to make allowances, to make it work.

CHAPTER 18

Marriage Is a Four Letter Word

In Toronto, there wasn't much difference between February and March. The snow slipped into rain but the city was still disgustingly cold, depressingly grey and miserable. The green beer on St. Patrick's Day was the only hint of spring.

Steven shivered as he closed the front door and dropped his keys in the dish on the hall table. The dish was tacky beyond belief, certainly not anything he would have chosen. He loved it, not for its artistic merit or its intrinsic value, because it had neither. It was a cheap flea market find, a ceramic Star Trek memorabilia plate. To anyone else, the dish was a deplorable piece of kitsch. To Steven, it was a concrete representation of the life that he and Daniel were building. Every time he dropped his keys on Spock's face, he smiled, thinking of the day they bought it:

"Steven, Breaking Bad or Orange is the New Black?" Daniel called out to Steven in the kitchen, and pointed the remote at the Netflix screen.

"Breaking Bad, but don't start it yet." Steven walked into the living room, a glass of wine in each hand and a manila folder under one arm. After weeks of waiting while Daniel looked for his keys, or worse, rummaging through the house looking for the damn things with him, Steven was ready to staple the keys to his partner's forehead. In the interests of keeping Daniel out of the nearest emergency room and himself out of jail, he had come up with a plan.

Unfortunately, Daniel's cooperation was vital. Without it, the whole house of cards crumbled to useless.

Daniel took his glass from Steven, and nodded at the folder. "Not more income tax forms?"

"No." Steven settled on the couch with Daniel and placed the folder between them. Taking a sip from his glass, he tapped the title on the front of the folder.

KEY SOLUTIONS
OPTIONS FOR CHANGE

Daniel scanned the words and looked at Steven. "Is this supposed to mean something to me?"

Ignoring Daniel's question, Steven posed one of his own. "Where are your keys, Daniel?"

"What?" Daniel was thrown off by the apparent non sequitur.

"When you came home today, where did you put your keys?"

Steven sounded like he was talking to a three year-old and it pissed Daniel off. "I don't know." His frown and exasperated tone of voice said, 'and I don't give a fuck!'

Steven nodded. "No, you never do."

"Hey! I can..."

Steven cut Daniel off. "I can't spend the rest of my life looking for your keys, Daniel." He smiled at his partner. "Please, I don't want to have an ulcer before I'm even thirty. You've got to help me out here." He tapped the folder again. "There are three options in here, three systems that will ensure you always know where your keys are. It's entirely your choice. Choose whichever one you think you can live with, but choose one, please, I'm begging you."

Daniel snorted. "Ulcers are caused by bacteria." He put his glass down and picked up the folder. "It's not that big a deal."

"Not to you, but, and I can't stress this enough," Steven held Daniel's eyes, "it is a very big deal to me."

"Fuck!" Daniel flipped the folder open. "So, if I don't do this I'm a selfish, inconsiderate bastard who doesn't care about you?"

Steven laughed and raised his glass in the air, toasting Daniel's interpretation. "Yeah, pretty much."

The folder contained three sheets of paper, each a print out of a Google Image. Daniel looked at the first one, a picture of a key rack hung on the back of a door, and snapped his eyes up to glare at Steven. "No way! Karen gave me one of these." Daniel shook his head. "No, not happening. Doug would never let me hear the end of it."

He turned the paper over and blinked at the next image, a little boy with a key on a chain around his neck. "Oh, you're fucking hilarious!" Daniel picked the picture up and turned it for Steven to see. "You want to pin my gloves to my sleeves too?"

"Well, obviously I'd get you a real chain, silver or white gold. I don't think yellow gold would work with your complexion." Steven's eyes teased, as he went all Queer Eye for the Straight Guy.

"Yeah, funny!" Daniel turned to the last option, an image of a bowl on a hall table by the front door. He looked up at Steven. "This is the one you want, isn't it?"

Steven nodded. "That's my preference, yes, but I'll work with whichever one you choose."

Daniel tapped the paper. "We already have a table like this, don't we?"

"Yeah, it used to be in your office, now it's in the basement."

Daniel snapped the folder shut and shoved it at Steven. "You're not my favourite person right now, Monaco."

"Thank you. I'm not kidding, I was going insane." Steven put the folder on the coffee table. "Last night I had a dream that we missed a flight because we couldn't find your keys."

"Oh, and we couldn't just take yours?" Daniel curled into his end of the couch and proceeded to inhale his wine.

Steven shrugged. "It was a dream. I'll find a bowl tomorrow."

"Uh-uh." Okay, maybe it was passive-aggressive but Daniel needed to grab some kind of victory here. "If I have to do this, then I'm picking the bowl."

Steven knew, he just knew, he was going to regret this. "Deal."

Unfortunately for Steven, their local mall was having its bi-annual antique show that weekend. After looking at booths of beautiful china plates, antique glass bowls, and distressed leather trays, Daniel picked up a ceramic plate and turned to Steven, his face lit with laughter. "You're a Trekker, right?"

Looking at his keys lying beside Daniel's in a dish that had all the quality of a gas station freebie, Steven remained convinced that it was the best seven bucks he'd ever spent. He hung his coat in the front hall closet. "Daniel?"

"Up here."

Steven took the stairs two at time. Striding down the hallway, *en route* to Daniel's office, he passed their bedroom and stopped so quickly that he almost tripped. Standing in the doorway, he noted the changes in the room since he had left it that morning. The blinds were drawn, the sheets were folded neatly at the foot of the bed, and there were lit pillar candles placed haphazardly around the room. Their bedroom was suddenly doing an excellent imitation of a spa. While he was still processing the new look, the *en suite* door opened, dark almost subliminal music, something with a heavy back beat flowed into the room, and Daniel stood there.

Steven's lips parted, but no sound emerged. He stared at Daniel, afraid to move, positive this was some kind of erotic hallucination. Daniel was naked, not your average, everyday, just-got-out-of-the-shower naked, no. He wore accessories, things that somehow made him look more naked. His body was decorated with hints of black leather: a collar wrapped around his neck, a cuff on his left wrist, and another one on his right ankle. Each distracting on their own, but what captured Steven's attention, what he couldn't look away from, were the delicate strands of black leather hanging from Daniel's right nipple. *A nipple clamp! Fuck! Fuck! Fuck!* Steven's cock was trying to rip its way out of his pants, even while his mind was babbling. *Oh my God! Oh my God! Oh my God!*

Daniel moved, padding towards him, and Steven couldn't tear his gaze off the bits of swinging leather. Daniel put his hands on Steven's shoulders, and slid them down, gripping his biceps. "Breathe, baby, breathe."

Steven inhaled raggedly, as he met Daniel's eyes. Reaching out, he laid his fingers lightly on Daniel's hips. "Daniel...Daniel!"

Daniel grinned, exultant with Steven's reaction. It was so worth pinching that damn clamp on to see Steven speechless. "Happy Birthday."

Steven's lips tilted into a smile, his hands tracing Daniel's sides, as he tried for coherent. "You look…" Steven licked his lips. "You look…" He raised one hand towards the nipple clamp. "Can I touch?"

Daniel chuckled, his arms around Steven, hands clasped low on his partner's back. "I think that's the whole idea, babe."

Steven traced the leather strips lightly, following them up to the silver clamp. He circled Daniel's nipple gently. "Does it hurt?"

"Not now." Daniel laughed as Steven winced.

Steven leaned in and licked at Daniel's nipple, flicking his tongue against the clamp, and Daniel hissed. He flashed his eyes up to check Daniel's expression. "You okay?"

"Mmmm." Daniel's eyes slid shut and his head tipped back as he arched into Steven. Threading his fingers through Steven's hair, he pulled the dark head back to his chest.

Nestling closer, Steven skimmed his hands down Daniel's back, settling on his ass. He flicked his tongue over Daniel's nipple, and sucked both it and the clamp into his mouth. Daniel moaned, his cock a solid, heated pressure along Steven's thigh.

"Steven?" Daniel's hands clenched on his partner's back, fingers clawing at his shirt.

Letting the clamp slip out of his mouth, Steven plucked at the leather strips with gentle fingers. "Yeah?"

"Oh, fuck!" The words slid past Daniel's lips, a whisper of surprise and arousal.

He had done this for Steven. Trying to find the perfect birthday present, he'd ended up slumped over his laptop, crumpled in defeat. He lived with the man for fuck's sake, he knew his favourite ice cream, the television shows he programmed into the PVR, his favourite restaurant, and precisely how he ordered his salad, no onions, hold the olives. He knew the man, how could he not know what Steven wanted? Staring at his computer keys, he smiled to himself as the thought occurred that there had been times when he knew exactly what Steven wanted. Not the kind of thing he could put in a box and wrap up…or was it? A few hits to Google, a few adult oriented website searches, the provision of a credit card number, and it turned out that what Steven wanted could be boxed, even better, it could be delivered!

So, yes, he'd done this for Steven. And, yes, he knew the man, so he wasn't surprised at Steven's reaction. He was surprised, however, at his own. He'd expected to feel like a complete dork playing at dress-up, self-conscious, and ridiculous. Forcing himself not to cringe as he walked out of their *en suite,* he had never felt like a bigger fool in his life, until he saw Steven's face.

Steven's eyes had burned over him, jumping from the collar, to the cuffs at wrist and ankle, to the leather hanging from his nipple, and oh, God!, he was hard before Steven ever touched him. Steven's lips on that stupid clamp, his fingers tugging on the leather tails...*Oh, fuck! Oh, fuck! Giving is its own reward!*

Tugging on Steven's shirt, he dragged it out of his pants and started on his belt, fingers shaking with impatience. "Steven! Get your fucking clothes off!"

❃   ❃   ❃

At the pharmacy, the next afternoon, Steven was surprised to see Julia's number flash across his cell screen, "Hello?"

"Steven, I'm sorry to bother you at work. Do you have a minute?"

"No problem, Julia. What's up?"

"What kind of birthday cake would you like? The bakery across the street does that brownie cheesecake that Daniel likes and a caramel crunch that is amazing. Or I can get an ice cream cake, whatever you want."

"You don't have to do anything special Julia."

Daniel's mother laughed. "Your birthday is special, Steven. So, pick your sugar overload."

While Steven was trying to decide on a birthday cake, Daniel was trying to ignore the insistent ring of his own cell phone. His fingers tapped over the computer keys, the words coalescing perfectly, the article already fully formed in his mind. He groaned with impatience when his phone stopped ringing only to vibrate on the desk instead.

From Sandy: what can I get Steven for his birthday?

Picking up the phone with a growl, Daniel punched in two words.

From Daniel: don't know

Dropping his phone on his desk, he went back to his article.

The phone started ringing again. "Jesus Christ!" Without even looking at the screen, he picked it up and snapped at his sister. "I'm working here, Sandy."

"What do you mean you don't know what Steven wants? You live with the man, how do you not know?"

"Because I'm not a fucking mind reader, okay?"

"Well, what did you get him?"

Daniel didn't answer that because he was suddenly submerged in images from last night: Steven's eyes, the leather strips on his nipple clamp dragging against the sheets as he knelt for Steven, Steven's hands bruising his hips as he pounded him into the mattress, the words Steven panted out as he buried himself in Daniel...the memory alone made his cock twitch!

"Daniel! Don't tell me you didn't get Steven anything for his birthday!" Sandy was appalled.

Daniel laughed. "Don't have a hemorrhage. I got him something."

"What?"

"None of your business."

"Oh." Sandy laughed. "That kind of birthday present. You don't have to tell me, I'll just ask Steven."

"Or you could try minding your own business."

"Daniel, when are you going to learn? The more you don't want me to know something, the more I want to know it. Remember Peter Miller when you were in ninth grade?"

"I remember you were grounded for a week."

"Yeah, but I found out your secret." Sandy cackled into the phone.

"You know it's very sad when your six-year-old daughter is more mature than you are."

Sandy laughed. "Insulting, but true. Can you at least tell me what kind of movies he likes, or music?"

Daniel sighed. "He watches Sci-Fi and he listens to pop, country, and jazz. Jesus! Just get him an iTunes gift certificate."

"See? Was that so difficult?" She hung up before Daniel could answer.

❉   ❉   ❉

That Friday night at Daniel's parents' house, after the dinner dishes were cleared, Julia walked into the dining room flanked by her grandchildren, her hands under the cake protectively, Lauren and Rhys holding the sides of the platter.

"Happy Birthday to you,
Happy Birthday to you,
Happy Birthday dear Steven,
Happy Birthday to you!"

Not everyone had the best voice, Glen had obviously taken lessons from a fog horn, but everyone sang.

Rhys knelt on the seat of his chair as Steven stood to blow out the candles. "You have to make a wish."

"Right." Steven smiled at both kids. "Like what?"

Lauren shook her head, she was pretty sure that birthday wishes were like the Tooth Fairy, just baby stories, but she didn't want to say that in front of Rhys. "Whatever you want."

"What do you think, Rhys?" Steven smiled at the boy leaning into the table, his face almost on top of the cake.

The four-year-old gave the request the seriousness it deserved. He thought for all of ten seconds and grinned at Steven. "Disney World?"

"Perfect!" Steven closed his eyes, and the kids held their own breath, doing their best to aid Steven's effort. Wish complete, Steven opened his eyes and looked directly into Daniel's, while he blew out his candles.

"If you get your wish, can I come?" Rhys' best friend had gone to Disney World over the Christmas break, and it had become something of an obsession with him.

Steven sliced a piece of cake and handed it to Daniel's nephew. "Well, it wouldn't be any fun without you."

Lauren handed Steven her plate. "I'm coming too."

"So, how does this birthday wish thing work?" Steven asked the kids as he cut slices for the adults. "Do the Disney World tickets come in the mail?"

"No." Rhys scrunched up his eyebrows. "I think an owl brings them, like in *Harry Potter*."

Hedwig didn't appear with the Disney tickets tucked under her wing and Rhys was vastly disappointed, but was eventually distracted by helping Steven open his presents.

In the kitchen, Sandy poured herself a second cup of coffee and smiled at her brother. "Steven says your birthday gift was very creative."

Karen put a container of fruit in the fridge and snapped the door shut. "Oh? What did you get him?"

Daniel closed the dishwasher and grinned at Sandy. "No, he didn't." He leaned against the counter. "You've got nothing. Steven didn't tell you anything."

"I didn't tell her anything about what?" Steven entered the kitchen carrying what was left of the cake.

"She's trying to find out what I got you for your birthday."

Steven put the cake on the island and leered at Daniel. "Best birthday present ever!"

The sisters descended on Steven, cornering him against the island, one on each side. "Really?" Karen threw a look over her shoulder at her brother and turned back to Steven. "What did he get you?"

Glancing over at a very nervous Daniel, Steven leaned closer to Karen, and lowered his voice. "It wasn't so much what he got me. It was more what he gave me."

Daniel pushed off the counter, alarm on his face. "Steven!"

Sandy put an arm out, blocking her brother, as he tried to reach his partner. "Uh-uh, Danny, let the boy talk."

"Monaco, you tell them anything and next year, I swear, you're getting socks!"

Steven ducked under Sandy's arm, and popped up beside his panicked partner. "Sorry, ladies."

Daniel put his arm around Steven's shoulders and practically pushed him towards the kitchen door. Turning his head, speaking over his shoulder, Steven grinned at Daniel's sisters. "Think black leather."

"Oooo! Way to go, little brother!" "Kinky!" Karen and Sandy laughed as Daniel glared at them before dragging Steven out of the kitchen.

"Shit! Steven, I warned you about sisters!"

✿　✿　✿

March rolled into April, and Daniel found himself standing with Steven in a ridiculous crowd of people at the opening night reception for Allan's gallery exhibit, sipping really bad white wine. "What a zoo!" He moved out of the way as a woman jostled his arm trying to get to the bar.

Brian squeezed through the crowd, smiling with relief when he found Daniel and Steven. "You'd think they were giving the damn pictures away! Where did all these people come from?"

Shaking his head, Daniel moved closer to Steven clearing a little more space for his father. "It looks like everyone Allan ever dated is here tonight."

Brian looked around, deciding that Daniel was probably right. The women certainly outnumbered the men. The room was jam packed with sparkly wisps of cocktail dresses, long legs in scary teetering heels, hair brushing naked shoulders or flowing down naked backs. "Could be."

Doug ploughed through the crowd. "Where's the bar?"

Steven pointed behind them, but Daniel shook his head. "Don't bother. All they have is wine, and it's pretty bad."

"No beer?" Doug looked wounded.

Steven laughed. "I think they have coffee."

Doug moved closer to Steven as a brunette in a plunging neckline brushed past him. His eyes followed the woman, a leer in his voice, as he parroted words he had heard someone gushing at Allan's work. "Powerful work! Great eye for detail."

Steven checked out the brunette Doug was drooling over. "An inspired capturing of the life esthetic."

Doug grinned. "Nice!"

Steven nodded. "I've been here awhile."

Doug turned to Brian. "How long do we have to stay?"

Brian shrugged. "Until our wives say we can leave."

Daniel's lips twisted into a grimace as he sipped at his wine and Steven took the glass out of his hands. "What are you doing?" He turned and put both of their glasses on the window ledge behind him. "I'll get you something decent to drink when we get out of here."

"Are you leaving?" Doug looked hopefully at Steven. If they left, he had a better chance of convincing Karen to leave.

Steven looked at Daniel, who checked his watch. "Another half hour should do it, I guess. Did you see Allan?"

Doug nodded. "Yeah, for like three seconds, that gallery owner guy was introducing him around."

Brian waved his hand at the assembled crowd. "That's what this whole thing is about. He has to schmooze the prospective buyers."

Karen and Sandy had no intention of leaving, they were busy nudging each other and whispering about every woman who passed, critiquing their outfits, and taste, or lack thereof. Julia took her third tour through the exhibit, this time walking with her sister-in-law, Allan's mother. "This is extraordinary, Brenda. He's so talented. Can you believe it? I'm so thrilled for him."

Across the room, Allan didn't even have to think anymore, the words came automatically. "Thank you, I'm pleased you could come." Jeremy Lichtner, the gallery owner, had introduced him to everyone he knew who might be tempted to take out their credit card, and it was working. There were a few red stickers sitting proudly under the titles of the photographs that had already sold. Every time Allan saw one, he felt...the whole thing was surreal.

"Allan?" Even in this tumult of noise, Allan had no trouble picking out that one particular voice.

Stephanie's dark hair popped through the crowd, and Allan smiled. "Excuse me." He nodded to Jeremy and Mr. Potential Collector and picked his not-girlfriend up, swinging her around. People next to them clutched their wine glasses and stepped out of the way. "Steph! You made it!"

Stephanie grinned as Allan put her down. "Of course, I made it. How many incredibly talented artists do I know?"

Allan actually blushed. "Have you been through the exhibit?"

"No, I just got here."

Allan put his hand at the small of her back and escorted her through the crowd. "Let me give you the two bit tour."

Daniel nodded at an overweight woman with a really bad dye job poured into a bondage style dress. "I went to high school with her."

Three heads turned to see who Daniel was staring at; Doug was the first to comment. "Allan never dated that."

Daniel smirked. "She was a lot younger then."

Brian jerked his chin up, indicating the woman. "I heard she's on her third husband. The last one paid for the…" Brian moved his hands to chest level, and the men all looked again.

Steven grinned, leaning into Daniel, keeping his voice low. "Floatation devices."

Doug appraised the strident curves. "Oh, yeah, they're going to keep her afloat!"

Not coincidentally, as the wine ran out, the crowd started to disperse, and Daniel tapped Steven's waist. "We're out of here, guys."

"Oh, thank God! I was ready to leave an hour ago." Doug turned to his father-in-law. "Glen's in the lobby with some of the guys from soccer. Let's find the girls."

Walking towards the exit, Steven turned his head to look back at Daniel. "We should find Allan and say goodbye."

Daniel groaned. "Can't we just sneak out?"

"No." Steven grinned and swerved around a body in front of him. "Daniel?"

Daniel stopped dead, and Steven turned back at the sound of Daniel's name. Recognizing Aidan immediately, he instinctively moved closer to his partner, his hand slipping to the small of Daniel's back.

"I thought you might be here." As impeccably gorgeous as ever, Aidan smiled at Daniel.

The smile was still stunning, the man even more so, but Daniel found himself unaffected. He recognized the really attractive man Aidan still was, but he wasn't invested the way he used to be. "Yeah, well, Allan would never forgive me if I missed this. I don't think you've met my partner, Steven Monaco."

Steven held his hand out to Aidan. "I'm the guy who answered that text you sent Daniel a while ago."

"Right." Aidan remembered the bitchy, possessive text clearly and his eyes narrowed as he swept them over the man at Daniel's side. Dark wavy hair, long eyelashes over dark eyes, broad shoulders, slender hips, nice…Aidan snapped his eyes up to find Steven smirking at him. He had definitely never seen this guy before, but there was something familiar about his voice, and the name…he knew that name from somewhere. His brows drew together as he tried to remember… "Steven Monaco, from Cloverleaf Pharmacy?"

"Yes. I'm one of the pharmacists there. We've spoken on the phone a few times." Steven watched, waiting for Aidan to make the connection. *Oh, yes, there it is, you've got it.* Aidan's eyes narrowed and his face froze with distaste. *Oh, fun!* Steven stepped into his partner, sliding his hand to Daniel's hip, a possessive bit of body language that Aidan did not miss. *Mine, asshole!*

"Yes." Aidan looked at his watch, suddenly in a major hurry to be somewhere else, anywhere else. "Daniel, nice seeing you again." He nodded at Steven and walked away.

Daniel grinned at Steven. "I don't think he likes you."

"Really?" Steven laughed as they continued their search for Allan. "I'm so hurt!"

❄   ❄   ❄

Even in Toronto, the snow melts eventually and the sun warms the leaves into green. By May, Daniel was back to playing soccer on Wednesday nights and biking with Allan on Saturday mornings. Steven was down to only one layer when he ran, and had graduated to the intermediate level in guitar. Four months into living together and everyone was happy.

"You do anything to screw up my Saturdays off, and I'll make you wish you were never born!" Sandy wasn't kidding. Steven took Rhys and Lauren with him and his guitar, every second Saturday when he entertained in the children's ward at the local hospital, and Sandy appreciated the child-free mornings.

"Do you have any idea what a miracle Steven is?" Karen agreed with her sister. She and Doug had the house to themselves for four hours twice a month, in the daytime, when both of them were awake! "I don't care if he wants you to alphabetize your socks, I don't care if he gives the worst blow jobs in the history of the universe, you screw this up and you're a dead man!"

Daniel grinned. "Steven is exceptionally gifted orally, thank you very much, and I have my own set of drawers which he's decided he never wants to look into."

"Good, I'm happy for you." Karen punched her brother.

"What the hell was that for?" Daniel rubbed his arm, glaring at his sister.

Sandy smiled and patted Daniel's cheek, as she answered for both of them. "Keep Steven happy because if he breaks up with you and our kids start whining that they're bored on Saturdays, we're dropping them off at your place."

His sisters were definitely team Steven, happy that Daniel was happy, but Julia was ecstatic. She didn't say anything to either Daniel or Steven, but she had a stack of bridal magazines in a basket in her *en suite*. She wanted to be prepared, just in case.

Brian dropped his toothbrush into its holder and watched his wife pat her face dry. "It hasn't even been a year yet. Give the boys a break." He knew what a sudden interest in bridal magazines meant. "Daniel was with what's his name for eight years and they never got married." Aidan was always 'what's his name' to Brian.

Julia sniffed disdainfully as she rubbed moisturizer into her face. "That's because Aidan wasn't the right one."

Brian stared at Julia in the mirror over their matching sinks. "And what makes you think that Steven is the right one?"

Julia caped her moisturizer and put it away. "Please! They finish each other's sentences, Daniel only eats fast food once a week now, because Steven worries about his cholesterol level, and Steven doesn't eat garlic bread anymore because Daniel doesn't like the smell on his breath. What do you think?"

"I think that Daniel's happy." Brian switched the light off in the *en suite* and followed his wife to bed. "Let's not push it."

Julia snuggled into her husband's side. "Who's pushing it? I haven't said anything to the boys."

"Good." Brian put his arm around his wife. "Keep it that way."

Julia didn't answer him and Brian sighed. She was going to say whatever she wanted to. Pulling her closer, Brian smiled to himself. He wouldn't have her any other way.

As it happened, Julia agreed with her husband. As much as she would like to see the boys married, this was something that Daniel and Steven had to come to on their own. It had to be something they wanted. It had to mean something to them, or it meant nothing. So, she didn't say anything to the boys. She didn't say anything because she didn't have to. Same-sex marriage was common enough in Toronto that she knew Daniel and Steven would inevitably, sooner or later, stumble into the marriage discussion.

After dinner one evening, Daniel played Angry Birds Space on his iPad while Steven aimed the remote at the TV and flicked through the channels. He stopped at one show, snorting derisively. "I can't believe people watch this crap!"

Daniel flicked his eyes toward the flat screen. "What?"

"The Bachelorette!" Disgusted with his fellow humans, Steven clicked onto the next channel.

Daniel shook his head, eyes back on his iPad. "Competing with a bunch of strangers for a woman you barely know, making a fool of yourself on network TV, yeah, that's the way to find a wife!"

Steven nodded. "They've finally revealed marriage as the glittering sham that it is!"

Daniel looked up, setting his game to pause. "You think marriage is a sham?"

"It's not much more than an elaborate hoax designed to finance the wedding industry. Cakes, dresses, tuxedos, it's big business."

Daniel's hands trembled as he closed his iPad and set it on the coffee table, turning to face his partner. "You don't think there's any validity to marriage?"

"Of course not!" Steven looked at Daniel, honestly surprised by the question. "It doesn't work, does it? Look at the divorce rate! It's an outmoded social construct that no longer has any relevance. Historically, it was designed to keep women in line, and cement property and trade agreements. The idea of love wasn't even connected to marriage until recent times."

Daniel waved the history lesson aside as irrelevant. "That may be how it started, but it means something different now. It signifies commitment, the intent to bond your life to someone else, to care for someone beyond all others."

"Right!" Steven couldn't believe that Daniel was that naïve. "It's a Hallmark moment, perpetuated by the same people who bring us Valentine's Day."

"My parents have been together almost forty years. They still hold hands, and giggle in the dark in their bedroom at night. I know that because my room was next door to theirs until I moved out."

"Your parents are the exception." Steven backed down, because yes, Brian and Julia loved each other, anyone could see that.

Daniel wasn't appeased. He stood up, his voice rising and his eyes cold. "What about Sandy and Doug, Karen and Steven, Kevin and Jonathan? They're just dupes taken in by the media? They just think they love each other?" Daniel waved a hand at Steven. "What about your parents? They're still together."

Steven looked up at his partner. He didn't understand how an offhand remark about a TV show had devolved into an argument so quickly. "Daniel, my parents aren't married. They've never been married. They don't believe in it."

Daniel nodded. "And you don't believe in it?" It wasn't really a question, Daniel already knew the answer.

"Well, no, I don't." Steven knew it wasn't what Daniel wanted to hear, but he couldn't lie to this man. Not now, not ever.

"Then what are we doing?" Daniel indicated them both, his hand gesturing between them.

"What do you mean?" Steven didn't follow the logical jump that Daniel had obviously made.

"This! Us living together! I thought we were building a life."

"We are. We are building a life." Steven stood up, reaching for Daniel. He was shocked and hurt when Daniel backed away from him. "I love you. You know that."

Steven watched as his Daniel disappeared. He watched, helpless as all the warmth and humour and life that was Daniel turned to a wall of rigid blankness. Undeterred by the frozen mask that used to be Daniel, Steven kept his hands to himself and spoke from his heart. "Daniel, I love you. You're a part of my life, a part of me. We're in this together."

"You love me, just not enough to stand up before our friends and family and say so." Daniel stared at Steven. "I'm such a fucking idiot!" His shoulders slumped in defeat, his voice empty, he turned away from Steven. "I am not going down that road again, Steven. I am not going to be the guy that's good enough until a better one comes along."

"Daniel!" Steven grabbed at Daniel's arm. "There is no one better. You're the man I love. You're the man I want."

Daniel shook him off. "Right!"

"Just because I don't believe in marriage, doesn't mean I don't believe in you, in us."

"Yeah, I've heard that before." Daniel strode out of the living room, plucked his keys out of the *Star Trek* dish in the foyer and walked out the front door.

Steven stood paralyzed in the empty living room, staring at the front door. *Fucking brilliant Monaco! If you hadn't bought that fucking plate, Daniel would still be here tearing the place apart looking for his keys!*

Chapter 19

Commitment

Daniel was halfway to his condo before he remembered that it wasn't his anymore. A young woman from New Brunswick was sleeping in what used to be his bed. *Shit! Shit! Shit!* He slammed his fist down on the steering wheel. *Now where the fuck, do I go?* There was no way he was going to either of his sisters, they would want to talk and he wasn't anywhere near ready to talk about this. His parents' place was out of the question. He couldn't bear to see the hope and the happiness die in his mother's eyes when he showed up without Steven. She liked Steven, they all liked Steven. Fuck, he liked Steven! The light changed and Daniel shoved a hand through his hair, pushing it out of his eyes as he hit the gas. He loved Steven and that was the fucking problem. He wasn't going to be that guy again, the one who cared, and tried, and gave. The one who got left…

Flashes from the past, Aidan's promises and betrayals, lit up in his mind like strobe lights on a construction site: PROCEED WITH CAUTION, DETOUR, DANGER, STOP! His hands clenched around the steering wheel tightly enough to turn his knuckles white. *Marriage is for breeders. Why would we want to imitate their failures? A signature on a piece of paper, a rubber stamp from the government, just useless hetero bullshit! I refuse to wedge myself into a conformist model, for what? So they can understand us? Accept us? We have each other. That's all we need. I met someone. I'm getting married.*

The words were long in the past, and he didn't give a fuck about Aidan anymore, but it still made his gut twist to think of how abysmally, terminally stupid he'd been. How had he not noticed, not known that Aidan… No, fuck this! Steven didn't believe in marriage, right, no problem, but Daniel wasn't sticking around until the day he suddenly decided he did. No, that hadn't been a fun game the first time around, he was definitely not signing up for round two!

Daniel considered going to Kevin's. Kevin and Jonathan wouldn't grill him for details. Actually, Kevin would try but Jonathan would shut him down. Staying with them was not even a possibility though, it would be too fucking painful. They had exactly the life he wanted with Steven, the life he had thought he would have with Steven until, he checked the digital clock on the dashboard, oh, about seventeen minutes ago.

Deciding there was only one person who wouldn't ask questions he didn't want to answer, who could be counted on not to go all Oprah on his ass, Daniel headed downtown. Parking his car, he hunched into his coat, ploughing through the wind tunnel between the high-rise condos, and pulled the lobby door open. Scrolling through the directory, he punched A. Fine and picked up the receiver. "Allan? Let me in."

"Daniel?"

"Yeah." The glass door clicked open and Daniel pushed through it, crossing the granite-tiled foyer, he punched the up button between the elevators. Slumped against the wall, eyes closed, he concentrated on not thinking, not thinking about anything, definitely not thinking about anyone.

Allan threw his front door open, a teasing smile on his face as he watched his cousin step off the elevator and start down the hallway. "Hey, man, what's up? You guys run out of lube?"

Daniel looked up and Allan stopped smiling. He followed Daniel into the condo and closed the door behind him. "Where's Steven?" The question was quiet, Allan's voice low; he already knew that he wasn't going to like the answer.

Daniel shook his head.

Okay, this is not good! Allan nodded. "You want to talk about it?"

"No." Daniel glanced around, avoiding Allan's eyes, and shoved his hands in his pockets. "Can I hang here for a few days?"

"Sure." *Oh, crap, this is really bad!* Allan turned, grabbed some towels from a closet, and opened the door to a small room littered with photography equipment and a couch covered in portfolios and photographs. Handing the towels to Daniel, he gathered everything off the couch and dumped it all on the desk next to an assortment of camera entrails. "Sorry, I never get around to sorting this mess out. The couch opens into a bed though."

Daniel dropped the towels on the couch and tossed his jacket beside them. "Thanks."

Allan pretended not to notice that Daniel had become an empty husk of himself. "You want a beer?"

While the cousins twisted the caps off beer bottles and settled in front of Allan's flat screen in his downtown condo, Steven sat in his echoingly empty house in suburbia, his own flat screen a meaningless shadow on the wall. He stared at his phone. He'd tried calling and texting, nothing. Daniel wasn't answering anything.

They'd had arguments before. Daniel would yell and Steven would wait out the storm and then say something to make him laugh and it was over. Or Steven would get pissed, and Daniel would nuzzle into him, until Steven ran out of synonyms for inconsiderate idiot. But this was different. Daniel wasn't just angry, he was hurt and Steven had no fucking idea why!

Steven stared at his phone, but all he saw was Daniel, mouth set in hard lines, eyes dead, walking out the front door. *He's coming back. Of course, he's coming back, idiot! He fucking lives here! He'll drive around, cool down, and come home.* Uncurling himself from the couch, operating entirely on autopilot, he turned the TV off and wandered into the kitchen. He found Daniel's coffee mug in the sink and slipped it into the dishwasher. *See, he's coming back.*

He walked upstairs and stood in the doorway of Daniel's office. He looked at the overflowing waste basket, the can of soda on the desk, and Daniel's sweatshirt tossed over the high-tech black web of steel and leather that Daniel thought was a ridiculous waste of money and Steven had talked him into buying anyway. *He'll be home any minute.* He took the sweatshirt and tossed it into the hamper in their bedroom. *He's probably on his way home now.*

He stood in the doorway of their *en suite* looking at Daniel's electric razor, soap, and toothpaste. Entering the washroom, he plucked Daniel's toothbrush out of its holder. He sat on the edge of the bathtub, turning the toothbrush over and over in his hands. *Oh God, where is he?*

Downstairs again, Steven retrieved his cell from the couch and tried again. Nothing, same as before, the call went straight to voice mail. *It's been over two hours, where the hell is he?* He paced a small circuit around the living room, pausing on each lap to stare out the window, hoping to see Daniel's car. He paced, and checked the window. He paced and listened for the sound of Daniel's key in the front door. He paced, and tried to make sense out of any of it.

Daniel was a fairly laid back guy, which is one of the things that Steven loved about him. Steven was not and never would be a 'go with the flow' kind of person, so he really appreciated that quality in Daniel. The point being, that Daniel didn't get bent out of shape when people didn't agree with him. It was totally out of character for Daniel to go ballistic over a simple difference of opinion. Obviously, Steven had inadvertently triggered a hidden explosive. He knew. He just fucking knew that Dr. Aidan Sleazebag had planted that explosive. He didn't have a fucking clue how to diffuse it, but he would figure it out. They would figure it out together, as soon as Daniel came home and fucking talked to him!

Checking his watch, he was surprised to see that it was after midnight. He absolutely refused to even consider that they were over. Just as he was thinking that maybe he should get in his car and try and track his partner down, a telephone ring pealed out into the quiet and Steven's heart jumped into his throat. *Jesus Christ! Calm the fuck down, moron! It's just the Face Time ring on your iPad. It's Stephanie calling from Vancouver. It's not Daniel. Daniel would call your cell.*

Grabbing his iPad, he flipped the cover open as he sank onto the couch. He swiped the screen, and opened the call. "Hey, Steph."

Stephanie didn't bother with small talk. "Daniel's at Allan's. What the hell happened?"

Oh, thank God! Of all the places Daniel could be, like hooking up with some faceless penis on Church Street or lying on a gurney in an emergency room, yeah, Allan's place was good. "When's he coming home?"

Stephanie paused and that's all the warning Steven needed. Stephanie was the 'barge in, ask questions later' type. She never hesitated. This was going to be bad. "I don't think he's coming home, Steven, at least not tonight. Talk to me."

Steven had to smile at the irony of her word choice, *talk to me.* That's exactly what he needed Daniel to do. "I don't know what the fuck happened. What did he tell Allan?"

"Nothing, he said he didn't want to talk about it. All Allan knows is that Daniel asked if he could stay for a few days."

He's not coming home! Steven started to stand and then fumbled to catch the iPad before it hit the floor. "I've got to go."

"Steven, wait!" Stephanie lowered her voice as Steven sat back down. "Give him some time. Allan says he's not talking. That means he's thinking. You may not know what happened but he does. And he needs time to process."

"I can't just sit here, Steph. I have to tell him…"

"He's not ready to listen, Steven. If he was, he wouldn't be at Allan's."

Well, fuck! She was right. Daniel hadn't heard anything he'd said, the words had bounced right off him, not getting through the protective shield he had raised. "I have to do something!"

"Go to sleep, go to work tomorrow. Give Daniel some time to remember that you're not Dr. Gorgeous."

"You know about Aidan?"

"I know that Allan wanted to gut him with rusty fishing tackle. I know that Daniel was the walking wounded until you, and that his whole family was worried about him."

"I want him here, Steph."

"I know, babe. He needs time to know that too."

"Okay, okay. If you hear anything…"

"I'll call."

Steven didn't get much sleep. He couldn't bring himself to lie down in their bed, not without Daniel. He paced the house and cleaned things, things that didn't need to be cleaned. He re-organized the fridge, the pantry, and the cutlery drawer. Finally, he curled onto the couch in Daniel's office. He fell asleep telling himself that Daniel was coming home. *He's in his car, he's around the corner. He's coming home.*

Even asleep, a part of Daniel knew that he didn't want to wake up. The mid-morning sun drifted under the blinds and slid across the hardwood floor as Daniel stretched against the sheets. No Steven lying curled behind him, no lingering coffee scent from the pot Steven made first thing in the morning, and no shower running in the *en suite*. Rolling onto his back, he opened his eyes to…not their room.

Allan's spare room, Allan's apartment. His brain woke up and filled in all the pain sleep had erased. *This is what happens when you look for more than sex. You get the world ripped out from under you! Happy ever after is for tweens who lose it over Twilight. It's a fucking plot point, it's not real. You're a writer; you should be able to tell fact from fiction. The fact is Steven is not committed to you. Move on.*

His bladder dragged him out of bed. In the washroom, he splashed water on his face and brushed his teeth with the spare toothbrush that Allan had given him last night. Padding into the kitchen, he found a Post-it note stuck to the coffee maker. Squinting, he finally managed to decipher Allan's messy scrawl.

Elle Canada Photo Shoot
Four Seasons Hotel
GET YOUR ASS DOWN HERE FOR 2 P.M.

"Fuck off." Scrunching the note up, he tossed it on the counter. Looking for a coffee mug, he opened the cupboard over the sink and found another note.

2 P.M.
OR I CALL YOUR SISTERS!

"Bastard!"

❄   ❄   ❄

At Cloverleaf Pharmacy, Janice was getting a little worried. Steven had been incommunicado all morning, staring at his phone as if it were a crystal ball. "Steven, you okay?" Her voice was low, her eyes concerned.

"Yeah, why?" Steven had to force himself to look at his colleague's face. His eyes kept straying to his cell phone.

"Well, you look kind of grey, you've been staring at your phone all morning, and you should have left for lunch." She glanced at the clock on the dispensary wall. "Nine minutes ago."

"Sorry, I'm a little out of it today." He slipped his phone into his back pocket and hung his lab coat up. "Those two prescriptions are for Mrs. Taraba. Make sure she understands the directions. She has a habit of taking everything at once. I'll be back by two."

He walked into the nearest Tim Hortons, and ordered coffee and a turkey on whole wheat. Taking a seat, he scrolled through his contact list and selected Steph's mobile.

"Steven?"

"Anything?"

"Not yet. He didn't say a thing last night. He just drank beer and stared at the TV. Allan's meeting him for lunch at two."

"He agreed to meet Allan for lunch, that's good."

"Agreed may be too strong a word. Allan left him a note threatening to call his sisters if he didn't show up."

"Yeah, that would work, although, no offense Steph, but Allan's not really my idea of a go-to guy for relationship advice."

Stephanie laughed. "I know. What's that expression? Those who can, do. Those who can't, teach. Let's hope Allan's a good teacher! Gotta go. I'll call you tonight."

Daniel spent what was left of the morning wandering Allan's apartment, staring out the windows and flicking through channels he didn't watch. He borrowed Allan's iPad and checked his email account to find various letters from editors and readers, all of which he ignored. At 1:30 P.M., muttering under his breath and cursing his cousin, he pulled on yesterday's clothes and drove down to the photo shoot.

Lunch ordered, Allan settled back in his seat, long fingers tapping on the table top. Daniel wanted to talk or he wouldn't be here. They both knew Allan's threat for the empty promise it was. Allan would never sic Daniel's sisters on him. "Okay, what did Steven do? Throw out your ratty sweat pants? Polish your desk? Handcuff you to the bed?" Allan's sense of humour went unappreciated. Daniel stared into his drink, moving it around on the table, overlapping the condensation rings in an intricate design. "Daniel!"

Daniel looked up. "Steven doesn't believe in marriage."

Allan waited, but apparently that was it. That was Steven's major crime. "So, neither do I, what's the big deal?"

Daniel sighed. "You don't get it."

"Explain it to me." Allan put his glass down and leaned into the table. "Because, so far, all I'm hearing is an episode of *Say Yes to the Dress*."

Daniel just waved that away, too depressed to even be insulted. "It's not about the wedding. It's about commitment."

"So, you think because Steven doesn't believe in white satin and flowers and little gold bands that he can't commit?"

"Gentlemen, be careful. The plates are hot." The waitress plunked their food down. "Anything else I can get for you?"

"No, we're good thanks." Allan smiled at the waitress and turned back to his cousin. "Since when are you all about the marriage vows anyway? You didn't have a problem shacking up with Aidan." Daniel flinched as if Allan had struck him. "Oh, shit! This is about that asshole, isn't it?" Allan jabbed his fork into his pasta. "Let me guess. Aidan didn't believe in marriage and Aidan left you, so, of course, Steven is going to leave you too."

"You forgot." Daniel hissed across the table. "Aidan said he didn't believe in marriage and then he left me to get fucking married!"

Allan swallowed a mouthful of pasta while he thought about that. "So, you think Steven is just stringing you along until Mr. Right shows up?"

"Not consciously, no. Steven's not like that."

Allan sat back in his chair. "Okay, answer me this all knowing and powerful Oz, say you and Aidan had been married, and he met this other guy, what would have happened?"

Daniel's eyes widened because knowing Aidan, he knew the answer. "He would have divorced me and married the other guy."

"Right!" Allan grinned in triumph. "The problem wasn't that Aidan was anti-marriage, the problem was that he was an untrustworthy, juvenile, selfish prick."

Daniel's fork hovered over his Caesar Salad, ideas ping-ponging around in his brain. He had never considered it from that angle. Married or not, the result would have been the same, Aidan would have left him. Married or not, Steven wasn't Aidan. It all came down to trust, didn't it?

Allan watched, knowing that Daniel had reached some kind of decision when he grimaced and stabbed at the lettuce in his bowl. He just hoped his cousin had reached the right decision. "So, can I have my spare room back now?"

Daniel speared a crouton and popped it into his mouth. "I didn't tell you I had lunch with Aidan a few months back, did I?"

Allan stared, his mouth open. "No, way!"

"Yeah, we ran in to each other in the PATH tunnels downtown." Daniel shrugged. "The guy he left me for, the one he was going to marry?"

"Yeah?"

"They never did get around to signing a marriage license. Ask me why."

"Why?"

Daniel smiled derisively, his eyes lit with malicious glee. "Because the love of his life, the man he intended to be with forever, wanted Aidan to join Doctors without Borders for two years." Daniel grinned. "They broke up."

"Aidan?" Allan's whole face broke into a grin. "Aidan, who practically lives in a spa, has Harry Rosen on speed dial, and can't function without Starbucks? Too bad he didn't go; I would pay money to see Aidan in a cinder block building without air conditioning." He pointed his fork at Daniel. "You know Steven's nothing like Aidan, right?"

"I know." Daniel pushed his plate away and sat back, a slow smile curving his lips. "When I first saw him standing outside Sandy's front door, I thought he was perfect." He shrugged, eyes getting in on the whole smiling thing. "He's not perfect, of course. He's just perfect for me." He looked across the table at Allan. "But there's no guarantee, is there? That he feels the same way, or that it's going to last?"

"No. There's no guarantee. Is that what you think marriage is, some magic Band-Aid that keeps everything from falling apart?"

"Yeah, maybe, a little bit."

Allan signaled the waitress, and dug out his wallet. "What are you going to do?"

"Man up."

After leaving Allan, and sitting in traffic on the Gardiner Expressway, Daniel finally made it home, home to Steven's house, their house. Dropping his keys on Spock's face, he smiled. Steven's esthetic ran towards earth tones and minimalism. He didn't let his Sci-Fi addiction influence his décor choices, but he'd compromised his good taste for Daniel.

Standing in the foyer, hands in his pockets, Daniel relaxed into the feeling of home. Nothing had changed since last night, nothing but Daniel, and that altered his perception of everything. It wasn't just the *Star Trek* plate, everywhere he looked he saw evidence of a joined life: his Wii beside Steven's Blu-ray player, his DVDs merged into Steven's collection, a throw his mother had made folded on the ottoman. In the kitchen his 'sugar toxic' cereals were lined up next to Steven's 'organic pulp' boxes. Both their favourite ice creams nestled together in the freezer, and his Tassimo sat on the counter beside Steven's juicer.

Walking upstairs, Daniel tossed the clothes he had been wearing since yesterday into the hamper and stepped into the shower. Doubts and insecurities slipped down the drain along with the shampoo and soap. Hitching a towel around his hips, he looked into the mirror as he shaved. *Maybe it isn't going to last forever. But it's working now, and I'm not going to sabotage my own happiness. Not with crap from my past, not if I can help it.*

Steven pulled into his driveway and parked beside Daniel's car. *He's here! He's back!* His hands clenched on the steering wheel, his eyes locked on Daniel's car. *What if he isn't back? What if he's in there packing?*

Steven winced, trying to hide from the image of Daniel pulling clothes off hangers and stuffing them into garbage bags.

His phone pinged with an incoming text message, and Steven jumped. He pulled his phone out, smiling as he read Stephanie's text.

From Stephanie: He's on his way home

From Steven: I know. I'm in the driveway. His car's here.

From Stephanie: So what are you waiting for?

From Steven: What if he's packing?

From Stephanie: He's not packing.

From Steven: What do you know?

From Stephanie: More than you do. Get in there. Love you.

From Steven: ☺

Letting himself into the house, he dropped his keys beside Daniel's. They looked so right, lying beside each other on that ridiculous plate. Tears pricked behind Steven's eyes and he blinked them back. He had been terrified that he would never see them nestled together on Spock's blue science uniform again. "Daniel?"

"Hey."

Steven looked up to see Daniel on the staircase, hair wet from the shower, towel around his hips. "You're home?" *Are we good? Are you staying?*

Daniel nodded. "Yeah." *I'm not going anywhere.*

That's all Daniel said, but that's all Steven needed to hear. Daniel took the last steps down as Steven crossed the foyer. They met at the bottom of the staircase. "Steven, I…"

Steven shook his head and, putting one hand flat against Daniel's chest, backed him up against the wall. "Later, we can talk later."

Opening his mouth under Steven's, Daniel was more than happy to postpone any discussion of his meltdown. He slid his arms around Steven's waist, under his jacket, hands linking into Steven's belt, pulling Steven into his body. *Yes! Good! Steven always felt so fucking good.*

Steven licked into Daniel's mouth, sucking at tongue and lips. He moved his hands down Daniel's back, tucked his fingers under the towel and tugged it off *Yes! You're not going anywhere, Daniel mine, ever!* Tossing the towel aside, he pulled off Daniel's mouth, kissing down his neck, and over his collarbone. Stepping back, he looked into Daniel's eyes as he dragged one hand down Daniel's torso and wrapped it around his cock.

Daniel's hands settled on Steven's hips and his eyes closed, only to snap open in surprise as Steven backed up, pulling Daniel with him, using his cock as a handle. "Hey! Don't damage anything we may need."

Steven smiled, but he didn't let Daniel go. In fact, he stepped up onto the first step, feeling his way, walking backwards. "Come with me," Steven tightened his grip on Daniel's shaft, "and no one gets hurt."

It was crazy, and ridiculously awkward, and it took forever for them to reach the top of the staircase. One step at time, his eyes burning into Daniel's, Steven backed up the stairs. He never let go, and Daniel never asked him too. Finally clearing the last step, they stopped on the upstairs landing.

Daniel glazed his hand over Steven's side and curled his fingers into the dip at the small of his back. "You going to let me go anytime soon?"

Steven swept his thumb over the flushed crown. "No." He locked his eyes on Daniel's. "I'm never letting you go."

Daniel didn't have to be a mind reader to know that Steven wasn't talking about his cock. "I'm not going anywhere, babe."

Steven pushed his fist down to the base of Daniel's cock, and slid it up again. "No, you're not, Daniel mine."

Daniel stepped into Steven, tucked his head into Steven's neck, smelling soap and skin and Steven. "Say it again."

One hand still wrapped around Daniel's cock, the other arm across Daniel's back, holding him close, Steven spoke the words softly. "Daniel mine."

"Yes." Daniel dragged his lips over Steven's neck, and pulling his head back, opened his mouth over Steven's. He didn't need rings and vows. He needed this, teeth and tongues, sliding lips and mingling breaths, he needed to be Steven's.

Backing out of his partner's hold, he pushed the jacket off Steven's shoulders, and down his arms. Steven let Daniel's cock go, and the jacket slid over his hands and hit the floor. Daniel grabbed Steven's tie, and pulled him into their bedroom. They attacked Steven's clothes together. Seconds later, his clothes in a heap on the floor, Steven hit the bed on his back, pulling Daniel down on top of him. He opened his legs and Daniel settled between them. Supporting himself on his elbows, Daniel stared down into dark-as-night eyes.

Steven reached one hand up into Daniel's hair, playing with the perpetually messy blond locks. "I missed you last night. I slept on the couch in your office. I couldn't be in here without you."

Dipping his head, Daniel kissed each eyebrow, each eyelid, and finally Steven's lips. "Who am I?" Steven frowned, not understanding the question. Daniel kissed him again, a warm gentle slide of lips. He looked down into Steven's eyes, his own filled with need. "Who am I, Steven?"

Tracing a hand over Daniel's jaw, Steven tried to read Daniel's eyes. He glided a thumb across Daniel's bottom lip. "Mine?"

"God, yes!" Daniel delved into Steven's mouth, slipping his arms under Steven, molding their bodies into one. "Yours Steven, please!"

The last words were whispered, gasped out between kisses. Steven wasn't entirely sure that Daniel even knew that he had said them. Conscious or not, the words were a guide to what Daniel needed. Steven brushed his hands down Daniel's back, and kneaded his ass. Tipping his hips up, he slid their cocks together. "Mine, Daniel, always mine."

The argument from last night wasn't forgotten. Rather, the anxiety that caused it and the resulting chasm that had separated them fueled their coupling. They ground against each other, mouths harsh and hands bruising, cocks hard and leaking, trapped between their bodies.

Steven tore his mouth away, and pushed his hands against Daniel's shoulders. Daniel pulled back, mouth still open, eyes wild. Not looking away from Daniel, Steven flailed his arm out, reaching for the end table, and the lube. Pumping some onto his fingers, he slicked the lube over Daniel's cock. Spreading his legs wider, he raised his hips. "Come home, Daniel."

They reclaimed each other with hard flesh and soft words. Eyes locked, they slammed into each other, grunts and gasps and sweat, and never letting go.

Slipping out of Steven, Daniel curled into his partner's side and traced his fingers through the spunk glistening wet against Steven's skin. Tipping his head back, looking at Steven, he licked his cum-coated fingers.

Not something Daniel had ever done before and while Steven thought it was one of the hottest things he'd ever seen, he wondered at the timing. "Have we run out of facecloths?"

Fingers clean, Daniel reached out to trace Steven's smile. "I just wanted all of you."

Pushing back against his pillows, Steven soothed one hand down Daniel's back. "Talk to me."

Daniel nodded, his head shifting against Steven's shoulder. He didn't say anything for quite a while, going over it in his mind, making sure he understood it himself before he tried to explain it to Steven. "Okay." Taking a deep breath, he moved out of Steven's arms, and sat cross-legged on the bed, facing his partner.

He placed his hand palm up on Steven's thigh, and Steven slipped his hand into Daniel's. "I told you that things just seemed to fall apart with Aidan and me. They did, that's true. What I didn't tell you was that our relationship didn't die a slow lingering death, limping along in silent dinners and token sex. It was murdered, a swift stab of hurt and betrayal." Daniel looked at Steven, a self-deprecating quirk to his lips. "Sorry, it's the writer in me."

Steven squeezed Daniel's hand. "I like your style, very visual. Don't leave me hanging."

Daniel gave Steven a real smile. "Yeah? Good." He shifted on the mattress, getting comfortable, his hand still entwined with Steven's. "I came home from dinner at my parents' one Friday and Aidan was waiting for me. He had met someone. He was leaving me to marry this guy, another doctor he interned with." Daniel shrugged. "Stupid, I guess, to be so shocked. I knew things weren't good but I thought it was stress, his intern hours, my trying to find work." Daniel held Steven's eyes. "The worst part, the part that made me feel like a complete idiot was that the whole time we were together, Aidan insisted that 'marriage was a heteronormative attempt to fit homosexuality into a mold that the social majority could accept'. He vehemently pronounced his refusal to 'imitate the straights'. And there he was, standing in our living room, telling me he's getting married!" Daniel looked down, playing with Steven's fingers. "So, I wasn't good enough to marry but some other guy was."

I knew it! I fucking knew that prick was behind this somehow! Steven tightened his fingers around Daniel's and waited for him to finish.

Daniel looked up, still twisting his fingers around Steven's, regret clear on his face. "When you said you didn't believe in marriage, all I heard was that you were leaving me. I'm sorry. I know that's not what you meant. I know you're not Aidan." His hand clenched around Steven's. "I just don't want to lose you, lose us."

Steven's lips tilted into his trademark crooked smile. "Daniel, you know what a nut job I am, how I keep my life organized and planned. I'm not good with surprises and I despise change. I couldn't even quit guitar lessons, how would I ever walk away from you?" Steven laid his free hand on Daniel's knee, and moved it up, caressing the muscled thigh. "What were you thinking? You're never going to lose me." He leaned over, tucked his head against Daniel's, his voice laughing into Daniel's ear. "I'm going to have a tracking chip inserted under your skin, like the one Brady has."

Daniel laughed and pushed Steven backwards onto the mattress, crawling on top of him. "I'm getting you a dog tag with my cell number on it. If found please call Daniel Fine."

Steven grinned up at Daniel, his hands playing over Daniel's shoulders and gliding down his arms. "So we're stuck with each other then?"

"Yeah." Leaning down, Daniel licked at one of Steven's nipples. "Too bad."

Laughing, Steven rolled them both over, tucking Daniel under him. He pinned Daniel's hands to the mattress, and pressed into his mouth. Straddling Daniel, he released his hands and worked his way across and down Daniel's chest, one kiss and nip at a time. The muffled sound of a text ping broke through the rustle of skin on sheets. Steven sat up astride Daniel's thighs and cocked his head, listening. The sound came from his pants still lying on the floor. "That's probably Stephanie."

Daniel nodded, "Yeah." He waved his hand over his torso indicating the path Steven had been nipping down his chest. "You were saying?" Steven grinned and leaned over Daniel again, teeth gliding down his happy trail. Daniel wriggled under him, impatient. Another ping rang out, louder; this time it was Daniel's phone on the night table. Steven flashed his eyes up along Daniel's body, and Daniel shrugged. "Probably Allan."

"Yeah." Steven rolled off Daniel and stretched out beside him. Pulling his leg up, he planted his foot on Daniel's hip, and pushed him off the bed.

Daniel hit the hardwood floor with a heavy thump. Sitting on the floor, gingerly twisting the shoulder that had taken most of the impact from the fall, he glared up at his partner. "What the fuck did you do that for?"

Steven grabbed a pillow and threw it at Daniel. "That is for running out on me last night." Stretching across the mattress, he grabbed a second pillow and threw it after the first. "That is for not coming home all night." Lying on his stomach, Steven reached over the edge of the bed and slapped a hand to the back of Daniel's head. "And that is for thinking, for even a second, that I was anything like that selfish, superficial, asshole ex of yours."

"Ow!" Daniel rubbed the back of his head. "You done now?"

"Are you going to walk out in the middle of an argument again?"

"No." Daniel peeked up at Steven from under his eyelashes, and sent him an 'oh, come on, you know I'm cute' smile.

"Then I'm done."

Daniel knelt up, crossed his arms on the mattress, and rested his chin on his arms, his face level with Steven's. "Is it safe to get back in bed now?"

Steven grinned at him. "Depends what you mean by safe."

Epilogue

"We're going to be late." Steven stood in the doorway of their *en suite*, watching as Daniel tried to push his hair into some kind of order. "Stop playing with your hair. It's not going to get any better." Steven didn't think you could improve on perfection, but he got a kick out of teasing Daniel.

Frustrated, Daniel met Steven's eyes in the mirror. "I should just cut it all off."

Steven moved up behind Daniel, crowding him against the sink. He brushed his hand up the back of Daniel's neck, and shuffled his fingers through the perpetually untidy mass of blond waves. "No."

Daniel turned in Steven's arms. "That's it? No."

Steven smiled. "What do you want me to say? I love your hair the way it is." Steven lowered his voice, wrapped his hand around the nape of Daniel's neck, and squeezed. "Or, I said no."

Daniel grinned, and rolled his hips suggestively against Steven's. "That second one sounds really," Daniel rolled his hips again, his cock trying to reach Steven through the towel, "Hot!"

Steven pressed Daniel back against the sink. "Perv!"

"Oh, I'm the perv?" Daniel reached up, threaded his fingers through Steven's hair, and closed his fist, tugging just a little too hard. He watched as Steven's head went back, his eyes closed and his hips thrust automatically.

Daniel loved everything about this; the fact that he knew this man well enough to know about the hair thing, the fact Steven trusted him enough to allow that knowledge and the fact that with a quick twist of his fingers he could unravel Steven, every fucking time! He leaned into Steven, licking up the side of his neck, and nipping just under his jaw as he tugged on his hair again.

Steven sighed, his eyes still closed, his arms pulling Daniel closer. His hands gripped Daniel's hips and in a sneak attack, he spun the blond around and delivered a swat to his terry-covered rear. "Uh-uh. Get dressed. We can't be the last ones there. We live across the street."

Daniel laughed and tossed his towel into the hamper as he crossed into the bedroom. He pulled a pair of black briefs out of his drawer and, knowing that Steven was watching him, made sure to bend over for much longer than absolutely necessary, while he stepped into them. He dragged them up his legs slowly and over his rump even more slowly, pausing half way, and looking over his shoulder at the man he was strutting the reverse-naked for.

Steven leaned against the door jamb in the *en suite* doorway, arms folded across his chest, eyes focused on Daniel's ass. "Oh, you're so going to pay for this when we get back home."

Still watching Steven over his shoulder, Daniel swayed his hips, one provocative slide. "You take Visa?"

Steven shrugged away from the door jamb and crossed the room to stand behind Daniel. He wrapped one arm around Daniel's chest pulling him flush against his own chest, and delved into the half raised underwear with the other hand. He stroked Daniel's shaft, while he nuzzled into his neck. "Teasing, it's a game for two."

Daniel tilted his head, exposing more of his neck to Steven's mouth, and moved his hands back, rubbing them over Steven's thighs. "We don't have to be on time. It's a buffet."

Steven bit Daniel's earlobe. "Yeah, it's a buffet that we promised to bring the watermelon for." He stepped away from the blond, with one last pat to a cock that Daniel was definitely going to have trouble tucking into his briefs. "Get dressed." He started out of the room.

Daniel grimaced as he pulled the soft cotton over hard flesh. "Sadist!"

Steven turned as he reached the bedroom doorway, and flashed a smile at Daniel. "Nope, I'm Italian."

Pulling open drawers, and flicking through hangars, his brows creased in concentration, Daniel tried to decide what to wear.

Dressing was a lot more complicated than it used to be. Over the past eighteen months since he'd moved in with Steven, he had replaced most of his ratty sweatpants and disintegrating T-shirts. Not because of any complaint Steven had made; the man didn't give a flying fuck what clothes Daniel wore, as long as he eventually took them off. He had gradually transformed his wardrobe because he had become a different person since he met Steven. He felt better about himself, about his life, about life in general, actually, and somehow that had translated into new clothes.

Smirking to himself, Daniel stepped into a pair of denim shorts. Distressed, pre-faded, and tight, they fell low on his hips and hugged his ass perfectly. They showcased a good amount of the thigh muscles that Steven had become addicted to. They were going to drive the man insane all afternoon. *Hah! Teasing is a game for two! Take that, Monaco!* He pulled on a white T-shirt emblazoned with a grinning black skull sporting a pair of black sunglasses.

"Daniel!" Steven yelled up the staircase.

Daniel slipped his feet into black leather sandals, grabbed his sunglasses, and sprinted out of the room. "Coming!"

Steven stood at the front door, all GQ perfect in black linen shorts and a crisp white shirt, cuffs folded precisely. He held the promised watermelon in the crook of one arm, his keys dangling from the other hand. He watched Daniel's legs come down the stairs. *Cargo shorts, that's what Daniel needs. Really long, really ugly cargo shorts that cover...* He swallowed and dragged his eyes off Daniel's thighs to meet hazel eyes sparking gold with laughter. Pretending that he could think of anything except taking Daniel right back upstairs, Steven cleared his throat. "You ready?"

"Almost." Walking into the kitchen, Daniel took a Canadian flag decal off the window and slapped it on his back pocket. "Don't want to be unpatriotic." He spun in a slow circle, giving Steven an excellent view of his ass, now highlighted by the red and white maple leaf sticker. Grinning at the look on Steven's face, Daniel pushed the front door open. "How long do I have to wait for you?"

Crossing the street, they wound their way through the cars parked in Sandy's driveway. Daniel unlatched the gate into the backyard and held it open for Steven. Brady jumped all over both of them, while Daniel tried to push him off and close the gate. "Sit, you crazy lump of fur, sit!"

Steven curled his fingers around Brady's collar. "Sit!" He didn't raise his voice, but Brady hunkered down immediately, his tongue hanging out of his mouth, his tail wagging.

Daniel leaned into Steven. "I know just how he feels."

Steven turned shocked eyes to the blond and laughed at the leer Daniel sent him. Whatever response he was going to make remained unsaid as Rhys yelled, "Danny and Steven are here!", and came barreling at them.

Steven had his hands full of watermelon and dog, so Daniel hoisted his nephew on to his shoulders. "What have you been eating, dude? You weigh a ton!"

"Nothing! Mom said I had to wait 'til you guys got here. I'm starving!"

"Uncle Steven! Watch!" Lauren checked to make sure she had Steven's attention and then she dived into the pool. Her head popped through the water and she swam to the side, hoisting herself to the edge of the pool. "Did I do it right?"

"Brilliant, Lauren, that was perfect!" Steven walked over to the pool, smiling down at the seven-year-old. "You're ready for your next badge, no problem."

"Yes!" Lauren grinned and pumped the air before she slipped back into the water. Steven turned to Glen, on life guard duty, watching his daughter from the comfort of a lawn chair. "She's half fish."

"She loves it. Those tips you gave her last week really helped."

"I can't believe I remembered anything useful. It's been a while."

"We're renting a cottage for two weeks at the end of August. You know, just before the kids go back to school. It's on a lake. You guys should come."

"Yeah, not a big fan of lakes." Steven shuddered. "There's always gushy stuff in there."

"Wuss! Wuss! Wuss!" Daniel went charging by, Rhys laughing on his shoulders.

"Who's a wuss?" Doug dragged a chair over to the pool.

"Me, although," Steven raised his voice so that Daniel could hear him, "he's not supposed to tell everyone that!" Voice back to conversational normal, he smiled at Doug. "Are you and Karen going up to Glen's cottage?"

"Hell, yes!" Doug popped the tab on his Coke Zero. "I'm trying to get a week off. You guys coming up?"

"Coming where?" Daniel dropped Rhys into Doug's lap, and Doug rolled him onto the ground, tickling the laughing five-year-old.

"Sandy and I are renting a cottage for the last two weeks in August. I was telling Steven you guys should come."

Daniel looked at Steven, and got a small nod of acceptance. "Sure, we can probably manage a weekend. Mom and Dad coming?"

"Steven! You adopting that watermelon or what?" Standing with one hand on the open patio door, Karen called across the backyard.

Steven waved. "Better go, not nice to keep a pregnant lady waiting."

Doug shuddered in an exaggerated pantomime of fear. "Not safe!"

Crossing the lawn, Steven slid the patio door open and found not Karen, but Daniel's mother. "Hi, Julia, where's Brian?"

Daniel's mother looked up from the salad she was tossing. "Oh, you know him, can't take the heat. He's soaking up the air conditioning in the living room."

"Do you want me to slice this?" Steven put the watermelon on a clear patch of counter near the sink.

Julia nodded. "If you don't mind, that would be great. Knives are in the second drawer, platters on top of the fridge."

Steven pulled a platter down and found a knife. "Where are the girls?"

Julia shook her head. "They're in the basement arguing over how much dessert to take out of the freezer. Karen's been baking all week."

"Think I'll stay up here then." Steven drew the knife along the length of the melon.

"Smart man!" She put the salad on the table and opened the fridge to get the dressing. "The heat and the waiting are getting to Karen."

"Can't be easy." Steven cut the watermelon into precise triangles.

"Three more weeks of this! How much bigger can I get? I'm the size of a hippo now!" Karen came up from the basement carrying a cherry pie, Sandy right behind her, a cake in each hand.

Steven put the sliced watermelon on the table and smiled at Karen. "But a really cute hippo."

Karen put her pie on the counter and walked over to Steven, talking to her tummy. "Hey, baby, say hi to Uncle Steven."

Steven put his hand on her stomach. "Hello, little one." He looked at Karen. "No name yet?"

Karen flopped onto a kitchen chair, one hand resting on her stomach. "Doug and I can't agree on anything. Every time I find one I like, he says he knew someone with that name who's a serial killer, or a drug addict."

Julia and Steven laid out napkins and cutlery while Sandy took clean glasses out of the dishwasher. "Just wait, once the baby's born, the name will come to you. You know, kind of like that old Kevin Costner movie." Sandy waved her fingers in the air and dialed her voice down to spooky. "Build it and they will come!"

In the kitchen, they explored baby names. By the pool, Glen pushed out of his lawn chair. "Daniel, keep an eye on Lauren. I've got to start the BBQ."

While Daniel watched his niece in the pool, and Glen fired up the BBQ, Doug played soccer with Rhys.

"Don't even think about it, Brady." Doug blocked the dog, who didn't understand why he couldn't play too. "Okay, Rhys, kick!"

Tongue lolling out of his mouth, Brady tracked the ball, totally focused until the sound of the latch rising on the backyard gate diverted his attention. He ran full tilt at the gate, barking at the intruders.

"Brady, sit!" Allan squeezed through the gate first, holding Brady off, so he wouldn't drool all over Stephanie.

Stephanie closed the gate behind her. "It's okay, I like dogs."

Allan grimaced. "This isn't a dog. This is one hundred pounds of crazy."

Stephanie reached out and scratched behind Brady's ear. "Oh, he's gorgeous!"

Spatula frozen in mid-flip, Glen stared as Allan introduced Brady to Stephanie. "No way! Allan what are you doing here?" Glen's yell got everyone's attention.

"Oh my God!" Daniel stood from his lawn chair, but he stayed by the pool, he couldn't leave Lauren. "I don't believe it!"

Kicking the soccer ball over to his son, Doug grinned at his wife's cousin. "Okay, how'd you do it?"

"What are you talking about?" Allan didn't do innocence at all well.

Glen shut the lid on the BBQ and joined Allan and Stephanie. "You know what we're talking about." Glen turned to Stephanie. "Allan has never, I mean never, shown up on time."

"Because he always gets lost." Doug watched as Rhys chased after the ball, Brady right beside him. "Steph drove here, right?"

"Oh, ye of little faith!" Allan laughed as they all walked towards the pool and Daniel. "I drove here, and I did not make even one wrong turn."

The three men looked at Stephanie for confirmation. She nodded and slipped her arm around Allan's waist. "It's true. Not even one U-turn."

"That's not possible!" Daniel looked from Stephanie to Allan, suspicious. "No way."

Doug nodded. "That's right. There's no way Allan made it here without getting lost. When he moved out of his parents' place, it took him two months to figure out where his apartment was."

Stephanie looked at Allan, and he nodded for her to speak. She cupped her hand by her mouth, as if she was revealing a national secret. "I bought him a GPS."

"Well, that explains it!" "I knew it!" "It's about freaking time!"

"Oh, right, we've only been telling you to get a GPS for years." Daniel's grin only emphasized the mocking tone in his voice. "But one word from Steph…"

"Yes, you all told me to get a GPS, but this angel," Allan wrapped his arms around Stephanie, "actually, bought me one."

Sandy slid the patio door open. "Glen is the...Allan! What are you doing here?" Taking the two steps down to the patio, Sandy smiled at her cousin. "I don't believe it!"

During lunch, while everyone else was talking, Steven leaned over to Stephanie. "This is a big deal, you know. Allan has never brought anyone to a family thing before."

Stephanie blushed. "Yeah, Julia told me the same thing, and Sandy, and Karen, even Brian." Stephanie raised her eyebrows, smiling at Steven. "I think it's because I bought him the GPS."

Steven laughed. "Yeah, that's it." He took a bite of his hamburger. "What's happening with the transfer?"

"There are two of us up for the same position, but I've got a little more experience." Stephanie shrugged. "I'm hoping."

On the other side of the table, Karen stole a roasted potato off Allan's plate, ignoring his protest. "Hey, I'm eating for two."

Allan looked at her baby bump. "You sure you're just eating for two?"

Karen stuck her tongue out at him and popped the potato into her mouth. "So, what's going on Allan?"

"What?" Allan knew exactly what she meant, but he didn't want to talk about it.

"You don't bring women to family things, remember? Makes them clingy, right?"

"It's no big deal." Allan frowned at his cousin. "Steph was in town and she knows all of you anyway through Steven, so I thought she'd like to come."

"Right!" Karen turned to her sister. "Are you buying this?"

Sandy grinned at Allan. "Nope!"

Karen shook her head at Allan. "So delusional!"

Allan leaned back in his chair and graced his cousin with a lazy grin. "So nosy!"

It got quiet after lunch, too much sun and too much food made everyone lazy. Brian fell asleep in the hammock that was strung between two trees in a corner of the yard. Glen took the kids for a bike ride. Everyone else either floated in the pool or lazed in the shade. Daniel looked around the yard; everyone but Steven.

Sliding the patio door shut behind him, Daniel crossed through the kitchen and walked down the hallway to the living room at the front of the house. He found Steven exactly where he knew he would be, standing in front of what Daniel liked to call Sandy's 'wall of shame'. His sister had a photo of every significant family event framed and hung on the fireplace wall.

Stepping behind Steven, he wrapped his arms around Mr. Perfect, and nestled their heads together. "Aren't you tired of looking at that picture yet?"

Steven leaned back into Daniel and shook his head. "No."

Daniel rubbed his cheek against Steven's. "You know we have the same one at home, right, only bigger?"

"I know." Crossing his arms over Daniel's, Steven smiled. "And there's one at your parents' place, and at Karen's."

Allan had taken the picture, of course, and it was excellent. Neither Daniel nor Steven had ever looked so good. It was idyllic, almost dreamlike, the two of them standing in the late June sunshine, holding hands and looking into each other's eyes.

"I'm sure this will wear off eventually, one day I'll pass this picture without even seeing it. But for now, it makes me smile every single time. We were so happy!"

"We're happy now."

"Yes, but look at that, that's magic!"

"Yeah, Allan's really good with a camera." Daniel ducked to the left but he wasn't quite quick enough, Steven's elbow got him just below his ribs. "Okay, you're right!" Laughing, he tucked his head next to Steven's again. "It wasn't what I expected. It was...powerful."

"Yes." Steven started out of the room. "And I look damn good in a tuxedo."

"Who was I, the ugly step-sister?"

Steven grinned at the blond walking beside him. "You looked okay."

Daniel stopped. "Okay? I looked okay?" He reached for Steven, but Steven sprinted into the kitchen and out the patio door. "That's right, Monaco, you better run!"

Lunch long over, the afternoon turning into evening, Allan and Stephanie got ready to leave. "Hey guys, we've got to go." Allan smiled, as Stephanie kissed Daniel and hugged Steven. "Steph's got a flight out to Vancouver tonight."

Steven pulled back from his friend, keeping her hands in his. "Text me as soon as you hear about the transfer."

Stephanie nodded. "You and Allan; got it."

As Allan and Stephanie moved away to say their goodbyes to the rest of the family, Steven turned to Daniel. "You ready to leave?"

"Yeah." He couldn't help smiling as he looked at the man standing beside him. Hours after they'd left their house, in the scorching heat of a July 1st day, after playing soccer with Rhys, and badminton with Lauren, Steven still looked perfect; shirt pristine and shorts unwrinkled. How was it even possible for linen shorts to not wrinkle? "Are we doing the fireworks at the park tonight?"

"Of course." Steven looked at the blond beside him. Messy hair, rumbling laugh, and shorts that hugged his ass, highlighting thigh muscles that...*Oh, yeah! We're leaving, like now!* "Would I miss our anniversary fireworks?"

Daniel brushed his fingers against Steven's. "Two years ago today."

Steven smiled. "In the park, remember, you held me for the first time?"

Daniel nodded. "You stumbled in the dark and I caught you."

Steven shook his head, lips tilting into a smile. "I didn't stumble."

Daniel's eyes went wide. "Why you manipulative control freak, you did that on purpose!"

"Well, I had to know, didn't I?"

"Know what?"

Steven leaned into Daniel, speaking low. "How you felt."

Daniel swallowed. "Don't move." He crossed the grass to where his mother and sister sat. "Mom, we're going. Sandy, see you in the park for fireworks." Turning, he bolted back to Steven.

Sandy caught her mother's eye and smirked. "Something tells me they're not going home to take a nap."

Julia laughed. "Daniel really shouldn't try to be discrete. He's not very good at it."

Closing the front door behind him, Steven threw his keys on top of Spock and kicked his loafers off. Turning to face Daniel, he unbuttoned his shirt and pulled it out of his waistband. Daniel tugged his T-shirt over his head and started on the button above his zipper.

"No, don't!" Steven tossed his shirt on the floor and knelt in front of Daniel. "Not yet." He put his hands on Daniel's knees and ran them up, sliding his fingers under the tight denim banding Daniel's thighs. Two years and Steven still had a thing for Daniel's legs, and his ass, and his cock. Two years and Steven still had a thing for Daniel, period.

Two years and Daniel still craved Steven's touch, his fingers, his lips, his cock. Two years and Daniel still craved Steven, period. His hands on Steven's shoulders, Daniel spread his legs, but Steven deliberately moved away from Daniel's groin. Hands moving in long vertical sweeps, he worked his way around the outside of his lover's thighs, inch by slow inch until his fingers were tracing up the back of Daniel's legs. On each sweep up, his fingers slid under the hem of Daniel's shorts, reaching as high as the tightness of the denim would allow.

"Steven." Daniel moved one hand into Steven's hair, tipping his head back, looking down into heated dark eyes, his own already changing colour, shifting to gold. The slow sweep of Steven's hands was making him crazy. They never quite reached any of the really good places. "Steven!"

"Always so impatient, Daniel mine." Steven grinned and slid his hands down, fingers tracing the back of Daniel's knees lightly.

Daniel snorted. "I'm not getting any younger you know."

Relenting, Steven placed his hands on Daniel's inner thighs, just above his knees. He kept his touch light, fingers grazing the soft blond hair that dusted Daniel's legs, as he moved his hands up. He stopped with his fingertips just brushing the hem of Daniel's denim shorts.

"You're killing me here." Daniel shifted his stance, trying to get Steven's hands higher.

Steven tucked his fingers just under the denim, and looked up at the man standing over him. "What did I say before we left, Daniel?

When you were sliding into your briefs like some kind of pole dancer?" Steven pushed his hands a fraction higher.

"Teasing is for two?" Daniel clenched his hand on Steven's shoulder. His body getting tight as Steven's fingers inched ever upwards.

"Yes, and?" Steven flexed his fingers, feeling the heat of Daniel's body.

"You were going to make me pay when we got home." Daniel thrust his pelvis. *Close, so close! Please!*

Steven looked up, needing to see the want in his lover's eyes. "I don't take Visa, Daniel." He pushed his hands under the denim shorts, his fingers grazing Daniel's cock through the cotton briefs. "But I will take you."

Daniel pumped his hips, feeling his cock shift against Steven's fingers. "Yes, God yes!"

Sitting back on his heels, Steven slipped his hands out from under the denim, and slid them all the way down Daniel's legs, linking his fingers around Daniel's ankles, waiting.

"Steven!" *Now! Now! Now!*

On his knees, his fingers tracing circles on Daniel's ankles, Steven looked up admiring the picture Daniel made. Cock full and thick behind his zipper, hips pumping the air, face flushed and eyes full of want, Daniel was everything Steven would ever need. "I will take you, if you ask me very nicely."

"Oh, fuck!" Steven wanted him to beg, and oh, God, he wanted to. Just the thought made his cock, still trapped inside his shorts, throb and leak. Steven made him burn. "Please! Fuck me!"

Steven pushed to his feet, hauled Daniel into his arms and commandeered his mouth. Daniel pressed into Steven's body, his arms locking Steven to him, feasting on Steven's lips. Not breaking the kiss, Steven pulled back enough to slip his hand between their bodies. He unzipped Daniel and pulled his cock out of its cotton nest. He fisted Daniel, sliding over the shaft in ever smoother glides as pre-cum slicked the way. Daniel moaned into Steven's mouth and thrust into his hand.

Pulling away from Daniel's lips, Steven dropped kisses along his jaw and down his neck. "That's better, Daniel mine." Leaning in, he nipped at Daniel's lower lip and, locking eyes with his lover, backed away. Bending, he snatched his shirt off the floor, and started up the staircase. He glanced over his shoulder, at Daniel standing bemused in the foyer. "Coming?"

Breathing hard, eyes glazed with want, Daniel watched Steven walk up the stairs. Wavy chocolate hair, strong back, slender waist, narrow hips, white shirt dangling from his right hand, and black linen shorts just grazing his ass. The shorts weren't tight, not like Daniel's. They only hinted at what they covered. Daniel took the stairs two at a time. He wanted what those shorts hinted at. Steven was so right; teasing was a game for two!

❈　❈　❈

Much, much later, when the sky turned full dark, they walked down to the park. Even amid the throngs of people waiting for the fireworks to start, Daniel didn't have any trouble finding the rest of the family. He led Steven to a clump of trees on a small rise, the same place the family parked themselves every year. Even after two years, Steven couldn't have found anyone. The trees all looked the same to him.

"Hey, look who's here!" Daniel grinned at his niece. "What are you doing up so late?"

Lauren grinned. "Mom said I was old enough to come."

Sandy shook her head. "After hours of pestering, I said if she was still awake she could come, big mistake!" Sandy only sounded like she was complaining. Fireworks were one of her favourite things and she was excited to share them with her daughter.

Karen stood in front of her husband, leaning into him, her hands resting on her bump. "What do you think, guys? Stephanie and Allan, they seem pretty serious. Well, you know, serious for Allan."

Daniel stood behind Steven, one hand on Mr. Perfect's hip. Steven shook his head. "I don't know what they're doing. Stephanie won't even say they're dating. But she's applied for a transfer to Toronto."

"Allan's never brought anyone to our place before. That has to mean something." Sandy held on to Lauren's hand. She didn't want her wandering off in the dark.

"Allan Skypes her every night." Daniel announced this with all the awe it deserved.

"No!" Sandy and Karen exclaimed together, and Steven nodded in confirmation.

"You can't win with you guys. You bug him to find someone special, and when he finally does, you bug him about that too." Doug still didn't get this family.

Karen patted his arm. "That's because we care."

Music started, flowing over the park from speakers hidden in the trees, and everyone looked up. Sandy squeezed Lauren's hand. "It's starting!" Rockets screamed into the air, and Lauren covered her ears, startled by the ferocity of the noise. Glen reached down and pulled her up, holding her high against his chest. Sandy grinned up at her daughter. "Isn't this great?"

Brilliant beauty streaked across the sky, explosions that lit up the night. Karen glanced at Doug to find him staring not at the sky, but at her. "You okay?"

His arm around her shoulder, Doug pulled her close. Smiling, he put his hand on her stomach. "Yeah."

Steven and Daniel stood together, eyes on the night sky. Daniel wrapped an arm across Steven's chest, pressing himself against Steven's back. Steven tilted his head, sent Daniel that crooked slide of a smile, and raised his arm, his left hand curling around Daniel's left wrist.

Crystals of colour erupted against the black sky. Light detonated around them, turning the night into day, reflecting off two simple gold bands. Steven's hand clasped Daniel's wrist, two hands, two rings, one life.

The End

About the Author

Aimer Boyz is a theatre and Sci-Fi geek. Her daughter still hasn't forgiven her for the "My Other Vehicle is a Romulan Warbird" bumper sticker!

A life-long reader, Boyz delved into Fan Fiction and morphed into a writer.

She lives in Toronto, with a family that pretends she's normal.